All Cloudless Glory

All Cloudless Glory

VOLUME II

THE LIFE OF
GEORGE WASHINGTON

MAKING A NATION

Harrison Clark

REGNERY PUBLISHING, INC.
Washington, D.C.

Library of Congress Cataloging-in-Publication Data

Clark, E. Harrison.
    All cloudless glory : the life of George Washington / E. Harrison Clark.
        p.   cm.
    Includes bibliographical references (p.   ) and index.
    Contents: v. 2. Making a nation
    ISBN 0-89526-445-5 (v. 2)
        1. Washington, George, 1732-1799. 2. Presidents—United States—Biography.
    3. Generals—United States—Biography. 4. United States. Continental Army—Biography.
    I. Title.
    E312.C56   1996
    973.4'1'092—dc20   95-37393
    [B]   CIP

Published in the United States by Regnery Publishing, Inc.
An Eagle Publishing Company
One Massachusetts Avenue, N.W.
Washington, DC 20001

Distributed to the trade by National Book Network
4720-A Boston Way
Lanham, MD 20706

Printed on acid-free paper.
Manufactured in the United States of America

10 9 8 7 6 5 4 3 2

Books are available in quantity for promotional or premium use. Write to Director of Special Sales, Regnery Publishing, Inc., One Massachusetts Avenue, NW, Washington, DC 20001, for information on discounts and terms or call (202) 216-0600.

Designed by Dori Miller
Maps by Chris Capell Computer Graphics

Endpapers: Paintings of Mount Vernon attributed to Edward Savage, 1792. Front: the west front with the circular driveway in the foreground. Back: the east front overlooking the Potomac. (Courtesy of the Mount Vernon Ladies' Association of the Union)

CONTENTS

LIST OF MAPS

ACKNOWLEDGEMENTS

MY SPECIAL THANKS go to my editor for this volume, Mrs. Patricia Bozell, to Mr. Alfred S. Regnery, and to Miss Barbara McMillan, the Mount Vernon librarian. I would also like to thank Mr. Richard Vigilante, Mr. David Dortman, Miss Jennifer Reist, and Miss Dori Miller of Regnery Publishing, Mrs. Ellen Miles and Miss Joanna Britto of the National Portrait Gallery, and Mrs. Karen Peters of Mount Vernon.

All Cloudless Glory

ONE

YORKTOWN TO NEWBURGH

1781–1782

THE YORKTOWN VICTORY brought Washington his greatest acclaim. Many of his countrymen began to speak of him as the Saviour and the Redeemer; the adulation continued till his death and long afterwards. For the next eighteen years he had but to move about the country to find soldiers parading, church bells ringing, cannon firing, choirs singing odes, and officials delivering tiresome addresses to the captive general. He bore it with characteristic grace and habitual modesty and good sense. Abigail Adams after his death expressed it in a precisely right phrase: "He never grew giddy..." Washington's own view of his victory was given in his November 18 letter to Robert Hanson Harrison, his old secretary, who had become Maryland's chief justice:

> *I thank you for your kind congratulations on the Capitulation of Cornwallis. It is an interesting event and may be productive of much good, if properly improved, but if it should be the means of relaxation and sink us into supineness... it had better not have happened. Great Britain, for sometime past, had been encouraged by the impolicy of our conduct, to continue the War, and should there be an interference of European Politicks in her favour, peace may be further removed from us than we expect, while one thing we are sure of, and that is that the only way to obtain Peace is to be prepared for War. Policy, Interest, Economy, all unite*

to stimulate the States to fill the Continental Battalions and provide the means of supporting them.

Mr. Custis's death has given much distress in this family...

After arranging with Mrs. Washington's brother, Bartholomew Dandridge, to be guardian of the Custis children and administrator of his estate, Washington left Mount Vernon with his wife for a triumphal procession north. His Alexandria neighbors were the first to greet him. He thanked them on November 19 for their "very kind and affectionate address." He added: "To make a peaceful return to the agreeable society of my fellow Citizens is among the most ardent of my wishes... The late success at York Town is very promising but... a vigorous prosecution of this Success will, in all probability, procure us what we have so long wished to secure, an establishment of Peace, Liberty and Independence." To all addresses from Congress, the states, and the cities, he reiterated the theme—there should be no relaxation of effort, for independence could still be lost.

As Washington moved north, the press reports moved from rapture to adoration. At Annapolis, on November 21, "All business ceased... and... on his appearance, people of every rank and age eagerly pressed forward to feed their eyes with gazing on the man, to whom, under Providence... they owed... their hopes of future liberty and peace..." On the following night "the city was beautifully illuminated, and an assembly prepared for the ladies, to afford them an opportunity of beholding their friend, and thanking their protector with their smiles. His excellency, to gratify the wishes of the fair, crowned the entertainment with his presence, and with graceful dignity and familiar ease, so framed his looks, his gestures, and his words, that every heart o'erflowed with gratitude and love, and every tongue grew wanton in his praise." On November 24: "Our illustrious and beloved commander in chief left the city, attended by innumerable prayers for his health, safety and happiness."

Philadelphia outdid Annapolis. The *Pennsylvania Journal* of November 28 described the arrival, two days previously, of "General WASHINGTON, our victorious and illustrious commander-in-chief, with his Lady. All panegyrick is vain and language too feeble to express our ideas of his greatness. May the crown of glory he has placed on the brow of the genius of America, shine with untarnished radiance and lustre, and in the brightness of its rays be distinctly seen—WASHINGTON, THE SAVIOUR OF HIS COUNTRY!" Charles Wilson Peale, who had painted Washington at various sittings over the years, prepared, for public exhibition, portraits of Washington and Rochambeau, "with rays of glory and interlaced civic crowns over their heads, framed with palm and laurel branches, and the words in transparent letters, SHINE VALIANT CHIEFS; the whole encircled with stars and flowers de luce."

Congress and the council and assembly of Pennsylvania poured verbal libations on Washington. He conveyed his reaction to General Stirling in a letter of November 30: "My Fear is that, from an Over-rating this Success, a Spirit of Relaxation will take place in our Measures, which should it be the Case, will prove very prejudicial to our future Operations or Negotiations, and may serve to protract a War already too long continued."

Under congressional pleading, the general and his wife settled down in the Benjamin Chew house, for a stay in the capital which lasted about four months. This was the first break he had had from the army since the spring of 1775. He wrote his old aide, James McHenry, who had been elected to the Maryland Legislature:

My stay in Town is merely to assist in and forward the several arrangements which are upon the Carpet, and I believe you are sufficiently acquainted with me to suppose that I do not fail to urge vigorous measures. I am happy in finding no want of disposition in Congress to adopt the measures required by their Committees and their executive Officers. The requisitions which they have made and which they will shortly make upon the States will evince this. It will afterwards lie with the States to determine whether we are, early in the next campaign, to take advantage of what we have gained in this, or whether we are, as usual, to suffer the enemy to bring their reinforcements from Europe, before we draw ours from the neighborhood of the Army, as it were.

Congress had appointed General Benjamin Lincoln as war secretary, following the surrender of Cornwallis. This was the first time Washington had a single executive, rather than a congressional committee, to deal with; this relieved him of some of his impossible burdens of detail. Washington knew that his own letters carried more weight with the states than appeals from Congress. He sent circular letters to the states on December 19, January 22, and January 31. The last letter said that the enemy was either going to wage war or to negotiate peace. In either case the United States should be strong. He noted that there had been a great wave of enthusiasm and patriotism "at the commencement of this glorious revolution," but that the "Spirit of Liberty... has sometimes seemed to slumber for awhile."

Washington particularly requested Pennsylvania and Virginia to increase the garrisons at Fort Pitt in order to protect the Ohio River regions. He informed them that he hoped to organize an expedition to proceed as far as Detroit in order to keep the British out of the region. In November, the enemy abandoned Wilmington, North Carolina, drawing its garrison to Charleston. On December 15 Washington wrote Greene:

> *Your private letter of the 22d. Ulto. came to my hands the day before yesterday, and giving fresh assurances of your attachment and regard for me, was received with affection and gratitude; as I feel myself interested in everything that concerns you, it is with unfeigned pleasure I hear the plaudits which are bestowed on your conduct by Men of all descriptions, public and private, and I communicate them to you with heart felt pleasure; there is no man that does not acknowledge your eminent services nor is there any one that does not allow you have done great things with little means...*

> *Mrs. Greene is now in this place on her way to So. Carolina. She is in perfect health, and in good spirits, and thinking no difficulty too great not to be surmounted in the performance of this visit, it shall be my endeavour to strew the way over with flowers. Poor Mrs. Washington, who has met with a most severe stroke in the loss of her amiable Son, Mr. Custis, is here with me, and joins me most cordially in every wish that tends to your happiness and glory.*

The Washingtons dined on Christmas with Robert Morris, Superintendent of Finance. On January 1, 1782, the Friendly Sons of Saint Patrick held a dinner for Washington and his general officers. Next day he and his wife went to an "elegant entertainment [attended by] a brilliant assemblage of ladies and gentlemen." Beaumarchais' *Eugénie*, "an elegant French comedy," was presented, plus a farce and various dances. It closed with a spectacle—thirteen pillars with heads of various generals on top. Biggest of all was Washington's; a cupid held a laurel over the motto: "Washington—the pride of his country and terror of Britain." On March 21 he attended a commencement at the University of Pennsylvania. Next day the Washingtons started north to join the army. They were accompanied out of the city by Joseph Reed and the Philadelphia Light Horse.

Washington's last act before leaving Philadelphia was to place Bushrod Washington, son of his favorite brother, John, as a law student under James Wilson, an authority on constitutional law. Washington had to give Wilson his note for the tuition rather than cash, promising that he would redeem it as soon as possible. Washington was to have the satisfaction, in 1798, of seeing Bushrod Washington take his seat on the United States Supreme Court, as successor to Mr. Justice Wilson.

THE KING IS UNBOWED

On November 3 George III received in audience Lieutenant Colonel Robert Conway, aide to Clinton, who had just arrived from America with the latest news. At six minutes to midnight, the king wrote to Lord North to report what Conway said:

> *His opinion seems to be that Lord Cornwallis will certainly leave the Chesapeake and return to Charles Town after having beat La Fayette, and that both these are likely events... On the whole he supposes we shall in a very few days hear from Lord Cornwallis, and he trusts Sir Henry Clinton will soon have somewhat decisive to communicate: this I own, gives me satisfaction, with such excellent troops if such an event can be effected I think success must ensue; I feel the justness of our cause; I put the greatest confidence in the valour of both Navy and Army and above all in the Assistance of Divine Providence: the moment is certainly anxious... If this Country will persist, I think an honourable termination cannot fail, for truth is ever too strong for such a conduct as France has held, and if we have any material success she will become sick of the part she has acted; duplicity can never withstand any disasters...*

On November 25 the news of Cornwallis' surrender reached Lord George Germain around noon. He got into his carriage, picked up the colonial secretary and the lord chancellor, and they called on Lord North. Lord George reported later that North had taken the news as if he had received a bullet in his breast. He walked up and down, crying out many times, "Oh God! It is all over." Germain then sent a note to the king on the event and went back to his office where the French newspapers had just arrived with confirmation of the defeat. About six that evening Germain had a reply from the king expressing his great concern at the news but assuring him it would not make the slightest difference in the prosecution of the war.

Parliament met two days later. The king's message breathed fire. The following day he asked every member of the cabinet individually to study how best to achieve a united effort. The war, he told North, had to go on, and Parliament should find the necessary means. No one ought to despond, said the king, but he soon found that he was almost alone in the kingdom in wanting to continue.

In Parliament, Charles James Fox opened fire directly on the sovereign: "Those persons who might chance to be ignorant that the speech... was the composition... of a cabinet council... would set it down as containing the sentiments of some arbitrary, despotic, hard-hearted, and unfeeling monarch... We have heard a speech breathing vengeance, blood, misery, and rancour...

What was its purport? 'Much has been lost; much blood, much treasure has been squandered; the burthens of my people are almost intolerable; but my passions are yet ungratified, my object of subjugation and revenge is yet unfilled, and therefore I am determined to persevere.'"

The younger Pitt and others fired steadily at Germain for losing an army, at Sandwich for his naval defeats, and at North for his loans at exorbitant interest. The London Livery told the king he had lost his army, his navy, and his dominions. The cabinet, under hot fire, prayed for some good news from somewhere, but the Spanish took Minorca, and the French, St. Eustatius. A British fleet came back to port after running from a much superior French force. Other posts fell and with them the independent votes which had backed North.

On February 22, 1782, George Washington's fiftieth birthday, General Henry Seymour Conway rose in the House of Commons. Conway was highly respected for his knowledge, integrity, and independence. He had long been a voice of reason. He had moved for the repeal of the stamp tax. He opposed all efforts to coerce America from 1774 to 1776, and he refused to fight the Americans. Now in an eloquent address he pleaded against further hostilities; he concluded by offering a resolution "that the war on the continent of North America might no longer be pursued for the impracticable purpose of reducing the inhabitants of that country to obedience." After stormy debate, the resolve was beaten by one vote, which everyone joked was Lord North's own.

The following day, Conway's cousin, Horace Walpole, wrote: "The power of the crown has increased, is increasing, and ought to be diminished; and it is diminished a good deal indeed. Lord Sandwich escaped on Wednesday but by a plurality of nineteen; and last night the American war survived but by one vote, which will not save its life." On February 28, the friend of liberty, Edmund Burke, wrote Franklin that Conway had succeeded:

> I congratulate you, as the friend of America; I trust, as not the enemy of England; I am sure, as the friend of mankind, and the resolution of the House of Commons, carried by a majority of nineteen, at two o'clock this morning, in a very full house. It was the declaration of two hundred and thirty-four; I think it was the opinion of the whole. I trust it will lead to a speedy peace between the two branches of the English nation, perhaps to a general peace... Mr. Laurens is released from confinement...

The king informed North that he was "hurt" and "mortified" by the vote. On March 4 North reported to the king that a further Conway resolve declaring "all those [to be] enemies of their country who should advise, or in any way attempt to prosecute an offensive war in America, for the purpose of reducing the colonies to obedience by force," had unanimously passed the House of Commons. Next day the house, without a dissenting vote, urged his majesty to conclude peace with America. The king wrote North to complain again that he was "hurt" by all his "trials of late." He said he would not "throw himself into the hands of Opposition." He hinted at other steps, meaning abdication. The king kept on being hurt, but on March 20 it was Lord North who resigned. A week later the Marquess of Rockingham became prime minister. The king drafted his abdication in favor of his oldest son but never handed it in.

On March 27, 1782, the new cabinet took office. Nearly every member— Rockingham, Camden, Grafton, Cavendish, Shelburne, Fox, Richmond, Keppel, and Conway—had been against the American war. The king wrote to Lord North: "At last the fatal day is come which the misfortunes of the times and the sudden change of sentiments of the House of Commons have drove me to, of Changing the Ministry, and a more general removal of the persons than, I believe, was known before... The effusion of my sorrows has made me say more than I had intended... Pray acquaint the Cabinet that they must this day attend at St. James's to resign..." On March 30 the cabinet asked the king to dispatch Sir Guy Carleton to America in place of Sir Henry Clinton.

From Passy, Franklin wrote Washington on April 3: "I have heretofore congratulated your Excellency on your victories over our enemy's generals; I can now do the same on your having overthrown their politicians. Your late successes have so strengthened the hands of opposition in Parliament, that they are become the majority, and have compelled the king to dismiss all his old ministers and their adherents. The unclean spirits he was possessed with are now cast out of him."

WASHINGTON AND KINGSHIP

On March 28 General and Mrs. Washington passed through Morristown where they had spent the grim winter of 1779–1780. There he wrote to Colonel Matthias Ogden, approving his plan to kidnap George III's son, Prince William, as well as Admiral Digby, who were in New York. Ogden was instructed not to offer "insult or indignity" to them and, after their capture, to "treat them with all possible respect." The plan fell through when the British got wind of it and redoubled their guards.

On May 22 Washington received a letter at Newburgh from Colonel Lewis Nicola, breathing veneration and suggesting that he be king. Nicola said that the war had certainly shown how weak the republic was; the army, in consequence, had suffered greatly from every sort of privation. Nonetheless the army had accomplished great things under a single head. Nicola went on to say that "the same abilities which have led us through difficulties, apparently insurmountable by human power, to victory and glory, those qualities that have merited the universal esteem and veneration of an army, would be most likely to conduct and direct us in the smoother paths of peace." Nicola said that some people connected the idea of monarchy with tyranny but he did not think that was necessarily true. There were strong arguments for having the head of state under a new American constitution be king in name as well as in fact. There was no mistaking the man he had in mind for the job.

This was one of Washington's busier days. He was drafting letters to the secretaries of war, finance, and foreign affairs, the governor of South Carolina, and his generals on the Hudson, in the south, and at Pittsburgh. He still found the time to dispatch his famous, blistering reply, the day he received the letter:

> *With a mixture of great surprise and astonishment I have read with attention the Sentiments you have submitted to my perusal. Be assured, Sir, no occurrence in the course of the War, has given me more painful sensations than your information of there being such ideas existing in the Army as you have expressed [which] I must view with abhorrence, and reprehend with severity. For the present, the communication of them will rest in my own bosom, unless some further agitation of the matter, shall make a disclosure necessary.*
>
> *I am much at a loss to conceive what part of my conduct could have given encouragement to an address which to me seems big with the greatest mischiefs that can befall my Country. If I am not deceived in the knowledge of myself, you could not have found a person to whom your schemes are more disagreeable; at the same time, in justice to my own feelings, I must add that no Man possesses a more sincere wish to see ample justice done to the Army than I do, and as far as my powers and influence, in a constitutional way extend, they shall be employed to the utmost of my abilities to effect it, should there be any occasion. Let me conjure you then, if you have any regard for your Country, concern for yourself or posterity, or respect for me, to banish these thoughts from your Mind, and never communicate, as from yourself or any one else, a sentiment of the like Nature...*

Washington often dictated his letters but this one he wrote with his own hand. That he was genuinely upset is indicated by his great number of mistakes in grammar and punctuation. He ordered his file copy endorsed by David Humphreys, his aide, and Jonathan Trumbull, Jr., his secretary, so that if any curious congressman heard of the story, he would have witnesses for the action he took.

Nicola was utterly undone by the roar of thunder and the bolts of lightning from his hero. In great distress next day he wrote Washington that he had experienced many misfortunes in his life but "nothing has ever affected me so much as your reproof." He assured Washington he had meant only good and not evil. On May 24 he wrote him again to say that, since receipt of the letter, he had been "greatly oppressed in mind and distressed" by it. He added that he had a large family to support, he was destitute from having served his country, and he had felt only that the army had to do something to remedy its dreadful situation. On May 28 he followed with a further letter saying "words cannot begin to apologize" for what he had written.

Nicola seems to have advanced only his own personal view on kingship, though Jefferson, the old maid who imagined so many things under the bed, came to believe that a whole cabal of army officers had wanted a Washington monarchy. Nicola did, however, reflect the widespread distrust in the army of the weaknesses of Congress and of the motives and even good sense and patriotism of its members. From this point, with little fighting to do, the rumbles of protest grew to roars and only the hand of Washington kept the army from another revolution. Within five years the forces of protest were constructively channeled into the Constitutional Convention where more than half the attending delegates had served under General Washington.

THE HUDDY AFFAIR

In December 1781 Cornwallis and Arnold sailed for England. Sir Henry Clinton passed a miserable winter in New York which was made more so by the intense cold and by rumors from London of the court's coolness to him. Clinton's final weeks in America were disturbed by an act of a small band of American Tories (or Loyalists, as they were called on the British side) under Captain Richard Lippincott. They had in their charge an American prisoner, Joshua Huddy, whom they accused of having killed a Tory by the name of Philip White. They hanged him in cold blood, attaching a placard to the body: "Up goes Huddy for Philip White." The evidence soon showed that Huddy had been a prisoner when White was killed. The cries of outrage from Congress, the army, and the civilian population were such that Washington had to threaten retaliatory measures unless the British punished Lippincott or delivered him to the Americans for trial. Washington ordered Brigadier Moses Hazen to select an "unconditional" British captain (that is, one not covered by such an agreement as the Yorktown surrender) for reprisal. On May 4 Washington informed the Board of War:

Keenly wounded as my feelings will be at the deplorable destiny of the unhappy Victim; no gleam of hope can arise to him but from the conduct of the enemy... I will receive no application nor answer any Letter [from them] on the subject, which does not inform me that ample satisfaction is made for the death of Capt. Huddy, on the perpetrators of that horrid deed.

Hazen, in violation of Washington's orders, picked by lot a nineteen-year-old British captain, Charles Asgill, who was clearly covered by the Yorktown cartel. British army officers, whether prisoners of the Americans or stationed in New York, were aroused to fury at the American Loyalists for having committed a deed for which one of their own might suffer. Sir Henry Clinton was also highly indignant at this deliberate murder, which he believed the Loyalists had done to disgrace the British. At the trial it turned out that the Loyalists had been exceedingly bitter over the surrender of Cornwallis and what appeared to be their abandonment by the British. It was the head of the Loyalist board, William Franklin, who had ordered the execution of Huddy. Because of this, Lippincott was acquitted.

In forwarding the verdict to Washington, the new commander, Sir Guy Carleton, told Washington that Clinton had regarded the act as "a great barbarity in itself, as well as a daring insult on his own authority." He had promptly undertaken measures for "punishment and prevention." Carleton said that he and Clinton agreed that the Loyalist board would have nothing further to do with prisoners. He added that he thoroughly disapproved of the execution and that he was ordering a further criminal investigation. Washington at once wrote Congress to report that this changed the situation, since his threat of retaliation had been made to prevent a repetition, and he asked Congress to decide about Asgill. Congress simply ignored his letter. Several weeks elapsed, and on September 30 Washington appealed to James Duane, a congressman:

I shall be obliged to you, or some friend in Congress, to inform me what has been, or is like to be done, with respect to my reference of the case of Captn. Huddy?

I cannot forbear complaining of the cruel situation I now am, and oftentimes, have been placed in by the silence [to call it by its softest name]* of Congress in matters of high importance, and which the good of the Service, and my official duty, has obliged me to call upon them (as the Sovereign power of these United States) to decide. It is only in intricate and perplexing cases I have requested their orders;

---

* Phrase omitted in letter sent.

being always willing to bear my proportion of public embarrassments, and take a full share of responsibility...

When I refer a matter to Congress, every proceeding on it, on my part, is suspended till their pleasure is transmitted; and for this it is well known I have waited with unexampled patience...

In the meantime, the captain's mother, Lady Asgill, appealed to the king and queen of France to save her son. Vergennes wrote Washington that his sovereigns hoped mercy might be extended and that he was sure he would wish to avoid "the disagreeable necessity of this retaliation." Washington forwarded it to Congress with a further request to let him release the prisoner. Congress immediately agreed. In November Washington gave Asgill a passport to New York, with a letter saying that Asgill's relief at the outcome could hardly be greater than Washington's own.

GENERAL CARLETON TALKS PEACE

In April Lord Dunmore reached New York, still claiming to be governor of Virginia, but this was no help to Clinton. On May 15 Sir Guy Carleton arrived to take command. Eight days later, Sir Henry Clinton, who had been in America nearly seven years, sailed for home. Governor Livingston of New Jersey, father-in-law of John Jay, commented: "As fertile as England is in the production of Blockheads, I think they cannot easily send us a greater blunderbuss, unless, peradventure, it should please his Majesty himself to do us the honor of a visit."

Sir Guy Carleton occupied an anomalous role as the new British commander in chief. There is no doubt that the unanimous parliamentary vote to stop the war with America was the will of the British nation. Even the king went along with the idea that all guns should be turned on the French. At the same time, the cabinet could not quite bring itself to believe that Americans did not still want, in their hearts, to be British. In consequence, Carleton was instructed to carry on no offensive operations and to save his army for work elsewhere. If attacked, he was to capitulate on condition that he be allowed to embark his troops. Above all he was instructed to be very kind to "His Majesty's American subjects," which apparently meant all of them, including Washington.

At the same time Britain was fighting France, America's ally. Carleton could not very well inform Washington that he was not permitted to fight by land. Equally, he could not always control his frontier Indians, nor the Royal Navy, so that it was neither peace nor war. As it turned out, he had a logistics problem of formidable magnitude. There were 38,000 British, German, and provincial troops of all ranks in America. With them were immense supplies and equipment. In addition large numbers of Tories wanted to leave, with their furniture, baggage, and slaves. The British did not have the shipping available for this tremendous movement. It took more than eighteen months to complete.

A peculiarity of British politics appeared at this point. Lord Shelburne, who had taken over Lord George Germain's job as colonial secretary, believed that peacemaking with America was in his department. Charles James Fox, the foreign secretary, considered it his province. Both sent delegates to Paris to sound out the Americans. Shelburne also dispatched his private secretary, Maurice Morgann, to New York, with instructions to confer with Congress for a reconciliation, though not on the grounds of independence. Morgann arrived with Carleton, who forwarded to Washington copies of the parliamentary authority, not yet enacted, to restore peace in America. He asked that Morgann be authorized to proceed to Philadelphia. Washington thought this procedure was dangerous and designed to lull Americans into a false security. He so wrote Congress, which refused to receive Morgann. In the meantime the Marquess of Rockingham died, and Lord Shelburne took over in early July as prime minister. By August Digby and Carleton were writing to Washington that "Mr. Grenville" (whose father had authored the stamp tax which began all the trouble) had gone to Paris, with authority to recognize the United States and to begin peace negotiations.

Lord Shelburne had a reputation in his lifetime for duplicity, which was greatly exaggerated. Later, as Marquess of Lansdowne, he became one of Washington's most fervent English admirers. (The "Lansdowne" portrait of Washington by Stuart hung in his house.) Shelburne was a man of broad vision, far in advance of his time. He believed in free trade, liberal and fair dealings with the world, and parliamentary and fiscal reform. When he swung over to independence for America, he decided to go overboard in being fair and generous, in order to rebuild American friendship and avoid all future disputes with the United States. His premiership was brief, but it was to be of inestimable value to America.

WASHINGTON CONFERS WITH ROCHAMBEAU

If the rest of the country tended further to relax into apathy after Yorktown, Washington had no such idea in his mind. Whether there was to be more war, or negotiations for peace, he was determined that the country's military strength be maintained. In May rumors of a great French naval defeat in the

West Indies reached him from his New York intelligence sources; by June its truth was confirmed.

Washington had planned to keep the French army in Virginia, ready to come north, if another allied fleet arrived and New York could be taken, or to move to South Carolina, to join Greene for an attack on Charleston. When Rochambeau heard from Luzerne that a remnant of the French West Indies fleet, under the Marquis de Vaudreuil, was heading to Boston for repairs, he determined, without consulting Washington, to move north. Washington, so informed by Luzerne, wrote Greene that this was not his idea. He informed Rochambeau, very politely, that it would be difficult for him to return south, if Charleston were to be attacked. He asked Rochambeau to meet with him in Philadelphia.

Before leaving for the capital, Washington took a brief holiday trip, his first in seven years, to Schenectady, Albany, and the Saratoga battlefields. The *Pennsylvania Gazette* of July 17 reported that, on his arrival in Albany on June 27, "the bells of all the churches began to ring, and continued their joyful peals until sun-set, when thirteen cannon were discharged from the fort and the city illuminated. Who is more worthy of our love and esteem than the GUARDIAN AND SAVIOUR of his country?" At Schenectady, three days later, "sixty of the principal inhabitants on horseback... attended him into the town amidst the ringing of bells, the firing of cannon and every other public demonstration of felicity." On July 2, at Albany, he went "on board his barge on his way to the army, amidst the benedictions of the multitude, leaving the citizens of this country strongly impressed with the ideas of a *great character*, in which are combined every public and private virtue."

Rochambeau and Washington had a cordial enough meeting in Philadelphia. Washington had to recognize the inevitable when Rochambeau stated that there could be no further French naval aid of any importance; therefore it was not going to be possible to attack Charleston and it would be better if the French joined him on the Hudson. Rochambeau's army moved north very slowly, taking two-and-a-half months to go from Virginia to Westchester.

Entirely by accident the two generals were in Philadelphia when the French minister was giving a ball in celebration of the birth of the dauphin, a young prince who, perhaps fortunately, was to die a natural death in 1789. It was the most exciting spectacle Philadelphia had seen, surpassing even John André's Meschianza. Luzerne, in preparing for it, had a special hall built under the direction of Pierre Charles L'Enfant, the French engineer who later designed the city of Washington. The French army sent up a battalion of chefs. Everyone who was anyone was invited, and those who were nobodies stood outside to watch. The humor of seeing a band of republican revolutionists scrambling for

tickets to attend a ball in honor of the birth of the heir to an absolute monarchy was not lost on Dr. Benjamin Rush. He was an inept physician, politician,
and military critic, but he was a born writer. He described the affair in a letter
of July 16, 1782, to a female friend:

> *For some weeks past our city has been amused with the expectation of a most splendid
> entertainment to be given by the Minister of France to celebrate the birth of the
> Dauphin of France... Hundreds crowded daily to see a large frame building which he
> had erected for a dancing room... This building... was supported by large pillars and
> was open all around. The ceiling was decorated with several pieces of neat
> paintings... The garden... was cut into walks and divided with cedar and pine
> branches into artificial groves... We were told that the Minister had borrowed thirty
> cooks from the French army... Eleven hundred tickets were distributed...*
>
> *For ten days before the entertainment nothing else was talked of in our city. The
> shops were crowded with customers. Hairdressers were retained; tailors, milliners,
> and mantua-makers were to be seen covered with sweat and out of breath in every
> street.*
>
> *Monday, July 15, was the long expected evening. The morning of this day was
> ushered in by a corps of hairdressers occupying the place of the city watchmen.
> Many ladies were obliged to have their heads dressed between four and six o'clock in
> the morning, so great was the demand and so numerous were the engagements this
> day of the gentlemen of the comb.*
>
> *At half-past seven o'clock [P.M.] was the time fixed... The approach of the hour was
> proclaimed by the rattling of all the carriages in the city... Near the Minister's house
> there was a collection of all the curious and idle men, women, and children of the
> city who were not invited... amounting, probably, to ten thousand people.*
>
> *The scene now almost exceeds description. The numerous lights distributed through
> the garden, the splendor of the room we were now approaching, the size of the
> company... the brilliance and variety of their dresses, and the band of music which
> had just begun to play, formed a scene that resembled enchantment... We entered
> the room... and here we saw the world in a miniature... here were the president and
> members of Congress, governors of states and generals of armies, ministers of
> finance and war and foreign affairs, judges of superior and inferior courts, with
> all their respective suites of assistants, secretaries and clerks...*
>
> *It was impossible to partake of the joy of the evening without being struck with the
> occasion of it. It was to celebrate the birth of a Dauphin of France. How great the*

revolution in the mind of an American! to rejoice in the birth of a prince whose religion he has been taught to consider as unfriendly to humanity. And above all, how new the phenomenon for republicans and freemen to rejoice in the birth of a prince who must one day be the support of monarchy and slavery!...

Nine days later, Washington left Philadelphia, visiting the Moravian settlements (which had rendered great service in the care of sick and wounded soldiers throughout the war) at Bethlehem, Pennsylvania, and Hope, New Jersey. He reached Newburgh July 27.

WASHINGTON AND CARLETON

Washington had no reason, after his long years of experience, to trust any peaceful British overtures. He kept his intelligence system operating in New York to find out what Carleton was planning. His August 14 instructions to Captain John Pray were clear and succinct:

The first great article of which the General requires to be ascertained is, the state of the British Naval Force at New York; and the arrival or sailing of any Fleet, Transports, Armed Vessels or single Ships of War. This information must, if practicable, be kept up constantly, until further Orders.

In order to obtain this intelligence with certainty and accuracy (without which it will be worth nothing at all) you should have some trusty and intelligent Person or Persons ready in the City to give the earliest notice of any Movement or alteration in the shipping... Money will be furnished for the payment of the actual expenses... but it is expected that the greatest compensation and reward which can be given to well disposed persons within the British Lines, who mean to remain after the enemy have abandoned New York, will be the promise of favour and security to those who shall recommend themselves in this way. It must also be impressed upon all those agents that they should be exceedingly exact and accurate in their accounts, that they should see every thing themselves and make a business of it, at this last hour, that they have intelligence thro' many different Channels and can detect any inaccuracy and falsehood...

The other objects to which you should attend unweariedly, are the number, state and disposition of the Troops... embarkations, arrivals, movements of any kind, indications of remaining in or evacuating the Garrison, European advices, domestic or other intelligence contained in the Newspapers, which might and should

*be obtained every day; to these should be added the British Orders and everything
else that can be interesting in a Political, Military or Naval light...*

A typical report of naval movements reached Washington a day or two after
they took place: "On Friday evening the 30th of August, the Warwick of 50
guns, with 5 large transport ships, with 1500 or 2000 troops on board, sailed
from New York harbour, bound for Halifax; and at 10 o'clock the next day, six
ships, supposed to be the same, were seen from the highlands of Middletown,
near Sandy Hook, standing to the eastward, with the wind at west."

Sir Guy Carleton's position was a difficult one since his home government
had tied his military hands while continuing to encourage its navy to warfare.
Dr. Benjamin Rush that summer complained that Philadelphia, in a few
months, had lost more than £800,000 through captures by British ships, the
proceeds of which were distributed as prizes to the Royal Navy. Washington
commented on this policy in a letter of July 10 to Tench Tilghman: "We have
nothing New in this Quarter. Sir Guy gives strong assurances of the pacific
disposition of his most gracious Majesty, by Land. Sir (that is to be) Digby gives
proofs, if he is deficient in assurances, of his Most gracious Majesty's good
intention of capturing everything that floats on the face of the Waters... To an
American, whose genius is not susceptible of refined Ideas, there would
appear some little inconsistency in all this; but to the enlarged and comprehensive Mind of a Briton, these things are perfectly reconcilable."

Washington on his trip north to Albany was informed of renewed Indian
raids in the Mohawk Valley under British officers from Canada. On September
8 he wrote Carleton, asking him to explain British policy:

*I cannot help remarking that your Excellency has several Times lately, taken occasion
to mention that "all hostilities stand suspended on your part." I must confess that, to
me, this Expression wants explanation. I can have no Conception of a suspension of
Hostilities, but that which arises from a mutual Agreement of the powers at War; and
which extends to naval as well as land operations. That your Excellency has thought
proper, on your part, to make a partial suspension, may be admitted; but whether this
has been owing to political or other motives, is not for me to decide. It is, however, a
well-known fact that, at the same Time, the British Cruizers on our Coasts have been
more than usually alert, and while Americans are admitted to understand their real
Interests, it will be difficult for them, when a Suspension of hostilities is spoken of, to
separate the Idea of its extending to Sea, as well as land.*

*I cannot ascribe the Inroads of the Savages upon our North Western Frontier, to the
Causes from whence your Excellency supposes them to originate; neither can I allow*

that they are committed without the directions from the Commander in Chief in Canada; for by prisoners and Deserters, it is apparent that those ravaging parties are composed of white Troops under the Command of Officers regularly commissioned, as well as Savages; and it would be a Solecism to suppose, that such parties could be out without the knowledge of their Commander in Chief.

Carleton assured Washington that any attacks from Canada were quite contrary to the instructions of the British government, and he would see to it they were stopped. He was as good as his word. On September 26 Washington forwarded to Congress an intelligence report from Quebec: "A number of Indians left a few days ago. They were told... they must not go to War, as the King had compassion on his American Subjects, they having expressed their sorrow for what they had done. The Seneca Sachem replied that the Americans and French had beat the English, that the latter could no longer carry on the War, and that the Indians know it well, and must now be sacrificed or submit to the Americans... The Indians after receiving considerable presents went home little satisfied with their Situation."

PURPLE HEART

In 1782 two awards were introduced into the American army, for enlisted men only. The first was a chevron, for each three years of satisfactory service. The other was a badge of military merit, in the form of a purple heart of cloth or silk, worn on the left breast. Only three men received the latter, by chance all Connecticut sergeants. The first was Daniel Brown, who led the advance on redoubt ten at Yorktown. The second was Elijah Churchill who, "with great gallantry," led the attacks on Forts St. George and Slongo on Long Island, where the watchword was "Washington and glory." The third was Daniel Bissell, selected for the honor by Washington himself for "having performed some important services, within the immediate knowledge of the Commander in chief, in which the fidelity, perseverance, and good sense of the said Sergeant Bissel were conspicuously manifested." At Washington's request, Bissell had deserted, in ostentatious fashion, for New York, where he obtained important assignments at British headquarters. He amassed a full report of the enemy's military strength, escaping with it to the camp of the American commander in chief.

THE IMPECCABLE ARMY

As it was to do for the next 136 years, the United States brought its army to a peak of perfection and then dissolved it.

Throughout the summer the troops went through training and more training. Washington reviewed each brigade individually, giving high praise, when possible, or quietly suggesting that they do more drilling to bring themselves to the standards of other brigades. After concluding his reviews, he expressed his appreciation of the "amazing contrast" between their past and present appearance.

On August 31 Washington conducted the first amphibious training operation in American history, when the whole army moved down the Hudson, "to try in what time a large number of Men could embark, debark, and move a given distance by water." Washington wrote Congress that it had been most successful.

When Rochambeau reached the Hudson on September 14, Washington paraded the army in his honor. According to Dr. Thacher's journal for September 14: "Count Rochambeau was most highly gratified to perceive the very great improvement which our army had made in appearance since he last reviewed them, and expressed his astonishment at their rapid progress in military skill and discipline. He said to General Washington, 'You must have formed an alliance with the King of Prussia. These troops are Prussians.' Several of the principal officers of the French army who have seen troops of different European nations, have... declared that they had seen none superior to the Americans." The Prince de Broglie recorded his "pleasure, astonishment and admiration." Another French officer wrote: "The most exact uniformity, the neat dress of the men, the glittering of their arms, their martial look, and a kind of military luxury gave a most magnificent appearance to this assemblage of citizens... The exactness, order and silence which distinguish veteran armies was here displayed; they changed their front, formed and displayed columns, with admirable regularity..."

THE UNPAID ARMY

Behind the army's brilliant facade was bleak despair which might have been assuaged by modest grants or loans from the French court but France had abruptly cut aid. Washington correctly predicted, in his letter of October 2 to General Lincoln, the war secretary, that the army's distresses would bring a train of evils:

Painful as the task is to describe the dark side of our affairs, it sometimes becomes a matter of indispensable necessity. Without disguize or palliation, I will inform you candidly of the discontents which, at this moment, prevail universally throughout the Army.

The Complaint of Evils, which they suppose almost remediless, are the total want of Money, or the means of existing from One day to another, the heavy debts which they have already incurred, the loss of Credit, the distress of their Families (i.e., such as are married) at home, and the prospect of Poverty and Misery before them. It is in vain, Sir, to suppose that military Men will acquiesce contentedly with bare rations, when those in the Civil walk of life (unacquainted with half the hardships they endure) are regularly paid the emoluments of Office... A Military Man has the same turn to sociability as a person in Civil life, he conceives himself equally called upon to live up to his rank; and his pride is hurt when circumstances restrain him. Only conceive then, the mortification they (even the Genl. Officers) must suffer when they cannot invite a French Officer, a visiting friend, or traveling acquaintance to a better repast than stinking Whiskey (and not always that) and a bit of Beef without vegetables...

The Officers also complain of other hardships which they think might and ought to be remedied without delay, viz., the stopping promotions, where there have been vacancies open for a long time, the withholding Commissions from those who are justly entitled to them...

...No one that I have seen or heard of, appears opposed to the principle of reducing the Army as circumstances may require; Yet I cannot help fearing the Result of the measure in contemplation, under present circumstances, when I see such a Number of Men goaded by a thousand stings of reflection on the past, and of anticipation on the future, about to be turned into the World, soured by penury and what they call the ingratitude of the Public, involved in debts, without one farthing of Money to carry them home, after having spent the flower of their days, and many of them their patrimonies, in establishing the freedom and Independence of their Country, and suffered every thing human Nature is capable of enduring on this side of death; I repeat it, these irritable circumstances, without one thing to soothe their feelings, or frighten the gloomy prospects, I cannot avoid apprehending that a train of Evils will follow, of a very serious and distressing Nature...

I wish not to heighten the shades of the picture, so far as the real life would justify me in doing, or I would give Anecdotes of patriotism and distress which have scarcely ever been paralleled, never surpassed in the history of Mankind; but you may rely upon it, the patience and long sufferance of this Army are almost exhausted, and that there never was so great a spirit of discontent as at this instant. While in the field, I think it may be kept from breaking out into Acts of Outrage, but when we retire into Winter Quarters (unless the Storm is previously dissipated) I cannot be at ease, respecting the consequences...

...You are too well acquainted, from your own service, with the real sufferings of the Army to require a longer detail; I will therefore only add that, exclusive of the common hardships of a Military life, Our Troops have been, and still are obliged to perform more services, foreign to their proper duty, without gratuity or reward, than the Soldiers of any other Army; for example, the immense labours expended in doing the work of Artificers, in erecting Fortifications and Military Works; the fatigue of building themselves Barracks or Huts annually; And of cutting and transporting Wood for the use of all our Posts and Garrison, without any expense whatever to the Public...

LETTERS

Washington's correspondence, except from John Hancock, was enormous that relaxed year of little fighting. Hancock, the general complained, went on ignoring him. Washington's letters could thunder or be gay and even flirtatious. His loudest complaint went to John Price Posey, son of the Thomas Posey who had imposed so much on Washington's good nature. When he heard from his brother-in-law that Posey had cheated the estate of Jacky Custis, Washington wrote him on August 7:

With a mixture of surprise, concern, and even horror have I heard of your treatment of the deceased Mr. Custis; in the abuse and misapplication of the Estate which he had committed, with much confidence I am sure, and I believe personal regard, to your management.

If what I have heard, or the half of it be true, you must not only be lost to the feelings of virtue, honor and common honesty; but you must have suffered an unwarrantable thirst of gain to lead you into errors which are so pregnant with folly and indiscretion, as to render you a mark for every man's arrow to level at. Can you suppose, Sir,...that the Heirs of Mr. Custis will not find friends who will pursue you to the end of the Earth?

Washington, in strong language, suggested that Posey make an immediate and complete accounting and settlement, in order to avoid further trouble, adding that if he did not, the affair "will be probed to the bottom; let the trouble and cost of doing it be what it may." More than four years later, Washington learned that Posey had also robbed him but he was far more restrained in his reaction than he had been to the depredations on his stepson's estate.

He wrote humorously to Gouverneur Morris on August 7: "I asserted pretty roundly to you, but not more confidently than it was asserted to me, that General Dalrymple had sailed for England. Since my return to this place, I have seen a letter from him to General Knox which, at the same time that it contradicts both assertions, announces his speedy departure for the Albion shore. If he should remain in New York after this, charge it to his act, not mine..." To McHenry, a physician who had been sick, Washington wrote that he wished he had medical books around to give him advice, having resolved to quit "the trade of General." By October 17 he, who was wondering as much as anyone else what was happening in Europe with regard to the peace, wrote McHenry: "In a time like this, of general uncertainty with respect to the designs of the British Court, it is not at all wonderful to find men inquiring at every corner for News; the North sends to the South, and the South to the North, to obtain it, but at present, all I believe, are equally ignorant."

PEACE

The small American army at home was now replaced in importance by the brilliant John Jay who, after being treated with calculated contempt at Madrid, had moved to Paris as peace commissioner. Although Jay was but one of four American ministers authorized to make peace, most of the burden fell on him. Henry Laurens was too sick after his release from the Tower of London to go to Paris; Franklin fell seriously ill in August, while John Adams' negotiations in the Netherlands kept him from Paris till October. Jay, whose great-grandfather had been expelled from France as a Protestant, took on, alone, three major powers—France, Great Britain, and Spain.

During the preliminary peace talks, Vergennes was fully candid with Spain but only slightly so with the Americans. The French position in relation to the United States was clear. America's independence was to be recognized by Great Britain, but only as part of a general peace treaty, which met all the demands of France and Spain. The United States was to be restricted as closely as possible to the Allegheny Mountains. Nova Scotia and Quebec were to be British but Quebec was to extend to the Ohio River, as defined by the Quebec Act of 1774. The Mississippi and the territory south of the Ohio were to go to Spain, which did not recognize the United States. Thus France proposed to make permanent two great American grievances against their former British rulers—the proclamation line and the Quebec Act. In addition France wanted to detach Maine from the United States. For generations, New Englanders had participated in the Grand Banks fishing; Vergennes proposed that they be excluded from such operations. Vergennes also wanted all Tories pardoned and their property restored to them.

France had cut off monetary aid to the United States and insisted that all her war loans be repaid by 1788. She also ordered her troops withdrawn from the United States, although the British still held American ports. France and Spain were preparing a siege of Gibraltar, in a final assault on British power; both countries agreed that no peace would be made until Spain regained the rock.

In his plans, Vergennes had taken everything into account, except the intransigence of John Jay, the high-mindedness of the Earl of Shelburne, and the naval abilities (when not fighting Americans) of Admiral Howe. In forcing Congress to surround John Adams with other commissioners, Vergennes, too, had not reckoned that, in the final play, they would all stand together.

When Lord Shelburne took over Lord George Germain's office, he directed Sir Guy Carleton to assure Americans that "the most liberal sentiments" had taken root in England; his treatment of them was to be so "open and generous... as... to captivate their hearts." Shelburne followed with further instructions of June 25 to endeavor to achieve reconciliation "on the noblest terms and by the noblest means." A few days later Shelburne became prime minister and never wavered from his professed ideals.

In July Franklin gave Richard Oswald, Shelburne's emissary, an outline of what he considered to be the necessary points for a peace treaty—recognition of independence, the withdrawal of troops, the restoration of Quebec to its old boundary, and freedom of the fisheries. Franklin also suggested that, for full reconciliation, Canada be given to the United States, war reparations be paid, and British ports be opened to American ships. The necessary points were acceptable to Shelburne and eventually became the basis of the peace treaty. By August, while Franklin was ill, Jay was in daily negotiation with Oswald, and through him, with Shelburne. At the same time, Jay found himself engaged in much more hostile discussions with France and Spain.

Earlier, when Franklin, Jay, and Oswald talked with Vergennes, Jay complained that Oswald's commission authorized him to negotiate with the American colonies. Vergennes waved this aside as unimportant. He assured Jay that American independence would be taken up at the final peace treaty (which, he did not add, could not be signed until Spain got Gibraltar). Vergennes also ordered Jay to negotiate with the Spanish ambassador about the western lands, dismissing Jay's objection that Spain had not recognized the United States. When Rayneval came along to act as interpreter between Jay and the Conde de Aranda, Jay found that the French *chef de cabinet* was arguing the Spanish case for the western lands.

In September, Oswald showed Jay an intercepted dispatch from François Barbé-Marbois, secretary of the French legation at Philadelphia. This outlined a proposal to keep the Americans from the fisheries and suggested that if the British were allowed to hold their western posts, America's dependence on France would increase. At almost the same time, after receiving a lengthy memorandum from Rayneval protesting against American claims to lands beyond the Alleghenies, Jay learned that Rayneval had gone to England for secret negotiations with Shelburne. At this time, although Jay did not know it, the French prime minister was writing about the Americans to Luzerne in Philadelphia: "It behooves us to leave them to their illusions, to do everything we can to make them fancy that we share them, and unostentatiously to defeat any attempts to which these illusions may carry them, if our cooperation is required. The Americans have all the presumption of ignorance, but there is reason to expect that experience will ere long enlighten them." So great was Vergennes' contempt for Americans that he failed even to send his usual spies to find out what they were doing.

In London Lord Shelburne had a difficult role, for he was a statesman of rare vision who had also to be a practical politician in a corrupt country. He was pushed by a powerful king who loathed the word independence; a large group of American Tories in England, who wanted both America and their property back; a divided cabinet; a Parliament split into many factions; and merchants, shippers, and fishermen who all wanted protection of one sort or another. While Shelburne kept to a straight line in dealing with America, his various zigs and zags, which were the despair of Jay and then of Adams and Franklin, arose from the political pressures he encountered from all sides.

Handling the king was the most difficult of all Shelburne's problems; his memoranda to George III were masterpieces of diplomacy. He praised and flattered and said how much he agreed with the king's discerning views but that he ought to point out the many difficulties in doing what he wanted and perhaps they should do things in Shelburne's way. The king had led North around, but Shelburne brought the king to his policies with tact and gentleness. From Shelburne's point of view, a generous peace with America was not only important for the future of both countries but would greatly strengthen his hand in negotiations with France.

When Jay heard that Rayneval, after holding a long conference with the Spanish ambassador, had left hurriedly for England, he rightly suspected the worst. Jay had already told Oswald that he could not negotiate further unless the king would recognize the United States. Jay now dispatched another British negotiator, Benjamin Vaughan, to London with perhaps the most important proposal ever made by an American diplomat: (a) Great Britain should immediately recognize the United States as a touchstone of sincerity; this would be cordially reciprocated by the Americans; and (b) France wanted America's independence postponed until her own terms were met; the United States would adhere to the French treaty, but it was a different thing for Americans to be guided by the French or American interpretation of the Treaty of 1778. Jay worked out with Oswald a formula for recognition, which might be acceptable to Shelburne and to George III, while keeping within the terms of the French treaty. Under it, Oswald would receive a commission empowering him to treat with the commissioners of "the United States of America" but *de jure* recognition could wait for the peace treaty. The United States would abandon any pretentions to Canada, provided the American boundaries extended to the Mississippi. Jay pointed out that neither Congress nor Great Britain could prevent American settlement there. The United States would insist on rights in the fisheries. In return for the backlands and fisheries, America would give Britain generous trading and commercial privileges, as well as freedom of navigation on the Mississippi.

Jay's message offered reciprocal friendship and advantages. Shelburne wrote a little later to Oswald that he was going to trust the Americans and that he hoped he was doing right, or "our heads must answer for it." Jay, too, had placed his own head in jeopardy, for he had violated the instructions of Congress and failed to inform Franklin of his move.

On September 13 Lord Shelburne reported at length to the king on his initial conversations with Rayneval. He described the very extensive demands of the French—for Spain, Gibraltar, and for themselves, various West Indian islands, Senegal for the slave trade, and a return of Dunkirk and her possessions in India. He added that Rayneval seemed "jealous rather than partial to America." The king told Shelburne how shocked he was by French demands and duplicity. Shelburne, on September 15, reported further conversations with Rayneval and then added, as if in afterthought:

> *...I am as clearly of opinion against a Peace as I ever was against American Independence, till in fact the Resolutions of the House of Commons decided the point. I am very clear that Your Majesty has within your Dominions Resources of every kind, if they could be brought forth. But Your Majesty knows, what I am mortyfy'd to allude to... The State of both Army and Navy; The few Subjects capable of supplying what is wanted in regard to both Services; The State of Ireland, and that of the House of Commons... This obliges me... to state as clearly as I am able the other side of the question...*

By September 19, having focused the king's fears on France, Shelburne was ready to hand him full cabinet approval of John Jay's formula for de facto recognition. When the king signed it, he did not realize that, for all practical purposes, he had recognized the independence of the United States. Shelburne's minutes said simply:

It is humbly recommended to Your Majesty that a new Commission be made out under Your Majesty's Great Seal for enabling Mr. Oswald to treat with the Commissions appointed by the Colonys, under the title of Thirteen United States, inasmuch as the Commissioners have offered under that condition to accept the Independence of America as the First Article of the Treaty.

Oswald received his commission in Paris on September 27 and showed it to Jay. With his only objection to negotiations removed, Jay urgently summoned John Adams from The Hague. On September 30 the king received word that the Franco-Spanish siege of Gibraltar had been smashed; soon afterwards Lord Howe's relief forces reached the rock.

Within the broad principles which had been accepted by the British government, the detailed peace negotiations were difficult for the English and Americans. They involved such questions as prewar debts, American demands for reparations, the boundaries of Maine and Florida, the claims of Tories to amnesty and property, fishing rights in British North America, restrictions on American commerce and navigation, and other points between countries which had been once intimately bound politically and economically. Many of the disputed points were slurred over rather than settled, and these became acute problems for Washington as president.

The negotiations were well advanced when John Adams arrived. He had precisely the same opinion of French duplicity as John Jay, and he heartily approved of all Jay had done. Franklin, recovered, protested that their congressional instructions required them to have the approval of the French court, but it soon proved that Franklin's was a rather *pro forma* remark. In the end he agreed to the secret negotiations; from then on the Americans worked as a team.

By November 19 the articles of the preliminary peace treaty between Great Britain and the United States were ready in Whitehall for transmission to Oswald. The secretary of state, Thomas Townshend, sent them to the king, adding that he would also send him the draft of the "Preliminary Articles and the Dispatches as soon as they are ready, without waiting for my seeing the latter: He cannot be surprised at my not having been overly anxious for the perusal of them, as Parliament having to my astonishment come into the idea of granting a Separation to North America, had disabled me from longer defending the just rights of this Kingdom. But I certainly disclaim thinking myself answerable for any evils that may arise from the adoption of this Measure as necessity not conviction had made me subscribe to it."

Next day Rayneval arrived in London to say that the French were unwilling to support the Americans in their "unreasonable demands," which the British prime minister duly reported to the king. On November 23 Vergennes informed his minister in Philadelphia that France had no intention of helping the "pretentious ambitions" of the United States to the Mississippi boundaries.

On November 30 Richard Oswald for Great Britain, and John Adams, John Jay, and Benjamin Franklin signed the preliminary treaty of peace. The United States, at least on paper, was free and independent from the Atlantic to the Mississippi.

On December 7, one of London's darkest and foggiest days, the king went before Parliament. His speech was clearly written by Lord Shelburne, for it called for an "entire and cordial reconciliation with the colonies" but the king read it in a tone which indicated that he, for one, wanted nothing of the sort. He then came to the terrible clause that, to attain reconciliation, "I did not hesitate to declare them free and independent states, by an article to be inserted in the peace treaty." Elkanah Watson, an American who was present, noted that at this point the king "hesitated, choked, and executed the painful duties with an ill grace which does not belong to him." Rayneval also noticed how embarrassed the king was and so reported to Vergennes. The king realized it, for he afterwards asked Lord Oxford: "Did I lower my voice when I came to that part of my speech?" The king then went on: "Religion, language, interest, affection, may and I hope will, yet prove a bond of permanent union between the two countries. To this end, neither attention nor disposition on my part shall be wanting." The old fox had given Lord Shelburne, three weeks before, his real opinion on losing the grapes:

> *I cannot conclude without mentioning how sensibly I feel the dismemberment of America from this Empire, and that I should be miserable indeed if I did not feel that no blame on that Account can be laid at my door, and did I not also know that knavery seems to be so much the striking feature of its Inhabitants that it may not in the end be an evil that they become Aliens to this Kingdom.*

That night, another American, John Singleton Copley, who had heard the speech, painted an American flag on the ship in the left-hand corner of his portrait of Elkanah Watson. Thus, said Copley, he had raised the first American flag in the port of London.

Vergennes received the details from Franklin after the signing. He was stunned. John Adams described it with more than his usual gracelessness: "No wrestler was ever so completely thrown upon his back as the Comte de Vergennes." The prime minister complained to Rayneval in London, to Franklin and to Fitzherbert, the British negotiator, in Paris, and to Luzerne in Philadelphia, but the deed was irrevocable. Rayneval particularly protested to Shelburne against the grant of the "backlands" which had been a cause of the war between France and Great Britain in 1756.

Vergennes was forced to speed up his own and Spain's treaty with Great Britain which, thanks to Shelburne, came out of the war better than anyone in England could have expected. Even George III agreed on this. Spain did not get Gibraltar. On January 20, 1783, the preliminary treaties and an armistice among Britain, France, Spain, and the United States were signed. Thereafter there were months of tedious negotiations before the final treaty was ready.

In England all the long years of war, followed by anger and frustration at the peace, now exploded onto Lord Shelburne. He had given too much to America, to France, to Spain. He had let down the Tories, the merchants, the businessmen. Lord North and Charles James Fox, bitter enemies, formed an unholy coalition to bring down Shelburne. On February 22, 1783, the first anniversary of General Conway's resolution, Shelburne told the king he would resign. He was never again in power. He knew that he had done the right thing and this was his monument. The day after he quit office, Benjamin Vaughan wrote from London to Franklin: "To you I need not point out any of the absurdities of the public proceedings; but you will now see who has been your friend, and upon what principles... I am much satisfied at having heard him say that he repented of nothing that he had done, that he would do it all over again, and that he sees that he alone had the resolution to go through with it. God be praised that it is done, and that no one asks to have it undone!"

Eight years later, on July 4, 1791, Shelburne, by then Marquess of Lansdowne, wrote to Washington, introducing his son, Lord Wycombe, to the president. He alluded modestly to a role which deserves to rank him among England's great ministers:

I cannot possibly suffer my son to go to America without soliciting your protection of him during his stay within the United States [where] he can meet with no conversation which will not confirm him in those principles of freedom, which have constituted my happiness thro' life. I shall always look upon that as the happiest moment of it, when I had the good fortune to have it in my power to be of some little use in fixing the boundary between the respective dominions in a manner which, tho' not desired by the alliance, must, I trust and hope, in the end lay the foundation of cordial friendship and good understanding.

Washington replied that the United States had "a grateful recollection" of Lansdowne's role in the peace treaty and he wished "that the same liberal policy" might again be pursued in England so that the two countries would be "reciprocally beneficial to each other."

THE FRENCH LEAVE AMERICA

Although the French government had at times acted more as an enemy than an ally, the French army in America behaved with honor and politeness, and Washington admired many of its officers as much as they did him. Congress, however, grumbled that the French army seemed to be leaving in too much of a hurry, while the British were in occupation of posts in Maine, New York, and the Northwest Territory. Even the pro-French members of Congress (the Gallicans, as they were known) thought this rather preposterous.

Most of the French army left the Hudson for Boston near the end of October. In early December, Rochambeau and Chastellux, who were to sail from Annapolis, returned to Newburgh to make their farewells in person. Because Washington's headquarters were so small and crowded, Chastellux and Rochambeau appeared on separate days. Chastellux wrote of his visit:

We crossed the North River as night came on, and arrived at six o'clock [December 5] at Newburgh... The headquarters... consists of a single house, neither spacious nor convenient, which is built in the Dutch fashion. The largest room in it, which had served as the owner's family parlor and which General Washington has converted into his dining room, is in truth fairly spacious, but it has seven doors and only one window... I found the company assembled in a rather small room which served, and when the hour of bedtime came, I found that the chamber to which the General conducted me, was this very parlour, in which he had just had a camp bed set up.

We assembled at breakfast the next morning at ten, during which interval my bed was folded up and my chamber became the sitting room... The smallness of the house and the difficulty to which I saw that Mr. and Mrs. Washington had put themselves to receive me, made me apprehensive lest M. de Rochambeau... might arrive... I therefore took it upon myself to send someone to Fishkill to request him to stay there that night... He did not join us until the next morning just as I was setting out...

On the 7th I took leave of General Washington; it will not be difficult to believe that this parting was painful for me; but I have too much pleasure in recollecting the real tenderness with which it affected him, not to mention it...

Washington may have admired Chastellux more than any other senior French officer, for a week later he sent Chastellux a letter even more emotional than his correspondence with Lafayette:

I felt too much to express anything the day I parted with you; A Sense of your public Services to this Country, and gratitude for your private friendship quite overcame me at the moment of our separation. But I should be wanting to the feelings of my heart, were I to suffer you to leave this Country without the warmest assurances of affectionate regard for your person and character. Our good friend the Marqs. de la Fayette prepared me... for those Impressions of Esteem which... your own benevolent Mind has since improved into a deep and lasting friendship, a friendship which neither time nor distance can ever eradicate. I can truly say that never in my life did I part with a Man to whom my Soul clave more sincerely than it did to you... It will be one of my highest gratifications to keep up a regular intercourse with you by Letter...

Congress, in gratitude for Yorktown, had ordered that two of the English cannons captured there be presented to Rochambeau in the name of the United States. Washington went to a great deal of trouble to have these orders carried out. The cannon were hauled from Yorktown to Philadelphia and then on to West Point when the French army moved north. Washington had to find an engraver and draw up an inscription. He and Knox decided it should be in Latin. Washington sent it on to Lincoln, the secretary of war, with instructions to ask a professor at the college in Philadelphia to put it into "elegant Latin." The inscription, after translation, was engraved at West Point. The cannon were eventually trundled back to Philadelphia, for delivery to Rochambeau on his way to France. Rochambeau thought it too risky to take them home before the peace and asked Luzerne to send them along after the war. Eventually they were placed at the Chateau de Rochambeau, on the Loir, where, a few years later, they were taken by revolutionaries. Washington's letter of farewell to Rochambeau, though not his final letter sent with the cannon, was forwarded the day he wrote to Chastellux:

I cannot, my dear Genl., permit you to depart from this Country without repeating to you the high sense I entertain of the Services you have rendered America, by the constant attention you have paid to the interests of it.

By the exact order and discipline of the Corps under your Command, and by your readiness, at all times, to give facility to every measure which the force of the Combined Armies was competent to.

To this testimony of your Public character I should be wanting to the feelings of my heart, were I not to add expressions of the happiness I have enjoyed in your private friendship. The remembrance of which will be one of the most pleasing Circumstances of my life.

My best wishes will accompany you to France, where I have no doubt of your meeting the Smiles and rewards of a generous Prince; and the warmest embraces of affectionate friends.

DISTRESSES

Washington had to turn from affectionate farewells to the growing distress and anger of the army. The day after he wrote his final letters to Rochambeau and Chastellux, he sent a communication to Joseph Jones, a Virginia congressman:

In the course of a few days Congress will, I expect, receive an Address from the Army on the subject of their grievances.

This Address, tho' couched in very respectful terms, is one of those things which tho' unpleasing, is just now unavoidable; for I was very apprehensive once, that matters would have taken a more unfavourable turn, from the variety of discontents which prevailed at this time.

The temper of the Army is much soured, and has become more irritable than at any period since the commencement of the War. This consideration alone, prevented me (for everything else seemed to be in a state of inactivity and almost tranquillity) from requesting leave to spend the winter in Virginia, that I might give some attention to my long neglected private concerns.

The dissatisfactions of the Army had arisen to a great and alarming height, and combinations among the Officers to resign, at given periods, in a body, were beginning to take place, when by some address and management, their resolutions have been converted into the form that will now appear before Congress. What that Honble. Body can, or will do in the matter, does not belong to me to determine; but policy, in my opinion, should dictate soothing measures; as it is an incontrovertible fact, that no part of the community has undergone equal hardships, and borne them with the same patience and fortitude, that the Army has done.

Hitherto the Officers have stood between the lower order of the Soldiery and the public, and in more instances than one, at the hazard of their lives, have quelled very dangerous mutinies. But if their discontents should be suffered to rise equally high, I know not what the consequences may be.

The spirit of enthusiasm which overcame everything at first, is now done away; it is idle therefore to expect more from Military men, than from those discharging the Civil departments of Government. If both were to fare equally alike with respect to the emoluents of Office, I would answer for it that the Military character should not be the first to complain. But it is an invidious distinction, and one that will not stand the test of reason or policy, that one set should receive all, and the other no part... of their pay.

On Christmas day, Washington wrote his quartermaster general that there was such a scarcity of fodder, his horses had not eaten for three days. His general officers could not get to headquarters, even on urgent business, "their horses being too weak to carry them." Even the mail was now coming long distances on the backs of his soldiers. That day, Robert Livingston, the secretary for foreign affairs, informed him of the Oswald commission to negotiate peace. This did not reach him until January 8 but he responded with a note of better cheer: "The Power given to Mr. Oswald... is more than I expected would have happened before the Meeting of Parliament; but as the Gentlemen on the part of America could not treat with Him unless such powers were given, it became an Act of necessity to cede them to effect their other purposes. Thus I account for the indirect acknowledgment of our Independence by the King; who I dare say felt some severe pangs at the time he put his hand to the Letters Patent. It is not however less efficacious or pleasing on that account."

It was only a momentary ray. On January he wrote to General Armstrong and to Tench Tilghman, giving them the news of the Oswald commission. To Armstrong he added: "The Army, as usual, are without Pay; and a great part of the Soldiery without Shirts; and tho' the patience of them is equally thread-bear, the States seem perfectly indifferent to their cries... If one were to hazard for them an opinion... it would be that the Army had encountered such a habit of encountering distress and difficulties... that it would be impolitic and injurious to introduce other customs in it." To Tilghman he said: "Upon the whole I am fixed in an opinion that Peace, or, a pretty long continuance of the War will have been determined before the Adjournment [of Parliament] for the Holidays, and as it will be the middle or last of Feby. before we shall know the result, time will pass heavily on in this dreary mansion in which we are fast locked by frost and Snow."

On January 14, a handsome new sleigh, built at General Knox's orders, was driven to his door for his use, thus enabling Washington and his wife to escape and get some air. A pleased Washington wrote Knox that he thought the sleigh "handsome, convenient and well executed. Shall I thank you for giving the Master Workman a couple of Guineas, to be laid out in liquour for those who have been engaged in this business?"

TWO

NEWBURGH TO MOUNT VERNON

1783

THE WEAKNESSES OF the American confederacy had long been Washington's particular crown of thorns. To John Jay they were an invitation to the wolves of Europe to prey. After describing French and Spanish intrigues to Robert Livingston, November 17, 1782, Jay wrote that Great Britain might well attempt once more to conquer America "if they again thought they could. I think we have no rational dependence except on God and ourselves." On September 24 of the following year, he wrote Gouverneur Morris: "I am perfectly convinced that no time is to be lost in raising and maintaining a national spirit in America. Power to govern the confederacy, as to all general purposes, should be granted and exercised. The government of the different States should be wound up, and become vigorous. America is beheld with jealousy, and jealousy is seldom idle."

As his army service drew to its close, a vigorous and newly politically minded Washington appeared. In brilliant papers to Congress and the states, in his farewell to his soldiers, in individual letters to his officers, confederate executives, state governors, congressmen, and friends, he stressed the danger that a divided country would be "the sport of European politics." His dominant theme, which reached every literate American, was summed up in his last toast as general of the armies: "Competent power to the Congress for general purposes." His countrymen expressed the idea more picturesquely: "Cement to the union... A hoop for the barrel."

BOREDOM

The comte de Vergennes had endeavored to dissuade Franklin and his fellow commissioners from informing Congress of the terms of the November 30 treaty. Franklin asked Vergennes what Congress would think if they heard of it from others. The commissioners seem to have thought the treaty would go quickly to Philadelphia in the *Washington*, Captain Joshua Barney commanding. There is no evidence that the French delayed Barney's departure but he did not sail from France until January 17. His crossing was long and stormy. He did not reach America until March 12 while Washington waited with impatient boredom for news.

From his bleak Newburgh house Washington wrote his old friend Bryan Fairfax on February 5: "At present, we are fast locked in Frost and Snow; without a tittle of news. We look wistfully to the East, and to the South for an arrival; supposing the first European Vessel will bring the Speech of the British King, the Addresses, and debates thereupon; the last of which I expect, will discover the Ultimatum of the national determination respecting the continuance of the War, or acceptance of Peace..." The same day he wrote General William Heath: "Without amusements or avocations, I am spending another Winter (I hope it will be the last that I shall be kept from returning to domestic life) amongst these rugged and dreary Mountains." On February 6, when congratulating Greene on the departure of the last redcoat from the south, Washington made one of his relatively rare reminiscences about the long war:

It is with a pleasure which friendship only is susceptible of, I congratulate you on the glorious end you have put to hostilities in the Southern States; the honor and advantage of it, I hope, and trust, you will long live to enjoy. When this hemisphere will be equally free, is yet in the womb of time to discover; a little while, however 'tis presumed, will disclose the determinations of the British Senate with respect to peace or War...

If Historiographers should be hardy enough to fill the page of History with the advantages that have been gained with unequal numbers (on the part of America) in the course of this contest, and attempt to relate the distressing circumstances under which they have been obtained, it is more than probable that Posterity will bestow on their labors the epithet and marks of fiction; for it will not be believed that such a force as Great Britain has employed for eight years in this country could be baffled in their plan of Subjugating it by numbers infinitely less, composed of Men oftentimes half starved; always in Rags, without pay, and experiencing, at times, every species of distress which human nature is capable of undergoing...

While waiting for peace, most of the general officers found urgent reasons to request leaves of absence—lawsuits, family troubles, financial problems, and plain ennui. When General St. Clair requested an extension of an already long leave, Washington, irked, wrote that if St. Clair expected to retain his command, he had better come back. "I do not here enter fully into a detail of the reasons which now make it particularly necessary for the Genl. Officers who have been long absent to join without loss of time; it will surely be sufficient to mention that out of nine Generals assigned to the command of the Troops in this Cantonment, seven are actually gone or have made applications to be absent at the same time, so that by gratifying their wishes, the whole weight of the business, and cares and troubles of the Army would devolve upon me, until a sunshine occasion, or a prospect of some brilliant operation would induce them to return and share the pleasures and honors of the service."

The chaplains, also bored, went off in great numbers. On February 15 Washington ordered Divine Service to be held every Sunday, in each brigade, for the "Homage and adoration which are due to the Supreme Being, who has through his infinite goodness brought our public Calamities and dangers (in all human probability) very near to a happy conclusion." He added: "The General has been surprised to find in Winter Quarters that the chaplains have frequently been almost all absent at the same time, under an idea their presence could not be of any utility at that season; he thinks it proper he should be allowed to judge of that matter himself, and therefore no future furloughs will be granted to chaplains except in consequence of permission from Headquarters..."

FAMILY TROUBLES

Almost invariably the bittersweet problems of Washington's family and domestic economy intruded, at even the happiest of times. His brother, Samuel, having had five wives, four of whom may have succumbed to tuberculosis, died in 1781, leaving seven children and stepchildren under fourteen along with numerous debts. His brother, John, wrote on November 12, 1782, giving the details. Washington replied the following January 16, referring first to Samuel, and then to complaints from his mother:

[Your letter] gave me extreme pain. In God's name how did my Brothr. Saml. contrive to get himself so enormously in debt? Was it by purchase? By misfortunes? Or sheer indolence and inattention to business? From whatever cause it proceeded, the matter is now the same, and curiosity only prompts the enquiry, as it does to know what will be saved, and how it is disposed of. In the list of his debts did it appear that I had a claim upon him for the purchase money of the Land I sold Pendleton on Bullskin? I have never received a farthing for it yet, and think I have been informed by him that he was to pay it.

I have lately received a letter from my Mother in which she complains much <u>of the Knavery of the Overseer at the Little Falls Quarter</u>, that She says she can get nothing from him. It is pretty evident, I believe, that I get nothing from thence, which I have the annual rent of between Eighty and an Hundred pounds to pay. The whole profit of the plantation, according to her Acct., is applied to his own use, which is rather hard upon me as I had no earthly inducement to meddle with it but to comply with her wish, and to free her from care. This, like every other matter of private concern with me, has been totally neglected; but it is too much while I am suffering in every other way (and hardly able to keep my own Estate from Sale), to be saddled with all the expence of hers and not be able to derive the smallest return from it. She has requested that I would get somebody to attend to it. I must therefore desire the favor of you to take it under your care. I know of none in whose hands it can be better placed, of none to whom it can be less inconvenient, and who is more interested in the good managemt. of the Land. For as it lyes directly in your Route to Berkley, and in the Neighbourhood of our friends, where you must always make a halt, it will give you very little additional trouble to provide an Overseer. Call upon him as you pass and repass, and settle the annual Accts. with him, so that I may have some knowledge of his transactions and a certainty that whatever is made goes towards payment of the Rent. I shall by this Post inform my Mother of this application to you...

While I am talking of my Mother and her concerns, I am impelled to mention something which has given, and still continues to give me pain. About two years ago a Gentleman of my acquaintance informed me that it was in contemplation that a move for a pension for her would reach the Virginia Assembly. That he did not suppose I knew of the measure, or that it would be agreeable to me to have it done; but wished to know my sentiments on it. I instantly wrote him that it was new and astonishing to me and begged that he would prevent the motion if possible, or oppose it if made; for I was sure she had not a Child that would not share the last farthing with her, and that would not be hurt at the idea of her becoming a Pensioner, or in other words receiving charity. Since <u>then</u> I have heard nothing of

<u>that</u> matter; but I learn from very good authority that she is, upon all occasions, and in all Companies complaining of the hardness of the times, of her wants and distresses; and if not in direct terms, at least by strong innuendos, inviting favours which not only makes <u>her</u> appear in an unfavourable point of view but <u>those</u> also who are connected with her. That she can have no <u>real</u> wants that may not be supplied I am sure of; <u>imaginary</u> wants are indefinite and oftentimes insatiable, because they are boundless and always changing. The reason of my mentioning these matters to you is, that you may enquire into her real wants and see what is necessary to make her comfortable. If the Rent is insufficient to do this, while I have anything I will part with it to make her so; and wish you to take measures in my behalf accordingly; at the same time I wish you to represent to her in delicate terms that impropriety of her complaints and acceptance of favours, even when they are voluntarily offered, from any but relations. It will not do to touch upon this subject in a letter to her, and therefore I have avoided it...

The general had become well accustomed to shocks but the reports on his farms and property from Lund Washington, his wartime Mount Vernon manager, quite upset him. Lund had encountered great difficulties because his markets overseas and many needed supplies had been cut by hostilities. He was required to supply all goods needed by Martha Washington as well as take care of many problems of her son and Washington's mother. During the war years he had not written much about the financial results of Mount Vernon's operations. Washington, on the other hand, had drawn only his actual expenses from Congress for his services. When hostilities ceased, he became increasingly concerned about conditions at home. On January 29, Lund gave him a few figures on the 1782 corn crop, adding: "I generally put off writing... I had rather be employed in the most laborious way than copying any writing... It causes me to keep irregular accounts." He suggested he might be able to persuade himself to write something by the next mail. A chill blast was returned from the north on February 12:

You do not seem to have considered the force and tendency of the words of yr. letter when you talk of the probability <u>only</u> of sending me "the long promised account the irregularity of them"; not you add "for want of knowledge in keeping them but neglect"; your aversion to writing, &ca. &ca. These are but other words for saying "as I am not fond of writing, and it is <u>quite</u> immaterial whether you have any knowledge or information of your private concerns or whether the accts. are kept properly or not, I have delayed, and do not know how much longer I may continue to delay bringing you acquainted with these accts., irregular as they are."

Delicacy hitherto, and a hope that you long ago would have seen into the propriety of the measure, without a hint of it from me, has restrained me from telling you that the annual Accts. of my Crops, together with the receipts and expenditure of my money, state of my stocks, &ca. ought to have been sent to me as regularly as the year came about. It is not to be supposed that all the avocations of my public duties, great and laborious as they have been, could render me totally insensible to the <u>only</u> <u>means</u> by which myself and my family, and the character I am to maintain in life hereafter, is to be supported, or that a precise acct. of these matters would not have been exceedingly satisfactory to me. Instead of this, except the Acct. rendered at Valley Forge in the year 1778 I have received none since I left home; and not till after two or 3 applications in the course of last year could I get any acct. of the crop of the preceding one; and then only of the Corn by the Post on Sunday last.

I have often told you, and I repeat it with much truth; that the entire confidence I placed in your integrity made me easy, and I was always happy at thinking my Affairs were in your hands, which I could not have been, if they had been under the care of a common Manager; but this did not exempt me from the desires which all men have, of knowing the exact state of them. I have now to beg that you will not only send me the Account of your receipts, and expenditures of Specie; but of every kind of money subsequent to the Acct. exhibited at Valley Forge, which ended sometime in April 1778.

I want to know before I come home (as I shall come home with empty pockets whenever peace shall take place) how Affairs stand with me, and what my dependence is.

I wish to know also, what I have to expect from the Wheat of 1781 and 82, as you say the two Crops are so blended that they cannot be rendered separately. How are settlements to be made with and justice done to the several Parties interested under these circumstances?

Lund Washington provided a confusing reply, indicating he had once offered to send the accounts but the general had not specifically stated that he wanted them. He added: "It is painful to me to make excuses for bad crops, but owing to one cause or another, we have not made a good one in my remembrance." Lund wrote again, forwarding some accounts, which Washington did not find encouraging. He replied on June 11: "You seem to have an unconquerable aversion to going from home; one consequence of which is, I expect I shall lose all my rents; for in a letter from my brother John in Berkeley, are these words: 'I fear you are suffering *greatly* in your rents, as I am informed many of the tenants are gone into the Western country; and understand there are many arrears of rent due to you.'... If your own wages... have not been received by you... which does not appear by the Accts. you have lately rendered to me; I shall be more hurt than at anything else, to think that an Estate, which I have drawn nothing from for eight years... should not have been able for the last five years, to pay the manager. And that, worse than going home to empty coffers, and expensive living, I shall be encumbered with debt. It is disagreeable to me, because I dare say it will be so to you, to make these observations, but as my public business is now drawing to a close, I cannot avoid looking towards my private concerns, which do not bear the most smiling countenance." Lund subsequently advised the general that Mount Vernon was going to need a new roof. The French officers, before leaving America, had all expressed the hope that he would come to France, but his financial troubles were to rule out this possibility.

NEWBURGH AND NEAR MUTINY

In August 1782 Congress repealed the suspension of Gates from command, as well as its earlier recommendation for a court of inquiry on his conduct at Camden. He reported to Washington in October; the general received him cordially and assigned him command of the right wing. Although chastened, Gates had not quite lost his taste for intrigue. In his activities he operated through his aide, Major John Armstrong, Jr., and his former aide, Colonel Walter Stewart, who had been made the army's inspector general.

On January 6 a committee of officers, headed by General McDougall, appeared before Congress to present a respectful petition on their deplorable financial position. Alexander Hamilton, now in Congress, was appointed chairman of a finance committee to work out plans for a national revenue which would meet the needs of the army. In the ensuing discussions, which eventually brought the army close to open revolution, Hamilton played a constructive role in maintaining an authoritative line of communication between Congress and the commander in chief.

Congress, so Hamilton informed Washington, was split into factions. There were those who feared the army. There were pro-British and pro-French groups; some were for states' rights while others advocated a national power and revenue. The government was totally broke and what, unless the states showed more sense, could the army do? By February 7 Hamilton was writing Washington: "I will not conceal from your Excellency a truth which it is necessary you should know. An idea is propagated in the army that delicacy, carried to an extreme, prevents your espousing its interests with sufficient warmth. The falsehood of this opinion no one can be better acquainted with than myself, but it is not the less mischievous for being false. Its tendency is to impair that influence which you may exert with advantage, should any commotions unhappily ensue, to moderate the pretensions of the army and make their conduct correspond with their duty."

The rumors that flew between Philadelphia and Newburgh multiplied, each inflaming the other. When Congress passed some stopgap resolutions on February 6, reports reached Newburgh to the effect that Congress hoped quickly to dissolve the army and thus evade its financial obligations. Not long afterwards, rumors circulated in Congress that the army had voted not to disband and to use whatever force was necessary to establish its claims. By February 20 it began to be clear that a secret hand, that of Gates, was at work. Hamilton had never forgiven Washington but he thoroughly disliked Gates. The essence of his private statements was to trust Washington, at all costs, in the crisis. As Madison reported it, Hamilton said that:

> It was certain that the army had secretly determined not to lay down their arms until due provision and a satisfactory prospect should be afforded on the subject of their pay... The Commander was already become extremely unpopular, among all ranks, from his known dislike to every unlawful proceeding; that this unpopularity was daily increasing and industriously promoted by many leading characters; that his choice of unfit and indiscreet persons into his family was the pretext, and with some the real motive; but the substantial one [was] a desire to displace him from the respect and confidence of the army, in order to substitute General [Gates]... Mr. Hamilton said that he knew General Washington intimately and perfectly; that his extreme reserve, mixed sometimes with a degree of asperity of temper, both of which were said to have increased somewhat of late, had contributed to the decline of his popularity; but that his virtue, his patriotism and firmness... might be depended upon never to yield to any dishonorable or disloyal plans...

On February 27 Joseph Jones of Virginia informed Washington of the many reports reaching Philadelphia that dangerous combinations were being formed in the army. On March 4 the general wrote Hamilton: "The predicament in which I stand as Citizen and Soldier, is as critical and delicate as can well be conceived. It has been the subject of many contemplative hours. The sufferings of a complaining Army on the one hand, and the inability of Congress and tardiness of the States on the other, are the forebodings of evil... Unless Congress have powers competent to all *general* purposes... the distresses we have encountered, and the blood we have spilt in the course of an Eight years war, will avail us nothing..." In a veiled reference, which he knew Hamilton would understand, he noted that the ideas propagated against him in the army arose from an easily traced source. This was the "old leaven" of the cabal—General Gates—who was operating "under a mask of the most perfect dissimulation and apparent cordiality."

On March 8 Colonel Walter Stewart arrived in camp from Philadelphia. Until then, according to Washington, there had been no serious agitation. Stewart stirred up the whole camp with his report that Congress intended to disband the army without doing it justice. Two days later the first of three anonymous letters circulated within the army; these became known as the Newburgh addresses. They were written by Gates' aide, John Armstrong, and circulated by Stewart and his assistant, Major William Barber. Armstrong, only twenty-four, drew up a rather juvenile harangue which had its emotional impact:

> *After a pursuit of seven long years, the object for which we sought is at length brought within our reach... Peace returns again to bless—whom? A country willing to redress your wrongs, cherish your worth, and reward your services?... Or is it rather a country that tramples upon your rights, disdains your cries, and insults your distresses...*

> *Change the milk-and-water tone of your last memorial. Assume a bolder style... and suspect the man who would advise more moderation and larger forbearance... Let two or three men who can feel as well as write, be appointed to draw up your last remonstrance... Tell them that the slightest mark of indignity from Congress must now operate like the grave and part you forever... Nothing shall separate you from your arms but death. . .*

Armstrong further suggested that, even if war continued, the army should retire, under Washington's leadership, "to some unsettled country." If peace came, their swords would establish justice for themselves. Washington simply issued an order that the meeting, called by the faction for March 11, was not to be held; he added that he was sure no officer would respond to an irregular call from an unknown person. He ordered, in its place, a meeting of all general and field officers, together with one officer from each company, to meet on March 15 to discuss their representations to Congress. Armstrong immediately put out another anonymous letter, noting that the commander in chief, who had, to this time, only expressed "good wishes" for their success with Congress, was now on their side. Washington then issued to the army such congressional resolves as he had received, respecting their willingness to meet their commitments. He also talked individually with all his principal officers, asking for restraint; from them he heard that emotions had run wild. Contrary to his original intention, and probably mistrusting Gates, he showed up at the meeting.

A month previously, Washington, who had read and written so much over eight years, received a new pair of glasses from David Rittenhouse of Philadelphia. He thanked him on February 16: "The Spectacles suit my Eyes extremely well, as I am persuaded that the reading glasses also will when I get more accustomed to the use of them. At present I find some difficulty in coming at the proper Focus; but when I do obtain it, they magnify properly and shew those objects very distinctly which at first appear like a mist blended together and confused."

When all his officers were assembled, Washington entered and went to the lectern. He said he had not originally planned to come but he now had with him a written paper. As he pulled it from his pocket, he also took out the Rittenhouse glasses and said: "Gentlemen, you will permit me to put on my spectacles, for I have not only grown grey, but almost blind, in the service of my country." Those present noticed involuntary tears start in his officers' eyes. The audience was his. He proceeded:

> By an anonymous summons, an attempt has been made to convene you together; how inconsistent with the rules of propriety! how unmilitary! and how subversive of all order and discipline, let the good sense of the Army decide.

> In the moment of this Summons, another anonymous production was sent into circulation, addressed more to the feelings and passion, than to the reason and judgement of the Army. The author of the piece is entitled to much credit for the goodness of his Pen and I could wish he had as much credit for the rectitude of his heart, for Men see thro' different Optics, [as] induced by the reflecting faculties of the Mind... The Author of the Address should have had more charity than to mark for Suspicion, the Man who should recommend moderation and longer forbearance, or, in other words, who should not think as he thinks, and act as he advises. But he had another plan in view, in which candor and liberality of Sentiment, regard to justice and love of Country, have no part; and he was right to insinuate the darkest suspicion [in order] to effect the blackest design.

> ...This much, Gentlemen, I have thought it incumbent upon me to observe to you, to shew you upon what principles I opposed the irregular and hasty meeting... not because I wanted a disposition to give you every opportunity consistent with your own honor, and the dignity of the Army, to make known your grievances. If my conduct heretofore has not evinced to you that I have been a faithful friend to the Army, my declaration of it at this time would be equally unavailing and improper. But as I was among the first who embarked in the cause of our common Country; as I have never left your side one moment, but when called from you on public duty; as

I have been the constant companion and witness of your Distresses, and not among the last to feel and acknowledge your merits; as I have ever considered my own Military reputation as inseparably connected with that of the Army; as my Heart has ever expanded with joy when I heard its praises, and my indignation has arisen when the mouth of detraction has been opened against it; it can <u>scarcely</u> <u>be</u> <u>supposed</u>, at this late stage of the war, that I am indifferent to its interests. But, how are they to be promoted? The way is plain, says the anonymous Addresser. If War continues, remove into the unsettled Country; there establish yourselves, and leave an ungrateful Country to defend itself. But who are they to defend? Our Wives, our Children, Our Farms... If Peace takes place, never sheath your Swords, Says he, until you have obtained full and ample justice; this dreadful alternative, of either deserting our Country in the extremest hour of her distress... or turning our Arms against it... has something so shocking in it that humanity revolts at the idea. My God! what can this writer have in view, by recommending such measures?...

There might, Gentlemen, be an impropriety in my taking notice... of an anonymous production, but the manner in which that performance has been introduced into the Army, the effect it was intended to have, together with some other circumstances, will amply justify my observations... With respect to the advice given by the Author, to suspect the Man who shall recommend moderate measures and longer forbearance, I spurn it, as every Man who regards that liberty and reveres that justice for which we contend, undoubtedly must; for if Men are to be precluded from offering their Sentiments on a matter which may involve the most serious and alarming consequences, reason is of no use to us; the freedom of Speech may be taken away, and dumb and silent, we may be led, like sheep, to the slaughter.

I cannot... conclude... without giving it as my decided opinion that [Congress] entertain exalted sentiments of the Services of the Army, and, from a full conviction of its merits and sufferings, will do it compleat justice...

For myself... a grateful sense of the confidence you have placed in me, a recollection of the cheerful assistance, and prompt obedience I have experienced from you... and the sincere affection I feel for an Army I have so long had the honor to Command, will oblige me to declare in this public and solemn manner, that in the attainment of compleat justice for all your toils and dangers, you may freely command my Services to the utmost of my abilities.

While I give these assurances... let me entreat you, Gentlemen, on your part not to take any measures which, viewed in the calm light of reason, will lessen the dignity, and sully the glory you have hitherto maintained... Let me conjure you... as you value your sacred honor, as you respect the rights of humanity... to express your utmost horror and detestation of the Man who wishes, under any specious pretences, to overturn the liberties of our Country, and who wickedly attempts to open the flood Gates [sic] of Civil discord, and deluge our rising Empire in Blood. By thus determining and thus acting, you will pursue the plain and direct road to the attainment of your wishes... You will give one more distinguished proof of unexampled patriotism and patient virtue... And you will, by the dignity of your Conduct, afford occasion for Posterity to say, when speaking of the glorious example you have exhibited to Mankind, "Had this day been wanting, the World had never seen the last stage of perfection to which human nature is capable of attaining."

Washington had once been considered no orator but he reached a peak here that he was to surpass on but few occasions. Leaving a stunned Gates in charge, Washington departed. Resolutions were quickly and unanimously passed expressing the confidence of every officer, including Gates, in Washington and Congress, and denouncing the "infamous" proposals of Armstrong.

One officer present, Major J. A. Wright, wrote: "[Washington] made a most excellent address; he appeared sensibly agitated, as the writer advises, 'to suspect the man who should advise moderation.' This expression... gave reason to suppose that it was a plan laid against his Excellency, as every one who knows him must be sensible that he would recommend moderation." Major Samual Shaw, who had seen him in battle and on many other occasions, said that he had never known him so truly great as at this meeting. "He stood single and alone. There was no saying where the passions of an army which were not a little inflamed, might not lead; but it was generally allowed that further forbearance was dangerous, and moderation had ceased to be a virtue. Under these circumstances he appeared, not at the head of his troops, but as it were, in opposition to them; and for a dreadful moment the interests of the army and its general seemed to be in competition. He spoke—every doubt was dispelled... What he says of the army may with equal justice be applied to his own character: 'Had this day been wanting, the world had never seen the last stage of perfection which human nature is capable of attaining.'"

Washington had forgiven Gates many times, but his sponsorship of the Newburgh addresses was too much. He considered the phrase, "Suspect the man who would advise moderation" as having originated with the second in command in the army. There is little doubt that Washington, who punned so often, deliberately inserted a plea to express detestation of "the Man who wickedly attempts to open the flood Gates of civil discord." Having thoroughly crushed Gates, Washington thereafter rarely spoke of him.

Major Armstrong had written that Washington expressed only good wishes that the army might get something. In fact, Congress and its executives had felt almost unbearable pressure from the commander in chief. Now Washington applied scalding heat. In transmitting the Newburgh resolves to the president of Congress on March 18, he said that they were "the last glorious proof of Patriotism [which] will not only confirm their claim to the justice but will increase their title to the gratitude of their Country." He continued, including a brief quotation from Armstrong:

> *If the whole Army has not merited whatever a grateful people can bestow, than have I been beguiled by prejudice, and built opinion on the basis of error. And "if" (as has been suggested for the purpose of inflaming their passions) "the Officers of the Army… are to grow old in poverty wretchedness and contempt," then shall I have learned what ingratitude is, then shall I have realized a tale which will embitter every moment of my future life. But I am under no such apprehensions, a Country rescued by their Arms from impending ruin, will never leave unpaid the debt of gratitude.*

Further letters followed in rapid succession to individual members, outlining the hunger, the cold, and the nakedness the army had suffered, the battles they had fought, and the jails they now faced if sent off penniless and in debt. Congress, on receipt of news of the great storm aroused by the Newburgh addresses had, with unexpected humor, appointed a committee, composed of those who opposed the army's claims, to meet their complaints. Soon, however, others took over, including two of Washington's former officers, Hamilton and Theodorick Bland. A makeshift revenue bill was presented to the states. In the end, the officers' and soldiers' claims were recognized, though they had to be content with treasury IOUs. These were funded into the national debt when Washington became president.

Washington also persuaded Congress to approve other rewards, which cost little but meant much to the army. All officers who had honorably served from January 1, 1776 on, were given a brevet one grade higher than they held at the conclusion of the war. Thus colonels could retire as brigadiers. For the enlisted men he proposed that the country make a free gift to them of the "arms and accoutrements" they had carried during the war. He wrote: "These constant companions of their Toils and Dangers, preserved with sacred Care, would be handed down from the present possessors to their Children, as honorable Badges of Bravery and Military Merit; and would probably be bro't forth, on some future Occasion, with Pride and Exultation… in the hands of Posterity." The final thing Washington did for his army was to sign all honorable discharges of officers and all badges of merit for enlisted men. Such signatures ran into the thousands.

PEACE

If Washington was interested in peace, so were his enlisted men. Private Joseph Plumb Martin, writing long afterwards, remembered the camp rumors as to what would be done with "General Washington's watch-chain." This was a 136-ton linked barrier across the Hudson at West Point which, as regularly as clockwork, was put in place when navigation opened in the spring and removed in the fall, before the river froze. That spring it was kept in the warehouse. On March 30 Washington had word of a general European armistice.

On April 6 Sir Guy Carleton informed Washington that he had just received the official peace intelligence from England. He would therefore declare a cessation of hostilities for April 8. Washington, in his turn, picked April 19, the eighth anniversary of the battle at Concord's rude bridge, for his proclamation. In joy as he wrote, he moved from army prose to a soaring flight of words, matched by no other founding father:

> *The Commander in Chief orders the Cessation of Hostilities between the United States of America and the King of Great Britain to be publickly proclaimed tomorrow at 12 o'clock at the New Building, and that the Proclamation [of Congress] which will be communicated herewith, be read tomorrow evening at the head of every regiment and corps of the army. After which the Chaplains with the several Brigades will render thanks to almighty God for all his mercies, particularly for his overruling the wrath of man to his own glory, and causing the rage of war to cease among the nations.*

> *Although the proclamation before alluded to, extends only to the prohibition of hostilities, and not the annunciation of a general peace, yet it must afford the most rational and sincere satisfaction to every benevolent mind, as it puts a period to a long and doubtful contest, stops the effusion of human blood, opens the prospect to a more splendid scene, and like another morning star, promises the approach of a brighter day than hath hitherto illuminated the Western Hemisphere; on such a happy day, a day which is the harbinger of Peace, a day which completes the eighth year of the war, it would be ingratitude not to rejoice! It would be insensibility not to participate in the general felicity.*

> *The Commander in Chief far from endeavouring to stifle the feelings of Joy in his own bosom, offers his most cordial Congratulations on the occasion to all the Officers of every denomination, to all the Troops of the United States in General, and in particular to those gallant and persevering men who had resolved to defend the rights of their invaded country so long as the war should continue. For these are*

the men who ought to be considered as the pride and boast of the American Army; And who, crowned with well earned laurels, may soon withdraw from the field of Glory, to the more tranquil walks of civil life.

While the General recollects the almost infinite variety of Scenes thro' which we have passed, with a mixture of pleasure, astonishment and gratitude; While he contemplates the prospects before us with rapture; he can not help wishing that all the brave men (of whatever condition they may be) who have shared in the toils and dangers of effecting this glorious revolution, of rescuing Millions from the hand of oppression, and of laying the foundation of a great Empire, might be impressed with a proper idea of the dignified part they have been called to act (under the Smiles of Providence) on the stage of human affairs; for, happy, thrice happy, shall they be pronounced thereafter who have contributed any thing, who have performed the meanest office, in erecting this stupendous <u>Fabrick</u> of <u>Freedom</u> and <u>Empire</u> on the broad basis of Independence; who have assisted in protecting the rights of human nature and establishing an Asylum for the poor and oppressed of all nations and religions. The glorious task for which we first flew to Arms being thus accomplished, the liberties of our Country being fully acknowledged and firmly secured by the smiles of heaven on the purity of our cause and the honest exertions of a feeble people (determined to be free) against a powerful Nation (disposed to oppress them) and the Character of those who have persevered through every extremity of hardship; suffering and danger, being immortalized by the illustrious appellation of the <u>patriot</u> <u>Army</u>; Nothing now remains but for the actors of this mighty scene to preserve a perfect, unvarying, consistency of character through the very last act; to close the Drama with applause; and to retire from the Military Theatre with the same approbation of Angels and men which have crowned all their former virtuous actions..."

THE ARMY MELTS AWAY

The address was much appreciated by the troops who failed to notice one of the concluding sentences: "Every considerate and well disposed soldier must remember that it will be absolutely necessary to wait with patience until peace shall be declared or Congress shall be enabled to take proper measures for the security of the public stores..." As Washington soon discovered, the soldiers could not distinguish between preliminary and final treaties. It was peace, they wanted to go home, and there was no way to stop them.

By the middle of June Washington was writing Lafayette: "We remain here in a listless state, awaiting the arrival of the definitive treaty; the uncertainty of which, added to the great expense of subsisting the Army, have induced

Congress to Furlough (which, in the present case is but another term for discharging) all the Soldiers who stood engaged for the War." Although Washington and Robert Morris tried to see that the soldiers had some small portion of their long missing pay in cash, they got only scrip. Many had to beg as they made their long hike from Newburgh to distant points. Washington had feared a clamor, and even a mutiny, but they went off quietly.

The situation was different in Lancaster, far from Washington's control. There, relatively new recruits, as he was careful to point out to Congress, complained about being discharged without pay. Eighty or so of them, under two sergeants, started for Philadelphia on June 17, in defiance of their officers. They intended to make their principal pleas, or threats, to the government of Pennsylvania, whose legislature shared Independence Hall with the Continental Congress. Hamilton, on behalf of Congress, appealed to the state's president, John Dickinson, to call out the militia but Dickinson refused. When the mutineers got to Philadelphia, they induced several hundred more men to join. On June 21 they surrounded the hall with fixed bayonets, shouting at both the state and national legislatures. Congress urgently asked Washington for help. He dispatched 1,500 troops under General Howe to Philadelphia. Before they arrived, Congress, muttering that the "majesty" of the United States had been "offended," removed itself to Princeton. The state government then called out its militia; with the approach of Washington's troops, the mutiny collapsed. Congress did not return to Philadelphia until 1790.

That autumn, in the congressional debates as to where the permanent capital should be, even Pennsylvania did not appear to want it in Philadelphia but offered Germantown. The majority of delegates appeared to think Maryland was more suitable and the choice should be between Annapolis and Georgetown.

PLEA FOR NATIONAL UNION

The commander in chief, his "sensibility" excited by seeing his veterans going off with pieces of paper they were expected to persuade the states to cash, decided on a plea to the whole country for a strong national government. On June 8 he finished a moving and forceful appeal under the modest title "Circular to the States." In it he announced his forthcoming retirement "for which I have never ceased to sigh through a long and painful absence." The address was lengthy:

> *The Citizens of America, placed in the most enviable condition, as the sole Lords and Proprietors of a vast Tract of Continent, comprehending all the various soils*

and climates of the World... are now acknowledged to be possessed of absolute freedom and Independence; They are, from this period, to be considered as the Actors on the most conspicuous Theatre, which seems to be peculiarly designed by Providence for the display of human greatness and felicity; Here, they are not only surrounded with every thing which can contribute to the completion of private and domestic enjoyment, but Heaven has crowned all its other blessings, by giving more opportunity for political happiness, than any other Nation has been favored with...

...Notwithstanding the cup of blessing... thus reached out to us, notwithstanding happiness is ours... yet... there is an option still left to the United States of America... whether they will be respectable and prosperous, or contemptible and miserable as a Nation; This is the moment when the eyes of the whole world are turned upon them, this is the moment to establish or ruin their Character forever, this is the favorable moment to give such a tone to our Federal Government, as will enable it to answer the ends of its institution, or this may be the ill-fated moment for relaxing the powers of the Union... exposing us to become the sport of European politics... for, according to the system of policy the states shall adopt at this moment, they will stand or fall... It is yet to be decided whether the Revolution was a blessing or a curse, not to the present age alone for, with our fate, will the destiny of unborn Millions be involved.

With this conviction of the importance of the present Crisis, silence in me would be a crime; there are four things... essential to the well being, I may even venture to say, to the existence of the United States as an Independent Power:

1st. An indissoluble Union of the States under one Federal Head

2dly. A Sacred regard to Public Justice

3dly. The adaption of a proper Peace Establishment, and

4thly. The prevalence of that pacific and friendly Disposition, among the People of the United States, which will induce them to forget their local prejudices and policies, to make those mutual concessions which are requisite to the general prosperity...

These are the pillars... Liberty is the Basis... It will be part of my duty, and that of every true Patriot to assert without reserve... that it is indispensable to the happiness of the individual States, that there should be lodged somewhere, A Supreme Power to regulate and govern the general concerns of the Confederated Republick without which the Union cannot be of long duration... Without an entire conformity to the Spirit of the Union, we cannot exist as an Independent

Power... It is only in our united Character as an Empire, that our Independence is acknowledged, that our power can be regarded, or our Credit supported...

...Honesty will be found on every experiment, to be the best and only true policy. Let us then as a Nation be just, let us fulfil the public Contracts, which Congress undoubtedly had a right to make... Let us strengthen the hands of Government and be happy under its protection; every one will reap the fruits of his labours, every one will enjoy his own acquisitions without molestation and without danger...

I now make it my earnest prayer, that God... would most graciously be pleased to dispose us all, to do Justice, to love mercy, and to demean ourselves with that Charity, humility and pacific temper of Minds, which were the Characteristicks of the Divine Author of our blessed Religion, and without an humble imitation of whose example in these things, we can never hope to be a happy nation.

The message's impact was immense. Governors and legislatures responded with their warmest thanks for Washington's services and advice to his country. Greene reported that Washington's words had a great impact in South Carolina, in contrast to the "feeble influence" of Congress. One newspaper said the report was "dictated by God." Even John Hancock wrote, which was perhaps his most unusual compliment.

Washington followed on November 2 with an address "To the Armies of the United States." This was his "affectionate farewell... of those he holds most dear." In it he recalled that the army had been originally composed of men who had been disposed to despise those from other sections, but they had become "one patriotic band of Brothers." He asked every officer and soldier to remember that the very existence of the nation, for which they had fought for so long, depended upon the country giving support and increased powers to the federal government. He asked them to exert every effort to effect "these great and valuable purposes." Twenty-three of the subsequent thirty-nine signers of the 1787 Constitution were to come from the revolutionary forces.

ORDER OF THE CINCINNATI

In May 1783 the organization of this society of revolutionary army officers created an uproar among those who were not eligible. The impetus for the society came from Knox, who sensed the strong desire among the officers that their friendships be maintained in the peace. Washington was automatically elected president. Its charter, as written by Knox, aimed to preserve the rights and liberties of the country, to work for national union, and to provide funds for the relief of widows and orphans of officers. Membership was to descend to the eldest male heir; this provision brought attacks from those who feared it might be an entering wedge to hereditary aristocracy. Its privileges were soon extended to the American navy and to France, which organized its own chapter.

The society, through the individual work of the order's members in the thirteen states, provided strong and constructive support to the calling of a national constitutional convention. Nine of the order signed the resulting Constitution, and two were in Washington's first cabinet.

PEACE ESTABLISHMENT

When Hamilton was appointed chairman of a congressional committee to propose a peacetime army, he asked Washington to submit his ideas. In his humorless way, Hamilton informed the general: "I will just hint to your Excellency that our prejudices will make us wish to keep up as few troops as possible."

Although Washington received the request towards the middle of April, he had ready a lengthy report for Congress on May 2. He suggested a small standing army of 2,631 officers and men, supplemented by an organization corresponding to Switzerland's "hardy and well organized militia service." He pointed out that the Swiss system had enabled her to retain independence and freedom for centuries.

Washington's far-ranging mind looked over the vast territories belonging to the United States. He advocated permanent forts at West Point, Penobscot, Lake Champlain, northern New England, Ticonderoga, Oswego, Fort Erie, Detroit, St. Mary's River, Fort Pitt, and the mouths of the Ohio, Kentucky, Illinois, and Scioto Rivers. He recommended that other posts in the Carolinas and Georgia be determined by those more familiar with the areas than he.

Washington in this paper and another which followed on September 7 outlined a peace policy providing for the orderly settlement and formation of new states, while assuring justice for the Indians. As he noted, there were huge areas of open land, hundreds of thousands of square miles, which the United States could not police. If the country neglected these, they would soon be overrun by land speculators and banditti, who would cause endless trouble with the Indians. He advocated that Congress establish a line beyond which no one could go without government approval. No further settlement should take place until there were satisfactory treaties with the Indians. Licensed traders only, checked for their integrity, should deal with them. Indian friendship should be gained by fair dealing.

In his proposal Washington also suggested that the land which is now Ohio should be the first to come under this policy. He sketched its boundaries, which come remarkably close to the present state lines. He thought that Detroit, though somewhat distant, should be included in the new territory because of the large number of French settlers there, who needed the protection of the American government. He also advocated opening the proposed new state to settlers from French Canada, who wanted to escape British rule, as well as to revolutionary veterans who had been promised land bounties. The latter would be useful in protecting the settlements.

As a part of his work on the peacetime military system, Washington sent General von Steuben to Quebec to confer with General Haldimand, the British commander in chief, and to arrange with him for the transfer of the western posts from British to American control. Haldimand, however, told Steuben that he had no instructions from London to yield them. The British did not give them up until Washington's second term as president.

CARLETON

Washington had much correspondence with Sir Guy Carleton on various terms of the peace treaty, which were not always clear to him nor to members of Congress. Washington particularly wanted New York evacuated, so he could go home. He had written to Chastellux in France on May 10: "We look forward with anxious expectation for the Definitive treaty to remove the doubts and difficulties which prevail at present, and our Country of our Newly acquired friends in New York... of whose Company we are heartily tired."

On May 6 Washington met Carleton at Tappan. Washington informed him that he had already given orders for the release of the German and British prisoners in American hands; they were to go to New York by land or by sea, as he preferred. Carleton said that he was doing everything he could to evacuate New York and had already sent some six thousand persons to Nova Scotia. He did agree to remove his troops from Westchester County, including what is now the Bronx. Becoming ill, Carleton returned to New York but not before his frigate had fired a seventeen-gun salute to General Washington and thus to the United States of America.

LETTERS FROM ENGLAND

Once the preliminary peace was signed, Washington's friends in England were free to write and many comrades from French and Indian War days sent him congratulatory letters. Strangers, some with unsurpassed gall, requested favors. On March 26 his old neighbor, George Fairfax, wrote from Yorkshire: "I cannot express the Joy, with which I take up my Pen to congratulate your Excellency upon the happy conclusion of the late diabolical war; my gratitude to Heaven exceeds all description... I wish you and your family may reap an ample harvest of honours and emoluments till time shall be no more. I have gloried in being called an American here, and I trust & hope, the People who have raised their reputation in the space of nine years from obscurity to the admiration of the world, will continue to act with Wisdom and moderation." Fairfax went on to say that one of his letters to Washington had been intercepted and sent to Lord North. It "like to cost me dear." He had fled Yorkshire, fearing arrest. Only his connections at court had saved him. He added: "Thank Heaven for you and my brave Countrymen, times are altered, and I am as much courted as I was despised as an American." People who had avoided him were now pressing for introductions to his distinguished friend, George Washington. To the letter the general replied on July 10:

With very sincere pleasure I receiv'd your favour... There was nothing wanting in this Letter to give compleat satisfaction to Mrs. Washington and myself, but some expression to induce us to believe you would once more become our neighbours. Your House at Belvoir, I am sorry to add, is no more, but mine (which is enlarged since you saw it) is most sincerely and heartily at your service till you could rebuild it.

As the path, after being closed by a long, arduous, and painful contest, is, to use an Indian Metaphor, now opened and made smooth, I shall please myself with the hope of hearing from you frequently; and till you forbid me to indulge the wish I shall not <u>despair</u> of seeing you and Mrs. Fairfax once more the Inhabitants of Belvoir, and greeting you both there, the intimate companions of our old Age, as you have been of our younger years...

I unite my prayers most fervently with yours, for Wisdom to these U States, and have no doubt, after a little while, all errors in the present form of their Government will be corrected and a happy temper be diffused through the whole; but like young heirs come a little prematurely, perhaps, to a large inheritance, it is more than probable they will riot for a while; but, in this, if it should happen, tho' it is a circumstance which is to be lamented (as I would have the National character of America be pure and immaculate) will work its own cure, as there is virtue at the bottom.

Washington said that it would hardly console Fairfax in the loss of his house to know how much everyone in Virginia had suffered. He recalled a story of an overseer employed by Mrs. Fairfax's father, who said the drought was so terrible he was like to starve but added: "Thank God my neighbours are as bad off as I am."

Robert Stewart, another old comrade to whom Washington had lent money so many years before, sent his "warmest and most sincere congratulations on that exalted fame which you so nobly won... The Poets and Historians of After Ages shall vie with each other in endeavouring to represent it in its true brilliance." He was afraid, he said, that his remarks might pain Washington's modesty but, although he was a British officer, he had praised Washington to everyone and had opposed the war. Stewart spoiled the letter by suggesting that he might like a job representing America at some pleasant European court. Washington sent a warm and friendly reply but noted that such appointments would go to those who had fought "with Halters about their Necks."

Others who wrote included Jacob van Braam, who had translated the terms of Washington's first and only surrender at Fort Necessity, and the Reverend Jacob Duché, who had once written Washington that his cause was hopeless but who now sent a moving appeal to be allowed to return to the United States. Washington replied to Duché: "Personal enmity I bear none, to any Man; so far therefore as your Return to his Country Depends on my private Voice, it would be given in favor of it with cheerfulness." Washington pointed out that the decision was up to the Pennsylvania state government.

A Scottish lady wrote to ask Washington to collect debts owing to her. He replied politely that he could not do this but would send her letter to someone who might help her. The elderly Countess of Huntingdon, a devout Methodist, wanted him to manage her scheme to convert the Indians. He declined courteously. The Countess of Tankerville and her son, Lord Tankerville, simply forwarded him a power of attorney to collect property they believed to be due them in Virginia. Her ladyship seems to have assumed that Washington would regard it as an honor to be her employee. He went to considerable trouble to find someone who could do the work.

INVITATION FROM FRANCE

The comte de Rochambeau sent Washington a charming note dated "à Paris le 13 Juillet 1783." He said:

> *Your letter, my dear General, of May 10 with which you honored me, gave me the greatest pleasure. I see you at the end of your long labors and with a desire to come to France. Try, my dear General, to carry out this project, let nothing prevent this idea, and come and receive, in a country which honors you and has always admired you, the great applause that we owe to a great man. You can count on a reception that will never be equalled. You will be received as you ought to be, after a revolution which has no parallel in history. Everyone is smiling in advance at the hopes you have aroused by your letter, and my heart already beats at the pleasure of embracing you.*
>
> *It seems to me that you ought to leave in the first days of October, after the equinox, to arrive here at the beginning of November. You will find the Court returned from Fontainebleau, you will pass your winter in the midst of the <u>fetes</u> of Paris and the Court, and we will carry you to our estates in the spring. Come, my dear General, and satisfy the wishes of a nation whose hearts are yours. You will eclipse all England, who are now arriving here for a change of air. We receive them well because we are polite and proper, but the French heart will receive General Washington."*

Washington had talked often of France, his wish to express his personal thanks for her aid, and his general desire to see the country, but he had now ruled out going to what he called "gayer scenes." He replied to Rochambeau on October 15:

> *With what words, my dear count, shall I express to you the sensibility of a heart which you have warmed by the flattering sentiments that are conveyed in your Letters of the 14th of April and 13th of July. Your Nation is entitled to all my gratitude. Your sovereign has a claim to my highest admiration, respect and veneration; and those Individuals of it who have been my companions in war, to my friendship and Love. Can it be surprizing then, that I should possess an ardent desire to visit your Country? But, as I observed to you in my Letter of the 20th of May, it is not yet clear to me, that I shall ever have it in my power to accomplish my wishes. My private concerns have been very much deranged by an absence of more than eight years, and require particular attention to put them in order.*

THE CHEERFUL WASHINGTON

Though he was not to see the splendors of Versailles, Washington was unusually ebullient as the time for going home approached. Jefferson and others commented that they had never seen him look happier nor more relaxed. Some of his remarks appear in records as do tales at which he laughed. His aide, Benjamin Walker, told everyone a story on himself. He had asked the general for leave of absence, saying that the Quaker girl, to whom he was engaged, had written that she would just die if he did not get it. Washington said: "Women don't die for such trifles." Walker asked what he should tell her, and Washington replied: "Why, tell her to add another page to the book of sufferings." To the man who said that Robert Morris, the finance minister, had his hands full, Washington said he wished it were his pockets. He burst into loud laughter at a story which, according to Dr. James Thacher, was told by Dr. John Thomas in Yankee twang: "What do you think Chambeau's soldiers call a hat? The tarnation fools, they call it a chapeau. Why, and be darn'd to them, can't they call it a hat and be done with it?"

His principal officers weighed themselves on August 19. It is a little difficult to see them as heads of a starving army, since the top nine weighed over a ton.

General Knox	280	pounds
Colonel Michael Jackson	252	pounds
Colonel Huntington	232	pounds
Colonel Henry Jackson	230	pounds
General Lincoln	224	pounds
Colonel Humphreys	221	pounds
Colonel Swift	219	pounds
General Washington	209	pounds
Colonel Cobb	186	pounds

General Huntington, at 132 pounds, was but a shadow at the bottom of the list.

Washington's boyish joy at returning home was reflected in the purchases he made for Mount Vernon. With Martha beside him to tell him what replacements were needed after eight years of war, Washington ordered nails, paint, glass, china, tea tables and urns, coffee pots, chairs and furniture of all sorts, blankets, and such items as olives, anchovies, fruits, and nuts. For his own reading pleasure, he chose from catalogues and advertisements, books which reflected his tastes as soldier and citizen. Among the first were biographies and memoirs of Gustavus Adolphus, Peter the Great, and Turenne. To these he added works by Locke, Voltaire, and Goldsmith, dictionaries of the arts and science; encyclopedias; histories of the world, Rome, and the Netherlands; travel books on France, Ireland, and Denmark; and—finally—a French grammar and dictionary, as though he had resolved on a heroic effort to acquire French. He asked Lafayette to procure china in France but cancelled this when he found that he could obtain what he needed in New York, at reduced prices, from forced sales by Tories and English merchants.

Although he had decided that he could not go to Europe, his curiosity about the great "empire," which Americans called their new country, was as great as when he was sixteen. He dreamed of a grand tour and invited Lafayette to come along, in a letter of October 12:

> *I have it in contemplation to make a tour thro' all the Eastern States, thence into Canada; thence up the St. Lawrence and thro' the Lakes to Detroit; then to Lake Michigan by land or water; thence thro' the Western Country by the river Illinois, to the river Mississippi, and down the same to New Orleans; thence into Georgia by the way of Pensacola; and thence thro' the two Carolina's home. A great tour this, you will say, probably it may take place no where but in imagination, tho' it is my <u>wish</u> to begin it in the latter end of April of next year; if it should be realized, there would be nothing wanting to make it perfectly agreeable but your Company.*

Such a trip would have been legendary, with Lafayette and Washington as an eighteenth-century Huck and Jim, paddling down the Mississippi, but it never came to pass. The British held on to the posts which they had agreed to surrender, and it was impossible to penetrate the area.

Washington's appetite for travel had been stimulated by the holiday trip he had taken north in July. He wrote Congress that he was bored with waiting for the peace treaty ("this distressing tedium") and with the many "troublesome demands" on him which he could not satisfy. With Governor Clinton to accompany him, he set out by horseback on July 18 and rode a little over 750 miles in nineteen days. He went as far north as Crown Point, returned to Schenectady, then rode along the Mohawk to Fort Schuyler, and on down to Lake Otsego. He returned to Newburgh by way of Albany. On his arrival, he found an invitation, which was in effect an order, to report to Congress at Princeton. He had to reply that his horses were so fatigued from his rapid journey that it might be a few days before they were rested enough for him to proceed south. Shortly afterwards, he wrote the president of Congress that Martha Washington had a fever and "is now in a very weak and low state." He noted that he had so many papers to pack that he would have further to delay his trip, and he hoped that Congress would forgive him. Not until twelve days after his return did he and his wife set out for New Jersey.

PRINCETON TO HARLEM

Washington received the usual addresses and praise from Congress upon his arrival in Princeton, but he found nothing to do. Congress was underrepresented and was unable to do anything effective about his recommendations for a peacetime army.

Washington learned in Princeton that Congress had unanimously passed an act for the erection of an equestrian statue of himself, to be designed "by the best artist in Europe." The act went on to say that the general was to be dressed in a toga, "holding a truncheon in his right hand, and his head encircled with a laurel wreath." Although it was now the law of the land that he appear in Roman dress, he did not care much for the idea. His August 1786 letter to Jefferson, who had asked how he wanted to be dressed for the Houdon statue, said, in effect, that he did not know much about art but "perhaps a severe adherence to the garb of antiquity might not be altogether so expedient as some little deviation in favor of the modern costume." He understood that Benjamin West's use of current dress "is received with applause."

Congress also decreed that the statue be erected "where the residence of Congress shall be established." Its members had already met in five cities and were debating several other possible locations. The irrepressible Francis Hopkinson suggested that it be placed on wheels, so that it could be hauled around wherever Congress moved.

Washington had to arrange to transfer his immense collection of war papers to his house. On October 8 he wrote Timothy Pickering that six wagons were available at Princeton to transport the papers, which were "very bulky." He could not yet estimate how many wagons would be required, but probably four or five. A biographer can only express the opinion that six wagons seem hardly enough but Jacob Hiltzheimer's diary for November 11 reported that number as passing through Philadelphia with the papers. Washington instructed Lieutenant Bezaleel Howe to take the wagons to Mount Vernon, located, he added, "ten miles below Alexandria." He said the papers were very valuable to him and Howe was not to use any ferries when the wind was high. Howe was ordered to have sentinels always on watch and the papers under lock and key at all times.

On the day following the dispatch of his papers, Washington set out for West Point to arrange with the state's governor to take over the administration of New York City when the British departed. On November 12 he received from Sir Guy Carleton his evacuation plan. On November 21 General Washington and Governor Clinton crossed the Harlem River onto Manhattan Island, his first return in seven years.

NEW YORK

The last redcoat left Manhattan November 25. The ever-faithful Knox, who had joined Washington eight-and-a-half years before as a twenty-four-year-old soldier, went ahead to the city, at the lower end of Manhattan, to take over its formal guard duties. Governor Clinton and Washington rode into town, wildly cheered by the citizens. They were accompanied by many New Yorkers, who had been exiled for more than seven years.

A long time before, in September 1777, a loyal Philadelphia lady, Deborah Logan, had written of the despair which gripped her heart when she saw the well-clad British troops march into her city and thought of the contrast between them and "our own poor, bare-footed, ragged troops." Now, a loyal New York lady wrote: "The troops just leaving us were as if equipped for show, and with their scarlet uniforms, made a brilliant display; the troops that marched in on the contrary, were ill-clad and weather beaten, and made a forlorn appearance; but then they were *our* troops, and as I looked at them and thought upon all they had done and suffered for us, my heart and my eyes were full, and I admired and gloried in them the more, because they were weather beaten and forlorn."

Washington resided in Fraunce's Tavern, which still stands, while waiting for Carleton to remove his troops from Staten and Long Islands. On November 28 the returning exiles gave Washington a dinner, as did the governor the following day. On December 2 fireworks were set off in the Bowery, a display which Washington called "splendid." On December 3 he nominated Knox to command what little was left of the American army. On December 4, informed that the British would quit the islands that day, Washington held a final lunch for his officers. His intelligence chief, Colonel Benjamin Tallmadge, who had gone on to the city in advance of the troops to secure all his agents, many of whom had been disguised as Tories, wrote of the farewell:

> At 12 o'clock, the officers repaired to Fraunce's Tavern, in Pearl Street, where Gen. Washington had appointed to meet them... We had been assembled but a few minutes when His Excellency entered the room. His emotion, too strong to be concealed, seemed to be reciprocated by every officer present. After partaking of a slight refreshment, in almost breathless silence, the General filled his glass with wine, and turning to the officers, he said: "With a heart full of love and gratitude, I now take leave of you. I most devoutly wish that your latter days may be as prosperous and happy as your former ones have been glorious and honorable."

After the officers had taken a glass of wine, Gen. Washington said: "I cannot come to each of you, but shall feel obliged if each of you will come and take me by the hand";

Gen. Knox being nearest to him, turned to the commander-in-chief, who, suffused in tears, was incapable of utterance, but grasped his hand; then they embraced each other in silence. In the same affectionate manner, every officer in the room marched up to, kissed, and parted with his General-in-chief. Such a scene of sorrow and weeping I had never before witnessed, and hope I may never be called upon to witness again. It was indeed too affecting to be of long continuance... Not a word was uttered to break the solemn silence that prevailed... The <u>simple thought</u> that we were then to part from the man who had conducted us through a long and bloody war, and under whose conduct the glory and independence of our country had been achieved, and that we should see his face no more in this world, seemed to me utterly insupportable. But the time of separation had come, and waving his hand to his <u>grieving children</u> around him, he left the room and passing through a corps of light infantry who were paraded to receive him, he walked silently on to Whitehall, where a barge was in waiting. We all followed in mournful silence to the wharf, where a prodigious crowd had assembled... As soon as he was seated, the barge put off into the river, and when out in the stream, our great and beloved general waved his hat, and bid us a silent adieu.

SOUTH TO MOUNT VERNON

Washington's three remaining aides, David Cobb, David Humphreys, and Benjamin Walker, offered to accompany him to Mount Vernon, but at Philadelphia, Cobb was detached by Washington because of his distance from home.

The general, as they travelled south, had to hear and answer one tedious address after another from the citizens of New Brunswick, the legislature of New Jersey, the merchants of Philadelphia, the president and council of Pennsylvania, the general assembly of Pennsylvania, the militia of Philadelphia, the magistrates of Philadelphia, the trustees and faculty of the University of Pennsylvania, the learned professions of Philadelphia, the American Philosophical Society, the burgesses and common council of Wilmington, the citizens of Baltimore, the general assembly of Maryland, the governor and council of Maryland, and the mayor and council of Annapolis. He and his aides managed to find something new to say in each reply.

On December 23 Washington dictated to Walker his last letter as commander in chief. This was to von Steuben, to whom Washington expressed the hope he would be pleased to have "this last letter... in the service of my country." He offered him his highest praise for his "zeal... abilities... and faithful and meritorious services."

The new president of Congress, which had now been transferred to Annapolis, was Thomas Mifflin, who had participated in the Conway Cabal and whose record as quartermaster general had not been distinguished. Nevertheless everything passed off gracefully. Banquets were held for Washington in Annapolis on December 20 and 22. On the night of December 22 the statehouse was illuminated and the Maryland General Assembly gave him a ball. James Tilton, who was present, noted that "the General danced every set, that all ladies might have the pleasure of dancing with him, or as it has since been handsomely expressed, get a touch of him." At noon next day, Washington, flanked by his aides, entered an extraodinarily crowded hall to resign his commission. The president said that Congress was ready to receive his communication; Washington rose and spoke:

> *The great events on which my resignation depended having at length taken place, I have now the honor of offering my sincere Congratulations to Congress and of presenting myself before them to surrender into their hands the trust committed to me...*

> *Happy in the confirmation of our Independence and Sovereignty... I resign with satisfaction the Appointment I accepted with Diffidence. A diffidence in my abilities to accomplish so arduous a task, which, however, was superseded by a confidence in the rectitude of our Cause, the support of the Supreme Power of the union, and the patronage of Heaven...*

> *While I repeat my obligations to the Army in general, I should do injustice to my own feelings not to acknowledge in this place the peculiar services and distinguished merits of the Gentlemen who have been attached to my person during the War. It was impossible the choice of confidential officers to compose my family should have been more fortunate. Permit me, Sir, to recommend [them] as worthy of the favorable notice... of Congress...*

> *I consider it an indispensable duty to close this last solemn act of my Official life, by commending the Interests of our dearest Country to the protection of Almighty God...*

> *Having now finished the work assigned me, I retire from the great Theatre of Action; and bidding an Affectionate farewell to this august body under whose*

orders I have so long acted, I here offer my commission, and take my leave of all the employments of public life.

President Mifflin made a suitable reply, and Washington handed him his commission of 1775. After reaching Mount Vernon, he wrote to ask if he might have it back as a souvenir for his family. Charles Thompson, secretary of Congress, replied that a congressional committee was at work preparing to return it to him in a gold box with a suitable inscription. Such are the ways of committees that Washington never received the commission, nor the gold box, nor—for that matter—did the Continental Congress erect the statue to him for which its members had voted.

The general and his aides reached Mount Vernon on the eve of the birth of the Prince of Peace.

THREE

MOUNT VERNON TO
PHILADELPHIA

1784–1787

WASHINGTON DID NOT, as he put it, "get translated into a private citizen," as easily mentally as he did physically. On February 20, 1784, almost two months after the ceremony at Annapolis, he wrote to General Knox:

I am just beginning to experience that ease, and freedom from public cares which however desirable, takes some time to realize; for strange as it may tell, it is nevertheless true, that it was not 'till lately I could get the better of my usual custom of ruminating as soon as I asked in the Morning, on the business of the ensuing day; and of my surprize, after having resolved many things in my mind, to find that I was no longer a public Man, or had any thing to do with public transactions.

I feel now, however, as I conceive a wearied Traveller must do, who, after treading many a painful step, with a heavy burden on his shoulders, is eased of the latter, having reached the Goal to which all the former were directed; and from his House top is looking back, and tracing with a grateful eye the Meanders by which he escaped the quicksands and Mires which lay in his way; and into which none but the All-powerful guide, and great disposer of human Events could have prevented his falling.

A particularly severe winter kept Washington largely indoors, and he chafed when he had insufficient exercise. He had usually been understaffed as a general. His aides suffered from the enormous amount of dictating, transcribing, and copying to which they were chained. Now Washington had no clerical staff. He found his accounts and papers in disorder. Many of his old problems as trustee and executor had never been settled. In addition, he had his six wagonloads of war papers to unload and sort out. They had been so hastily stuffed into boxes, during his frequent moves, that Washington called them "a mass of confusion."

Washington expected his friends to write and give him their gossip. If they neglected him, they got a humorous complaint, sometimes with a barb stuck in it. (He pleaded with Jefferson, in Congress, on March 3: "If you have any News that you are at liberty to impart, it would be charity to communicate a little of it, to a body.")

What Washington had not expected was the extent to which total strangers in Europe and America felt free to write. Some were distinguished and deserved and got polite answers. Others wanted favors, loans, or old records. Two persons wrote to accuse him of keeping money owed them by people of whom he had never heard. The Reverend Jonathan Boucher, quite like his old self, wrote to express his doubt that America would be as happy as it had been under the king. Washington replied to almost everyone, though in many cases he did not bother making file copies, as his aides had done during the war. Most tedious were the old estate and trustee matters, for he had to go through endless papers and, as he did for George Fairfax, make numerous handwritten copies of letters that the latter had not received during the war.

By February 7, 1785, the general, searching hard for a secretary, was describing his burden to David Humphreys who was now in Paris: "What with letters (often of an unmeaning nature) from foreigners. Enquiries after Dick, Tom, and Harry who *may have been* in some part, or at *sometime* in the continental service. Letters, or certificates of service, for those who want to go out of their own States. Introductions; applications for copies of Papers; references of a thousand old matters with which I *ought* not to be troubled, any more than the Grand Mogul, but which must receive an answer of some kind, deprive me of my usual exercise; and without relief, may be injurious to me as I already begin to feel the weight, and oppression of it in my head, and am assured by the *faculty*, if I do not change my course, I shall certainly sink under it." At the same time, Washington pointed out to Humphreys that he had sent but two short notes from France and his next letter had better not be so "laconic."

Practically everyone Washington had ever met considered himself an old and dear friend and welcome at Mount Vernon. Friends and acquaintances brought or introduced strangers, sometimes so many that Washington did not even catch their names and wrote that, among others, Mr.— and Mr.— had dined with him. Even worse were those who dropped in without introduction. He sourly recorded: "A Mr. Martel (or some such name) a Frenchman came in and dined... A Person calling himself Hugh Patten dined here... A Count de Cheize D'Artingnon (so calling himself)" dropped in unannounced and made himself at home for two days.

Not everyone was even grateful. A twenty-two-year-old Dutch boy, Karel van Hogendorp, sent on by Jefferson, wrote that he had been very well entertained at Mount Vernon, but he had not liked the general, who was a cold person and quite stupid. Hogendorp's unconsciously revealing account indicates the suffering he imposed. He wrote that he had to carry on almost all the conversations with Mrs. Washington and her friends. He did the same with her husband, noting that the more he showed "vivacity and enthusiasm" in his talks, the more the general looked embarrassed. Hogendorp added that Washington seemed to have difficulty in following his shifts in topics, from which it would appear that he had turned his mind to other matters.

Washington wrote his mother that he seemed to be running "a well-resorted tavern." His genuine friends were as welcome as their letters but he had an enormous amount of chaff with his wheat and a heavy expense. At times there were as many as eighteen house guests. With the fifteen or more house servants, the place, as Washington also noted to his mother, was pretty noisy. This induced him, as soon as he had a secretary, to spend as much time as possible out of doors.

TO PHILADELPHIA

Washington had called a first general meeting of the Society of the Cincinnati for May 1784. Though he disliked leaving his house, its president had no choice but to make the long trip to Philadelphia. He left Mount Vernon by carriage on April 26, arriving in Philadephia on May 1. This was the day the American army had devoted to celebrating King Tammany, the Delaware chieftan and friend of liberty. After the war, societies of St. Tammany were organized in various American cities. The Philadelphia sons were delighted with the opportunity of firing noisy cannon on his arrival and drinking numerous healths to George Washington.

Washington faced a difficult problem at the meeting. There had been a loud uproar, fairly nationwide, against the society because of its hereditary membership, fear of a veterans organization, and the admission of foreigners.

Washington's initial reaction was that the society should be disbanded, but he finally decided that its motives were pure and it was needed for charitable aid to the widows and orphans of officers. He consulted at length with Jefferson, who was most fearful of the men who had fought so long for their country. Washington then suggested various changes in the charter to make it acceptable to all Americans. He asked that any political phrases in the constitution be stricken out, the hereditary descent be cancelled, and a separate French society be organized. His fellow officers, who had been distressed and surprised by the clamor, generally went along with his views and made changes in the national constitution. The state charters were not amended; the hereditary proposals of 1783 prevailed. Contrary to the fears of Jefferson, the society never became a political organization.

On his return trip to Virginia, Washington visited Washington College at Chestertown. The students presented a play about Sweden's hero: *Gustavus Vasa.* A few lines were tacked on the end, drawing attention from "Swedish woes" to the "more than Danish" fury which America had suffered. The actor pointed out that a Potomac hero "gave us PEACE, where War and Rapine raged." According to the official college report, "tears rolled from every eye and applause from every heart."

On June 2, back home, Washington wrote General Knox to say how impatient he had been to get to Mount Vernon after leaving Philadelphia on May 18. However, such were the difficulties of travel then, that he had had to wait from eight in the morning of May 20 to the following evening before he could cross the Chesapeake by ferry.

LAFAYETTE RETURNS

When Washington wanted someone to visit him, he was likely to be persuasive. He wrote to Charles Thompson, January 22, 1784, asking him as one of his "late Masters" in Congress to come and stay. He added: "Mrs. Washington, if she knew I was writing to you in the stile of Invitation would, I am certain, adduce arguments to prove that I ought to include Mrs. Thompson; but before she should have half spun the thread of her discourse, it is more than probable that I should have nonplused her, by yielding readily to the force of her reasoning."

For Madame de Lafayette, Washington prepared an effusion nearly as gallant as a French courtier might have mustered:

> *Madam: It is now, more than ever, I want words to express the sensibility and gratitude with which the honor of your felicitations... has inspired me. If my expression*

*was equal to the feelings of my heart, the homage I am about to render you would
appear in a more favourable point of view, than my most sanguine expectations
will encourage me to hope for...*

*Great as your claim is... as the wife of my amiable friend to my affectionate
regards... the charms of your person, and the beauties of your mind, have a more
powerful operation. These, Madam, have endeared you to me, and every thing
which partakes of your nature will have a claim to my affections. George and
Virginia (the offspring of your love), whose names do honor to my Country and to
myself, have a double claim...*

*Mrs. Washington... feels very sensibly the force of your polite invitation to Paris,
but she is too far advanced in life, and is too much immersed in the care of her little progeny, to cross the Atlantic. This, My Dr. Marchioness, is not the case with
you. You have youth... and must have a curiosity to see the Country, young, rude
and uncultivated as it is; for the liberties of which your husband has fought, bled,
and acquired much glory. Where every body admires, every body loves him. Come...
and call my Cottage your home... You shall taste the simplicity of rural life. It will
diversify the Scene and may give you a higher relish for the gaieties of the Court,
when you return to Versailles...*

Lafayette's wife, with three small children, decided against the trip, but the
marquis, now raised by Louis XVI to be major general in the French army,
arrived in New York in August. On his way south to Mount Vernon, he had a
triumph nearly as great as Washington received wherever he went. He
reached Mount Vernon on August 17, with letters from Chastellux and
Rochambeau, and the talk of Europe. He could tell Washington of the dinner
he attended where all the marshals of France stood and drank a toast to
General Washington. Lafayette stayed till the end of the month. There is little
documentation on the visit except Washington's reference to the "round of
company" which prevented him from answering letters.

Washington met Lafayette again at Richmond, after the general had
returned from his western trip, and brought him back to Mount Vernon on
November 24. He sent a note to Henry Lee at Stratford to say how anxious the
marquis was to see him and to come over, as soon as convenient, "prepared to
stay a few days." Since Lafayette was about to return to France, Washington
prepared letters to his friends there, including one to Madame de Lafayette:
"The Marquis returns to you with all the warmth and ardour of a newly
inspired lover. We restore him to you in good health, crowned with wreaths of
love and respect from every part of the Union." Another went to Virginia de

Washington's Western Tour

September 1784

Lafayette: "Permit me to thank my dear little correspondent for the favor of her letter of the 18th of June last, and to impress her with the idea of the pleasure I shall derive in a continuation of them. Her papa is restored to her with all the good health, paternal affections and honors her tender heart could wish. He will carry a kiss to her from me (which might be more agreeable from a pretty boy), and give her assurances of the affectionate regard with which I have the pleasure of being her well-wisher." He accompanied Lafayette as far as Annapolis, taking his final farewell on December 1. A week later he sent him a gloomy note:

In the moment of our separation... and every hour since, I felt all that love, respect and attachment for you, with which length of years, close connections and your merits have inspired me. I often asked myself... whether that was the last sight I ever should have of you? And tho' I wished to say no, my fears answered yes. I called to mind the days of my youth, and found they had long since fled to return no more; that I was now descending the hill I had been 52 years climbing, and that tho' I was blessed with a good constitution, I was of a short lived family, and might soon expect to be entombed in the dreary mansions of my fathers. These things darkened the shades and gave a gloom to the picture, consequently to my prospects of seeing you again; but I will not repine, I have had my day...

It is unnecessary, I persuade myself, to repeat to you, my Dr. Marquis, the sincerity of my regards and friendship, nor have I words which could express my affection for you...

Along with the letter, he sent another for Lafayette to take to France and give to Luzerne. In flowery language he expressed his appreciation for the special invitation, which had been extended him by the king and queen of France, to visit Versailles. He wrote: "I fear my vows and earnest wishes are the only tributes of respect I shall ever have it in my power to offer them in return."

Lafayette answered Washington as he was about to sail: "No, my beloved General, our late parting was not by any means a last interview. My whole soul revolts at the idea, and could I harbour it an instant, indeed, my dear General, it would make me miserable. I well see you will never go to France. The unexpressible pleasure of embracing you in my own house, of well coming you in a family where your name is adored, I do not much expect to experience. But to you, I shall return... My firm plan is to visit now and then my friends on this side of the Atlantick, and the most beloved of all friends I ever had, or ever will have... Adieu, adieu... it is with unexpressable pain that I feel I am going to be severed from you... Adieu, adieu."

With a growing family and troubles in France, Lafayette did not return to Mount Vernon for forty years. Mrs. Washington's grandson, George Washington Parke Custis, who had been only three when Lafayette departed, was there to receive him. At Washington's tomb, Custis delivered what was intended to be a moving oration. With the Custis knack for saying the wrong thing, he referred to Lafayette as a "setting sun," and invited him, as soon as he had set, to join Washington in the sepulchre. Lafayette murmured, in reply, that he had no words with which to express his feelings.

TRAVELLER AND REPORTER

By the time he reached Philadelphia for the Congress of 1774, Washington had covered more American territory than any delegate there. His military activities in the revolution carried him to nine of the thirteen states. Between 1784 and 1799 his travels took him westward again to the Ohio region and from Maine to Georgia. His diaries, which he resumed in the fall of 1784, and his letters contain lengthy reports of the political sentiments of the people, but his notes on their daily life are often far more interesting. It would be possible, from these alone, to construct a quite complete account of the economic and social life of late eighteenth-century America.

Washington wrote that mail took three to four days from Philadelphia to Alexandria in 1785. Scheduled stage coaches ran three times a week from Norfolk as far north as Portsmouth, New Hampshire. The stage took ten to twelve days from Richmond to Boston. There was a good wagon road, 150 miles west, from Alexandria to Cumberland. Most people preferred to travel south of Virginia by ship, since the roads and inns were so bad in the Carolinas and Georgia. Washington noted in the mid-eighties that meat prices fluctuated seasonally from a minimum of 3-1/2 to 5-1/2 cents a pound, horses sold for $8 to $30, cows for $12, flour for $18 a barrel, while whisky was 40 cents a gallon at Pittsburgh. Land cost $10 an acre near Mount Vernon and $3 an acre in western Pennsylvania. One hundred shad in season could be bought at Alexandria for $2.50. Wages for workmen ran around a dollar a day. His records indicate what books the principal booksellers were advertising, and the prices for staples, gloves, furniture, wallpaper, and Peale portraits.

Washington's years on the frontier let him converse as an equal with frontiersmen and Indians. He could gossip extensively with the farmers of the country and certainly did so from a great variety of notes he made on agriculture wherever he travelled. He was able to talk with manufacturers, for he had made cloth, bricks, flour, and brandy. He could chat with ferrymen, for he owned a ferry, as well as with horsemen, hunters, carpenters, gardeners, fishermen, soldiers, sailors, surveyors, and inventors, whose activities he had touched at some point in his career.

SIMPSON, CANALS, AND THE WEST

More than thirty years before, Lawrence Washington had noted that the closeness of the Potomac and Ohio Rivers would be significant in the development of the West. George Washington thereafter had travelled over much of the region and, at twenty-two, canoed the Potomac from Cumberland to the falls above Georgetown. By 1769 he was endeavoring to promote a series of lock canals to improve transport and communications westward. Subsequently he went west to the Kanawha River and made the first attempt at organized settlement there. After buying land in western Pennsylvania, he spent much capital attempting to increase wheat growing and milling in the region. He now turned back to his old dreams.

Washington, in Cambridge, had referred to the extreme "stupidity" of Gilbert Simpson, the miller who had drained his pockets pretty heavily, while offering one excuse after another. Nine years later, hardly back at Mount Vernon, he requested an accounting from Simpson on February 13:

> *It now behooves me to look into my own private business, no part of which seems to call louder for attention, than my concerns with you. How profitable our partnership has been, <u>you best can tell</u>...*

> *[My reports indicate] I ought to have a good deal of wealth in your hands... All agree that it is the best Mill, and has had more custom than any other on the west side of the Alleghany Mountains; I expect something very handsome therefore from that quarter. I want a full settlement of this Account from the beginning, clearly stated [and] a full and complete settlement of our Partnership accounts... supported by vouchers... The world does not scruple to say that you have been much more attentive to your own interest than to mine. But I hope your Accots. will give the lie to these reports... and that you have acted like an honest, industrious and frugal man...*

On April 27 Simpson replied with a note quite like the old ones. He complained about everything, the prevalence of smallpox, the troubles he had, and his lack of cash. He said that he resented Washington's letter and was therefore asking for "a settlement and a separation." He hoped there would be a "crown of bliss and felicity" reserved somewhere for the general and his wife.

The existing documentation is scanty but it appears that Simpson may have come to Mount Vernon, for he wrote Washington from the mill on July 31: "I got safely home and found everything well... there has been no rane... which has almost don for our corn our winter crops are very light." There followed more complaints. Meanwhile Washington had written Simpson that he intended to let the mill and land to someone else, for he could no longer tolerate such "waste of property and losses, as I have hitherto sustained by my partnership with you." At the same time Washington made enquiries about his other Pennsylvania lands and found that squatters, taking advantage of his long absence, had settled down on them and were beginning to think of ways to get permanent possession.

In early March, Jefferson wrote Washington a long letter outlining his views on opening navigation to the Ohio. Many of these coincided with Washington's thoughts. Jefferson noted that he had written the Virginia Assembly, asking if a few thousand pounds could be set aside for this purpose. He feared that public bodies would be slow and wasteful. Could not Washington crown his achievements by taking the lead in this enterprise? Washington did not quite say no. He had Jefferson's proposal in mind when he decided that his western lands and the Simpson mill needed personal inspection. He spent a good deal of time that summer getting ready for a trip west and in arranging for supplies and boats for the Ohio River. He invited his old friend, Dr. James Craik; his nephew, Bushrod Washington; and Craik's son, William, to go along. Three servants and six horses for Washington's use were with the party. As he began the trip on September 1, he also resumed his diary.

The party proceeded via Falls Church and Leesburg to Charles Town. Though Washington had his rent collection and other business with his tenants in Berkeley County, he spent a good deal of time asking his old friend, General Morgan, and many of the leading citizens, about roads and rivers west. At Bath (now Berkeley Springs) and Martinsburg, he repeated his enquiries on the principal branches and runs leading into the Potomac, Monongahela, Little Kanawha, Ohio, and Youghiogheny rivers.

At Berkeley Springs, Washington was a fascinated watcher of an early experiment by James Rumsey in improving water transport. Rumsey shares with John Fitch credit for the first steamboats, which they launched separately in 1787. At this time Rumsey was still experimenting with water-current–induced propulsion. According to Washington's diary, Rumsey made him swear to keep his secret. He then demostrated his model, which Washington found to run "prety swift... it might be turned to the greatest possible utility in inland Navigation; and in rapid currents." Washington gave Rumsey a certificate that the invention appeared highly useful. This much annoyed John Fitch who trotted to Mount Vernon, the following year, with his designs.

As Washington moved north from Berkeley Springs, he went over ground he had covered during his first western expedition, his first diplomatic mission, and his subsequent battles with the French and Indians. There was no introspection in his diary, which records notes of every conversation he had on roads, paths, creeks, runs, rivers, and obstacles to navigation, but nothing about the past.

Washington's first stop was with the eighty-two-year-old Thomas Cresap. It had been over 36 years since Washington, the youth with his love of trees and good land, had first visited Cresap's house, where he wrote his account of the "comical" and liquor-inspired Indian "War Daunce." From Cresap's he rode to old Fort Cumberland, over whose status Dinwiddie and Loudoun had caused him so much anguish, then up the old Braddock Road, which he had travelled with the redcoated army. The party moved on through the Shades of Death to Laurel Hill, where Washington had once expressed his fear that the Forbes army would lose its laurels. On they rode to the house of Thomas Gist, brother of Christopher Gist, who had accompanied the twenty-one-year-old Washington to Fort Le Boeuf. At the Gist house a tired young Washington had rested on his way back to Williamsburg. In anticlimax to the ride through the great scenes of his younger years, the general reached Simpson's mill on September 13. He found, contrary to the reports he had received at Mount Vernon, that the situation was a mess. He summed it up:

> ...I do not find the land in _general_ equal to my expectation of it—some part indeed is as rich as can be, some other part is but indifferent—the levellest is the coldest and of the meanest quality—that which is most broken is the richest; tho' some of the hills are not of the first quality.

> The Tenements with respect to the buildings are but indifferently improved—each have Meadow and are arable, but in no great quantity—the Mill was quite destitute of water—the works and House appear to be in very bad condition—and no reservoir of water—the stream as it runs, is all the resource it has—formerly there was a dam to stop the water; but that giving way, it is brought in a narrow confined and trifling Race... In a word little Rent, or good is to be expected from the present aspect of her.

Washington held a public auction for the disposal of his share of the Simpson stock but was disappointed in the proceeds, about £47, towards his total investment in the enterprise of around £1,200. He was forced to let the land for shares in wheat. In addition Washington held conferences with the squatters on his land at Washington's Bottom, west of Pittsburgh. Many had been living there rent-free for years. When he visited the area, everyone refused to deal with him and said that he could try to sue to make them leave. Washington was forced to do this but it necessitated an intensive search of old records in Pennsylvania and Virginia. Some of the latter had been destroyed in Benedict Arnold's raiding expeditions, but Washington was eventually able to establish his full right to the land through a court order.

While he was conducting his business at the mill, the commanding officer at Fort Pitt confirmed rumors Washington had picked up that the Indians along the Ohio were in an ugly mood. He was warned against travelling there and promptly cancelled his trip to the Kanawha, where his previous settlements had presumably been knocked out by Indians. On the rest of his trip he pretty well confined himself to investigations of the area's transport and land use. He wrote in his diary that he found much of the intelligence given him to be unreliable, either from ignorance or design. He mentioned that information on the best and shortest route for portage or roads was always by way of the informant's property. He diligently checked and cross-checked every statement and, wherever possible, made personal observations.

At Gist's settlement, the general decided that he, his nephew, and a guide would set off across wild and often trackless country to examine the tributaries to the Potomac and Ohio Rivers. On September 25 Washington "lodged," as he put it, on the ground in a heavy storm with only his cloak to cover him. That morning he rode through heavy rain and a wet and gloomy forest to a farmhouse, where he could get only boiled corn for breakfast. He rode high up and over the Allegheny Mountains and down a steep and dangerous path to the valley. Three days later an exhausted Washington spent an entire day resting at Fort Pleasant, "having had a very fatiguing journey thro' the Mountains, occasioned not more from the want of accomodation and the real necessaries of life than the showers of Rain which were continually falling and wetting the bushes—the passing of which, under these circumstances was very little better than swimming Rivulets."

On the trip Washington discovered that the source of the north branch of the Potomac, which flowed into the Chesapeake and then to the Atlantic Ocean, was only ten miles from the head of the Youghiogheny River, which flowed to the Ohio and on into the Mississippi. This confirmed what his long-dead brother, Lawrence, had surmised.

In five more days of riding, marred frequently by rain, Washington reached Mount Vernon October 4, having covered, by his usually accurate measurements, 680 miles in a little over a month. While the trip was still fresh in his mind, he added to his diary notes extensive computations on the general geography and the distances from Detroit to Philadelphia and Detroit to Richmond. To these he added a series of "reflections" on the facts he had gained. He noted how enthusiastic he had become about navigation on the Potomac. Virginia stretched to the Ohio River; there was an immense fertile country between the Blue Ridge and the Allegheny Mountains, "but how trifling when viewed upon that immeasurable scale which is inviting our attention!"—the great Ohio Valley. To bring its trade to the Potomac would be cheaper and simpler than to any point to the north. Crops grew in the area with ease but the people had no incentive to grow more than they needed, without good inland transportation to the seaboard and thence to foreign markets. With it, the area would be of immense economic, commercial, and political importance.

The United States, he went on to himself, was occupied on its flanks and rear by formidable powers who would do anything to win the trade and allegiance of these people. The western settlers "from my own observation—stand as it were on a pivot—the touch of a feather would almost incline them any way" (to the United States, Great Britain, or Spain). They would meet the United States more than halfway, if their country did its part. "Our clearest interest... is to open a wide door, and make a smooth way for the produce of that Country to pass to our Markets..." In short, transport and communications would cement the settlers forever to the American union and promote the country's economic development to the fullest.

POTOMAC NAVIGATION COMPANY

In writing to Jefferson, March 29, 1784, Washington expressed keen interest in resuming his earlier work on improving navigation westward on the Potomac River. He noted that, before the war, because Virginia's funds were limited, he had proposed a private joint-stock company. The legislature would not approve even a private company, unless the James River were included as a sop to those with interests there. Virginia could not move without Maryland. His bill ran into opposition at Annapolis, when the merchants of Baltimore became alarmed, "perhaps not without cause, at the consequence of Water transportation to George Town of the produce which usually came to their Market."

Although he complained to Jefferson about his prewar difficulties, Washington, refreshed and enthusiastic from his trip, decided once more to try his dream scheme. He did not quite realize that, this time, whatever he wanted from a legislature, he was almost certain to get. What emerged was a pioneer public–private corporation to promote economic growth. As a by-product,

Washington devised a mechanism for bringing states to act together on matters of common interest. In stages that are perceptible, Washington launched himself from directing a canal company to heading a nation.

Washington polished his notes six days later into a long letter to Benjamin Harrison, Virginia's governor. He suggested that the state give consideration to forming, jointly with Maryland, a public or private corporation, and to the appointment of a Maryland–Virginia commission to survey all means to open navigation and trade westward to the Ohio. The governor answered at once that he not only liked the plan but that Washington's letter was "so much more explicit than I could be" that he had handed it directly to the assembly. The members, he reported, seemed so impressed that he thought the survey would be quickly authorized. By the middle of November, Washington was in Richmond with Lafayette and orally reported his findings to the assembly. On January 10, James Madison sent Thomas Jefferson, in Paris, a letter on Washington's efforts:

> *...The earnestness with which he espouses the undertaking is hardly to be described, and shews that a mind like his, capable of great views, and which has long been occupied with them, cannot bear a vacancy; and surely he could not have chosen an occupation more worthy of succeeding to that of establishing the political rights of his Country than the patronage of works for the extensive and lasting improvement of its natural advantages; works which will double the value of half the lands within the Commonwealth, will extend its commerce [and] link its interest with those of the [future] Western States...*

The bill to establish the Potomac Navigation Company provided for a joint-stock company, with 500 shares at $440 each, and authorized the company to collect tolls at various points. It was proposed, if Maryland agreed, that both states spend public funds on the road, from the end of navigation to the Cheat River. Pennsylvania was to be asked to cooperate on a road to the Youghiogheny. Virginia also authorized an intrastate company to develop the James.

Washington's ideas were speedily implemented. By December 13 the act had been approved in principle, and Virginia commissioners were appointed to discuss the bill in Annapolis. Washington was made chairman of the delegation whose other members were General Gates and Thomas Blackburn. The former, to say the least, was a surprising appointment, but the members of the Virginia Assembly could hardly know all the internal politics of the American revolutionary army. (Washington wrote privately to Knox: "My bosom friend Genl. Gates, being at Richmond, contrived to edge himself into the Commission.")

Blackburn did not appear. Gates and Washington went to Annapolis, where Gates fell ill, leaving Washington with the whole negotiation. Much of the talk was on the complex question of tolls, whether they should be by weight, value, or a combination thereof. In addition, he agreed to Maryland's suggestion, which had not been in the original bill, that each state bear 10 percent of the cost by buying shares. On December 28 Washington wrote to Madison in Richmond: "The Bill passed this Assembly with only 9 dissenting voices; and got thro' both Houses in a day, so earnest were the members of getting it to you in time. It is now near 12 at Night, and I am writing with an aching head, having been constantly employed in this business since the 22d. without assistance from my Colleagues: Genl. Gates having been Sick the whole time, and Colo. Blackburn not attending."

Since the legislature at Richmond was scheduled to adjourn in the near future, Washington himself galloped back to Virginia with the papers. He wrote to Samuel Chase of Maryland on Januray 5: "When I found your Express at Mount Pleasant, and was unable to procure another in Marlbro', I commenced one myself, got home before dinner, and dispatched one of my servants to Hooes Ferry immediately. He placed the packet into the hands of the Express there waiting, before nine o'clock next morning; on Friday the business with ease might have been laid before the Assembly..."

On January 4 the bill was ratified by Virginia, which placed in the act an unexpected clause, presenting to General Washington the state's 10 percent of the Potomac company shares, and fifty shares in the James River company, in gratitude for his wartime services and for promoting so beneficial an act. On February 8 the books of the new company were open to public subscription. By summer the needed sums, for all practical purposes, were subscribed. The directors elected Washington president of the company, a job at which he spent long and active hours. Washington was, however, very "agitated" by the act of the Virginia legislature in awarding him the shares, since he wanted neither to accept them nor to offend his state. On January 22, 1785, he wrote the governor:

The attention and good wishes which the Assembly have evidenced by their act... are more than mere compliment; there is an unequivocal and substantial meaning annexed. But believe me sir, notwithstanding these, no circumstance has happened to me since I left the walks of public life, which has so much embarrassed me. On the one hand, I consider this act... as a noble and unequivocal proof of the good opinion, the affection, and disposition of my Country [Virginia] to serve me; and I should be hurt, if by declining the acceptance of it, my refusal should be construed into disrespect... or that an ostentatious display of disinterestedness or public virtue, was the source of the refusal... Not content then with the bare consciousness of having, in all this navigation business, acted upon the clearest conviction of the political importance of the measure; I would wish that every individual who may hear that it was a favorite plan of mine, may know also that I had no other motive for promoting it, than the advantage I conceived it would be productive of to the Union...

How would this matter be viewed then by the eye of the world; and what would be the opinion of it, when it comes to be related that G W—exerted himself to effect this work and G W—has received 20,000 dollars, and £5,000 Sterling of the public money as an interest therein?

There was much more to the letter. Washington said he would take the views of all his friends, prior to the next meeting of the assembly. He did so in long letters. Knox made the sensible suggestion that the stock be used for the widows and orphans of revolutionary war men in Virginia. Washington accepted the idea of putting the shares to a charitable purpose, but he eventually decided they should go to educational institutions. The Virginia Assembly passed a subsequent act empowering Washington to place them in trust for this purpose.

Maryland and Virginia appointed commissioners of high caliber. They often dropped in on Mount Vernon, conveniently located between Annapolis and Richmond. By March they had agreed so amicably that they decided to continue the meetings, in order to discuss trade and other related questions. Some of these involved Pennsylvania and Delaware, and it seemed natural to ask them to participate. Other states became interested. Congress was too weak to act on general matters but there was nothing to prevent individual states from asking for a meeting. A majority soon did so, and Congress then ratified the proposal. Thus Washington had sliced America's Gordian knot. When a date was set for all the states to meet in Constitutonal Convention, it seemed only right to ask the president of the Potomac Navigation Company to attend.

FARMER

The various Mount Vernon farms, amounting at their peak to over 8,000 acres, composed a more complex operation and employed more people than the United States government in its initial stages under the new constitution.

Before the war Washington had tried to introduce at Mount Vernon a more systematic agriculture than was generally employed in Virginia. After the revolution he decided that American agricultural practices were, at best, crude and primitive.

The country could not progress unless scientific methods were introduced and information on them widely disseminated. When Arthur Young, England's foremost agricultural expert and editor of the *Annals of Agriculture*, opened correspondence with him, Washington was delighted. He wrote Young on August 6, 1786:

> *Agriculture has ever been amongst the most favourite amusements of my life, though I never possessed much skill in the art, and nine years total inattention to it, has added nothing to a knowledge which is best understood from practice; but with the means you have been so obliging as to furnish me, I shall return to it (though rather late in the day) with hope and confidence.*
>
> *The System of Agriculture (if the epithet of system can be applied to it), which is in use in this part of the United States, is as unproductive to the practitioners as it is ruinous to the land-holders. Yet it is pertinaciously adhered to. To forsake it; to pursue a course of husbandry which is altogether different and new to the gazing multitude, ever averse to novelty in matters of this sort, and much attached to their old customs, requires resolution; and without a good practical guide, may be dangerous... Your Annals shall be this guide. The plan on which they are published, gives them a reputation which inspires confidence; and for the favor of sending them to me, I pray you to accept my very best acknowledgments. To continue them, will add much to the obligation.*

Washington followed with other critical remarks to Young on American agriculture, many sounding remarkably like those applied by twentieth-century agricultural experts to underdeveloped countries. Virginia, he wrote on November 1, 1787, was as backward in agricultural matters as any place in America. Tobacco, given first preference, had ruined the soil. For other crops, corn was always grown first, followed by wheat on the same soil,

> *after which the ground is respited (except from weeds, and every trash that can contribute to its foulness) for about eighteen months; and so on, alternately, without any dressing; till the land is exhausted; when it is turned out without being sown with grass seeds, or any method taken to restore it; and another piece is ruined in the same manner. No more cattle is raised than can be supported by lowland meadows, swamps, &ca; as very few persons have attended to sowing grasses, and connecting cattle with their Crops...Our lands, as I mentioned in my first letter to you, were originally very good; but use, and abuse, have made them quite otherwise.*

Washington ordered special English plows from Young, which he found very satisfactory, and numerous varieties of seeds. He followed his advice on barn-building. On the basis of Young's articles and his own experiments, he introduced practices of later centuries, such as green manuring, the prevention of soil erosion, and crop rotation. He tried various types of fertilizer, from the usual dung to river bottom muck and plaster of Paris. He wrote of his great variety of crops, including some from the tropics, most unsuitable to Virginia: papaws, pepper, oats, buckwheat, rye, barley, wheat, millet, spelt, flax, corn, beans, sweet and Irish potatoes, cabbages, pumpkins, carrots, asparagus, peas, turnips, parsnips, and Jerusalem artichokes. He also grew clover, luzerne, and vetches. To his food and fiber crops he added such fruit trees as pear, crab-apple, cherry, apricot, apple, plum, fig, and sour oranges.

Washington hired a farmer from England, James Bloxham, as his manager, but he wrote to Young that the Englishman could not adapt very easily to American conditions. He made no allowances for eight years of war and destruction and for the generally primitive methods. Washington said that Bloxham had been hired to improve cultivation. Had America been as advanced as England he would not have been needed.

Washington was probably mistaken in thinking his soil had once been good but had been ruined by bad practices. It most probably had never been of more than mediocre quality though it had certainly deteriorated over the years. Washington had the usual problems with the American climate, late sharp frosts after he had planted, too-heavy spring rains, followed by long periods of severe heat and drought. These peculiarities increased plant diseases, and he complained of rust, cheat, and speck, together with chinch bugs and the Hessian fly (which had made its appearance about the time of the arrival of German troops who got the blame for it). The area was also a source of human diseases. A nearby "Hell Hole" was a breeder of malarial mosquitoes, and the general and his fieldhands alike suffered from "agues and fevers."

From his description of stock-feeding practices, it would appear that Washington was one of the first Americans to sow ground covers and grasses for cattle feeding. His inventory of November 1785 indicated that he had 130 horses, 336 cattle, and 283 sheep. He was never able to count his pigs, since they ran wild, but the number was substantial, for in December of the same year, he killed and dressed 128 hogs, to yield nearly eight tons of meat.

There is no accurate account of the total number of persons living and working at Mount Vernon, but probably close to four hundred had to be fed and clothed whether crops were good or bad. The working force consisted of free and indentured whites and of Negro slaves. Of the 322 Negroes on the place, not much more than a third formed the working force, the rest being old, sick, or children. As many as 30 percent were in the skilled or semiskilled class: cooks, waiters, bricklayers, overseers, seamstresses, weavers, gardeners, and stonemasons. The rest were field hands. Among the whites, some of whom were working out their passage to America, were millers, brewers, coopers, blacksmiths, tailors, bricklayers, carpenters, and cradlers (mowers). In addition, seasonal labor was hired for harvesting and fishing. One physician was kept on a retainer to treat the workers, while Washington's own physician, Dr. James Craik, and others, were called in from time to time on serious cases. Although he had had to fire his miller for constant drinking (with regret because he was a good one), Washington could tolerate a certain amount of it, and did so with a gardener, Philip Bater. Under an agreement, signed by Washington and Bater on April 23, 1787, the latter was to be allowed:

> *Four dollars at Christmas, with which he may be drunk 4 days and 4 nights; two Dollars at Easter to effect the same purpose; two Dollars also at Whitsuntide, to be drunk two days...*

GIFTS

Washington was given some French hounds by Lafayette, which he trusted to the care of future President J. Q. Adams. The latter did not at all relish being kennelmaster across the Atlantic, even for Washington, but the dogs did reach Mount Vernon. The king of Spain also sent a gift which Washington was exceedingly anxious to have—a pair of jackasses which could breed both their own race and mules for heavy labor.

The king, perhaps unintentionally, was thrifty enough to pay their freight only to England. One jackass died at sea and the other reached Gloucester, Massachusetts. Washington named it Jack Ass before its arrival and sent an overseer to Boston in October 1784 to bring it to Mount Vernon, with its Spanish groom. Eventually he had a very large bill both from the sea captain who got it to America and for the expenses of the trip to Mount Vernon. There Jack Ass was renamed Royal Gift.

---

* The following trees, shrubs, and plants were recorded by Washington as having been planted by him at Mount Vernon in 1784–1787. They do not include food and fiber plants, which are listed in the text: Holly, English walnut, oak, hemlock, aspen, linden, hickory, elm, ash, pistachio, mahogany, palmetto, poplar, hickory, locust, maple, cedar, spruce, white pine, redbud, dogwood, catalpa, honey locust, persimmon, horse chestnut, cypress, chestnut, filbert, acacia, weeping and yellow willows, sassafras, mulberry, buckeye, pecan, and magnolia. Also hollyhock, yew, mock orange, lilacs, fringe tree, laurel, jasmine, blackhaw, honeysuckle, boxwood, and spicebush.

Though Washington wrote very solemn letters of thanks to the Spanish minister to the United States, the American minister at Madrid, and the Spanish foreign minister, behind the scenes there was some pretty unroyal humor about the animal. The following April Washington informed his nephew, Bushrod, that, thus far, Royal Gift had shown little inclination to administer to a plebeian race. He wrote Lafayette in May:

The Jack which I have already received from Spain in appearance is fine; but his late royal master [Charles III, aged seventy], tho' past his grand climacteric, cannot be less moved by female allurements than he is; or when prompted, can proceed with more majestic solemnity to the work of procreation.

To Colonel Fitzhugh, who enquired about having his mares bred, he replied that, like the king, the jackass could hardly "perform seldomer," but he hoped that when Royal Gift "becomes a little better acquainted with republican enjoyments, he will amend his manners, and fall into our custom of doing business." Richard Sprigg, who had a small jenny, which was not of as good quality as the Spanish, sent her over to the Washington farm. This time Royal Gift was successful. Washington wrote Sprigg on June 28: "Tho' in appearance quite unequal to the match, yet, like a true female, she was not to be terrified at the disproportionate size of her paramour, and having renewed the conflict twice or thrice, it is to be hoped the issue will be favourable." The Sprigg jenny foaled a jack, the first of this breed in America.

Washington asked a ship, which anchored off Mount Vernon in order to pick up flour for sale in Surinam, to buy a jenny for him there. This seems to have been the source of the one he acquired by late June. He noted that she finally inspired Royal Gift to administer to his mares and thus to breed mules for farm work. More jacks and jennies arrived from Malta, gifts of Lafayette, and Washington was able to advertise stud services. The new Washington breed performed more work, on less feed, than horses, and was invaluable to the new country.

LANDSCAPE ARCHITECT

Over the previous forty years Washington had often expressed his love of trees. (His references to birds, however, describe only their destructive work on his crops and fruit trees.) To Sir Edward Newenham, member of the Irish Parliament for Dublin, he wrote on April 20, 1787:

The manner in which you employ your time at Bell Champ (in raising nurseries of fruit, forest trees, and Shrubs) must not only contribute to your health and amusement, but it is certainly among the most rational avocations of life; for what can be more pleasing than to see the works of one's own hands, fostered by care and attention, rising to maturity in a beautiful display of those advantages and ornaments which, by the combination of Nature and taste of the projector... is always regaling to the eye...

I should have much pleasure in admiring your skill in the propagation and disposal of these things in a visit to Bell Champ, but declining health and an anxious wish to spend the remainder of my days in retirement will fix me to Mount Vernon.

Washington, from his wartime headquarters, had often sent anxious enquiries and instructions to Lund Washington on the planting of trees and shrubs around his gardens. With the spring of 1785, he was free to indulge the hobby which he called his "innocent amusement." Much of his diary records are devoted to his planting. His letters teem with polite requests to everyone he knew from New York to South Carolina and in Madeira, France, Ireland, and England to send him seeds for his botanical garden. With his artistic eye, he could blend the best of nature with the best of man. His views were practical— never move a tree or shrub that had grown in a forest, into the open, for it would not adjust—and esthetic—he thought his arrangement of white dog- wood in a circle around the flowering redbud or Judas tree to be "very pretty." He ended up with an extraordinary variety of trees and shrubs, though he mentioned few flowers.[*] Some were native plants which he used entirely for decorative effects. The more exotic ones he put into his botanical garden. To this he added a greenhouse, as well as a sweeping grass bowling green, in the middle of the carriage approach to Mount Vernon.

VISITORS

Visitors of infinite variety continued to pour in. "A Mr. Noah Webster" and Mason Weems, who were each to gain a certain immortality, came to call. John Fitch dropped by to explain his steamboat. Old army comrades, Lee and Lincoln, visited him; Madison and Monroe appeared to discuss state and national problems. The governors of Maryland and Virginia sought his advice. The head of the Pennsylvania Cincinnati brought him 250 diplomas to sign. The "celebrated Mrs. Macauley Graham," a formidable Whig authoress, arrived from England.

The writers who came failed to leave adequate impressions of Mount Vernon, but two visiting merchants did so. One was an Englishman, Robert Hunter, who came with Richard Henry Lee on November 16, 1785. Hunter, who considered Washington "the first man in the world," was enthusiastic about him as farmer and landscaper. He wrote:

I... took a walk about the General's grounds, which are really beautifully laid out. He has about 4,000 acres, well cultivated, and superintends the whole himself. Indeed, his greatest pride now is to be thought the first farmer in America. He is quite a Cincinnatus, and often works with his men himself; strips off his coat and labours like a common man.

The General has a great turn for mechanics. It's astonishing with what niceness he directs everything in the building way, condescending even to measure the things himself, that all may be perfectly uniform. The style of his house is very elegant, something like the Prince de Condé's at Chantilly... only not quite so large... He is making a most delightful bowling green before the house... The situation is a heavenly one, upon one of the finest rivers in the world. I suppose I saw thousands of wild ducks upon it...What makes it still more pleasing is the amazing number of sloops that are constantly sailing up and down the river...

By then, Washington had a secretary, William Shaw, who did not stay very long, but who told Hunter something about Washington's life. Shaw mentioned the astonishing numbers of letters that poured in from all over. Washington got up before sunrise and, after spending part of the morning answering them, rode out to superintend his farms. He dined at three and then spent two or more hours on his accounts and letters until tea time. He often worked thereafter until bed at nine. Because the Lees were there, Washington gave more than his usual time to relaxing in company. The delighted Hunter wrote:

At three, dinner was on the table... very neat and plain. The General sent the bottle about pretty freely after dinner, and gave success to the navigation of the Potomac for his toasts, which he has very much at heart, and when finished will, I suppose, be the first river in the world...

After tea General Washington retired to his study... If he had not been anxious to hear the news of Congress from Mr. Lee, most probably he would not have returned to supper but gone to bed at his usual hour, nine o'clock—for he seldom makes any ceremony. We had a very elegant supper about that time. The General with a few glasses of champagne got quite merry and, being with his intimate friends, laughed and talked a good deal...We had a good deal of conversation... about Congress, the Potomac, improving the roads, etc. At twelve I had the honour of being lighted up to my bedroom by the General himself.

An earlier visitor that year had been an American merchant, Elkanah Watson, who arrived on January 23. Watson had heard George III make the speech to Parliament, which had brought the king so much misery and Washington so much joy. He could hardly have failed to entertain the Washingtons with an account of it. Watson appeared when the family was dining and wrote: "This was the first time I had contemplated him in his private relations. I observed a peculiarity in his smile, which seemed to illuminate his eye; his whole countenance beamed with intelligence, while it commanded confidence and respect. I found him kind and benignant in the domestic circle, revered and beloved by all around him... Smiling content animated and beamed on every contenance in his presence."

Watson had arrived with a bad cold. When he got to bed that night he started coughing heavily. A little while later he noticed a lighted candle in his room. Washington was by his bedside with hot tea, a gesture which greatly moved the twenty-six-year-old Watson.

Washington talked at length of his canal schemes and of the need to open the West. Watson added: "Hearing little else, for two days, from the persuasive tongue of this great man, I was, I confess, completely under the influence of the canal mania, and it kindled all my enthusiasm." According to Washington's diary records, Watson stayed only one night at Mount Vernon but the effect was lasting. He became one of the leaders in the promotion of canals in New York State, helped to organize the Erie canal, and forty years after his visit wrote a history of his state's canal system.

Washington told Watson a funny story about one of his visitors, Joseph Wright, a minor artist, and son of the American, Patience Wright, who, during the war, ran both a wax museum and an intelligence service for Washington in London. Wright asked to make a medallion of Washington, and the rather reluctant general agreed to let his face be covered with plaster. Washington went on: "Whilst in this ludicrous attitude, Mrs. Washington entered the room, and seeing my face thus over spread with the plaster, involuntarily exclaimed. Her cry excited in me a disposition to smile, which gave my mouth a slight twist or compression of the lips, that is now observable in the busts Wright afterwards made."

Virginia and Congress had each decided that the best artist in Europe should be engaged to execute a statue of Washington but only the state carried the project to completion. Virginia's governor asked Jefferson to do the selecting, and he replied on January 12, 1785, that there was no question who should be employed, "the reputation of Monsr. Houdon... being unrivalled in Europe." He had consulted the sculptor who "was so anxious to be the person who should hand down the figure of the General to future ages, that without hesitating a moment he offered to abandon his business here, to leave the statues of kings unfinished, & to go to America to take the true figure."

The following October 2 Washington and his wife were awakened by a clatter downstairs. It was Jean-Antoine Houdon, who had arrived from Alexandria by water, with three assistants and an interpreter. Everyone knows the intelligent and sensitive face of Washington, as executed by Houdon, but neither the general nor the artist left more than scanty records of the meeting. Fortunately the visit made a lifelong memory for Nelly Custis, Martha Washington's six-year-old granddaughter. Martha had involuntarily exclaimed a little less than two years before, on seeing her husband covered with plaster by Joseph Wright. The horrified Nelly one day saw the general laid out on a table, covered with a sheet, and immediately assumed he was a corpse. She went into the room and found Houdon "engaged in putting on plaster to form the cast. Quills were in the nostrils. I was very much alarmed until I was told that it was a bust, a likeness of the general and would not injure him." This letter, acquired by Mount Vernon, was the first documentary evidence that their clay bust was made from a life mask.

On October 17 Houdon left by the stage for Philadelphia, and Washington for a meeting of directors of the Potomac Company. The two never met or corresponded again but Houdon's son-in-law stated the visit to Mount Vernon always shone for him "with special radiance." By the time his statue reached Richmond in 1796, Washington's national views had won him an intense hatred in his own state.

On July 30, 1785, Washington noted in his diary that he had "dined with only Mrs. Washington, which I believe is the first instance of it since my retirement from public life." On August 6, 1786, he wrote that he was "at home all day without Company."

On May 29, 1786, Tobias Lear, an honors graduate of Harvard, who had been cordially recommended by the president of the college and by General Lincoln, arrived at Mount Vernon. He had been engaged at a salary of $200 a year to be Washington's private secretary and tutor to Mrs. Washington's grandchildren. It was a fortunate choice for the general, since Lear stayed with him until 1793, and then returned to Mount Vernon after Washington's presidency.

LIFE AND DEATH

Death was ever-present in the eighteenth century, and it struck hard at the Washington family and friends. Four months after her husband returned to Mount Vernon, Martha Washington had news of the death of her mother and brother. On August 1, 1786, Washington wrote Jefferson in Paris:

> *You will probably have heard of the death of Genl Greene before this reaches you, in which case you will, in common with your Countrymen, have regretted the loss of so great and so honest a man. Gen. McDougall, who was a brave Soldier and a disinterested patriot is also dead... Colo. Tilghman, who was formerly of my family, died lately and left as fair a reputation as ever belonged to a human character. Thus some of the pillars of the revolution fall. Others are mouldering by insensible degrees. May our Country never want props to support the glorious fabrick!*

In early 1787, Washington learned of the death of his favorite brother, John. He was always a little gloomy whenever he heard of the deaths of younger people and also when he fell ill. At the beginning of September 1786 he himself had a severe attack of malaria which he dosed heavily with quinine. It was accompanied by so bad an eruption on his face that, for days, he had to use scissors rather than a razor for his whiskers. This was followed soon afterwards by what he described as severe rheumatic pains which he had never previously experienced. These plagued him for months. Not long before he was to set off for the Constitutional Convention, he complained that he was hardly able to turn in bed or raise his hand to his head.

While death and illness were around, there were always new people coming up. Martha's grandchildren and quantities of nieces and nephews on both sides gave the general and his wife plenty to do, much joy, and many headaches. Martha Washington was totally maternal by instinct and spoiled all children, though her granddaughter, Nelly, complained that she was stricter with her than with her brother. Washington thundered at them when they did wrong and was extraordinarily kind and playfully humorous when they behaved. Nelly was his favorite. She wrote, after his death, how often she had made him laugh in "sympathy with my joyous and extravagant spirits." Her brother became a problem child, as his father had been before him, and Washington commented that he seemed to be able to command men, but not boys.

Washington saw to the education of two nephews, sons of his dead brother, Samuel, by placing them in school at Georgetown. They ran up such high bills that he removed them to Alexandria. One of them, George Steptoe

Washington, was subsequently reprimanded by his uncle for "disobedience, Perverseness, [and] disobliging conduct." Another nephew, Fielding Lewis, Jr., was chided for "your disrespectful conduct towards me, in coming into this country and spending weeks therein without ever coming near me." He summed up his niece, Harriott Washington: "She dabs her clothes in every hole and corner." Nonetheless, he spent a great deal of individual time and effort to see them brought up and educated. Another nephew, George Augustine Washington, who had served in the war as Lafayette's aide but had acquired the Washington family's tuberculosis, was sent on a long and expensive trip to the West Indies to recover his health. Washington was delighted when he married Martha Washington's niece, Fanny Bassett, and had them live at Mount Vernon. He also took care to see that another nephew, Bushrod, received the best legal education. Others were given loans or grants which Washington could not afford, plus advice or help.

Mount Vernon was something of a matrimonial bureau, for not only did Martha's niece marry George's nephew, and Tobias Lear marry two of Martha's nieces (one having died), but Martha also married her granddaughter to another nephew of Washington. Martha made sure there would always be a plentiful supply of babies for a growing country, leaving to her husband the task of achieving a peaceful nation in which they could grow up.

ENEMIES, FOREIGN AND DOMESTIC

No very certain figures exist of the number of American-born Tories who left for Canada, Nova Scotia, or Great Britain. Certainly many of the refugees were British-born officials, placemen, or merchants, while numerous Americans who fled to England during the war years returned quietly after the peace. They and others who had remained gradually forgot the past, settled down to be republicans, and intermarried with the patriots. Consequently many a daughter of the revolution is also a daughter of a united empire loyalist.

In determining policy for Quebec and Nova Scotia, the British government took care to see that no revolution could happen again. The existing inhabitants were given short shrift. In Nova Scotia Tories took command of the council and of the lower house. For Canada (a word largely meaning Quebec), the British government appointed a military governor, Sir Guy Carleton, former commander at New York, after making him Baron Dorchester. Lord Beauchamp remarked at the time: "Peers are made by dozens. The King, nobody knows why, has put Carleton into the list."

Carleton kept power in his hands, until he could arrange for its sharing with

Tories who could be trusted. He appointed lifetime councillors from their ranks. To free the crown and church from dependence on local revenues, he reserved one-seventh of the land for each of these bodies. He made additional generous land grants to those who fled the United States. By the time assemblies were permitted in upper and lower Canada, control was in the hands of crown, church, and gentry. British policies contrasted strongly with those established by Congress in the Northwest Ordinances of 1785 and 1787. These provided for the carving of new territories into acreage for public sale and settlement, the reservation of part of the land to finance public schools, and the establishment of new and fully equal states, when a territory had 60,000 people.

Lord Dorchester had an even more important task than setting back the Canadian clock. This was to reinstitute a hostile policy designed once more to keep Americans behind the Alleghenies. Britain had already refused to make a commercial treaty with the United States, while an order in council excluded American shipping from the West Indies trade. Dorchester, before leaving New York, had written that the United States seemed unlikely to survive as an independent power. George III, that same year, predicted that it would be many years before America, without a monarch, would have a stable government.

As governor of Canada, Dorchester commanded the British forts still held on American territory. Using these as cover, he promoted Indian attacks against the defenseless western settlements. John Jay, the American foreign secretary, remarked that Dorchester could easily outbuy the Indians, since the United States was so poor. Henry Knox, the war secretary, could do little, with his few hundred troops, to guard thousands of miles of frontier. When Prince William visited Canada in 1787, Dorchester took him to a great Indian council at Montreal. The prince wrote to George III that they said how pleased they were to see in him the same blood as their "Great Father in the East." They hoped he would again view them as his "favoured children," after the evil late rebellion in the south.

The only valid excuse which Britain could muster for holding forts on American territory lay in the failure to settle the prewar commercial debts owed by Americans to her merchants. When Jefferson visited Adams in London in 1786, the pair devoted much time to discussions with Duncan Campbell, chairman of the merchant group. Jefferson pointed out that America wanted to meet her just debts but the country had been ravished by a long war and needed time to pay. While there were differences on wartime interest, every sign appeared that they would reach an amicable agreement. Campbell went off happily to talk to the British secretary of state. He never again appeared. Jefferson assumed that the proposals had been overruled by the British government, which needed a reason to hold the posts.

Dorchester reestablished a British secret service system in the United States under his aide, Major John Beckwith, who had been assistant to John André. Its aim was to win friends for Great Britain, to get all useful intelligence, and to detach Vermont, Kentucky, and the territories north of the Ohio from American control. In 1787 Beckwith informed Quebec and London that William Smith, president of Columbia College and a member of Congress, told him the United States government was held in such contempt from Maine to Georgia that there was hardly an American who did not long to see monarchy restored.

In the meantime, while Spain was also holding American forts and stirring up Indian attacks in Tennessee and Georgia, a little American revolution broke out in New England, where British trade restrictions had caused a recession, Massachusetts, at the same time, reverted to a specie system which brought hardship to her western farmers who found their debts multiplying, while their produce sank in value. To the annoyance of Samuel Adams, now grown more conservative, the courts were closed, committees of correspondence were established, and armed rebellion, led by Daniel Shay, broke out. General Benjamin Lincoln, Washington's former officer, smashed the disorder with state militia. In New Hampshire, the state's president, General Sullivan, also had to call out the militia to establish peace. The Canadian government, carefully watching these developments, told the Indian nations to be patient and wait for the breakup of the American union.

WASHINGTON COMMENTS

Although the general wrote Jefferson in 1786 that he did not have much opportunity to get news, since he was mostly working on his canals and farms, this was only rhetoric. David Humphreys, who visited him the following year, said that Mount Vernon was the focal point for all New World intelligence. Washington kept himself well informed on domestic and international developments, while his own western visit had shown him how fragile were the ties of the settlers there to the United States.

As early as August 11, 1784, he noted to Jacob Read: "Tho' it is undoubted that the British Cabinet wish to recover the United States to a dependence on that Government; yet I can scarce think they ever expect to see it realized... unless *our* want of wisdom, and perserverance in error, should in their judgement render the attempt certain... Her prospect of success must diminish as our population increases, and the government becomes more consistent; without the last of which, indeed, anything may be apprehended... Nothing,

I confess, would sooner induce me to give credit to a hostile intention on the part of G. B., than their continuing (without the shadow of reason, for I really see none) to withhold the Western Posts... and sending... Sir Guy Carleton over as Viceroy..."

By June 30, 1785, he was writing George Fairfax in England: "With respect to the commercial system which G. B. is pursuing... the Ministers, in this as in other matters, are defeating their own ends, by facilitating those powers in Congress which will produce a counteraction of their plans, and which half a century without, would not have invested the body with. The restriction of our trade, and the additional duties which are imposed upon many of our staple commodities, have put the commercial people of this country in motion; they now see the indispensable necessity of a general *controlling* power, and are addressing their respective Assemblies to grant this to Congress." Following Knox's report to him of the troubles in Massachusetts, he replied on December 26, 1786:

I feel, my dear Genl. Knox, infinitely more than I can express to you, for the disorders which have arisen in these States, Good God! who besides a tory could have forseen, or a Briton predicted them! were these people wiser than others, or did they judge us from the corruption and depravity of their own hearts? The latter I am persuaded was the case, and that notwithstanding the boasted virtue of America, we are far gone in everything ignoble and bad...

That G. B. will be an unconcerned Spectator of the present insurrections (if they continue) is not to be expected. That she is at this moment sowing the Seeds of jealousy and discontent among the various tribes of Indians on our frontier admits of no doubt, in my mind. And that she will improve every opportunity to foment the spirit of turbulence within the bowels of the United States, with a view to distracting our governments, and promoting divisions, is, with me, not less certain... We ought not therefore to sleep nor to slumber. Vigilance in watching, and vigour in acting, is, in my opinion, become indispensably necessary...

CALL TO CONVENTION

Virginia, after its meeting with Maryland, invited other states to discuss trade regulations. Under the leadership of Madison, joined by Hamilton of New York, commissioners from Virginia, Pennsylvania, New Jersey, New York, and Delaware, met at Annapolis in September 1786. Washington, though ill, wrote Colonel John Fitzgerald on September 9: "Have the Commercial

Commissioners met? Have they proceeded to business? How long is it supposed their sessions will last? and is it likely they will do anything effectual?"

The meeting, five days later, called unanimously for a general convention of the states to meet the second Monday in May 1787 to "render the constitution of the federal government adequate to the exigencies of the Union." It was a successful call, so much so that seven states had selected their delegates, before Congress got around to approving the resolution in February.

On December 6 the new governor of Virginia, Edmund Randolph, notified Washington that Virginia was sending an exceedingly strong representation to Philadelphia. To lend the delegation, as Madison put it, "a very solemn dress and all the weight which could be derived from a single state," General Washington, by unanimous vote of the assembly, had been chosen chairman. When the list of delegates from America's largest state was printed throughout the country, HIS EXCELLENCY GENERAL WASHINGTON was automatically capitalized. The second largest state, Pennsylvania, selected its president, Benjamin Franklin, as her chairman, and the choices seemed good omens for the meeting.

Washington was not at all sure he would go. First and foremost in his mind was that, by odd chance, the triennial meeting of the Cincinnati had been called to meet in Philadelphia the first Monday in May 1787. On October 31 Washington had written to all the state societies, declining again to be president and explaining that he could not attend, since it was becoming more and more inconvenient for him to be absent from his farms:

> *The numerous applications... which are made to me in consequence of my military command; the multiplicity of my correspondences... the variety and perplexity of my private concerns... the arduousness of the task, in which I have been... engaged, of superintending the opening of the navigation of the great rivers in this State; the natural desire of tranquility and relaxation from business, which almost every one experiences at my time of life... and the present imbecility of my health, occasioned by a violent attack of the fever and ague succeeded by rheumatic pains... will, I doubt not, be considered as reasons of sufficient validity to justify my conduct in the present instance.*

The same reasons operated in Washington's mind when the governor's notification arrived. To these were added a recollection of his 1783 statement that he was withdrawing forever from public office, as well as the idea that his former officers would be greatly chagrined, if he attended one meeting and not the other. He sent a candid letter to Madison explaining also that the failure of many of the state societies of the Cinncinati to amend their charters, to remove hereditary membership, made his situation especially "delicate."

Washington wrote Randolph on December 21 that in all probability he would not be able to attend and it would be better for Virginia to select someone else. The governor on January 4 replied that he and the council had decided to leave Washington's name as it was. "Perhaps the obstacles now in view may be removed before May; and the nomination of a successor, if necessary at all, will be as effectually made some time hence as now. Perhaps too (and indeed I fear the event) every other consideration may seem of little weight, when compared with the crisis, which may then hang over the United States."

Beyond every argument which he could convey to his friends was one he was too embarrassed to mention. He was in such critical need of money that he could not meet his taxes. His total efforts to restore his farms and income and to make up for nine years of neglect were far from succeeding. When his mother applied for money, he wrote her on February 15, 1787:

> *In consequence of your communication to George [Augustine] Washington of your want of money, I... send you 15 guineas, which believe me is all I have, and which indeed ought to have been paid many days ago to another...I have now demands upon me for more than 500, three hundred and forty odd of which is due for the tax of 1786; and I know not where or when, I shall receive one shilling with which to pay it... Those who owe me money cannot or will not pay it without suits, and to sue is to do nothing; whilst my expenses... for the absolute support of my family and the visitors who are constantly here, are exceedingly high; higher indeed than I can support without selling part of my estate, which I am disposed to do, rather than run in debt... but this I cannot do, without taking much less than the lands I have offered for sale are worth...*

In early March he was asking through his friends whether, if he did not go, he might be considered as not a warm republican. On March 28 he informed the governor that so many people seemed anxious for him to attend that, if his health permitted, he had about decided to participate. Once over the hurdle of decision, he was able to write to James Madison on March 31 with something of his old vigor: "It gives me great pleasure to hear that there is probability of a full representation of the States in Convention... My wish is that the Convention may adopt no temporizing expedient, but probe the defects of the constitution to the bottom, and provide radical cures; whether they are agreed to or not; a conduct like this, will stamp wisdom and dignity on the proceedings..."

On April 27, Washington wrote Knox that, though his arm was still in a sling, he had been getting ready to get to Philadelphia in time for the Cincinnati meeting. He had just had word of the critical illness of his mother and sister and was setting off for Fredricksburg and was therefore forwarding the papers needed for the meeting. The alarms turned out to be exaggerated, and he returned to Mount Vernon. On May 3 he rode over all his plantations with his nephew and new manager, George Augustine, explaining his management problems.

On May 9, 1787, shortly after sunrise Washington left Mount Vernon to cross the Potomac to Maryland. That night he recorded that he had a violent headache and sick stomach and had to rest at Elkridge. Two nights later high winds delayed his crossing of the Susquehanna, forcing him to spend the night at Havre de Grace. At Chester, May 13, he found the officers of the Cincinnati, who had been waiting impatiently to escort their president into Philadelphia.

FOUR

THE CONSTITUTION ADOPTED

1787–1788

I T IS PROBABLY not true that the only duty performed by the elect Light Horse Troop of Philadelphia was that of escorting General Washington into and out of the city. As they had done for twelve years, they welcomed and saluted him on May 13 as he rode into town with three of his revolutionary generals. The guns boomed, the church bells chimed, and great crowds were out at the boarding house of Mrs. House, where he had engaged rooms. He was mercifully spared any speeches. Mr. and Mrs. Robert Morris "warmly and kindly pressed" him to come and be more comfortable at their house a few doors away. He accepted; while his baggage was being removed to the Morris house, he rode off to call on the president of Pennsylvania, Doctor Franklin. This was their first meeting since 1775.

Washington had once before had a long and dreary wait in Philadelphia for Lord Loudoun, the British commander in chief. Now he passed boring days without his wife (who, he said, had become much too domestic to travel again), waiting for the various state delegations to show up. It had been a hard winter; the primitive roads were in bad condition, and travel was slower than ever. On his arrival only two states were represented—Pennsylvania and Virginia. The following day therefore he attended the Cincinnati, where he was unanimously reelected president.

By May 18 there was still no quorum. Washington recorded that he dined that day at a club, had tea with the Morrises, then went with Mrs. Morris "and some other ladies to hear a Mrs. O'Connell read (a charity affair). The lady being reduced in circumstances had had recourse to this expedient to obtain a little money. Her performance was tolerable." By Sunday he was reduced to visiting the Morrises' country farm. On Monday he dined "at Mr. Bingham's in great splendor." On May 23 he again rode into the country. In the afternoon he dined at Mr. Chew's and "drank tea there in a very large circle of ladies."

While waiting, Washington wrote long and anxious letters to George Augustine Washington, urging him, because of his health, not to work too hard, but at the same time forwarding detailed questions on every aspect of his farming operations. He added that he had bought and was forwarding Mrs. Washington's buckles and knives, and he asked George to send up his new umbrella.

THE CONVENTION

The representatives from states as far as South Carolina having reached Philadelphia, New Jersey managed to get its delegates across the Delaware on May 25. This made a quorum of seven states, and the convention proceeded to business.

The host state, Pennsylvania, had agreed to nominate Washington as president, with Franklin as sponsor. The latter was too ill to appear, and Robert Morris, Washington's host, had the honor. John Rutledge of South Carolina seconded the nomination and, since he was present, suggested that it not be discussed but be made unanimous. This was immediately done, and Morris and Rutledge escorted Washington to the president's seat. This was the chair, with its gilded sun on the back, used by every president of Congress and which is still in Independence Hall.

The country had as usual given a reluctant Washington a particularly gruelling job. This one was to last for almost four months, during one of the hottest summers on record. Some idea of what it involved may be gathered from Clinton Rossiter's estimate that the six delegates who talked the most made 900 speeches. Washington had to hear every one, many doubtless repetitive. Never has a future president received such an education in constitutional law and in diversity of opinion.

Washington made one of his usual little talks, expressing his thanks for the honor, his lack of qualifications, and his hope that the convention would indulge his errors. From then on he presided with grace and no known errors. The convention, after imposing total secrecy on its members, elected a committee composed of Hamilton, Charles Pinckney, and Chancellor Wythe to formulate rules and orders. Rhode Island, the smallest state, had refused to attend and, for its intransigence, was called Rogue Island in Boston. Other delegates subsequently straggled in. Not till June 2 were twelve states represented by a quorum of their delegates.

The French chargé d'affaires, Louis Otto, after reading a list of the members, informed the French foreign minister that even Europe had never seen "an assembly more respectable for the talents, knowledge, disinterestedness, and patriotism of those who compose it." Otto's observations were especially noteworthy, for France was also having a convention to consider constitutional and fiscal reform, the Assemblé des Notables, which Lafayette promptly dubbed the "not-ables."

The American convention was extraordinary for the diversity of experience of its members, who had often combined three or more careers. Thirty-two of the fifty-five had served in some capacity in the military forces, ranging from chaplain to commander in chief. Four had been on Washington's personal staff. Two were war governors of states devastated by the British. Forty-two men had served in the Continental Congress, and two had been its president. Eight had signed the Declaration of Independence. Practically every man from Washington down had also been in his colonial or state government, and many had worked on revising their own state constitutions after independence. A majority had enjoyed a college education at home or abroad. Princeton topped the list with nine graduates including James Madison, Jr., who had done much homework in preparation for the event. Harvard came in fourth after Yale and William and Mary.

New York State, then fifth in population, sent the oddest delegation. Washington's old and trusted friend, Governor George Clinton, was opposed to more than modest changes in the Articles of Confederation, since his state was happy in taxing products moving to the port of New York. Clinton arranged that two men, Robert Yates and John Lansing, Jr., who were opposed to any newfangled laws, be a majority for New York at the convention. In a complication arising from New York political intrigue, Alexander Hamilton was added to the group. Both Yates and Lansing did oppose the federal plan and then, seeing the convention move far from their position, withdrew in early July.

Hamilton, in his turn, made what was easily the most inept proposal to the convention. On June 18 he advocated a lifetime president to be elected by electors who, in turn, had been elected by electors, who had been chosen by the voters. The president was to appoint all state governors. Senators were to be elected for life by electors, while the lower house was to be chosen by the people. Congress was to be permitted to pass all "laws whatsoever," subject only to executive veto. Hamilton drew up a "constitution" modeled on his proposal which is noteworthy only for its clumsiness. There have been various conjectures as to why Hamilton left the convention on June 29, not to return again until August. It appears most likely that his effort at constitution making, having fallen with a dull thud, caused him to depart in high dudgeon. He remarked to Washington in a letter of July 10 that his attendance there seemed to be "a waste of time." From July 10 on New York was either unrepresented, or had but one man present, and therefore had no quorum and no vote.

With secrecy imposed, Washington's diary automatically became mum as to the proceedings. In the absence of news, some gazettes republished Washington's 1783 "Circular to the States," which pleaded for national union. A wild rumor appeared in the press that the convention had chosen a younger son of George III to be king. The convention authorized a public statement that a monarchy had never been considered. Benjamin Franklin got a mild chiding from one of the delegates for nearly revealing state secrets when, with others present in his garden, he exhibited a two-headed snake and began humorously comparing it with the problem of choosing one or two branches of Congress. In far-off Paris, Jefferson denounced the secrecy, perhaps because of an inordinate curiosity as to what was happening.

James Madison had brought to Philadelphia an outline of a proposed new constitution to substitute for the old Articles of Confederation. He discussed it point by point with the Virginia delegates. The plan was introduced into the convention by the state's governor on May 29. Thereafter Madison had the author's exquisite pain, which Jefferson had experienced with his declaration, of seeing it torn apart word by word. In the end, Madison put much of the flesh on his remade skeleton, which enabled it to grow into a living organism.

On June 4 Franklin predicted that whoever would be chosen to head the union "will be a good man," and everyone, with the possible exception of Washington, knew whom he had in mind. However, this was at a very early stage in the proceedings. Many still thought of "the National Executive" as a committee or council with a presiding officer. As the convention worked on, every delegate, including those who had never known him, had the fullest opportunity of observing and talking to the president. In the end the nation's presidency was tailored to the man who sat there "like patience on a monument," but the fullest safeguards were built around the office, in case his successors should be more ambitious or venal. Jefferson had once remarked that the horseflies from nearby stables tended to speed up debates in Independence Hall but they had no noticeable effect in 1787. Washington wrote Knox during a steamy August that any defects in the convention's work "cannot, with propriety, be charged to the hurry with which the business has been conducted."

SOCIAL LIFE

Washington had some social life after his duties, which generally occupied him six days a week. He attended a Roman Catholic Mass, and he heard Bishop William White preach. White, just consecrated by the Archbishops of Canterbury and York, had been chaplain of Congress and a leader in a revolution in the American branch of the Church of England. Washington dined with many prominent Philadelphians but also spent long hours reading and writing in his rooms. Mrs. Morris wrote later that she had never had a quieter guest nor one who gave less trouble. For the most part, days and nights were of a most routine nature, except for dinner parties and occasional rides to the country.

Washington inspected the most famous botanical gardens in America, belonging to William Bartram. As an experienced botanist and landscape designer, he did not think much of the garden, which he described as "not laid off with much taste, nor was it large." He also examined some experiments in using plaster of Paris as fertilizer on nearby farms. Having been told it should always be applied during a waxing moon, he added, "but this must be whimsical." Peale did his portrait once more.

During an interval from July 27 to August 6, the convention adjourned in order to give the Committee on Detail time to provide a first draft of a constitution. Washington went fishing, and his diary had a happier sound. He and Gouverneur Morris rode to a point near Valley Forge to catch trout. He examined his old encampment and found the works in ruins and woods growing where the army's log cabins had been. He made notes on raising buckwheat and its use in feeding cattle and laying "fat upon hogs." He continued fishing after Mr. and Mrs. Robert Morris came to join the party. They all returned to Philadelphia August 1. On August 3, in company with the three Morrises, he went over to Trenton to try the fishing there. He commented, "In the Evening fished, not very successfully." Next day he hooked some perch.

On August 5 he returned to Philadelphia and his grind. Thereafter, until September 15, little happened outside the convention. On August 19, a Sunday, he went to his old camp at Whitemarsh and dropped by the Chew house, the center of the Germantown battle. The only other item of interest he recorded was: "Visited a Machine at Doctr. Franklin's (called a Mangle) for pressing, in place of ironing, clothes from the wash. Which Machine from the facility with which it despatches business is well calculated for Table cloths and such articles as have not pleats and irregular foldings and would be very use-ful in all large families."

THE CONSTITUTION

Washington's highly discreet letters during the convention gave only hints of his feelings. To Jefferson he wrote on May 31: "The business of this Convention is as yet too much in embryo to form any opinion of the result. Much is expected of it by some; but little by others; and nothing by a few." On June 3 he wrote George A. Washington: "The sentiments of the different members seem to accord more than I expected they would as far as we have yet gone." On July 1 he informed David Stuart who had married Jacky Custis' widow: "I have had no wish more ardent, through the whole progress of this business, than that of knowing what kind of government is best calculated for us to live under... To inform the judgment, it is necessary to hear all arguments that can be advanced. To please all is impossible, and to attempt it would be vain... Demagogues, men who are unwilling to lose any of their state consequence, and interested characters in each, will oppose any general government." To Hamilton, who had left the convention, he wrote on July 10: "The state of the Councils which prevailed at the period you left this city... are now, if possible in a worse train than ever... I am sorry you went away. I wish you were back." On August 15 he told Lafayette: "There are seeds of discontent in every part of the Union; ready to produce other disorders if the wisdom of the present Convention should not be able to devise, and the good sense of the people be found ready to adopt a more vigorous and energetic government... "

Most of the work fell on the few who were hard working, able, and anxious to see a working union and constitution. Fewer than half the delegates attended consistently. The latter included Franklin, who came early to the state house in order to do duty as the state's president before the meeting. Death and illness, private or official business, called away others for short or long periods. Antiunionists quit the proceedings.

The first draft of the Constitution, presented by the Committee on Detail on August 6, was elephantine in comparison with the final version. The debates continued. Hours of meetings were lengthened. As the broiling heat of August persisted, speeches got shorter and compromises grew more accept-able. More antinational delegates departed, making it easier for the unionists to proceed.

The "National Executive" (some members having urged that three or more heads were better than one) slowly became "the president." An original proposal to give him a single seven-year term was beaten down to four. Though many objected, he could, in the end, be reelected. In a compromise between "national" and "state" interests, an electoral system was instituted for the president, rather than an election by Congress or popular vote. A proposal that judges and ambassadors be appointed by the Senate was fortunately changed, giving this power to the president, with the Senate reduced to advice and consent. Considering what all the delegates thought of George III, the president, who became chief of state and government as well as commander in chief, was a surprisingly strong figure. Nonetheless, everywhere in the documents were checks on his power by a strong Congress and an independent judiciary. The people could refuse to reelect the president. If they could not wait four years, a two-thirds vote in the House and Senate, under defined procedures, could remove him from office.

On September 8 a five-member Committee on Style was appointed to redraft the early version and to incorporate changes made by the voting states. Three committee members, Abraham Baldwin, James Madison, and Gouverneur Morris, all testified in later years that Morris was the man who did the drafting. In four memorable days he produced a masterpiece of clarity where intentions were clear and of ambiguity where the convention so determined. As an editor, Morris was notable. "We the People of the States of New Hampshire, Massachusetts, Rhode-Island and Providence Plantations, etc. etc." became "We the People of the United States," a change which brought howls from states' righters. Other wordy clauses were sharply cut. "The Executive Power of the United States shall be vested in a single person. His style shall be, 'The President of the United States of America'; and his title shall be, 'His Excellency,'" became "The Executive Power shall be vested in a President of the United States of America."

On September 17 the convention met for the last time. In a final motion to increase the size of the House of Representatives, in order to give more power to the people, the president rose and made his first speech. As indirectly quoted, Washington said that "the smallness of the proportion of Representatives had been considered by many members of the Convention an insufficient security for the rights and interests of the people. He acknowledged that it had always appeared to himself among the exceptional parts of the plan; and late as the present moment was for admitting amendments, he thought this of so much consequence that it would give much satisfaction to see it adopted." It was done immediately.

Two delegates, Edmund Randolph and George Mason of Virginia, the state which had started the whole business, announced they would not sign, as did Elbridge Gerry of Massachusetts. Hamilton stated that he would subscribe as New York's only delegate present. The first signature on the engrossed copy was "G. Washington—president and deputy from Virginia." He was followed by thirty-eight others from twelve states. Copies were ordered printed for dispatch to Congress and the states. The members then adjourned to await the anticipated uproar. Washington became a little more loquacious in his diary:

> *Met in Convention, when the Constitution received the unanimous assent of 11 States and Colo. Hamilton's from New York (the only delegate from thence in the Convention) and was subscribed to by every Member present except Govr. Randolph and Colo. Mason from Virginia, and Mr. Gerry from Massachusetts.*

> *The business being thus closed, the Members adjourned to the City Tavern, dined together, and took a cordial leave of each other; after which I returned to my lodgings, did some business with, and received the papers from the Secretary of the Convention, and retired to meditate on the momentous work which had been executed, after not less than five, for a large part of the time six, and sometimes 7 hours sitting every day, except Sundays and the ten days adjournment... for more than four months.*

TO MOUNT VERNON

Washington forwarded copies of the Constitution to Lafayette and Jefferson. He then exited from Philadelphia with as much haste as his packing and natural politeness permitted. The following morning he took "leave of those families in which I had been most intimate, dined early (abt. 1 o'clock) at Mr. Morris's... and reached Chester where we lodged, in Company with Mr. Blair, [delegate of Virginia] who I invited to a seat in my Carriage till we should reach Mount Vernon." The pair ran into a nasty accident at Christiana bridge, described by Washington:

> *The rain which had fallen the preceding evening having swelled the water considerably, there was no fording it safely, I was reduced to the necessity therefore of remaining on the other side or of attempting to cross on an old, rotten and long disused bridge. Being anxious to get on I preferred the latter, and in the attempt one of my horses fell 15 feet at least, the other very near following, which, had it happened, would have taken the Carriage with baggage along with him, and destroyed the whole effectually. However by prompt assistance of some people at a Mill just by, and great exertion, the first horse was disengaged from his harness, the*

2d. prevented from going quite through and drawn off and the Carriage rescued from hurt.

Washington got to Mount Vernon September 22 "about sun set, after an absence of four months and 14 days." The following day, a Sunday, there were a dozen or so people for dinner and Washington did not go out to his farms. Early Monday morning he was out inspecting them, and he did this every day thereafter. There had been an exceptionally severe drought and his crops were meager. To add to his troubles there was an early and severe frost on October 14, which turned his buckwheat, peas, potatoes, and pumpkins "quite black."

Washington's acute financial position was much worsened by bad luck and weather. At the end of October he concluded that he would have to buy at least £500 in grains for his large but usually self-supporting establishment. On December 11 he wrote David Stuart "that at no period of my life have I ever felt the want of money so sensibly as now; among other demands upon me, I have no means of paying my Taxes."

From the time of his return from Philadelphia until the following summer, the greater part of his correspondence was devoted to trying to collect money owed him and to letters expressing anxiety about the ratification of the Constitution. Occasionally his two concerns overlapped. One of his largest debtors was John Francis Mercer, who had represented Maryland at Philadelphia. Mercer, an antifederalist, quit the convention in disgust when he saw the way things were moving. Before leaving, he informed Washington that as soon as he got home, he would send him £200 in part payment of his debts. The money never arrived, and Washington put increasing pressure on him to pay, so he could keep the sheriff away. While this was going on, Mercer's loud trumpetings against the Constitution were being carried across the Potomac to Mount Vernon, making him doubly irksome to the general.

With everything else on his mind, more impending trouble came in the form of a blunt letter, which David Humphreys sent him on September 28. This told Washington what everyone was expecting: "What will tend, perhaps, more than anything to the adoption of the new system will be an universal opinion of your being elected president of the United States and an expectation that you will accept it for a while." Washington was not one who generally tried to conceal the worst from his wife. He probably showed her the letter, since Humphreys announced he was coming for a long visit. She had borne a lot for her country, and there was now, apparently, more to come.

REVOLUTION BY DEBATE

The Constitution has meant many things to many people in the two centuries since its adoption. The five men most directly concerned with its operations in its first years differed widely on its meaning at the time of ratification. In his reply on October 10 to Humphreys, in which he ignored the comment about his being president, Washington wrote:

> *The Constitution that is submitted is not free from imperfections, but there are as few radical defects in it as could well be expected, considering the heterogeneous mass, of which the Convention was composed, and the diversity of interests that are to be attended to. As a Constitutional door is opened for future amendments and alterations, I think it would be wise in the People to accept...*

Adams wrote to Jefferson from London on November 10: "It seems to be admirably calculated to preserve the Union, to increase Affection, and to bring us all to the same mode of thinking... I hope the Constitution will be adopted..." Jefferson wrote Adams three days later from Paris: "How do you like our new constitution? I confess there are things in it which stagger all my dispositions to subscribe to it. The house of representatives will not be adequate to the management of affairs either foreign or federal. Their President seems a bad edition of a Polish king... Once in office, and possessing the military force of the union, without either the aid or check of council, he would not be easily dethroned..." Hamilton summed up his view to the convention September 6 when he said he disliked the whole scheme but he would vote for it. "It is better than nothing." John Jay wrote to Adams October 16: "[The Constitution] is much better than the one we have, and therefore... we shall be the gainers by the exchange, especially as there is reason to hope that experience and the good sense of the people will correct what may prove to be inexpedient in it. A compact like this, which is the result of accommodation and compromise, cannot be supposed to be perfectly consonant to the wishes and opinions of any of the parties."

The convention politely forwarded the Constitution to the Congress for approval and transmission to the states. In an unprecedented gesture, the delegates asked that the proposed Constitution "be submitted to a convention of delegates, chosen in each State by the people thereof... for their assent and ratification." This was an invitation to the most open free debate and to revolution by popular vote.

To say that the American people debated is to use understatement. Nothing else was discussed for months. Every gazette, legislature, dinner party, and tavern echoed with talk. For those who could not make head nor tail of the document, many papers pointed out that WASHINGTON and FRANKLIN had signed it, which should be sufficient guarantee of its goodness. It was the most bloodless revolution in history, though it is possible a few noses dripped red when feelings among a free and enlightened people ran high.

Washington's correspondence in the next eight months leaped to great volume as he moved to push ratification. The leading federalists in each state kept in the closest possible touch with each other. Letters in immense quantity were interchanged among Langdon in New Hampshire; Lincoln, Knox, and King in Massachusetts; Hamilton in New York; Madison in Virginia; and the Pinckneys in South Carolina. Washington was all unrestrained impatience to get news from any and all of them.

The first stages in the states were almost too easy. Delaware quickly and unanimously ratified, thus becoming "the first state," whose governor precedes all other state executives. New Jersey and Georgia ratified without opposition, while Pennsylvania and Connecticut approved by wide margins. The battle then grew harder. New York had been expected to be very troublesome, but Virginia also turned out to be difficult, while much opposition appeared in New Hampshire, Massachusetts, and North Carolina.

In New York State the battle was long. During his absence from the convention in July, Hamilton had attacked Governor Clinton in an unsigned article and impugned his motives. In a counterattack in September, a friend of Clinton wrote in the *New York Journal:* "I have also known an upstart attorney, palm himself upon a great and good man, for a youth of extraordinary genius, and under the shadow of such a patronage, make himself at once known and respected, but being sifted and bolted to the brann, he was at length found to be a superficial, self-conceited coxcomb, and was of course turned off, and disregarded by his patron." Hamilton wrote Washington that his feelings had been hurt by this, and he wanted a letter from him saying it was not true. Washington replied that he was much concerned at such a dispute between Clinton and Hamilton, for he had "the highest esteem and regard" for both. He added that the newspaper charges were "entirely unfounded." The quitting "was altogether the effect of your choice."

From all this, and the many attacks on the Constitution in the New York press, Hamilton decided on the more constructive approach of enlightening the people on what the document meant. He enlisted the help of James Madison and John Jay in developing the famous *Federalist Papers,* which appeared from September to May. Washington, after studying the writings with care, forwarded them to David Stuart, asking him to have them published in a Richmond paper. He also forwarded for publication a Pennsylvania speech by James Wilson, defending the new Constitution.

The federalist leaders in each state convention wrote those in other states, outlining the principal arguments of their opponents and how they were answered. They also revealed the use, when necessary, of political tricks. Massachusetts, determinedly democratic, had assembled nearly ten times as many delegates as signed the Constitution. John Hancock, the governor, whose sloth was exceeded only by his vanity, veered like a Boston winter weathervane, being for the Constitution one day and against it the next. The federalists informed him that Virginia, in all probability, would not ratify, and Washington could not therefore be president. Hancock, as the only man of stature next to him, would get his office. He decided for the Constitution, which carried by a rather small margin. Federalist express riders raced with the news to the neighboring capitals, Concord and Poughkeepsie.

Washington was exceedingly anxious to see Maryland ratify, as a good example to Virginia. The opponents there expected to use a tactic which had worked in New Hampshire—to vote to adjourn the state convention. Washington heard that this would also be tried in Virginia. He wrote his friends across the Potomac, under no circumstances should they permit this. On May 2, in glee, he informed Madison in Richmond that Maryland had approved by a huge majority: "Mr. Chace, it is said, made a display of all his eloquence. Mr. Mercer discharged his whole artillery of inflammable matter; and Mr. Martin did something; I know not what, but I presume with vehemence, but no converts were made, no, not one. So business after a very short Session, ended; and will if I mistake not, render yours less tiresome."

South Carolina quickly followed, and only one more state was needed to complete the nine necessary to union. It became a race between Virginia and New Hampshire. Washington had sent Tobias Lear, who came from the latter state, to report to him from Concord. By June 17 Washington had assurances from Lear that New Hampshire would ratify.

In Richmond the lineup was formidable for and against. Partly under Washington's prodding, the governor swung to support of the Constitution. Patrick Henry used all his flaming arguments against it. The quiet Madison displayed remarkable knowledge and debating skill. George Mason railed against the Constitution. It was ratified on June 25, though by but ten votes. Most of the opposition came from the western counties, now Kentucky and West Virginia, which voted, seventy-two years later, to stay in the Union. James Monroe, an opponent, wrote Jefferson that Washington's influence had carried the state. When it was over, Patrick Henry said he would support the union peaceably, as all good citizens should, and would work for changes within a constitutional framework. This gesture of magnanimity greatly pleased Washington. Alexandria held a celebration, after hearing the reports from Richmond, which was made even more cheerful by news that New Hampshire had ratified and ten states were in the Union. Washington reported to Lear on June 29:

> *Your letter of the 2d. instant came duly to hand and obliged me by its communications. On Friday last (by the stage) advice of the decision of the <u>long</u> and <u>warmly</u> (with temper) contested question, in the Convention of this State, was received, 89 ayes, 79 noes, without previous amendments; and in the course of that night Colo. Henley, Express from New York on his way to Richmond, arrived in Alexandria with the news of the ratification by the State of New Hampshire. This flood of good news almost at the same moment, gave, as you will readily conceive, abundant cause for rejoicing in a place, the Inhabitants of which are <u>all</u> federal. The cannon roared, and the Town was illuminated yesterday, as <u>magnificent</u> a dinner as Mr. Wise could provide (to which this family were invited and went), was displayed before the principal <u>male</u> Inhabitants of the Town; whose Ears were saluted at every quaff with the melody of federal guns. And on Monday, the business it seems is to recommence and finish, with fiddling and Dancing, for the amusement, and benefit of the Ladies.*

Only New York and North Carolina had yet to vote. The area around New York City sent a solid federal delegation to the state convention, while the opposition came from upstate. The New York convention, the longest of all, lasted nearly six weeks. Madison from Richmond and Langdon from New Hampshire sent urgent expresses to Hamilton, when their states ratified, in order to influence New York's vote. In the end, Hamilton carried the convention by the narrowest of all squeaks—three votes. This was done primarily by a threat that southern New York would secede from the state and join the Union. This, said Hamilton, would leave the upstate area without a friend, an ally, a port, or a source of taxes. Hamilton also made "Flag and mother" speeches when, according to his notes of July 17, he spoke of "Franklin... Washington... Heroes who have died... sister states... Mankind... Heaven." The economic threats doubtless carried greater weight. Washington wrote Hamilton on August 28, giving him high praise for the *Federalist Papers:*

> *As the perusal of the political papers under the signature of Publius has afforded me great satisfaction, I shall certainly consider them as claiming a most distinguished place in my Library. I have read every performance which has been printed on one side or the other... I have seen no other so well calculated... to*

produce conviction on an unbiased Mind, as the <u>Production</u> of your <u>triumvirate</u>.
When the transient circumstances… which attended this Crisis shall disappear,
That Work will merit the Notice of Posterity…

In anticlimax, North Carolina rejected the Constitution, but eleven states were ready to start and Congress had taken steps to admit Kentucky to the new Union. Washington had written John Armstrong on April 25, 1788:

Upon the whole I doubt whether the opposition to the Constitution will not
ultimately be productive of more good than evil; it has called forth, in its defence,
abilities which would not perhaps have been otherwise exerted, that have thrown
new light upon the science of Government, they have given the rights of man a full
and fair discussion, and explained them in so clear and forcible a manner, as
cannot fail to make a lasting impression upon those who read the best publications
on the subject.

The debates had certainly educated everyone. By the time they were over, nearly every American considered himself an expert on constitutional law; it was not going to be an easy country to govern. The great split was the beginning of a two-party system. Those who were against the Constitution formed a large nucleus of an opposition party, while those who later disagreed with the federal government's operations had a solid group with which to coalesce.

As the ratifications proceeded, the volume of letters pouring into Mount Vernon rose sharply. Many came from disinterested persons who believed that the country required Washington as president. Others expressed eagerness to have office under him. He responded to all that he did not want to be president, it was too great a sacrifice once again to leave Mount Vernon, while there was no assurance there would not be as great an opposition to his presidency as there had been to the Constitution. To those who wanted office, he added that, under the circumstances, a discussion of such matters was impossible.

FIVE

THE FIRST NATIONAL
ELECTION

1788–1789

I N THE MEANTIME, Great Britain had moved forward with policies
designed to confine Americans behind the mountains and to subordinate the Northwest Territory to Canada, two earlier grievances which had
helped to bring on revolution and war. The operations were directed by "His
Majesty's Government in America," the Canadian arm of Whitehall. Britain
was served by a large network of officials, army officers, Indian chiefs, traders,
unreconstructed Tories, and American friends and dupes. The seven forts
held by the British commanded the straits of Detroit, Mackinac, and Niagara,
as well as Lake Ontario, the Saint Lawrence River, and Lake Champlain. Lord
Dorchester had been commanded to hold them and, if attacked, to repel war
by war.

Dorchester was also ordered by London to support all Indian "rights" in
northern New York and west of Pittsburgh. This policy avoided open hostility,
while encouraging Indian warfare to prevent American settlements beyond
the mountains. The Indians were provided with gold, provisions, arms, and
ammunition. Numerous renegade Americans were employed to manage
them. They included Sir John Johnson in the Mohawk Valley as well as the
notorious Girty brothers and Alexander McKee and John Butler, who operated farther west.

London had further aims, to detach all American territory loosely tied to the confederacy, particularly Kentucky and Vermont. George Beckwith's espionage network employed Sir John Temple, British consul at New York; Peter Allaire, a New York merchant; Dr. John Connolly, who had spent four years in an American prison for intelligence work; as well as Dr. Edward Bancroft, who had been secretary to Franklin's Paris mission while on George III's payroll. Another member was Ethan Allen, who wrote Dorchester in 1788 that he was sure his 15,000 Vermont militia, leagued with the antifederalists, could prevent the ratification of the Constitution.

Connolly worked in Kentucky to attach it to Britain. This was a fertile area since most of its delegates had voted against ratification in Richmond. As early as 1786, Washington wrote Henry Lee that there were in Kentucky "many ambitious and turbulent spirits… who from the present difficulties in their intercourse with the Atlantic States, have turned their eyes to New Orleans, and may become riotous and ungovernable, if the hope of traffick with it is cut off by treaty."

In his negotiations with the Spanish minister, John Jay was unable to budge him on opening the Mississippi to American trade. The minister did agree to consider a commercial treaty, a move eagerly welcomed by New England, which was suffering a depression. Jay suggested that Congress set aside the question of navigation to New Orleans, in return for a trade treaty. There were not enough votes for this in Congress and the negotiations collapsed, but the proposal itself alarmed the Kentuckians.

While operating in Kentucky, Connolly picked up information on the activities there of another American, James Wilkinson, who was on Spain's payroll. Wilkinson, whose remarks about Gates and Conway had broken open the Conway Cabal, moved to Kentucky after the war. He began there an intrigue with the governor of Louisiana, who agreed to let Wilkinson move his goods to New Orleans and to have a pension, provided he would assist the Spanish to control the area east of the Mississippi. Wilkinson took the oath to Spain and returned to Kentucky to stir up the inhabitants against the United States. His address to the citizens there was forwarded by Connolly to Dorchester, with a note predicting that it could be detached from the United States if Britain could persuade Spain to open the river to Kentucky's products.

PAX VIRUMQUE

The general who had so long borne the arms of his country was the American who most loved peace. Between 1785 and 1789, particularly to his French friends, he expounded a consistently peaceful philosophy and a dream that

America would take the lead in making a better world for everyone. On July 25, 1785, he wrote Lafayette:

> *As the clouds which overspread your hemisphere are dispersing, and peace with all its concomitants, is dawning upon your Land, I will banish the sound of War from my letter. I wish to see the sons and daughters of the world in Peace and busily employed in the more agreeable amusement of fulfilling the first and great commandment, <u>Increase and Multiply</u>, as an encouragement to which we have opened the fertile plains of the Ohio to the poor, the needy and the oppressed of the Earth. Any one therefore who is heavily laden, or who wants land to cultivate, may repair thither and abound, as in the Land of promise, with milk and honey. The ways are preparing and the roads will be made easy...*

He followed with a further letter to Rochambeau on July 31, 1786:

> *It must give pleasure to the friends of humanity... to find that the clouds which threatened to burst in a storm of War on Europe, have dissipated... As the rage of conquest, which in times of barbarity stimulated Nations to blood, has in a great degree ceased; as the objects which formerly gave birth to Wars are daily diminishing; and as mankind are becoming more enlightened and humanized, I cannot but flatter myself with the pleasing prospect that more liberal policies and more pacific systems will take place amongst them. To indulge this idea affords a soothing consolation to a philanthropic mind, insomuch that, altho' it should be founded in illusion, one hardly wishes to be divested of an error so grateful in itself, and so innocent in its consequences.*

Washington happily congratulated Chastellux on April 25, 1788, on his unexpected marriage to a lady-in-waiting to the Duchesse d'Orléans:

> *In reading your very friendly letter... I was, as you may well suppose, not less delighted than surprised to come across those plain American words "my wife." A wife! Well my dear Marquis, I can hardly refrain from smiling to find you are caught at last. I saw, by the eulogium you often made on the happiness of domestic life in America, that you had swallowed the bait and that you would as surely be taken (one day or another), as you [are] a Philosopher and a Soldier... Now you are well served for coming to fight in favor of the American Rebels, all the way across the Atlantic Ocean, by catching that terrible Contagion, domestic felicity, which... like the small pox or plague, a man can have only once in his life... at least with us in America, I don't know how you manage these matters in France...*

While you have been making love, under the banner of Hymen, the great personages in the North have been making war... under the infatuation of Mars. Now, for my part, I humbly conceive, you have had much the best and wisest of the bargain. For certainly it is more consonant to all the principles of reason and religion (natural and revealed) to replenish the earth with inhabitants, rather than to depopulate it by killing those already in existence, besides it is time for the age of Knight-errantry and mad-heroism to be at an end.

He wrote again on November 27 to Chastellux, reintroducing Gouverneur Morris to him. Morris, in spite of having but one leg, was famous as a ladies' man. Washington therefore noted: "As for Mr. Morris only let him be once fairly presented to your French Ladies, and I answer for it, he will not leave the worst impression in the world, of the American character, for taciturnity and improper reserve." Chastellux never received the letter, for he died suddenly in October. Morris seems to have met all the French ladies he needed, without help. Jefferson sent him with a note to an old friend, Maria Cosway, in London, and got back her reply: "I am quite in Love with Mr. Morris. Are all Americans so engaging as those I know? Pray take me to that country."

Washington's French friends followed American political developments with close attention and as soon as they read the new Constitution they pushed for him as president. Rochambeau wrote that he longed to see Washington president of a strong confederation, while Lafayette said that he thought perhaps the president had too many powers but so long as Washington was to have the office, it would be all right. To Lafayette, on April 28, 1788, Washington gave the first indication that he might be forced to accept, against all inclination, but that it was not decent for him to talk about it, as there was always the story of the fox and the grapes. He followed this with another letter of June 19:

There seems to be a great deal of bloody work cut out for this summer in the North of Europe. If war, want and plague are to desolate those huge armies that are assembled, who that has the feelings of a man can refrain from shedding a tear over the miserable victims of Regal Ambition? It is really a strange thing that there should not be room enough in the world for men to live, without cutting one another's throats. As France, Spain and England have hardly recovered from the wounds of the late war, I would fain hope they will hardly be dragged into this...

I like not much the situation of affairs in France. The bold demands of the parliament, and the decisive tone of the King, shew that but little more irritation would be necessary to blow up the spark of discontent into a flame, that might not easily be quenched. If I were to advise, I would say that great moderation should be used on both sides. Let it not, my dear Marquis, be considered as a derogation from the good opinion that I entertain of your prudence, when I caution you, as an individual desirous of signalizing yourself in the cause of your country and freedom, against running into extremes and prejudicing your cause... It is a wonder to me that there should be found a single monarch, who does not realize that his own glory and felicity must depend on the prosperity and happiness of his People. How easy it is for a sovereign to do that which shall not only immortalize his name, but attract the blessings of millions...

... I expect that many blessings will be attributed to our new government... When the people shall find themselves secure under an energetic government, when foreign nations shall be disposed to give us equal advantages in commerce from dread of retaliation, when the burdens of war shall be in a manner done away by the sale of western lands, when the seeds of happiness which are somewhere shall begin to expand themselves, and when everyone... shall begin to taste the fruits of freedom, then all those blessings (for all these blessings will come) will be referred to as from the fostering influence of the new government. You see that I am not less enthusiastic than ever I have been in a belief that peculiar scenes of felicity are reserved for this country... Indeed, I do not believe that Providence has done so much for nothing...

... I hope, some day or another, we shall be a storehouse and granary for the world...

On January 29, 1789, as his presidency approached, he wrote Lafayette:

I will content myself with only saying that the elections have been hitherto vastly more favorable than we could have expected, that federal sentiments seem to be growing with uncommon rapidity and this increasing unanimity is not less indicative of the good disposition than the good sense of Americans. Did it not savour so much of partiality for my countrymen, I might add that I cannot help flattering myself that the new Congress on account of the... respectability and varied talents of its Members will not be inferior to any Assembly in the world...

... I can say little or nothing new, in consequence of the repetition of your opinion on the expedience there will be, for my accepting the office to which you refer... Nothing short of a conviction of duty will induce me again to take an active part in public affairs; and in that case, if I can form a plan for my own conduct, my endeavours shall be unremittingly exerted... to establish a general system of policy, which, if pursued, will ensure permanent felicity to the Commonwealth. I think I

see a path, as clear and direct as a ray of sunlight, which leads to the attainment of that object. Nothing but harmony, honesty, industry and frugality are necessary to make us a great and happy people. Happily the present posture of affairs, and the prevailing disposition of my countrymen promise to co-operate in establishing those four great and essential pillars of public felicity...

While you are quarreling among yourselves in Europe; while one King is running mad, and others acting as if they were already so, by cutting the throats of their neighbours, I think you need not doubt, my dear Marquis, we shall continue in tranquility here. And that population [growth] will be progressive so long as there shall continue to be so many easy means for obtaining a subsistence, and so ample a field for the exertions of talents and industry.

Washington's final word to France was to Rochambeau the same day:

Notwithstanding it might probably, in a commercial view, be greatly for the advantage of America that a war should rage on the other side of the Atlantic; yet I shall never so far divest myself of the feelings of a man interested in the happiness of his fellow-men, as to wish my country's prosperity might be built on the ruins of other nations. On the contrary, I cannot but hope that the Independence of America, to which you have so gloriously contributed, will prove a blessing to mankind. It is thus you see, My dear Count, in retirement, upon my farm, I speculate upon the fate of nations; amusing myself with innocent Reveries that mankind will, one day, grow happier and better.

WASHINGTON LEAVES THE PLOW

July 4, 1788, was celebrated throughout the nation as a day of hope. Enough states had ratified so that the new government was certain to come into being. That day, there were in all probability only two Americans (or three, if John Hancock is included) who did not hope the general would become president—Washington and his wife. A new song, "Great Washington shall rule the land," was first sung at York. In nearby Frederick, the Independence Day toast was "Farmer Washington—May he, like a second Cincinnatus, be called from the plow to rule a great people."

Cincinnatus was far from happy at the thought. He was having more difficulties that spring and summer than he had ever encountered with the Mount Vernon farms. The severe drought of the previous year, which had brought him so much financial loss, was followed by a wet and windy spring.

Washington's June diary noted the thinness of his wheat and buckwheat crops. That July 4 he was out all day in "dripping Rains," finding his grain crops too wet to cut and bind. Twenty days later there was a heavy, driving rain through the night. This was followed by a hurricane which lasted all day. Washington's trees were uprooted and felled, and many of his fences and crops were ruined. He noted that the Potomac tide, which rose four feet above any previous high-mark, drove all his boats onto the shore and drowned some of his shoreland. A miniature ship, *The Federalist,* which had been presented to Washington by the people of Baltimore, was smashed and sunk.

Washington's diaries for 1788 are the most extensive and the most tedious of any he kept during his life. No one on his farms was out for longer hours nor worked harder than he that year. It was as though he were trying, by sheer grit, to overcome personally all the difficulties that nature placed in his way, while blanking from his mind the imperious calls from the country. His financial condition grew worse. His January plea to John Francis Mercer to make his promised payments said that he had put the sheriff off three times on taxes. Though he had offered to finance the schooling of George Washington Craik, his physician's son, and had scraped together some money for this, he informed Dr. Craik on August 4:

> *I also send you Thirty pounds Cash for one year's allowance for the Schooling of your Son G.W. I wish it was in my power to send the like sum for the other year, which is now about, or near due; and that I could discharge your account for attendance and ministration to the Sick of my family; but it really is not; for with much truth I can say, I never felt the want of money so sensibly since I was a boy of 15 years old, as I have done for the last 12 months, and probably shall do for 12 Months more to come.*

A further drain on his purse was the schooling of the sons of his dead brother Samuel. He described this to another nephew, Bushrod Washington, on November 17: "What the abilities of my deceased brother Samls. Estate toward paying his debts may be, I am unable to say; but I much fear that the management of it is in very bad hands; as the hours of your Uncle Charles are, I have reason to believe, spent in intoxication… My Money (tho' it is exceedingly distressing to me to apply it that way) and my credit, is at stake for the board, the Schooling, clothing &ca. of George and Lawe. Washington, in Alexandria; without being able to receive from the Estate more than a little driblet now and then, entirely inadequate to the demand. My advance for them, at this time, in money and credit, is considerable…"

Congress, after a long summer's wrangle on where to locate the capital of the new government, decided on September 13 to leave it just where it was—in New York City. With this decision came a call for election of the president, vice-president, senators, and representatives, to meet and form the new government on March 4, 1789. Because of the slowness of communications, this did not give the faraway states too much time to organize their electoral machinery. New York, at the doorstep of Congress, did not even manage to vote for president.

Electioneering was intense for the vice-presidency and the twenty-two Senate and fifty-nine House seats. In general, the federalists thought in terms of John Adams as vice-president because he was a New Englander while Washington was a Southerner; Adams was also a Federalist, and had a long record of patriotic service. Another factor was that after his resignation as minister to Great Britain, he was out of a job.

Hamilton and others quickly discovered a flaw in the Constitution. If Adams received as many votes as Washington, then neither would be elected, and the new House of Representatives would have to decide who would be president. Hamilton therefore persuaded his neighboring states to give a few votes to other candidates, while providing a majority to Adams. Other states decided that they would compliment their own citizens by giving them a vote. Out of this chaos, Washington, as expected, received every vote, whereas Adams failed, by one, to have a majority, a result which he called "scurvy." No fewer than eleven men received votes for vice-president, including three from Massachusetts—Adams, Hancock, and Lincoln—and three exceedingly obscure Georgians.

Exactly when Washington faced the inevitable cannot be pinpointed. In October he informed Hamilton that the question filled him with gloom. That same month he repeated to Lincoln the despair he felt in facing "an unexplored field, enveloped on every side with clouds and darkness." He had hoped his public statement of 1783, that he would never again go into public office, would have been accepted by the people and thus give him "a last anchor of worldly happiness in old age." In early December he wrote John Trumbull, using the same phrase, "clouds and darkness," and indicating the sacrifice he would have to make. Nevertheless, in the same letter he noted how pleased he was by the selection of the first fourteen senators and the many distinguished people who were going into the House of Representatives. On December 19 James Madison arrived at Mount Vernon to spend six days in conference with Washington, while he made his final decision.

On January 29 Washington wrote to General Knox, the war secretary, in New York, that he had seen an advertisement in the *New York Daily Advertiser* for American broadcloth, the first manufactured in the country. He asked him to get enough cloth for a suit for himself and a riding habit for Mrs. Washington. On February 16, 1789, Knox replied that he had ordered the cloths from Hartford. "The moment they come to hand I will forward those for you and Mrs. Washington. It appears by the returns of elections hitherto obtained, which is as far as Maryland southward, that your Excellency has every vote for president..."

Virginia, with Patrick Henry an elector, also voted unanimously for Washington, though Henry and two others gave their votes to Clinton for vice-president. The votes from South Carolina and Georgia followed for Washington, and he was president-elect of the United States of America.

In early February, he received from Francis Hopkinson a book of music, dedicated to Washington, along with a humorous letter to which Washington replied: "We are told of the amazing powers of musick in ancient times; but the stories of its effects are so surprizing that we are not obliged to believe them unless they have been founded upon better authority than Poetic assertion... My dear Sir... you have not acted with your usual good Judgement in the choice which you have made of a Coadjutor, for should the tide of prejudice not flow in favor of it (and so various are the tastes, opinions and whims of men that even the sanction of divinity does not ensure universal concurrence) what, alas! can I do to support it? I can neither sing one of the songs, nor raise a single note on any instrument to convince the unbelieving..."

Washington wrote on May 13 that Hopkinson's subsequent reply made him "laugh heartily." It was obviously intended as advice to the president-elect, for Hopkinson wrote: "Orpheus was a legislator and civilizer of his country. In those days laws were promulgated in verse and sung to the harp, and the poets by a figure in rhetoric have attributed the salutory effects of his laws to the tunes to which they were play'd and sung."

On March 4 Washington wrote to Richard Conway in Alexandria to explain that he was terribly short of cash, he had not been able to sell his lands nor to collect money due him, and he was faced with the necessity of borrowing. Could Conway lend him £500 (which he later upped to 600)? Conway advanced the funds, enabling the president-elect to move to New York. On March 7 Washington rode to Fredericksburg to make a last call on his mother who was slowly dying of cancer.

The president-elect had now to wait while the House and Senate assembled with a quorum to make the official count. A severe winter delayed the new members in many states. Washington wrote to Knox on March 2 that the Virginia delegates were just about setting off. While waiting he drafted elaborate summaries of Mount Vernon's farm problems for his managers, as well as a proposed inaugural address. A report by Knox on the delays in New York was met with Washington's reply, April 1, that he considered them "a reprieve... My movements to the chair of Government will be accompanied by feelings not unlike those of a culprit who is going to the place of his execution... so unwilling am I, in the evening of a life nearly consumed in public cares, to quit a peaceful abode for an Ocean of difficulties, without that competency of political skill, abilities and inclination which is necessary to manage the helm... Integrity and firmness is all I can promise..."

On April 6 John Langdon, president of the Senate *pro tempore*, announced that both houses had met, the votes of all electors had been counted, and "His Excellency George Washington, Esq., was unanimously elected, agreeable to the Constitution, to the Office of the President of the said United States of America." Congress immediately dispatched Charles Thompson, who had been for fifteen years secretary of the old Continental Congress, to Mount Vernon, with the official notification and the duty of accompanying the president-elect to New York.

Thompson reached Mount Vernon shortly after noon on April 14 and read the document to Washington, who formally accepted. He wrote Senator Langdon that he would leave Mount Vernon for New York on April 16. In the meantime, by joint resolution, the Senate and House voted that the house lately occupied by the president of Congress, be prepared as the residence of the president of the United States.

THE TRIUMPHANT PROCESSION

Midmorning on April 16 Washington climbed into his waiting carriage. He recorded the event in his diary: "About ten o'clock I bade adieu to Mount Vernon, to private life, and to domestic felicity, and with a mind oppressed with more anxious and painful sensations than I have words to express, set out for New York in company with Mr. Thompson, and Colonel Humphreys, with the best disposition to render service to my country in obedience to its call, but with less hope of answering its expectations."

At Alexandria his fellow citizens had prepared a farewell dinner. The mayor, Dennis Ramsay, said that he would avoid the usual speech praising Washington as a great soldier and patriot, for his services to his neighbors had been "less splendid but more endearing... The first and best of citizens must leave us—Our aged must lose their ornament!—Our youth their model!—Our agriculture its improver!—Our commerce its friend!—Our infant Academy its patron!—Our Poor their Benefactor!—And the interior navigation of the Potowmack—an event replete with the most extensive utility, already, by your unremitted exertions, brought into partial use—its 'Institutor and Promoter'... Go, and make a grateful People happy... To that Being who maketh and unmaketh at will we commend you... May he restore to us again the best of men..." To this Washington replied:

> *Although I ought not to conceal, yet I cannot describe, the painful emotions which I felt in being called upon to determine whether I would accept or refuse the Presidency of the United States.*
>
> *The unanimity of the choice, the opinion of my friends, communicated from different parts of Europe, as well as of America, the apparent wish of those who were not altogether satisfied with the Constitution in its present form, and an ardent desire, on my own part, to be instrumental in conciliating the good will of my countrymen towards each other have induced an acceptance.*
>
> *Those who have known me best (and you, my fellow citizens, are from your situation, in that number) know better than any others that my love of retirement is so great, that no earthly consideration, short of a conviction of duty, could have prevailed upon me to depart from my resolution "never more to take any share in transactions of a public nature." For, at my age, and in my circumstances, what possible advantages could I propose to myself, from embarking again on the tempestuous and uncertain ocean of public life?*
>
> *I do not feel myself under the necessity of making public declarations, in order to convince you Gentlemen of my attachment to yourselves, and regard for your interests. The whole tenor of my life has been open to your inspection; and my past actions, rather than my present declarations, must be the pledge of my future conduct.*
>
> *In the meantime I thank you most sincerely for the expression of kindness contained in your valedictory address. It is true, just after having bade adieu to my domestic connections, this tender proof of your friendship is but too well calculated still farther to awaken my sensibility, and increase my regret at parting from the enjoyments of private life.*
>
> *All that now remains for me is to commit myself and you to the protection of that beneficent Being who, on a former occasion, has happily brought us together after a long and distressing separation. Perhaps the same gracious Providence will again indulge us with the same heartfelt felicity. But words, my fellow-citizens, fail me: unutterable sensations must then be left to more expressive silence; while from an aching heart, I bid you all, my affectionate friends and kind neighbours, farewell!*

According to the report of the *Pennsylvania Packet* from Georgetown,

> *The Most Illustrious the President of the United States of America... arrived at about 2 o'clock, on the banks of the Potomack, escorted by a respectable corps of gentlemen from Alexandria, where the George-Town ferry boats, properly equipped, received his Excellency and suite, and safely landed them under the acclamations of a large crowd of their grateful fellow-citizens, who beheld their Fabius in the evening of his days, bid adieu to the peaceful retreat of Mount Vernon, in order to save his country once more. From this place his Excellency was escorted by a corps of gentlemen... to Mr. Spurrier's tavern, where the escort from Baltimore took charge of him.*

The roaring Baltimore welcome included a speech containing the best single tribute paid Washington in his lifetime: "We behold an extraordinary thing in the annals of mankind, a free and enlightened People, choosing by a free election, without one dissenting voice, the late Commander-in-Chief of their Armies to watch over and guard their civil rights and privileges." Great crowds accompanied him to the Delaware line where that state's citizens took over, shouted their acclaim, and read an address to "The President General of the United States of America." At this point we can let the Reverend Mason Locke Weems take him as far as Trenton, where, seventy-two years later, Abraham Lincoln was to recall Weems' great impact on him as a boy:

> *"On reaching the western banks of Schuylkill," said a gentleman who was present, "I was astonished at the concourse of people that overspread the country, apparently from Gray's ferry to the city. Indeed one would have thought that the whole population of Philadelphia had come out to meet him. And to see so many thousands of people on foot, on horseback, and in coaches, all voluntarily waiting upon and moving along with <u>one</u> man, struck me with strangely agreeable sensations. Surely, thought I, there must be a divinity in goodness, that mankind should thus delight to honor it."*

> *His reception at Trenton was... planned... by the ladies... It was near this place that the fair sex in '76 suffered such cruel indignities from the enemy; and... it was here that Providence in the same year enabled Washington severely to chastise them for it... Under their direction, the bridge over the Sanpink... was decorated with a triumphal arch, with this inscription in large figures:*

> *DECEMBER 26, 1776*
> *THE HERO WHO DEFENDED THE MOTHERS*
> *WILL ALSO PROTECT THE DAUGHTERS*

He approached the bridge on its south side, amidst the heartiest shouts of congratulating thousands, while on the north side were drawn up several hundreds of little girls, dressed in snow-white robes, with temples adorned with garlands, and baskets of flowers on their arms. Just behind them stood long rows of young virgins, whose fair faces, of sweetest red, and white, highly animated by the occasion, looked quite angelic—and, back of them, in crowds stood their venerable mothers. As Washington slowly drove off the bridge, the female voices all began, sweet as the first wakings of the Eolian harp, and thus they rolled the song:

> *Welcome, mighty chief! once more*
> *Welcome to this grateful shore…*

While singing the last lines they strewed the way with flowers before him.

Completely charmed by this welcome, Washington wrote them from Trenton: "General Washington cannot leave this place without expressing his acknowledgements to the Matrons and Young Ladies who received him in so Novel and grateful a manner at the Triumphal Arch in Trenton, for the exquisite sensation he experienced in that affecting moment. The astonishing contrast before his former and actual situation at the same spot, the elegant taste with which it was adorned for the present occasion, and the innocent appearance of the *white-robed Choir* who met him with the gratulatory song, have made such impressions on his remembrance as, he assures them, will never be effaced."

At Elizabethtown there was a newly constructed barge, manned by twenty-six pilot-oarsmen dressed in white. Every ship in New York harbor was decorated with flags and bunting. Many followed the president-elect's barge, with singing and music. French, British, Spanish, and American ships fired salutes. Almost the entire population of New York had massed at the lower end of the island to roar a welcome. All the bells of the city rang. So heavy were the crowds that it was only with the greatest difficulty that Washington could get to the house prepared for him. The governor of New York gave him a formal dinner. That night the city was illumined but rain forced the cancellation of the fireworks planned by the Spanish and French missions. His former aide, Samuel Blatchley Webb, said he had never seen so much "joy" on every face. In the midst of his happy countrymen, one man, alone, viewed the delirium with a somber eye. The president-elect wrote in his diary: "The display of boats, which attended and joined on this occasion, some with vocal and others with instrumental music on board, the decorations of the ships, the roar of the cannon, and the loud acclamations of the people, which rent the sky as

I passed along the wharves, filled my mind with sensations as painful (contemplating the reverse of this scene, which may be the case after all my labours to do good) as they were pleasing."

SIX

THE GOVERNMENT
IS ORGANIZED

1789–1790

SINCE HIS EARLIEST days at Mount Vernon, when he discussed the Ohio Company's plans with his brother, Lawrence, Washington's mind had been concerned with the economic progress of Virginia, particularly in its western portions. More than four decades later, still at Mount Vernon, he drafted a comprehensive program for the development of a new nation with "an extent of fifteen hundred miles." It appears to have been intended as his inaugural address as president. The original manuscript of seventy-two pages existed intact until the late 1820s, when it came into the hands of an unscrupulous vandal, Jared Sparks, a managing editor. Finding it had not been delivered, Sparks cut it into pieces, to give souvenirs to his friends. The fragments, which have been put back together over the years, amount in readable form to less than a quarter. From these, nonetheless, it is possible to reconstruct a considerable portion of America's first economic development program, which was also the first in the world.

As expected from his bitter years, when he had to fight without money, Washington gave his first attention to the national credit and the "load of debt... left upon us." In the government's initial planning, revenues would have to come from import duties and excise taxes, for the support of the federal government and payments on the national debt. He hoped that these could be made "as little burdensome on the people as possible." Fortunately, an ocean separated America from Europe. The country could therefore avoid "the burden of maintaining numerous fleets and Armies… a singular felicity in our national lot." The federal government should, however, give every encouragement to the development of the merchant marine and the fisheries. Not only would these provide increasing national wealth but also be a source of sailors for the navy in any emergency. So long as the country was still impoverished by the war, he would not recommend an increase in the size of the regular army. However, there would be a need for arsenals, dockyards, and a well-trained and organized militia.

Washington then proceeded to his economic measures. He proposed national assistance to increase the production of wool, cotton, flax, and hemp to up to ten times the current level. While there would be a comparative advantage in importing the highest quality manufactures, the country should stimulate its own fabrication of agricultural products as well as leather, fur, iron, and wood, which were available in abundant supply. He advocated a great improvement in the postal system and in postroads to promote inter- state trade, which, he foresaw correctly, would be of much greater importance than international commerce. He proposed that the federal government carry newspapers and periodicals throughout the Union, without charge, in order to disseminate information to the people.

The president-elect also suggested federal assistance to institutions of higher education, a patent and copyright system, as well as uniform national coins, weights, and measures. He proposed a bill of rights. He advocated a fed- eral judiciary system which would have "a supreme regard for equal justice and the inherent rights of the citizens."

The whole of the address was much broader and more inclusive but even the fragments suggest a constructive development program. Washington probably decided that he had best not present so sweeping a program as he entered office. His countrymen were still pretty sensitive to tyranny, and too much strong and apparent leadership at the beginning might be considered dangerous. He therefore cancelled the address and substituted for it a general statement. The plans remained, however, and were very largely carried through during his two administrations.

INAUGURATION

Washington's New York house had been hastily readied for him, though there were still some noisy repairs during his first days of residence. Visitors were an overwhelming problem since everybody dropped by, even before breakfast, "to pay their respects to the President." Washington realized that he would soon be nothing but the principal New York attraction for curiosity seekers. He made early restraining rules which aroused some outcries about royalty.

Congress set April 30 for Washington's oath of office. Since Great Britain had forbade colonial manufacturing, Washington, in conscious symbolism, put on a plain brown suit, which had been made at Mount Vernon from the American broadcloth ordered by Knox from Hartford. Its buttons bore the federal eagle, which was rapidly becoming a prominent feature of American decorative arts.

At nine in the morning the churches of the city opened for prayers for the president and government. At noon a committee of Congress, with an honor guard, almost all of whose officers had been revolutionary soldiers, arrived at Washington's house. He drove through the streets, lined with most of New York's thirty thousand people who were out to cheer him. Congress had always received him seated when he was a general, but all now rose as he entered. Having greeted them and sitting briefly, Washington was notified by the vice-president, John Adams, that they would proceed to the balcony of Federal Hall for the administration of the oath before the people.

As he came out onto the balcony, Washington could see every inch of space on the streets, in the windows, and on the roofs occupied by his people who applauded wildly when they saw him. He bowed to them and then faced the chancellor of New York, Robert Livingston, who was flanked by Vice-President Adams, Governor Clinton, and such old revolutionary companions as Steuben, Knox, St. Clair, Humphreys, and Webb.

Livingston, having handed the Bible to him, said: "Do you, George Washington, solemnly swear that you will faithfully execute the office of President of the United States and will, to the best of your ability, preserve, protect, and defend the Constitution of the United States?" Washington repeated the oath, adding, "So help me God." He then bowed to kiss the Bible. The chancellor turned to the people and said: "Long live George Washington, President of the United States."

Washington returned to the congressional chambers where he read his rather brief inaugural address. Fisher Ames of Massachusetts recorded an impression of his delivery: "His aspect grave, almost to sadness; his modesty, actually shaking; his voice deep, a little tremulous and so low as to call for close attention; added to the series of objects presented to the mind, produced emotions of the most affecting kind upon the members. I... sat entranced."

Washington's address was extraordinarily modest. It included a touching appeal to his countrymen not to look upon him as omnipotent or a deity. The deeply religious speech was also a call to virtue and unity among a people not always virtuous, and always fractious:

I was summon'd by my country, whose voice I can never hear but with veneration and love, from a retreat which I had chosen with the fondest predilection, and in my flattering hopes, with an immutable decision, as the asylum of my declining years, a retreat which was rendered every day more necessary as well as dear to me, by the addition of habit to inclination and of frequent interruptions in my health to the gradual waste committed on it by time. On the other hand, the magnitude and difficulty of the Trust to which the voice of my Country called me, being sufficient to awaken in the wisest and most experienced of her Citizens, a distrustful scrutiny into his qualifications, could not but overwhelm with despondence, one, who (inheriting inferior endowments from Nature and unpracticed in the duties of civil administration) ought to be particularly conscious of his own deficiencies. In this conflict of emotions, all I dare aver is that it has been my faithful study to collect my duty from a just appreciation of every circumstance, by which it might be affected. All I dare hope is that if in executing this Task, I have been too much swayed by a grateful remembrance of former instances or by an affectionate sensibility to this transcendant proof of the confidence of my fellow Citizens; and have thence too little consulted my incapacity as well as disinclination for the weighty and untried cares before me; my error will be palliated by the motives which misled me, and its consequence be judged by my Country, with some share of the partiality in which they originated.

It would be peculiarly improper to omit in this first official act, my fervent supplications to that Almighty Being who rules over the Universe, who presides in the Councils of Nations and whose providential aids can supply every human defect, that his benediction may consecrate to the Liberties and happiness of the People of the United States, a Government instituted by themselves for these essential purposes... No People can be bound to acknowledge and adore the invisible hand, which conducts the affairs of Men, more than those of the United States...

There is no truth more thoroughly established than that there exists in the economy and course of nature, an indissoluble Union between Virtue and Happiness, between duty and advantage, between the genuine maxims of an honest and magnanimous policy, and the solid rewards of public prosperity and felicity: Since we ought to be no less persuaded that the propitious smiles of Heaven, can never be expected on a Nation that disregards the eternal rules of order and right, which Heaven itself has ordained: And since the preservation of the sacred fire of Liberty, and the destiny of the Republican model of Government, are justly considered as deeply and finally staked on the experiment intrusted to the hands of the American people.

Following the address, Washington, with Congress and the invited guests, walked throughout the streets to St. Paul's Chapel, where the Right Reverend Samuel Provoost, Episcopal bishop of New York, conducted a brief worship, made the more blessed because he was not impelled to a sermon. Washington returned by carriage to his house. That evening he went with his secretaries, Humphreys and Lear, to watch the fireworks at the battery. So many people were out in the town that his carriage could not get back to his house at number three Cherry Street. The president walked home through the crowds.

Both Senate and House had been at work before Washington's arrival. The vice-president of the United States, John Adams, started his duties as president of the Senate with considerable seriousness. He had apparently assumed that, in the latter office, he would direct the proceedings and that his advice and counsel would be welcome at all times. It did not take very long for the Senate to indicate they expected him to be a silent and impartial presiding officer, voting only in a tie. This was a difficult task for an Adams. He complained how hard it was to listen without being able to talk back. The day after Washington's address, Senator William Maclay, a bitter little man from Pennsylvania, was on his feet in violent protest against his reference to the president's "most gracious speech." Adams, he said, was trying to make a king out of George Washington. Another senator replied that if Americans were never to use any British terms, they were going to be rather hard put to write or talk. The United States thus started its first day of operation with a quarrel, and a silly one at that, but the Senate's reply referred to the president's speech as "excellent" rather than "gracious."

In addition to a new House and Senate, some elements of the confederate government remained. The secretaries of foreign affairs and war, Jay and Knox, continued to act until new departments could be established by law. The old Treasury Board functioned, as did the Post Office. There were a handful of government clerks, an army of fewer than nine hundred men, and no money.

While many persons that spring and summer complained of the length of the debates and the slowness in organization, everything proceeded with what now appears to be remarkable speed. Washington had the aid of the noteworthy James Madison, a member of the House, with whom he had held so many discussions at Mount Vernon. Although, in deference to his countrymen's feelings about kingly rule, he had avoided presenting a solid initial program, he worked quietly and effectively with leaders of the Senate and House behind the scenes. There were divergencies in details on every measure that passed Congress but on broad aims there was general agreement and in fact little choice but to establish a revenue, permanent government departments, and a judiciary. The federalists generally were as anxious for a bill of rights as the antifederalists, the more so because it would serve to attach the latter more firmly to the Union.

WASHINGTON'S ILLNESS

Washington had come through the triumphant procession to New York in a rarely pessimistic and gloomy mood. This deepened as adulation approached mass hysteria. The newspapers spoke of "our adored ruler and leader" and, in one case, suggested that he was on the borderline between the human and divine. Published poetry referred to him as actually divine. Roman emperors might believe such claptrap, but for Washington, the thought that his countrymen expected him to be a living god served only to deepen his human worries. To Edward Rutledge of South Carolina he wrote six days after his inauguration:

> *I cannot fail of being much pleased with the friendly part you take in every thing which concerns me; and particularly with the just scale on which you estimate this last great sacrifice which I consider myself as having made for the good of my Country. When I had judged, upon the best appreciation I was able to form of the circumstances which related to myself, that it was my duty to embark again on the tempestuous and uncertain Ocean of public life, I gave up all expectation of private happiness in this world. You know, my dear Sir, I had concentrated all my schemes, all my views, all my wishes, within the narrow circle of domestic enjoyment. Though I flatter myself the world will do me the justice to believe that, at my time of life and in my circumstances, nothing but a conviction of duty could have induced me to depart from my resolution of remaining in retirement, yet I greatly apprehend that my Countrymen will expect too much of me.*

> *I fear, if the issue of public measures should not correspond with their sanguine expectations, they will turn the extravagant (and I may say undue) praises which they are heaping upon me at this moment, into equally extravagant (though I will fondly hope unmerited) censures. So much is expected, so many untoward circumstances may intervene, in such a new and critical situation, that I feel an insuperable diffidence in my own abilities. I feel, in the execution of my arduous Office, how much I shall stand in need of the countenance and aid of every friend to the Revolution and of every lover of good Government. I thank you, my dear Sir, for your affectionate expressions on this point...*

He said much the same thing more briefly in answer to an address from the city of New York on May 9: "The partiality of my Countrymen in my favor has induced them to expect too much from the exertions of an individual. It is from their cooperation alone, I derive all my expectations of success." Martha Washington, following her husband north, with her two grandchildren, arrived on May 28. She described the acclaim she had received in a letter to her niece on June 8:

> *My dear Fanny… In Philadelphia… [we] were met by the President of the state with the city troop of Horse… Was met on Wednesday morning by the President at Elizabethtown with the fine barge you have seen so much said of in the papers… Dear little Washington seemed to be lost in a maze at the great parade that was made for us all the way we came. The Governor of the state met me as soon as we landed. I thank God the President is very well… The House he is in is a very good one and is handsomely furnished… My first care was to get the children to a good school, which both are very pleased at… My Hair is set and dressed every day, and I have put on white muslin Habits for the summer. You would I fear think me a good deal in the fashion if you could but see me…*

A week after Martha wrote this letter, the president took to bed with a serious illness. He had a fever which lasted for several days before a great and severely painful carbuncle formed on his thigh. He was attended by Dr. John Bard and his son, Dr. Samuel Bard, who were considered among the most eminent of New York's physicians. It was the younger Bard who summoned all his courage and, under his father's directions, performed the operation of cutting open the tumorous mass to drain the infectious matter. By July 4 Washington had improved sufficiently to receive the members of the Cincinnati, but he had to lie down in his carriage thereafter when he drove out for air.

On September 8 the president wrote his own physician, Dr. Craik: "My disorder was of long and painful continuance, and though now freed from the latter, the wound given by the incision is not yet closed… After the paroxysm had passed, I had no conception of being confined to a lying posture on one side six weeks, and that I should feel the remains of it more than twelve. The part affected is now reduced to the size of a barley corn, and by Saturday next (which will complete the thirteenth week) I expect it will be skimmed over. Upon the whole, I have more reason to be thankful that it is no worse than to repine at the confinement." The bill subsequently presented by the Bards indicates that he was under treatment until October 2.

The French minister at New York, the comte de Moustier, suggested, in a letter of June 24 to Jefferson in Paris, that Washington's illness was of emotional origin: "The President of the United States has run the risk of being the victim of his devotion to the good of his country. A complete change of life, a great preoccupation of mind... an unease caused by the novelty of a role difficult to play, especially when he wants to displease no one, something we of the more common sort believe to be impossible... Such circumstances have altered a vigorous health; fortunately the fire has gone to the surface."

Abigail Adams had arrived from Braintree to join the vice-president while Washington was sick. She called on Martha Washington, and the two women easily renewed their friendship. Abigail wrote to her sister: "She received me with great ease and politeness. She is plain in her dress but that plainness is the best of every article. Her hair is white, her teeth beautiful, her person rather short than otherwise... Her manners are modest and unassuming, dignified and feminine, not the tincture of hauteur about her... I found myself much more deeply impressed than I ever did before their Majesties of Britain." When Washington, propped up in bed, was able to receive Mrs. Adams, she wrote how pleased she was by his modesty and "easy affability." Later, when he was up and happily chatting with the ladies, Abigail noted that the president talked to them "with a grace, ease and dignity that leaves royal George far behind."

THE GOVERNMENT IS COMPLETED

Although Washington was ill much of the time, the executive and judicial systems were organized, and most of them in active operation by early October. Perhaps the most overworked of all persons were the secretaries to the president, especially Tobias Lear, for the presidential papers, all drafted in longhand, and copied for filing, ran into the thousands and presidential appointments into the hundreds. In addition, prior to the organization of the Department of State, the president was the chief means of communication with each of the states. Further, almost every college, religious society, city council, and state legislature, as well as innumerable citizens at home and abroad, felt impelled to write lengthy congratulatory letters and addresses, which were all politely answered. The most impressive of the private letters came from his former partisan officer, Colonel Armand, the Marquis de la Rouerie, who wrote from France that he wished Washington could command the whole world.

On June 8 the president asked the acting department heads—Foreign Affairs, War, Treasury, and Post Office—to provide him with as "clear account of their work... as may be sufficient... to impress me with a full, precise, and

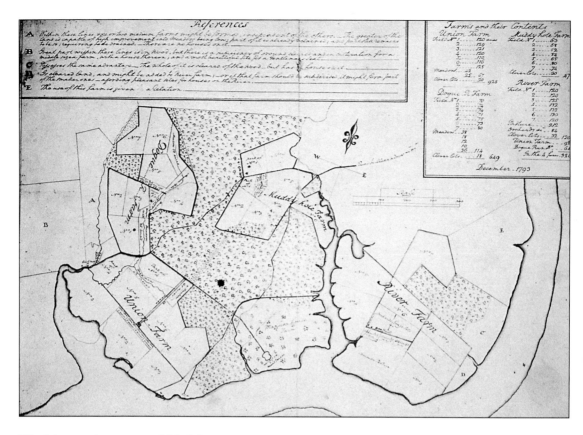

Washington's survey of his Mount Vernon farms (December 1793). *(Courtesy Huntington Library)*

John Adams, by John Trumbull, Vice President 1789–1797, President 1797–1801.
(National Portrait Gallery)

Thomas Jefferson, by Gilbert Stuart, Minister to France 1785–1789, Secretary of State 1790–1793, President 1801–1809. *(National Portrait Gallery)*

Henry Knox, by Charles Peale Polic, after Charles Wilson Peale, Secretary of War under the Confederation and the Constitution 1785–1794. *(National Portrait Gallery)*

John Jay, by John Trumbull, after Gilbert Stuart, Secretary of Foreign Affairs 1785–1789, Chief Justice of the United States 1789–1794, Special Envoy to Great Britain 1794, Governor of New York 1795–1801. *(National Portrait Gallery)*

Patrick Henry, by James Longacre, after James Sully. After early opposition to the new Constitution, Henry came to uphold it and was elected a Federalist Congressman in 1799, dying shortly thereafter. *(National Portrait Gallery)*

Gouverneur Morris, by James Sharples, Minister to France 1792–1794, reported faithfully to Washington on the Terror. *(National Portrait Gallery)*

James Madison, by Chester Harding, Member of Congress 1789–1797,
President 1809–1817. *(National Portrait Gallery)*

James Monroe, by John Vanderlyn, Senator 1790–1794, Minister to France 1794–1796, President 1817–1825. *(National Portrait Gallery)*

John Quincy Adams, by George Bingham, appointed by Washington as Minister to the Netherlands 1794, President 1825–1829. *(National Portrait Gallery)*

distinct general *idea* of the affairs of the United States." Knox provided substantial information on the Indian situation, John Jay forwarded bulky reports on his foreign correspondence, while the postmaster general sent him a not too complete statement on postal finances. The most impressive document was provided by the Treasury Board, which forwarded, over a period of weeks, 250 folios, outlining the entire history of the currency after 1775, the current state of the national and state finances, and the foreign and domestic debts. This information was so complete that Hamilton was able to use it as a prime source for his subsequent report on the public credit.

On July 4, 1789, the president signed the first federal revenue act, a combination of *ad valorem* and specific tariff duties. Additional tonnage revenue acts, discriminating in favor of American-owned and -built vessels, followed. The states had adopted the British colonial port collector and naval officer system, which was now, in turn, nationalized. State officers became federal when authorizing legislation passed. On August 3 Washington nominated ninety-five collectors, surveyors, and naval officers, for ports ranging from Passamaquoddy, Maine, to St. Mary's, Georgia. Included on the list, as collector for Boston, was General Benjamin Lincoln, an appointment which, according to a friend of Lincoln, "renewed his youth and happiness."

One nomination precipitated the first conflict between the president and the Senate. Benjamin Fishbourne, appointed as naval officer at Savannah, was summarily rejected, without explanation, the only one on the list so treated. Washington wrote a dignified complaint, pointing out the reasons why he had nominated Fishbourne, which were to be his general criteria for all appointments. He had personally known him as a brave and resourceful revolutionary officer. He had been elected repeatedly to the Georgia Assembly which, in turn, had chosen him for the state council which elected him its president. Georgia had subsequently made him Savannah's naval officer. Washington noted that Fishbourne was endorsed for the office by numerous prominent Georgians. The Senate did not back down, and Washington nominated another officer. Subsequently the president learned that there had been charges made against his nominee in the state and these had been brought onto the Senate floor.

Legislation followed in rapid order. On July 27 the president signed the act to establish a Department of Foreign Affairs. The title was later changed to Department of State when a parsimonious Congress decided the occupant could administer both internal and external affairs. The War Department was approved on August 7. On August 18 Washington nominated a governor, General St. Clair, and a secretary and judges for the Northwest Territory, then, largely, Ohio. He also nominated commissioners to negotiate treaties with the

Indians. In September the acts establishing a federal judiciary, Treasury, and Post Office were signed by the president.

Between September 11 and 29 Washington made the most sweeping series of nominations ever made by a president of the United States when he sent to the Senate for confirmation the whole of the federal judiciary, the cabinet, and many other officers. On September 11 he designated Hamilton and Knox to head the Treasury and War departments, together with four principal officers of the Treasury, and the "surveyor of Town Creek." On September 24 he sent up nominations for a chief justice of the United States, John Jay, four associate justices, ten federal district judges, and twenty district attorneys and marshals. The following day he added two more district judges, four attorneys and marshals, and the names of Thomas Jefferson as secretary of state, Edmund Randolph as attorney general, and Samuel Osgood as postmaster general. On September 29 he named forty-five officers for commissions or promotions in the army. With a speed never equalled since, the Senate approved every nomination, and on September 29 both Houses adjourned. The United States government was in full operation and, for the first time, had proper officers and a revenue which began to accrue almost as soon as Washington forwarded commissions to the port collectors.

To add to an impressive beginning, which included the approval by Congress of constitutional amendments for a bill of rights, the United States enjoyed a summer of full crops, while Europe, including England, had grain shortages. Vessels streamed to America from Britain, France, Spain, and Portugal, buying wheat and flour at almost any price. In addition, according to William Short, chargé at Paris, over two hundred American ships went to France, Portugal, and the Baltic. In 1789 the port of New York alone reported the arrival of one thousand ships and smaller vessels. The government collected nearly $800,000 in the first five months of the new federal tariff. United States obligations rose by a third in the domestic money markets; at Amsterdam they went to par.

The costs of administration were smaller than the revenue.

Salaries and supplies were:

The President	$ 25,000
The Vice-President	5,000
Twenty federal judges	69,700
House and Senate	183,100
Treasury Department	28,000
Department of State	5,950

The army, with 887 officers and enlisted men, cost the government $160,887. The president's allowances had to cover his expenses as chief of state, his rent, entertaining, and travel, as well as the wages and board of four or five secretaries and as many as twenty servants. As usual, George Washington was to end up out of pocket from his public service.

SOCIAL LIFE

The first president, like all early heads of the republic, was supposed to be better than any king on earth, but no better than his commonest countryman. Unlike many of his successors, Washington could, with equal grace, sleep on a cold, wet hillside or preside at dinners made more cheerful by claret and champagne. As president he behaved pretty much as he always had, but with an eye to the dignity of the "United States," a term which he used on his letterheads. To conserve his time he established set social functions. He held a one-hour open-house for "respectable characters [male]" on Tuesday afternoon, while Mrs. Washington organized a similar affair for mixed company on Friday evenings. The Washingtons gave formal dinners each Thursday for members of Congress and the government. None of these affairs, which mixed up political enemies and strangers, was considered very lively. Washington kept Sundays free of official engagements to spend the day with his family.

In the middle of one of these dinners, September 1, when General von Steuben was at his most cheerful, a letter was delivered to the president announcing that his mother was dead of cancer. The *Gazette of the United States* announced that hers had been a life of "virtue, prudence and Christianity, worthy the mother of the greatest Hero who ever adorned the annals of history." Washington wrote his sister, Betty Lewis: "Awful and affecting as the death of a Parent is, there is consolation in knowing that Heaven has spared her to an age, beyond which few attain… When I was last at Fredericksburg, I took a final leave of my Mother, never expecting to see her more."

In a country where there was a movement to drop "Mister" as too formal a title, rumors circulated that the president's house was beginning to resemble a European court. These were stimulated to some extent by the social columns of the fawning *Gazette*, which relished reporting the names of titled guests who attended the Washingtons' receptions. Dr. David Stuart reported that stories about "the court" were being vigorously circulated in Virginia by opponents of the Constitution. Everyone was quoting Patrick Henry's early assertion that the document "squinted towards monarchy." It was also stated that Adams, who had suggested to the Senate that the president be called "His high mightiness," was using a state coach with a team of horses. Washington himself had become too snobbish to accept dinner invitations. The president replied on July 26:

> *Had I not adopted [rules], I should have been unable to have attended to <u>any</u> sort of business unless I had applied the hours allotted to rest and refreshment to this purpose, for by the time I had done breakfast, and thence till dinner, and afterwards till bed time I could not get relieved from the ceremony of one visit before I had to attend to another; in a word, I had no leisure to read or answer the dispatches that were pouring in upon me from all quarters... The late Presidents of Congress were involved in insuperable difficulties... for [their] table was considered as a public one, and every person, who could get introduced, conceived that he had a <u>right</u> to be invited to it. This, although the Table was always crowded (and with mixed company, and the President considered in no better light than as a Maitre d'Hotel) was in its nature impracticable and as many offences given as if no table had been kept...*

> *So strongly had the citizens of this place imbibed an idea of the impropriety of my accepting invitations to dinner that I have not received one from any family (though they are remarkable for hospitality, and though I have received every civility and attention from them) since I came to the city, except dining with the Governor on the day of my arrival, so that, if this should be induced as an article of impeachment, there can be at least <u>one</u> good reason for my not dining out; to wit never having been asked to do so...*

Washington added that, as far as he knew, John Adams never used more than two horses but he regretted that he had ever brought up the question of titles, for he foresaw that it would arouse great opposition.

Since Washington worked so hard, his wife found her life far less attractive than at Mount Vernon, as she wrote that fall:

> *I lead a very dull life here and know nothing that passes in the town. I never goe to any publick place. Indeed I think I am more like a state prisoner than anything else... I sometimes think the arrangement is not quite as it ought to have been; that I, who had much rather be at home, should occupy a place with which a great many younger and gayer women would be prodigiously pleased... I am still determined to be cheerful and to be happy, in whatever situation I may be; for I have also learned from experience that the greater part of our happiness or misery depends upon our dispositions, and not upon our circumstances.*

Her husband, still athletic at fifty-seven, decided as soon as his recovery was complete, to get a lot more exercise. He also resumed his diaries on October 1. On October 3 he took a long walk. Two days later he was out on horseback for two hours and walked a further hour. On October 7 and 9 he again rode for two hours. On October 10 he went for a full day's excursion in the country. With John Adams and others, he took a barge to William Prince's fruit gardens and nurseries at Flushing. The comment by landscaper Washington was succinct: "These gardens, except in the number of young fruit trees, did not answer my expectations. The shrubs were trifling, and the flowers not numerous."

Washington also visited the Morrisania estate of Gouverneur and Lewis Morris, the latter the lord of the manor. The former had boasted to Washington about his barn. Farmer Washington was even briefer: "It was not of a construction to strike my fancy—nor did the conveniences of it all answer their cost." From there the party went to Harlem where Mrs. Washington, Mrs. Adams, and the Adamses' daughter, Mrs. Smith, were waiting. They dined at a tavern and returned to lower Manhattan.

In his diary, at this period, Washington noted the discussions he held on the possibility of sending a diplomat to London, to sound out the British on the peace treaty. He also discussed the desirability of a trip through the New England states, but in a *pro forma* manner because he had already made up his mind.

THE MORRIS MISSION

The president's policies, as he was to maintain them throughout his years in office, aimed to establish permanent peace with all nations. This would ensure domestic tranquility, and the steady growth of population, internal and external trade, and manufactures, until the country was strong enough to maintain its independence against any potential enemies. With strength, patience, and firmness, the United States would free itself of the British and Spanish occupying forces.

After numerous discussions with his cabinet, Madison, and Jay, the president determined on October 10 to send Gouverneur Morris to London as his personal representative, empowered to discuss the implementation of the 1783 treaty and to negotiate diplomatic representation and a treaty of commerce. Morris' instructions, which Washington drafted that day, were clear and succinct:

> *My letter to you, herewith enclosed, will give you the credence necessary to enable you to do the business, which it commits to your management...*

Your inquiries will commence by observing that, as the present constitution of government, and of the courts established in pursuance of it, removes the objections heretofore made to putting the United States in possession of their frontier posts, it is natural to expect, from the asssurances of his Majesty, and the national good faith, that no unnecessary delays will take place. Proceed then to press a speedy performance of the treaty respecting that object.

Remind them of the article by which it was agreed that negroes, belonging to our citizens, should not be carried away, and the reasonableness of making compensation for them. Learn with precision, if possible, what they mean to do on this head.

The commerce between the two countries you well understand... You doubtless have heard that, in the late session of Congress, a very respectable number of both Houses were inclined to a discrimination of duties, unfavorable to Britain, and that it would have taken place but for conciliatory considerations and [to await negotiations for a commercial treaty].

Request to be informed, therefore, whether they contemplate a treaty of commerce with the United States... Let it be strongly impressed that the privilege of carrying our productions in our vessels to those Islands, and of bringing the production of those Islands, to our own ports and markets, is regarded here as of the highest importance; and you will be careful not to countenance any idea of our dispensing with it in a treaty. Ascertain, if possible, their views on this point; for it would not be expedient to commence negotiations without previously having good reasons to expect a satisfactory termination of them.

It may also be well for you to take a proper occasion of remarking that their omitting to send a minister here, did not make an agreeable impression...

It is, in my opinion, very important that we avoid errors in our system of policy respecting Great Britain; and this can only be done by forming a right judgment of their disposition and views. Hence you will perceive how interesting it is that you obtain the information in question, and that the business may be so managed that it may receive every advantage which abilities, address and delicacy can promise and afford.

Washington left the following morning for his New England tour. The secretary of the Treasury was among those who, as a mark of respect, accompanied the president part way out of town. Very probably that same day, he returned and began the extraordinary discussions and negotiations with the head of British intelligence in the United States, which have had no subsequent parallel.

THE YANKEE TOUR

No travel diaries of eighteenth-century America are as vivid as those of Washington on his five tours as president—to New England, through Long Island, to Rhode Island, south to Georgia, and to western Pennsylvania. In spite of the crowds, Washington was always able to look closely at the economy, noting what the farmers, merchants, seamen, and manufacturers were doing, and what the roads, inns, and people were like. In one way he had changed little since his youth, for he loved natural scenery, trees, good land, and beautiful women, and he found an abundance of these on his trips. There are few strictly political observations but he had a sharp and observing eye and ear for what the people liked and disliked. The tours were a great education for him, and they did an immense amount to cement the Union. Not until 1817 did any president venture so far out in the country.

CONNECTICUT AND MASSACHUSETTS

Washington began his trip on October 15 in the golden clear days of autumn. He was accompanied by two aides, William Jackson and Tobias Lear, and six servants. He crossed Kingsbridge, which separated Manhattan from the mainland, and spent the night in Rye at "the Tavern of a Mrs. Haviland... who keeps a very neat and decent Inn." He made copious notes as his party proceeded. The thirty-one miles from Manhattan north were "very rough and stony, but the Land strong, well covered with grass and a luxuriant crop of Indian Corn" mingled with pumpkins. He wrote that he had passed about 120 beeves and many sheep being driven to the New York market. The towns, East Chester, New Rochelle, and Mamaroneck, were scarcely distinguishable, as such, from the surrounding farming areas. Next morning he was again on stony roads which bounced his carriage around. He had breakfast at an inn which was only "tolerable good." He described the area from Horse Neck (Greenwich) to Fairfield:

> *Superb landscape... a rich regalia. We found all the Farmers busily employed in gathering grinding and expressing the Juices of their apples; the crop of which they say is rather above mediocrity. The average crop of Wheat... is about 15 bushels to the acre... often 20, and from that to 25. The Destructive evidences of British cruelty are yet visible both in Norwalk and Fairfield; as there are the chimneys of many burnt houses standing in them yet. The principal export from Norwalk and Fairfield is Horses and Cattle—salted Beef and Pork—lumber and Indian Corn to the West Indies, and in a small degree Wheat and Flour.*

Washington crossed by the ferry at Stratford, recorded that vessels navigated the river up to Derby and that the town had established a factory for the manufacture of duck (a type of cloth), while there were grist and saw mills at Milford. He also noted "a handsome Cascade over the tumbling dam; but one of the prettiest things of this kind is at Stamford, occasioned also by damning the water for their mills; it is near 100 yards in width, and the water now being of a proper height, and the rays of the sun striking upon it as we passed, had a pretty effect upon the foaming water as it fell."

Leaving Milford the party was lucky enough to take the lower road. They thus missed a committee of the state legislature which had expected to read a long address to the president. They arrived in New Haven, free of officials, and walked at length around the town. They did not escape, however, for five hours later Washington had to stand and listen to them. They were followed by the Congregational ministers, the governor, the lieutenant governor, and the mayor of New Haven, who each said more or less the same things.

Since Washington arrived at New Haven on a Saturday afternoon, he was faced for the first time with Connecticut's laws against Sabbath travel. He spent Sunday in the town, attending the Episcopal Church in the morning and the Congregational in the afternoon. He invited the principal officers of the state and city to dine with him at his tavern, which he marked as "good." He questioned them about the manufacture of glass and linen.

At 6 A.M. Monday Washington rode to Wallingford where he examined the silkworm and mulberry tree experiments and samples of their heavy silk, which he pronounced "exceeding good." Going on to Middletown, he found the prospect from the heights over the Connecticut River to be "beautiful." He noted that the three principal towns on the river had around sixty-four trading vessels. "The Country hereabouts is beautiful." At Hartford Washington inspected the woolen manufactory and ordered another suit of broadcloth for himself, as well as bolts of a product called "Everlastings" for his servants' breeches. Washington rode on to Windsor where he inspected the United States arsenal and powder plant. There, a large party from Massachusetts waited to escort him to Springfield. As he left Connecticut, he recorded his impressons:

> There is a great equality in the People of this State. Few or no opulent men—and no poor—great similitude in their buildings—the general fashion of which is a Chimney (always of Stone or Brick) and door in the middle, with a stair case fronting the latter, running up by the side of the former—two flush stories with a very good show of sash and glass windows—the size generally is from 30 to 50 feet in length, and from 20 to 30 in width, exclusive of a back shed, which seems to be added as the family increases.

*The farms, by the contiguity of the Houses, are small, not averaging more than
100 acres. These are worked chiefly by oxen (which have no other feed than hay)
with a horse, and sometimes two, before them, both in Plow and Cart. In their light
lands, and in their sleighs, they work Horses, but find them much more expensive
than oxen...*

CONFUSION AT BOSTON

News that the president of the United States was on his way to Boston put the
state and city governments there in a frenzy. As Christopher Gore wrote
Tobias Lear: "The people of Boston are, beyond all conception, enraptured
with the idea of beholding their deliverer and protector." Gore, in response
to Lear's request, had engaged a house for the president, who had decided
always to stay at public inns or rented lodgings when travelling. Thus he did
not have to choose among clamorous hosts and hostesses nor subject them to
great crowds of curiosity seekers.

As it turned out, the vice-president, John Adams, the governor, John
Hancock, the lieutenant governor, Sam Adams, the executive council, the
state legislature, and the councils of Boston and Cambridge all worked to give
Washington a memorable welcome. They provided one he was scarcely likely
to forget.

Messengers galloped from Boston and Cambridge with invitations and
instructions. The governor asked Washington to stay at his house, the citizens
of Boston requested him to stay at another house, and an aide from the
Middlesex militia informed him they would escort him through the county to
a ceremonial reception at Cambridge. The governor had decided that the
president of the United States should make his first call in Boston on the
governor. He ordered, or Sam Adams and the state council volunteered, to go
and meet Washington and escort him from Cambridge to Hancock's house.
In the meantime the selectmen of Boston were working on their plans to
escort the president into Boston.

On Saturday, October 24, a raw New England day, the president and his
party set out at 8 A.M. from Marlborough, Massachusetts. Following his usual
pattern, Washington got out of his carriage at the Cambridge town limits and
mounted his horse to enable the people to see him better. He was in his place
at ten o'clock, punctually as planned, for his Cambridge reception. The militia that were to do honor to him did not show up until eleven. Washington
had to wait in the cold until they could perform their maneuvers. When these
were over, Lieutenant Governor Adams and the executive council of

Massachusetts moved to escort Washington across the neck to Boston. The selectmen of Boston had, however, determined that they were to do honors in the town. They appeared with their carriages and numerous schoolchildren to give Boston's official welcome, thus blocking the state party. The president had to sit patiently on his horse while the committees argued and brawled. Eventually the sheriff of Boston and his troopers broke through, scattering committees and children, and letting the president proceed.

In some sort of order, the city having won, the parade assembled, the state lined up behind the city, and the whole escorted the president to the Boston State House. Washington recorded seeing banners reading "To the man who unites all hearts," "To Columbia's favorite son," and "Boston relieved March 17, 1776." Washington climbed to the balcony where, as he wrote, "a vast concourse" was out to cheer him, many of whom, because of the contretemps, had waited hours in the cold.

When this was over, Samuel and John Adams, together with the state council, accompanied the president to his lodgings. Washington had agreed to go to dinner at the governor's house, but since the governor had not deigned to call on him (as Fisher Ames expressed it, Hancock did not like the idea that he had any "superior"), the president politely declined to go. Instead he dined in his own house with the vice-president of the United States. Governor Hancock, squirming, sent the lieutenant governor and members of the council to explain that he was too ill to call on Washington. The president replied that he would be glad to have the governor come when he recovered.

In the morning the president had begun to sneeze violently. Nonetheless, he attended an Episcopal service. When he returned to his lodgings, there was a note from the governor saying he was prepared to "hazard every thing, as it respects his health" to call on the man whom the governor referred to as "the President," a term borne also by the head of Harvard. With that glint which came often to his eye, Washington replied:

> *The President of the United States presents his best respects to the Governor, and has the honor to inform him that he shall be at home 'til two o'clock.*
>
> *The President of the United States need not express the pleasure it will give him to see the Governor; but, at the same time, he most earnestly begs that the Governor will not hazard his health on the occasion.*

The humorous Washington Irving could not bear to think that Washington was also humorous. His biography cautiously noted that the final sentence "almost savors of irony." Hancock appeared, his gouty foot carefully done up in cloth, as he was supported up the stairs by his servants. By the time he got back to his house, the rags were off and he skipped up the staircase without help. That afternoon the president attended a Congregational church and the vice-president again dined with him. Next day Washington was confined to his quarters with a bad cold and an inflamed eye. That evening, with even subtler irony, he presented them and himself at the governor's house.

On Tuesday, feeling a little better, he heard an oratorio at King's Chapel and received addresses from the town clergy, the governor and council, the town of Boston, the president of Harvard, the state Cincinnati, and others. During their meeting the town council requested that Washington sit for a picture so that it could be copied for various Boston ladies who wanted one in their houses. He promised that he would send a portrait from New York by John Trumbull, or another painter, since he did not have time to pose. The governor gave him a dinner that afternoon at Faneuil Hall. Hancock invited the vice-president also but in a manner which John Adams thought entirely too casual and he cut the dinner dead.

On October 28 Washington inspected factories. In one, he wrote, there were twenty-eight looms "and 14 girls spinning with Both hands (the flax being fastened to their waist). Children (girls) turn the wheels for them, and with this assistance each spinner can turn out 14 lbs. of Thread pr. day." The girls worked from eight in the morning to six at night. The whole factory produced thirty-two pieces of duck a week, each from thirty to forty yards long. Plans were under way to increase the number of workers and production. He told the manager that he had corralled all the best-looking girls in town. Washington also visited a factory where they made cards, including playing cards, which employed nine hundred hands.

In the evening, after visiting several ships, including French warships, he attended the Boston assembly where more than one hundred ladies were present. "Their appearance was elegant and many of them very handsome." This view of Boston was perhaps the best way to end a stay which had begun badly. John Adams, not often given to praise, was delighted with the president's trip and his popularity in his own state's capital. He wrote that Washington was very much "in character and consequently charming to all."

CAMBRIDGE TO NEWBURYPORT

After visiting Harvard, its library of 13,000 volumes, its laboratory and museum, Washington headed north. He found the bridges at Charlestown and Malden "useful and noble—doing great credit to the enterprising People of this State." He insisted on going to Marblehead which had not been on his itinerary. He wrote that 800 men and boys were engaged in commercial fishing in about 110 town vessels. He inspected the harbor and "their fish brakes for curing fish." Marblehead disappointed him: "The Houses are old; the streets dirty; and the common people not very clean."

At Salem the president was greeted by a Quaker chairman of the welcoming committee who merely said: "Friend Washington, we are glad to see thee, and in behalf of the inhabitants bid thee a hearty welcome to Salem." If Washington thought he was to be spared the full routine, he was mistaken, for singers stepped forth to sing an ode, after which he had to hear another long address. In the evening Salem did better, for the town held another dance for him "where there was at least an hundred handsome and well dressed Ladies. Abt. Nine I returned to my lodgings." He liked Salem, finding it "a neat Town and said to contain 8 or 9000 Inhabitants. Its exports are chiefly Fish, Lumber and Provisions. They have in the East India Trade at this time 13 Sail of Vessels."

The following morning Washington crossed the bridge to Beverley, commented on its handsome appearance, its length (nearly a third of a mile), and "the inconceivable low price at which it had been built"— about $11,000. He noted that all Massachusetts bridges of any importance had drawbridges and many had foot paths. At Beverley he inspected the "cotton Manufactory, which seems to be carrying on with spirit by the Mr. Cabots... They have the new Invented Carding and Spinning Machines... A number of Looms (15 or 16) were at work with spring shuttles, which do more than double work. In short, the whole seemed perfect and the cotton stuffs which they turn out, excellent of their kind; war and filling both are now of Cotton."

Newburyport, which he visited next, had prepared a noisy welcome, still remembered in its annals, which John Marquand recalled in *Timothy Dexter Revisited*. The local militia met him, the church bells rang, and the artillery fired the federal salute of thirteen guns. The smoke lifted to show a band and male chorus, as well as trumpeters, drummers, and cannoneers enthusiastically ready to serenade the president:

He comes! He comes! The HERO comes!
Sound, sound your Trumpets [loud blasts] beat,
* beat your Drums; [thunderous rolls]*
From port to port let Cannons roar [Boom, boom, boom]
He's welcome to New England's shore.
Welcome, welcome, welcome, welcome,
Welcome to New England's shore.

The second verse, with its line, "Loud, loudly rend the echoing air," probably barely conveys a sense of what happened when band, singers, trumpets, drums, and cannon all joined together. Marquand says that Washington was moved to tears. If so, this was the only sign he gave, as he sat on his white horse looking at the astonishing scene, that he was struggling not to laugh. Marquand continued:

> *Following the song a procession marched up the street, made up of all the social orders of the town. Following the musicians marched the selectmen, the marshal and the high sheriff. Then came the ministers, the physicians, the lawyers, the magistrates, the town officers, and the Marine Society. Behind the Marine Society were tradesmen, manufacturers, ships' captains, sailors, and finally schoolmasters with their scholars. Upon approaching the president, the parade divided its ranks to right and left, allowing the honored guest to pass through. Then they joined ranks again and followed him. The teachers, we are told, led four hundred and twenty scholars, each bearing his quill pen.*

At the Tracey house Washington was given an address of welcome to which he responded as usual with some graciously stilted words, and he was then given dinner. That night the militia came around and fired muskets under his windows. The citizens followed with fireworks including rockets. The next morning the president left Newburyport quietly.

NEW HAMPSHIRE

There was no Hancockian nonsense in New Hampshire. At the state line, October 31, the governor (General Sullivan), the lieutenant governor, members of the governor's council, both United States senators, the state marshal, as much of the state's cavalry as could be mustered, and "many officers of the Militia in handsome (white and red) uniforms of the manufacture of the State" were present to greet Washington, who wrote: "With this cavalcade, we proceeded and arrived before 3 o'clock at Portsmouth where we were received with every token of respect and appearance of cordiality, under a discharge of artillery. The streets, doors and windows were crowded there, as at all other Places; and alighting at the Town House, odes were sung and played in honor of the President."

Washington invited all the officials to dine with him at his tavern. Next morning, another Sabbath, he followed his usual custom, attending the Episcopal church in the forenoon and the Congregational in the afternoon.

After church he found time to write a few letters. He spent three more days in New Hampshire, which he recorded in some detail:

(November 2) "I went in a boat to view the harbour of Portsmouth; which is well secured from all winds; and from its narrow entrance from the Sea and passage up to the Town, may be perfectly guarded against any approach by water. The anchorage is also good... I stopped at Kittery [Maine]. From hence I went by the old Fort (formerly built while under the English government) on an Island, which is at the entrance of the harbour, and where the Light House stands... We were saluted by 13 guns... We proceeded to the Fishing banks, a little without the Harbour, and fished for Cod; but it not being a proper time of tide, we only caught two, with which... we returned to town. Dined at [Senator] Langdon's, and drank tea there, with a large circle of Ladies, and retired a little after seven o'clock...

(November 3) Sat two hours in forenoon for a Mr. [Gülager], A Painter, of Boston... Having walked through most parts of the town, returned by 12 o'clock, when I was visited by a Clergyman of the name of Haven, who presented me with an Ear and part of the stalk of the dyeing Corn, and several pieces of Cloth which had been dyed with it, equal to any colours I had ever seen... This Corn was blood red...

About 2 o'clock, I received an Address from the Executive of the State of New Hampshire, and in half an hour after dined with him and a large company, at their assembly room, which is one of the best I have seen anywhere in the United States. At half after seven I went to the assembly, where there were about 75 well dressed, and many of them handsome ladies—among whom (as was also the case at the Salem and Boston assemblies) were a greater proportion with much blacker hair than are usually seen in the Southern States. About nine, I retired to my quarter...

(November 4) About half after seven I left Portsmouth... without any attendance, having earnestly entreated that all parade and ceremony might be avoided... Before ten I reached Exeter, 14 miles distance. This is considered as the second town in New Hampshire, and stands at the head of the tide-water of Piscataqua River; but ships of 3 or 400 tons are built at it. Above (but in the town) are considerable falls, which supply several grist mills, 2 oil mills, a slitting mill, and a snuff mill. It is a place of some consequence, but does not contain more than 1,000 Inhabitants. A jealousy subsists between this town (where the legislature alternately sits), and Portsmouth; which, had I known it in time, would have made it necessary to have accepted an invitation to a public dinner, but my arrangements having been otherwise made, I could not.

MRS. COOLIDGE AND MR. TAFT

Washington proceeded south to Haverhill, Massachusetts, "in a beautiful part of the country," thence to Andover and on to Lexington to "view the spot on which the first blood was spilt in the dispute with Great Britain, on the 19th of April, 1775."

At this point the New England weather turned nasty and the president changed his route in order to pass the night at Watertown. There, he remarked, "We lodged at the house of a Widow [Mrs. Nathaniel] Coolidge, and a very indifferent one it is."

The president had no better luck the following day. Having covered thirty-six miles in threatening weather, over "amazingly crooked" road built, he said, to suit "the convenience of every man's fields," and having been given wrong directions which took him miles out of his way, the tired president was glad to stop for the night at the house of Samuel Taft at Uxbridge. Washington remarked that "though the people were obliging, the entertainment was not very inviting." He got out before dawn.

In his courteous way, Washington wrote a note of thanks next day, November 8, to Taft from Hartford, noting that he had been informed that he had named one son for the president and a daughter for Martha Washington, "and being moreover very much pleased with the modest and innocent looks of your two daughters, Patty and Polly, I do, for these reasons, send each of these Girls a piece of chintz. And to Patty, who bears the name of Mrs. Washington, and who waited upon us more than Polly did, I send five guineas, with which she may buy herself any little ornaments she may want... As I do not give these things with a view to have it talked of... the less there is said about the matter the better you will please me, but that I may be sure the chintz and money got safe to hand, let Patty, who I dare say is equal to it, write me a line thereof directed to 'The President of the United States' at New York."

Patty was more than equal to her task though it took her several weeks to figure out how to address a president. In Uxbridge, or elsewhere, she found a book from England which explained how to write to high personages. On December 28 she dispatched her letter:

May it please your Highness:

Agreeable to your commands, I, with pleasure, inform the President that, on the 20th inst., I received the very valuable present...

And I want to express gratitude to you, Great Sir, for the extraordinary favour &

honour, conferred on me and our family... while your Highness was pleased to honour my Papa's house with your presence...

My most ardent desires are that the light of heavens blessing may... ever rest on him who stands at the head of our United Empire... Papa and Mama with sincere thanks and duty desire to be remembered to your Highness... May it please your Highness...

Mercy Taft

Pray pardon me sir if I mention the mistake in my name, you see, sir, it is not Patty.

CONNECTICUT

As he moved south from the Tafts', Washington found an "intolerable bad road, and a poor and uncultivated country" on the Massachusetts side. On Sunday, November 8, he spent a peculiarly disagreeable day. He got breakfast at a bad inn on the Connecticut side and, finally, lodged Saturday evening at Ashford, which condemned him to pass the Sabbath there. He summed it up: "I stayed at Perkins' tavern (which, by the bye, is not a good one) all day—and a meeting-house being within few rods of the door, I attended morning and evening service, and heard very lame discourses from a Mr. [Enoch] Pond."

Talk of snows, worry about Mrs. Washington, and a general desire to get to New York to see what was going on caused the president to hurry home as rapidly as the bad roads permitted. On Monday, he travelled thirty-four miles to Hartford, twenty-four of them over "hilly, rocky, and disagreeable roads." He still found time to question the farmers about their crops and yields and where and what they marketed. Next day he reached New Haven where he met Elbridge Gerry, just arrived by stage coach from New York, who assured him his wife was in good health. On Wednesday he was nine miles beyond Fairfield and on Thursday at Rye. On Friday afternoon, November 13, "between two and three o'clock arrived at my house at New York, where I found Mrs. Washington and the rest of the family all well—and it being Mrs. Washington's night to receive visits, a pretty large company of ladies and gentlemen were present."

Shortly after returning, the president received an invitation from a minor, but rather pushy, New York family, to come to a burial service for a relative. He declined, feeling that if he went to Mrs. Isaac Roosevelt's service, he might be expected to attend too many others of people he did not know.

The trip did Washington great good. The gloom, with which he had moved to New York, and which had affected his health, seems to have entirely disappeared. The time he spent out-of-doors, riding and walking, brought renewed vigor. Though John Trumbull noted that he returned "all fragrant with the odor of incense," his own observations, rather than the public and tiring demonstrations, lifted up his spirits. He found the high caliber of his appointments to office had won universal admiration. People were pleased to have a respectable national government. Everywhere that Washington looked he could see strength and growth in the economy. The removal of the dead hand of colonialism had stimulated shipbuilding, manufacturing, and commerce. He heard reports of ships trading from New England to China and the Indies. He saw and talked with the people, egalitarian and prosperous, who were proud of their farms, handicraft, and new machinery. Washington sensed that the demonstrations of affection for the president had been their way of showing pride in themselves.

PROMOTING MANUFACTURING

Nine days after returning to his office, Washington wrote to Beverley Randolph, the governor of his own state, in an initial endeavor to get the south to move forward with New England:

From the original letters, which I forward herewith, Your Excellency will comprehend the nature of a prospect for introducing and establishing the Woolen Manufactory in the State of Virginia. In the present state of population and agriculture, I do not pretend to determine how far that Plan may be practicable and advisable; or in case it should be deemed so, whether any or what public encouragement ought to be given to facilitate its execution. I have, however, no doubt as to the good policy of encreasing the number of Sheep in every way. By a little Legislative encouragement, the Farmers of Connecticut have, in two years past, added one hundred thousand to their former stock. In my late tour through the Eastern States, I found that the Manufacturers of Woolens... preferred the Wool raised in Virginia for its fineness, to that raised in the more Northern parts of the Continent. If a greater quantity of Wool could be produced, and if the hands (which are often in a manner idle) could be employed in the manufacturing of it; a spirit of industry might be promoted, a great diminution might be made in the annual expenses of individual families, and the Public would eventually be exceedingly benefitted.

Under these impressions, I have thought proper to transmit the Proposal; and will only add that, if it should be judged expedient to submit the project to the Legislature, or if any private Company should engage in promoting the business, the necessity of keeping the Manufacturer's name concealed would undoubtedly occur: as a premature knowledge of it might not only frustrate the success of the Project, but also subject the person principally concerned to the most distressing consequences.

The United States, in its early development, did not have the technical and financial aid which it gave away so freely in the twentieth century. The reverse, in fact, was true as far as Great Britain was concerned. That country had passed legislation making it a criminal offense to export certain types of machinery and plans, or to encourage and promote the emigration of skilled engineers and mechanics. The laws were not entirely enforceable. Machinery, plans, and mechanics did cross the Atlantic but in a clandestine manner. One of Washington's most accomplished wartime intelligence officers, Thomas Digges, his friend and neighbor across the Potomac, aided in this traffic. Digges had operated from London during the revolution, sending out important intelligence. He had also helped American prisoners to escape, using them as couriers to convey information to Washington. The British so trusted him that they dispatched him as a peace emissary to John Adams in the Netherlands. Washington gave him high praise in 1794 for his work.

It is not clear whether the Virginia proposal came from Digges but it appears probable. He loathed slavery, as did Washington, and was anxious to promote manufacturing and European settlement in Virginia and Maryland. When Governor Randolph, much interested, asked the president's aid in getting the plans out of England, he had to reply that he had gone as far as he was able to do in sending the information. He could not actively assist in the violation of foreign laws.

SECRETARY HAMILTON

The first surviving letter by Hamilton was written at fourteen to Edmund Stevens: "To confess my weakness, Ned, my ambition is [so] prevalent that I contemn the grov'ling and condition of a Clerk... and would willingly risk my life tho' not my character to exalt my Station... I mean to prepare the way for futurity... We have seen such schemes successful when the Projector is Constant. I shall conclude saying I wish there was a War."

Hamilton's earlier experience as a shipping clerk was to be of value to the

United States, whose revenues, in the first years, came very largely from import duties. Much of his time after becoming secretary of the treasury was devoted to routine but complex matters. These included establishing forms and regulations for the customs collectors, deciding disputed points of law, building revenue vessels, and providing lighthouses and navigational aids. In addition, by order of the House of Representatives, he prepared a report on the public finances, providing for the settlement of the large internal and foreign debt.

By the time Hamilton took office, the government already had a revenue larger than its operating expenses. In addition, the president had obtained a very full documentation of the debt which he could give the secretary. What Hamilton formulated thereafter was a proposed debt settlement of great complexity, but a tax program to pay for it of utmost simplicity. In essence, the country's consumers of alcoholic beverages were to foot the bill. The secretary pointed out that such a tax was not only a dependable source of income but had a certain moral value as well. His estimate of the national consumption of spirits at that period is rather staggering. It was about three-and-a-half times per capita what it would be in the late twentieth century.

HAMILTON AND THE BRITISH

After the execution of John André, his deputy, George Beckwith, succeeded him as head of British intelligence. A much subtler operator than André, he remained with Sir Guy Carleton until the British departed New York in 1783. He reappeared in the United States in 1787 and 1788, getting such intelligence as he could, which would aid London in dividing the former colonies, and returning a large portion of the country to British control. While Washington was on his way north to take the oath as president in April 1789, Carleton, now Lord Dorchester, reported from Quebec to his home government that many settlers in Kentucky and Tennessee wanted independence. They would welcome English protection as well as an occupation of New Orleans, provided they could trade through that port. Dorchester noted that whoever controlled the navigation of the Mississippi would be master of the lands beyond the Alleghenies.

On June 7 Dorchester informed London that he intended to supply arms to Americans in the West, to assist their trade through Great Lakes ports, and to enlist their cooperation should the British attack New Orleans. While this proposal was being implemented, the English were studying a project to link Vermont with Quebec by a canal to the Chambly River. Ira Allen, a brother of Ethan, was working to bring Vermont back under English control. In

September 1789 Beckwith returned once more to New York, to direct the extensive activities of British intelligence. One of his first calls was on Senator Schuyler of New York, with whom he had previously held conversations. He insinuated that his government was not pleased with the American tonnage and revenue acts, which had passed before Hamilton assumed office. The British were quite prepared to take action.

When Schuyler reported this to Hamilton, the secretary of the treasury called Beckwith to his office. This talk and their most important future conferences were to take place while the president was away from the capital: in October 1789, from August to October 1790, and May to July 1791. In these, Hamilton was to endeavor to frustrate not only the president's policy of impartiality to all countries but his plans to develop the country's economic potentials by a great increase of manufactures and the merchant marine. In reporting to London and Quebec, Beckwith stated that Hamilton opened the talk by saying, "I have requested to see you on this occasion from a wish to explain certain points, relative to our situation, and from a desire to suggest a measure, which I conceive to be both for the interest of Great Britain, and of this country... I have always preferred a connexion with you, to that of any other country... We must be for years, rather an agricultural, than a manufacturing people, yet our policy has had a tendency to suggest the necessity of introducing manufactures... Doubtless their increase will be proportioned to your conduct... We wish to form a commercial treaty with you, to every extent, to which you may think it your interest to go..." In succeeding points, which are here rearranged to follow, in order, Washington's instructions to Morris, Hamilton observed:

> On our side there are... two points unadjusted, the Western Forts [two were on Lake Champlain] and the negroes, although as to the latter I always decidedly approved Lord Dorchester's conduct on that occasion... The reply of your cabinet to our application on that subject was perfectly satisfactory...

> We may have a matter of great importance to settle with Spain, I mean the navigation of the Mississippi; this is of the first moment to our territories to the westward, _they must have that outlet, without it they will be lost to us_... Our country is already sufficiently large, more so than prudence might wish, as its extent tends to increase our difficulties in certain points, and to weaken our government... Connected with you, by strong ties of commercial, perhaps of political friendships, our naval exertions, in future wars, may in your scale be greatly important and decisive. These are my opinions... which I have long entertained...

... I do think a treaty of commerce might be formed of advantage to both countries. I am of opinion, that it will be better for Great Britain to grant us admission into her Islands under certain limitations of size of vessels so as merely to enable us to [trade] there... and... under such restrictions as to prevent the possibility of our interfering with your carrying trade to Europe...

... The ideas I have thrown out may be depended upon, as the sentiments... of General Washington....

In the discussions Hamilton assured Beckwith the United States would never attack Canada, thus removing an important British fear. Hamilton indicated he was heartily against any commercial discrimination against Great Britain and intimated that Washington was also opposed. Beckwith said that Britain's national honor would force her to repel any trade hostility, even in opposition to Britain's own discrimination, and he blasted James Madison who had introduced the bill. Hamilton agreed that Madison had "little knowledge of the world" and that Britain would be acting wisely, and in honor, if she retaliated against the United States. Beckwith told Hamilton to make sure anyone the president chose to go to London had no French bias, a remarkable piece of impudence on the part of a military spy. At the end, Hamilton sought, and got, Beckwith's assurances that he would not repeat his conversation anywhere in the United States. He gave him full liberty to forward his views to the British cabinet.

When Gouverneur Morris appeared in London to present his case on behalf of the United States, which he did in exact accordance with the president's instructions, he was surprised at the cool contempt with which he was received. This was the first of the years in which Hamilton thwarted the president's efforts to achieve a peaceful settlement of all issues with Great Britain. Six days after Beckwith left New York, and before they heard of the appointment of Morris, the British cabinet forwarded to Lord Dorchester approval of his plan to form the western American settlements into a political unit, independent of the United States.

BACK TO WORK

Problems and correspondence had accumulated for Washington on his New England trip. Not all of his nominees to office accepted. His old secretary, Robert Hanson Harrison, whom he had placed on the Supreme Court, declined the post. In bad health, he died the following year. Washington went over the report of the commissioners whom he had sent to negotiate a peace treaty with the southern and warlike Indians. He noted: "Gave it one read-ing—and shall bestow another and more attentive one on it." Next day he held long conversations with the commissioners on their negotiations with the Creek chief, Alexander McGillivray, who was trying to play Spain and Great Britain against the United States, to find out who would bid highest.

On November 25 Washington went to the theater taking as his guests Mrs. Adams, the two New York senators and their wives, Senator and Mrs. Pierce Butler of South Carolina, Mr. and Mrs. Hamilton, and Mrs. Nathanael Greene. The theaters always trumpeted his appearance in a way to assure a full house. They had begun a custom of playing a tune on his entry, "The President's March," which later had the words, "Hail, Columbia." The *New York Daily Advertiser* wrote: "On the appearance of THE President, the audi-ence rose, and received him with the warmest acclamations—the genuine effusions of the hearts of FREEMEN." The program included, as an epilogue, a short humorous sketch, *Darby's Return*, by William Dunlap, one of the first plays written by a native American. It was an account by a soldier, returned to Ireland, of the war in America and the new government. The humor has not stood the test of time but three lines on the Constitution had merit:

> *A revolution without blood or blows*
> *For as I understood, the cunning elves,*
> *The People all revolted from themselves.*

The president was a regular churchgoer and noted it each Sunday in his jour-nal. He issued the first presidential Thanksgiving proclamation on October 3. On November 26 he wrote, probably without irony: "Being the day appointed for a thanksgiving, I went to St. Paul's Chapel, though it was most inclement and stormy—but a few people at Church." On December 11 he noted: "Being rainy and bad, no person except the Vice-President visited Mrs. Washington this evening." December 29 was worse: "Being very snowing, not a single per-son appeared at the Levee."

Though he made such notes, the president, from his diary comments, seems to have begun to enjoy his office more than he anticipated. He went on frequent walks, carriage rides with his wife and her grandchildren, and horse-back rides as far as Harlem. His dinner parties included officers of the gov-ernment, senators and representatives, old military comrades, governors, bishops and other clergy, and Péter Van Berckel, the Dutch minister who was the only fully accredited diplomat after the return of the French minister to Paris. When out on his horse he frequently stopped to call informally on various people who had come to his house.

The business which most occupied his attention was with Henry Knox, his war secretary. Reports in abundance reached the capital of Indian raids and atrocities from Pennsylvania to Georgia. Negotiations for peace treaties with the Indians bogged down. The president, in consequence, was greatly interested in revising the militia and defense system of the United States. He drafted his proposal himself after obtaining the views of Knox and von Steuben. He reviewed Hamilton's first report to Congress on the state of the public debt and shortly afterwards ordered Adam Smith's *Wealth of Nations*. He also wrote the first State of the Union message for delivery in January.

THE SECOND SESSION

Congress, scheduled to meet January 4, 1790, did not have a quorum that day. Washington sent a note to say that he would be glad to meet them at a time and place "convenient for Congress… to make some oral communications at the commencement of their session." Two days later Congress had its quorum, and Washington set January 8 for his message. He described the rather impressive ceremony in his diary:

> *According to appointment, at 11 o'clock, I set out for the City Hall in my coach, preceded by Colonel Humphreys and Majr. Jackson in uniform (on my two white horses) and followed by Mssrs. Lear and Nelson, in my chariot, and Mr. Lewis, on horseback, following them. In their rear was the Chief Justice of the United States and the Secretaries of the Treasury and War Departments, in their respective carriages, and in the order they are named. At the outer door of the hall I was met by the door-keepers of the Senate and House, and conducted to the door of the Senate Chamber; and passing from thence to the Chair through the Senate on the right, and House of Representatives on the left, I took my seat. The gentlemen who attended me followed and they took their stand behind the Senators; the whole rising as I entered. After being seated, at which time the members of both Houses also sat, I rose (as they also did) and made my speech… On this occasion I was dressed in a suit of clothes made at the Woolen Manufactory at Hartford, as the buttons also were.*

Though the speech was short, it contained much more meat than his inaugural address. Washington read it with a far clearer and more confident voice. Pleased with his country's progress, he now felt free to ask for a much broader program of national security and economic development:

> *I embrace with great satisfaction, the opportunity which now presents itself, of*

congratulating you upon the present favourable prospects of our public affairs. The recent acquisition of the important State of North Carolina to the Constitution of the United States (of which official information has been received)—the rising credit and respectability of our Country—the general and increasing good will towards the Government of the Union—and the concord, peace and plenty, with which we are blessed, are circumstances auspicious in an eminent degree, to our national prosperity...

Among the many interesting objects, which will engage your attention, that of providing for the common defense will merit particular regard.—To be prepared for War is one of the most effectual means of preserving peace.

A free people ought not only to be armed but disciplined—to which end a uniform and well digested plan is requisite. And their safety and interest require that they should promote such manufactories as tend to render them independent of others for essentials, particularly military supplies.

The proper establishment of the Troops, which may be deemed indispensable, will be entitled to mature deliberation. In the arrangements which may be made respecting it, it will be of importance to conciliate the comfortable support of the Officers and Soldiers, with a due regard to economy.

There was reason to hope that the pacific measures adopted with regard to certain hostile tribes of Indians would have relieved the Inhabitants of our Southern and Western frontiers from their depredations. But you will perceive from the information contained in the papers, which I shall direct to be laid before you (comprehending a communication from the Commonwealth of Virginia) that we ought to be prepared to afford protection to those parts of the Union, and if necessary, to punish aggressors.

The interests of the United States require that our intercourse with other nations shall be facilitated, by such provisions as will enable me to fulfill my duty in that respect... [with] a competent fund designated for defraying the expenses incident to the conduct of our foreign affairs.

Various considerations also render it expedient that the terms on which foreigners may be admitted to the rights of Citizens should be speedily ascertained by a uniform rule of naturalization.

Uniformity of the Currency, Weights and Measures of the United States is an object of great importance, and will, I am persuaded, be attended to.

The advancement of Agriculture, Commerce, and Manufacturing by all proper means, will not I trust need recommendation. But I can not forbear intimating to you the expediency of giving effectual encouragement as well to the introduction of new and useful inventions from abroad, as to the exertions of skill and genius in producing them at home; and of facilitating the intercourse between the distant parts of our country by due attention to the Post-Office and Post-Roads. Nor am I less persuaded that you will agree with me in opinion that there is nothing which can better deserve your patronage than the promotion of Science and Literature. Knowledge is in every country the surest basis of public happiness...

Whether this desirable objective will be best promoted by affording aids to seminaries of learning already established, by the institution of a national university, or by any other expedient, will be worthy of a place in the deliberations of the Legislature.

...Adequate provision for the support of public credit is a matter of high importance to the national honour and prosperity...

I have directed the proper Officers to lay before you such papers and estimates as regards the affairs, particularly recommended to your consideration and necessary to convey to you that information of the State of the Union, which is my duty to afford...

This was to be the longest legislative session of Washington's administration. In his quiet way the president presented the most comprehensive program which the federal legislature has ever received. Congress was to revise the general defense system, provide for payment of the national debt with new taxes, establish naturalization laws, uniform money, new weights and measures, a patent office, interstate roads, better postal service, a permanent foreign service, and aid to higher education and science. To these points in his message, Washington subsequently added proposals for copyright laws, a national census, the assumption of state debts, the establishment of a permanent national capital, and a national banking system. The executive was soon transmitting formal reports on treaties with the Indians, a proposal to reorganize the militia, the cession by North Carolina of lands to the federal government, a report on the public credit, and new nominations for federal offices.

In less formal language, Washington described to the enthusiastic English Whig, Catherine Macauley Graham, January 9, 1790, how the United States was doing:

On the actual situation of this Country under this new Government I will... make a few remarks. That the Government, though not absolutely perfect, is one of the best in the world, I have little doubt. I have always believed that an unequivocally free and equal Representation of the People in the Legislature, together with an efficient and responsible Executive, were the great Pillars on which the preservation of American Freedom must depend... So far as we have gone with the new Government (and it is completely organized and in operation) we have had greater reason than the most sanguine could expect, to be satisfied with its success.

Perhaps a number of accidental circumstances have concurred with the real effects of the Government to make the People uncommonly well pleased with their situation and prospects. The harvests of wheat have been remarkably good, the demand for that article from abroad is great, the increase of Commerce is visible in every Port, and the number of new manufactures introduced in one year is astonishing. I have lately made a tour through the Eastern States. I found the country, in a great degree, recovered from the ravages of War, the towns flourishing, and the People delighted with a government instituted by themselves and for their own good. The same facts I have also reason to believe, from good authority, exist in the Southern States. By what I have just observed, I think you will be persuaded that the ill-boding Politicians who prognosticated that America would never enjoy any fruits from her Independence, and that she would be obliged to have recourse to a foreign Power for protection, have at least been mistaken.

SEVEN

NEW YORK TO PHILADELPHIA

1790

A LTHOUGH HAMILTON'S BUDGET always placed his department ahead of the foreign office, the president considered the secretary of state to precede the head of the Treasury. When he originally offered the post to Jefferson on October 13, 1789, the latter, after examining his proposed responsibilities, replied: "When I contemplate the extent of that office, embracing as it does the principal mass of domestic administration, together with the foreign, I cannot be insensible of my inequality to it; and I should enter on it with gloomy forebodings."

Washington had received persuasive enough letters when he wrote in similar vein. He replied that he knew no one who could fill the post better than Jefferson. His appointment had given "extensive and very great satisfaction to the public." The domestic duties were, in fact, divided among the cabinet members. Adjustments would be made, if they were too great for the Department of State. It was Jefferson's option to return to Paris but Washington hoped Jefferson would report to the capital. The organization of the foreign service depended on his acceptance of the office.

When the secretary of state reached New York, he found that his entire staff was to consist of four clerks, a messenger, and an interpreter. Washington had underplayed the work involved. Jefferson found himself running the foreign office during war and revolution abroad, organizing a permanent diplomatic and consular service, administering the mint and the patent office, and working on weights and measures and a national census.

LEGISLATION

The president had now taken the lead, which he had originally planned to do in his inaugural address, in recommending legislation in widely varied fields of endeavor. The details were to be worked out either in Congress or in conferences between the legislative and executive branches. Many proposals were expected to be noncontroversial, but the census was originally rejected by the Senate as a form of make-work for bookkeepers. The president let the toughest major issues, where feelings ran high, be fought out in the Senate and House. He wrote that he occasionally signed legislation that he might have voted against, had he been in Congress. What he wanted, however, and what he got were generally in close agreement.

The first session of the First Congress had passed extensive legislation. The second was even more productive. Although Congress was criticized as dilatory, the laws came out with speed. Before Washington's first year in office was completed on April 30, North Carolina had been admitted to the Union and its federal officers appointed; the budget for 1790 ($551,491.71) had been approved; and acts had authorized a national census, uniform naturalization, a patent office, and a permanent army. Washington was disappointed that the regular army was set at only 1,680 officers and men, inasmuch as he faced trouble on many frontier points. Between May and August 1790, laws established a foreign and consular service, a territorial government south of the Ohio River, a Library of Congress, a copyright office, the placement of the permanent capital for the United States, and the admission of Rhode Island to the Union. Further legislation authorized the purchase of West Point, higher import duties, a revenue cutter service, and treaties with the Indians. In addition acts passed for the settlement of all United States debts.

Fiscal legislation was the most troublesome, but not all of it was controversial. The French finance minister, Jacques Necker, told William Short, the American chargé at Paris, that the United States ought to regard its war debts to France as the most sacred of all its obligations. No such reminder was needed. As a matter of national honor, all Americans agreed that the debt to France should have priority over payments to its own citizens. The Senate and House unanimously approved this at the beginning of debates which, on other parts of the debts, lasted for six months.

The internal debt of the old Continental Congress consisted of six types of obligations totalling, with arrears of interest, $40 million. The unsettled war charges owed by the various states were calculated at $18 million. Adding the foreign loans brought the total to $70 million. Hamilton's report on public credit recommended that the federal government assume the whole burden and raise taxes on spirits sufficiently high to pay the interest. In his first and subsequent reports, Hamilton added small taxes on sugar, salt, tea, and coffee. As nearly as can be calculated from Hamilton's reports, he urged taxes high enough to yield a federal revenue of $3.6 million. All but $600,000 was to be used for debt payments. His suggested settlements were clumsy but they were somewhat modified and improved in Congress.

Hamilton stated "the proper funding of the present debt will render it a national blessing," if "the creation of debt [is] always accompanied with the means of extinguishment." This was to be done by sinking funds. Hamilton, in his report to Congress, made two proposals, the first fraudulent and the second disingenuous. Hamilton proposed "that the net product of the post-office, to a sum not exceeding one million of dollars," be applied to debt redemption. The gross annual receipts of the Post Office at this time, as Hamilton knew, were only $29,000, and the service probably ran at a deficit. Hamilton also proposed that additional foreign loans be floated, to act as a sinking fund, thus implying that debts can be reduced by borrowing. His proposals for debt settlement, including the payment by the federal government of state war debts, nearly blew the Union apart. Neither the rich nor taxes were popular, and the proposals for the latter seemed designed to benefit the former. Speculation in federal and state securities had started almost as soon as it was clear that the new government would be organized under Washington. When Hamilton's proposals were announced (and, many thought even before, thanks to leaks to friends by Hamilton's assistant, William Duer), there were scrambles by foreign and domestic cash-holders to acquire securities, especially state obligations which had been selling as low as ten cents on the dollar.

No one had thought much about taking care of the soldiers during the war but politicians suddenly grew alarmed that those brave men who had been forced to sell their notes at discounts to speculators would thus have lost what was due them from the government. Madison proposed discriminating among the original and subsequent holders, but this failed of congressional assent. The individual states calculated how they would fare and were for or against assumption accordingly. New England was all for it and threatened to leave the Union if it did not pass. Virginia, which calculations some years later showed to have come out very well under assumption, was strongly against it, as a benefit to the north. There were cries throughout the Union against speculators as harpies and bloodsuckers. Even in such centers of commerce and banking as New York, Philadelphia, and Boston, which were supposed by many states to be the principal beneficiaries, there was violent newspaper opposition. The respected *Pennsylvania Gazette,* particularly indignant, attacked Hamilton in rhyme: "Soldiers and farmers don't despair—Untax'd as yet are earth and air."

Since much of the fiscal system was adapted from British practices, anti-English feelings came to the surface. There was also the fear, which Jefferson subsequently exploited, that the corrupting practices of the British govern-ment and Parliament would come to the purer air of America.

The president kept out of the controversy as much as he could. The Constitution had provided the Senate and House as the national cockpit and he was willing to accept what a majority finally determined. In his private let-ters he expressed regret at the warmth of the debates, the scurrility of the newspapers, and the narrowness of the margin by which, he predicted in April, a compromise would pass.

THE COMPROMISES

Jefferson, arriving in the midst of the discussions, followed them with interest. At this time, he still held on to a certain realistic objectivity and his reporting of events in these months has a degree of reliability. On April 6 he wrote William Short in Paris that Congress had approved a settlement of the foreign debt but the vote of the necessary funds had to await congressional determi-nation of the domestic debt question. On May 3 he informed Washington that two of the American loans had gone above par at Amsterdam. On May 30 he told his son-in-law, Thomas Mann Randolph, that the question of removing the government to Philadelphia had been voted down in the Senate, 13–11, while assumption of state debts was "so equal on the former trial that it is very possible that with some modifications it may prevail." On June 6 he wrote his daughter that the House had voted to remove to Philadelphia; with the vice-president's vote, this might carry the Senate. On the same day Jefferson told Short that the senators who opposed a removal from New York were waiting for the new senators from Rhode Island to appear. To delay a vote they had referred the bill for a permanent capital to a Senate committee. He again noted that funds for the foreign payments were delayed by the assumption bill. On June 13 Jefferson wrote Elizabeth Eppes that the House had voted overwhelmingly to remove to Baltimore. "It is very doubtful whether the Senate will concur. However it may very possibly end in a removal either to that place or Philadelphia."

By June 13 Jefferson was writing to William Hunter that he thought the Baltimore vote might open the way to the government's temporary residence at Philadelphia and its permanent removal to Georgetown. The same day Jefferson informed George Mason that he thought there ought to be some compromise on the assumption of state debts: "I think it is necessary to give as well as take in a government like ours." By June 20 he was writing Monroe:

> *Congress has long been embarrassed by two of the most irritating questions that can be raised among them, 1. The funding of the public debt, and 2. The fixing on a more central residence… It has become probable that unless they can be reconciled, there will be no funding bill agreed to, our credit (raised by late prospects to be the first on the exchange at Amsterdam, where our paper is above par) will burst and vanish, and the states separate to take care everyone of itself… In the present instance I see the necessity of yielding for this time to the cries of the creditors in certain parts of the Union, for the sake of the Union, and to save us from the greatest of all calamities, the total extinction of our credit in Europe… It is proposed to pass an act fixing the temporary residence for 12 or 15 years at Philadelphia, and that at the end of that time it shall be transferred to Georgetown. In this way there will be something to displease and something to soothe every part of the Union, but New York…*

The compromise involved many of the states. The proposed debt settlements for Delaware, Virginia, and North Carolina were adjusted upwards. New England got the assumption it wanted. Pennsylvania was to have the capital for ten years. The South, meaning Maryland and Virginia, was to have the permanent capital on the Potomac. The residency bill passed in July and the debt settlement in August, although details of the states' debts were left for the next session.

Jefferson's letter mentioned that only New York failed to get what it wanted and had lost the national capital. This weakened Hamilton's New York political basis. It also played a role a few months later when Aaron Burr was chosen to replace Schuyler in the Senate. As it was to turn out, Hamilton had greatly underestimated the vigor of the country's economic development and growth. He had expected that as much as 80 percent of the federal revenue would be needed to service the national debt. By 1792 only a third of the federal receipts went to interest and principal. The great increase in the accruing revenues gave the president a needed flexibility in building the nation's maritime and military strength.

DOCTOR STUART

Washington continued to ask David Stuart to keep him informed on political conditions and sentiments in Virginia. What the president got were Stuart's views of Virginia politics, critical comments on everything he thought the federal government was doing, a physician's opinions on constitutional law, and a great deal of gossip. On March 15 he blasted the "eastern states" (New England) for acting in solid phalanx against Virginia. He disliked Madison's plan of discrimination in the debt settlement and denounced the proposed assumption of state debts as unconstitutional. On June 2 he wrote that he thought Congress was lazy, working only four hours a day, and, "like School-boys," taking Saturday as a holiday. Stuart sent on Patrick Henry's supposed remark that he did not wish to be a senator, for he was too old to learn all the fashionable graces expected at Washington's court. "From this expression I suspect the old patriot has heard some extraordinary representations of the etiquette established at your levees." He also quoted Colonel Theodorick Bland to the effect that there was more pomp at his house and "Washington's bows were more stiff" than anything that could be seen at the British court.

Washington took Stuart's rather humorless harangues more seriously than they deserved, very probably because Virginia was the largest state and his own. He replied on March 28: "If the southern States are less tenacious of their interest, or, if whilst the eastern move in a solid phalanx to effect their views, the southerners are always divided, which of the two is most to be blamed?... Common danger brought the States into confederacy, and on their union our safety and importance depend. A spirit of accommodation was the basis of the present constitution, can it be expected then that the Southern or Eastern part of the Empire will succeed in all their measures?" The president followed with another letter on June 15, acid in its humor:

Your description of the public Mind in Virginia gives me pain. It seems to be more irritable, sour and discontented than... in any other State in the Union, except Massachusetts; which, from the same causes, but on quite different principles, is tempered like it.

That Congress does not proceed with all that dispatch which people at a distance expect... is not to be denied... Can it well be otherwise in a country so extensive, so diversified in its interests? And will not these different interests naturally produce... long, warm, and animated debates? Most undoubtedly; and if there was the same propensity in Mankind to investigating the motives, as there is for censuring... it would be found the censure so freely bestowed is oftentimes unmerited and uncharitable, for instance, the condemnation of Congress for sitting only four hours in the day. The fact is, and this is, and has been for a considerable time, from ten o'clock in the forenoon until three, often later... after which the business is going on in Committees...

In a letter of last year, I informed you of the motives, which <u>compelled</u> me to allot a day for the reception of idle and ceremonious visits... That I have not been able to make bows to the taste of poor Colonel Bland (who, by the by, I believe never saw one of them) is to be regretted especially too, as (upon those occasions) they were indiscriminately bestowed, and the best I was master of; would it not have been better to throw the veil of charity over them, ascribing their stiffness to the effects of age, or to the unskillfulness of my teacher, than to pride and dignity of office, which God knows has no charm for Me?...

DEATH OF FRANKLIN

Benjamin Franklin, who had first entered public service in 1736, retired as head of Pennsylvania's government in 1788, after seeing the Constitution ratified. Hearing that the president had been ill, Franklin wrote him from his own sick bed on September 18, 1789:

For my own personal Ease, I should have died two years ago; but tho' those Years have been spent in excruciating Pain, I am pleas'd that I have liv'd them, since they have brought me to see our present situation. I am now finishing my 84th year and probably with it my career in this Life; but in what ever State of Existence I am plac'd hereafter, if I retain any Memory of what has pass'd here, I shall with it retain the Esteem, Respect, and Affection with which I have long been, my dear Friend, Yours most sincerely...

Washington replied a week later:

Would to God, my dear Sir, that I could congratulate you upon the removal of the excruciating pain under which you labour! and that your existence might close with as much ease, as its continuance has been beneficial to our Country, and useful to mankind!... If to be venerated for benevolence; If to be admired for talents; If to be esteemed for patriotism; If to be beloved for philanthropy, can gratify the human mind, you must have the pleasing consolation to know that you have not lived in vain; And I flatter myself that it will not be ranked among the least grateful occurrences of your life to be assured that, so long as I retain my memory, you will be thought on with respect, veneration and Affection by Your sincere friend.

Franklin's last public service was to send Jefferson, a few days before his death, a geographical description of a boundary in dispute between Great Britain and the United States. He died quietly on April 17, 1790, leaving a codicil to his will: "My fine crab-tree walking stick, with a gold head curiously wrought in the form of the cap of liberty, I give to my friend, and the friend of mankind, General Washington. If it were a sceptre, he has merited it and would become it."

THE PRESIDENT'S ILLNESS

On May 12 William Jackson, one of Washington's secretaries, sent an urgent letter to Clement Biddle, in Philadelphia, by express rider: "The inclosed letter from Doctor Bard to Doctor Jones is transmitted to you with a view to ensure secrecy, certainty, and dispatch in the delivery of it... I need not repeat the necessity of delivering the letter with Privacy, and keeping the object of it a secret from every person, even Mrs. Biddle. Doctor Jones may want your aid to accelerate his arrival at New York." Doctor Jones set off for New York the following day, two hours after he had received the letter.

Washington's illness was sudden and violent. He had written in his diary May 9: "Indisposed with a bad cold, and at home all day writing letters on private business." This developed into severe pneumonia. On May 12 his condition was critical, as three top New York physicians worked on him. Three days later he appeared to be worse, and Dr. Samuel Bard summoned Dr. Jones from Philadelphia. At the president's house that day everyone was in tears. Abigail Adams, knowing that only Washington could keep the still feeble government going, was badly shaken. Jefferson wrote his daughter, Martha Randolph, on May 16: "Yesterday the President was thought by the physicians to be dying. However about 4 o'clock in the evening a copious sweat came on, his expectoration which had been thin and ichorous, began to assume a well digested form, his articulation became distinct, and in the course of two hours it was evident he had gone thro' a favorable crises. He continues mending today, and from total despair we are now in good hopes of him." On May 27 Jefferson informed William Short in Paris that two of the three physicians present that day had considered that he "was in the act of death. A successful effort of nature relieved him and us. You cannot conceive the public alarm on this occasion. It proves how much depends on his life."

On June 7 the two tall Virginians, Washington and Jefferson, the latter having been suffering from severe headaches, went off on a three-day, deep-sea fishing trip. The *Pennsylvania Packet* carried a June 12 dispatch from New York: "The President... returned from Sandy Hook the fishing banks where he had been for the benefit of the sea air, and to amuse himself in the delightful recreation of fishing. We are told he had an excellent sport, having himself caught a great number of sea bass and black fish." Washington's physicians again urged him to get more exercise. His July diaries repeatedly note that he was out on horseback from five to seven every morning.

RELATIONS WITH GREAT BRITAIN

Washington's proposals to increase the army, in view of repeated Indian attacks, were reported to Quebec by British agents, in a manner calculated to alarm Lord Dorchester. The reports suggested that the United States intended to seize the frontier posts and other treaty rights by force. As a result George Beckwith came hurrying down from Canada in March to pick up military intelligence and to talk to his American contacts. From his conversations, Beckwith concluded, and so informed Dorchester, that the troops were being added primarily for defense against Indian attacks and to strengthen the hands of the federal government. Eventually they would operate offensively, but so far as he could see there would be no threat to the British-held posts that year.

During their conversations Hamilton warned Beckwith that Jefferson, the new secretary of state, had taken office the day before. This factor, he said, introduced a strongly pro-French element into the American government. In a further conversation, in which Beckwith sought assurances that the United States sincerely desired a close political and commercial connection with England, he asked Hamilton in mid-April whether the secretary's communications to him were, in fact, authorized by General Washington, the responsible chief of state. Hamilton replied: "I am not authorized to say to you in so many words, that such is the language of the President of the United States: to a gentleman who has no public character, such a declaration cannot be made but my honor and character stand implicated in the fulfillment of these assurances." While Hamilton thus destroyed whatever fragment of character and honor he claimed, he also introduced a very confusing situation for Dorchester and Beckwith. Lord Dorchester began pushing for a policy towards the United States, which was at variance with that of the British government.

THE MORRIS MISSION

On March 28 Gouverneur Morris, the president's emissary, presented Washington's letter of credence to the British foreign secretary, the Duke of Leeds. His Grace remarked astutely that America was quite far away. The question of sending a minister to New York was a difficult one, but Morris would hear something in due course. He was dismissed. At this time, the British government was concentrating its thoughts on an incident at Nootka Sound, in what is now British Columbia, and Spain had seized two ships in the territory she claimed as hers; the British were preparing to go to war over this, in order to break Spain's stranglehold in the Pacific.

The United States was considered of little importance, and official policy to the country had already been determined. The posts were to be held and treaties of commerce and friendship reserved for those areas which Great Britain planned to detach from the United States. Hamilton's assurances that there would be no American commercial restrictions against Britain, and no attack on British posts, had little real influence on British policy. A month after his initial interview and several subsequent written requests, Morris received a brutal note from Leeds: "We cannot but lament every circumstance which can have delayed the Accomplishment of those engagements (comprized in the Treaty) in which those States [the U.S.] were in the most solemn Manner bound and should the Delay in fulfilling them have rendered their final Completion impracticable, we have no Scruple in declaring our Object is to retard the fulfilling of such subsequent Parts of the Treaty as depend entirely upon Great Britain, until redress is granted… or a fair and just compensation obtained for the non-Performance of those Engagements on the part of the United States…"

Morris wrote a flawlessly diplomatic reply, in much better English. He asked the duke to be more precise in explaining British policy, which was exactly what the foreign secretary did not want to do. Morris wrote Washington that Leeds' "Confusion of Language… resembles the Stammering of one who endeavors to excuse a Misdeed which he has resolved to commit… It seems pretty clear they wish to evade a commercial treaty… I have construed into Rejection his Grace's abstruse Language leaving him the Option to give it a different Interpretation. I do not expect that he will, tho he may perhaps write an explanatory comment more unintelligible than the last."

A few days later a war crisis burst on London. The British had already directed a huge impressment of seamen, some of whom turned out to be Americans. In view of a probable war with Spain, the government instructed Lord Dorchester to send an agent to the United States to obtain military

intelligence and to see whether there was any chance of American cooperation in case of war. The navigation of the Mississippi, Dorchester was assured,
would be of much greater importance to the United States than the forts.

Morris' letter reached Leeds at a point when Britain did not want too many
enemies. By May 21 Morris was closeted with the prime minister and foreign
secretary. This time Morris played cold. When Leeds said that he had misinterpreted his letter and Britain was interested in discussing the possibility of a
commercial treaty, Morris replied that "it appeared idle to form a new treaty,
until the parties should be thoroughly satisfied about that already existing." A
long wrangle followed on violations, with Pitt maintaining that Britain had to
hold the posts as a guarantee that the United States would observe the treaty.
Morris replied: "We do not think it worth while to go to War with you for these
posts, but we know our rights, and will avail ourselves of them, when Time and
circumstances may suit."

While Morris' firmness had little immediate effect on British policy, the gov-
ernment took a few positive steps. Some impressed Americans were released.
Pitt also ordered Dorchester to restrain Indian massacres of American settlers.
Morris' warnings, planted at a suitable time, pushed the British government
along towards reaching its later decision to give up the posts, if war came.
Spain had been counting on French support but France, with revolution
spreading, could offer no help. By autumn Spain had knuckled under, and
Britain, for the moment, was triumphant.

In reporting to Washington on his May 21 conversation, Morris proposed
that, in case of war, Britain or Spain be forced to pay a high price for
American neutrality. He suggested that negotiations with Madrid proceed at
once. After receiving the letter, Jefferson worked on what was the beginning
of a neutrality policy designed to let the United States take the utmost advantage from the warring powers. In August he sent an American consul to
London, to obtain intelligence on British policy. He also ordered the
American chargé at Madrid, William Carmichael, to press Spain with full
force, if war broke out, to grant the United States the Mississippi navigation,
as well as a port of deposit at new Orleans. To give Carmichael support as well
as information on the new government's policies, the president dispatched his
secretary and former aide, Colonel David Humphreys, to Madrid. Jefferson
also wrote informally to the Portuguese ambassador at Paris to see if diplomatic relations could be established with Lisbon. Jefferson's most urgent
worry, frequently expressed, was that Britain might seize all Spanish territories
to the west and south and encircle the United States.

BECKWITH AND HAMILTON

On July 5, a Monday, the official celebration of American independence was held. Members of the government, House and Senate, the Cincinnati, and others called on Washington. The president went to St. Paul's Church, where Brockholst Livingston, according to Washington's diary, made an oration "to show the different situation we are now in, under an excellent government of our own choice, to what it would have been if we had not succeeded in our opposition to the attempts of Great Britain to enslave us; and how much we ought to cherish the blessings which are within our reach, and to cultivate the seeds of harmony and unanimity in all our public Councils. There were several other points touched upon in a sensible manner." Washington's diary the same day continued:

> *I was informed this day by General Irvine (who recd. the acct. from Pittsburgh) that the Traitor Arnold was at Detroit and had viewed the Militia in the neighborhood of it twice. This had occasioned much Speculation in these parts— and with many other circumstances—though trifling in themselves led strongly to a conjecture that the British had some design on the Spanish settlements on the Mississippi and of course to surround these United States.*

The British government had instructed Dorchester that his agents in the United States were to have no official or public character. The Canadian governor, in turn, gave secret orders to Beckwith to obtain intelligence on American relations with Spain and France, "the characters of military men... military arrangements... any increase of troops, their position and movements, the number and magnitude of deposits of military stores and provisions, and the arming of any ships for War..." Beckwith was instructed to be particularly attentive to Vermont and to the actions of French and Spanish agents.

In addition to his secret instructions, Dorchester handed Beckwith an open but rather caustic letter which he was permitted, at his discretion, to show to American authorities. In it he expressed the hope there would be no "alteration in the good disposition of the United States to establish a firm friendship and alliance with Great Britain." The same letter denounced America for its treaty violations and its "misrepresentations" of British activities, arising, he surmised, from the "unsettled state of their government" and from French influence. Dorchester expressed concern that the Spanish were stirring up the Indians, and he blasted anti-British statements by Americans in the Northwest Territory.

Beckwith and Hamilton conferred on the morning of July 8. In the course of the conversation, Beckwith showed Hamilton his nonsecret instruction, which he may have permitted him to copy. Hamilton decided at this point to make a partial disclosure to Washington of what he had been doing. In preparing his memorandum for the president, Hamilton doctored both Dorchester's letter and Beckwith's oral statements. He quoted the former's note referring to "the agency of Mr. Morris," but he added gratuitously that Beckwith had said that "Mr. Morris had not produced any regular credentials, but merely a letter from the President." Hamilton then stated that Great Britain and its cabinet were interested in an "alliance" with the United States and that Dorchester deplored both the Indian attacks and the "intemperate language" of Americans in the Northwest Territory. He inserted the unfounded remark that Beckwith suggested, with some indirection, that he was speaking for the British cabinet.

Washington was so interested in the Hamilton memorandum that he copied it as a whole in his July 8 diary. Dorchester, as Julian Boyd has pointed out, referred in his letter only to the "good disposition *of the United States*" (italics his) to form an alliance. The president of course had no such idea in mind. Neither Washington nor Jefferson were entirely fooled by Hamilton's memorandum, but their suspicions tended to be directed towards Great Britain rather than their colleague.

Washington commented in his diary that all the Beckwith communication signified was:

> *We did not incline to give any satisfactory answer to Mr. Morris, who was* <u>*officially*</u> *commissioned to ascertain our intentions with respect to the evacuation of the Western Posts within the Territory of the United States, and other matters into which he was empowered to enquire, until by this unauthenticated mode we can discover whether you will enter into an Alliance with us and make Common cause against Spain. In that case we will enter into a commercial Treaty with you and* <u>*promise perhaps*</u> *to fulfill what they already stand engaged to perform. However, I requested Mr. Jefferson and Colo. Hamilton, as I intend to do the Vice President, Chief Justice and Secretary at War, to resolve this matter in all its relations in their minds...*

Next day Washington recorded in his diary that troops and militia under General Harmar had moved from Kentucky into Ohio to prevent Indian raids, which he did not need to mention, were clearly instigated by Lord Dorchester. Subsequent to his conversations with various officials on July 14, the president instructed Hamilton, as he noted in his diary of July 14, "to treat [Beckwith's] communications very civilly—to intimate, delicately, that they carried no marks official or authentic nor in speaking of Alliance, did they convey any definite meaning… In a word, that the Secretary of the Treasury was to extract as much as he could from Maj. Beckwith and to report to me, without committing, by any assurances whatever, the Government of the U. States, leaving it entirely free to pursue, unreproached, such a line of conduct in the dispute as her interest (and honour) shall dictate."

It appears to have been an unfortunate error on the part of the president not to require the secretary of state to attend all discussions with Beckwith. Even the bifurcated tongue of Hamilton would have been hard put to cope in such a situation. The secretary of the treasury proceeded at once to violate the president's instructions. On July 15 he talked to Beckwith who recorded Hamilton's statements for his government:

I have communicated to the President, the subjects on which we have conversed… You must be sensible that official formality is wanting, but it is conceived that His Lordship would not have gone the length he has without being acquainted with the general views of your administration.

In the present stage of this business, it is difficult to say much on the subject of a Treaty of Alliance; Your rupture with Spain, if it takes place, opens a very wide political field; this much I can say, we are perfectly unconnected with Spain.

The Speeches… of any person whatever in the Indian Country… suggesting hostile ideas respecting the forts, are not authorized by this government.

Lord Dorchester's conduct with respect to the Indians is held by us to be a strong proof of His Lordship's disposition to harmony and friendship.

It appears to me that, from the nature of our Government, it would be mutually advantageous, if this negotiation could be carried out at our seat of Government, as it would produce dispatch and obviate misconceptions.

There is one thing more I wish to mention to you; I do it altogether as one gentleman to another, and I trust it will be so considered.

I have decided on doing it at this time from the possibility of my not having it in my power to come to such an explanation hereafter.

If it shall be judged proper to proceed on this business by the sending or appointing a proper person to come to this country to negotiate on the spot, whoever shall then be our Secretary of State, will be the person in whose department such negotiation must originate, and he in turn will be the channel of communication with the

President; in the turn of such affairs the most minute circumstances, mere trifles, give a favorable bias or otherwise to the whole. The President's mind I can declare to be perfectly dispassionate on the subject. Mr. Jefferson our present Secretary of State is I am persuaded a gentleman of honor, and zealously desirous of promoting those objects, which the nature of his duty call for, and the interests of his country may require, but from some opinions which he has given respecting Your government, and possible predilections elsewhere, there may be difficulties which may possibly frustrate the whole, and which might be readily explained away. I shall certainly know the progress of the negotiation from day to day, but what I come to the present explanation for is this, that in case any such difficulties should occur, I would wish to know them, in order that I may be sure they are clearly understood, and candidly examined; if none take place the business will of course go on in regular channels...

In this I am steadily following up what I have long considered to be the essential interest of this country...

Hamilton's report to the president did not mention most of what he had said to Beckwith. He prepared a twisted version of a portion of it for Washington, notably where he quoted Beckwith as repeating "assurances" of Lord Dorchester's "disposition to discourage Indian outrages." He suggested that Beckwith stated that Britain's efforts, in case of war with Spain, would be directed against South America. Hamilton also reported that he had told Beckwith: "As to alliance, this opens a wide field. The thing is susceptible of a vast variety of forms. 'Tis not possible to judge what would be proper or what could be done unless points were brought into view. If you are in a condition to mention particulars, it may afford better ground for conversation. I stopped here for an answer. Major Beckwith replied that he could say nothing more particular than he had done. This being the case (continued I) I can only say... we shall be disposed to pursue whatever shall appear under all circumstances to be our interest as far as may consist with our honor."

Beckwith did not confine his conversations to Hamilton, nor was he the only secret agent at work in America. The British government that summer and autumn was flooded with reports, some of such critical importance that they went directly to the prime minister. Beckwith forwarded the views of Thomas Scott, member of Congress for western Pennsylvania, who urged the British to take New Orleans. Their consul at Norfolk reported that western North Carolina was eager to raise men and to cooperate with the British in freeing the western areas from Spanish domination. Senator Johnson of Connecticut warned Beckwith that the British should never trust Jefferson.

Peter Allaire, a New York merchant, reported, in a message read by Pitt, that the whole great West and Florida would fall to England with a few thousand troops. One of the richest areas on earth could thereby be "forever" bound to Britain "in spite of Congress and all the world."

By early September Beckwith and Sir John Temple, British consul at New York, had written London that Colonel David Humphreys was on his way to Europe on some secret mission. Temple guessed that he might be going to France or Spain. Beckwith followed September 25 with an intimation from Hamilton that "in case of a rupture with Spain, the probable effect, which such an event may produce upon the navigation of the Mississippi, attracts the very particular attention of this government." On almost the same day Hamilton told Beckwith: "We consider ourselves perfectly at liberty to act with respect to Spain in any way most conclusive to our interests, even to the going to war with that power, if we should think it advisable to join you." This would have astonished the peace-loving president who was anxious to avoid war at almost any cost.

JEFFERSON ACTS

During Hamilton's last conversations with Beckwith, the president and secretary of state were absent in Virginia. Nevertheless instructions had gone out looking to the national interest. Washington and Jefferson felt that the gravest danger faced by the new federal Union was British encirclement. If that country, having posts in the North and the Midwest, and substantial control of the western Indians, moved to eject Spain from Louisiana and the Floridas, the United States would once again be surrounded by a hostile power controlling the seas.

Washington had two purposes in mind in sending Morris to London. He hoped he could negotiate a peaceful settlement with Britain. If not, he would be able to provide an accurate evaluation of the attitude of the British government, as a basis for American policy. Morris concluded that nothing could be done by negotiation. His assessment was based not only on conversations with the prime minister and the Foreign Office, but also with officials of the Board of Trade, members of parliament, the French ambassador, and Charles James Fox, leader of the opposition. John Adams, long experienced with the British, said that Morris had described exactly what could be expected. Having started negotiations with Lisbon and instructed Carmichael at Madrid to press for the opening of the Mississippi, Jefferson wrote to Gouverneur Morris on August 12:

You have placed their proposition of exchanging a Minister on proper ground. It must certainly come from them, and come in unequivocal form; with those who respect their own dignity so much, ours must not be counted at nought... Besides what they are saying to you, they are talking to us through Quebec; but so informally that they may disavow it when they please... They talk of a Minister, a treaty of commerce <u>and</u> <u>alliance</u>. If the latter object be honorable, it is useless; if dishonorable, inadmissible. These tamperings prove they view a war as very possible; and some symptoms indicate designs against the Spanish possessions adjoining us. The consequences of their acquiring all the country from the St. Croix to the St. Mary's are too obvious to you to need development. You will readily see the dangers which would then surround us. We wish you to intimate to them that we should contemplate a change of neighbours with extreme uneasiness; and that a due balance on our borders is not less desirable to us, than a balance of power in Europe has always appeared to them. We wish to be neutral, and we will be so, <u>if they will execute the treaty fairly, and attempt no conquests adjoining us</u>... If the war takes place, we would readily wish to be quieted on these two points, offering in return an honorable neutrality; more than this they are not to expect. It will be proper that these ideas be conveyed in delicate and friendly terms; but that they be conveyed, if the war takes place; for it is in that case alone, and not till it be begun, that we would wish our dispositions to be known; but in no case need they think of our accepting any equivalent for the posts...

So concerned was Washington that the British might move troops across the United States from Detroit to Spanish territory, that he took the unusual step on August 27 of asking the chief justice, the vice-president, and the members of his cabinet to send him written memoranda as to what should be done if the British requested permission to do this or, as more probable, if they did it without leave.

The answers were as varied as the personalities of the respondents. While Knox hedged, he made the shrewd guess that Spain would not go to war without France and that country might be too "convulsed" to join. Adams and Jefferson wanted strict neutrality with vigorous protests to the British court. The latter also thought America might be forced to join Spain and France, but this eventuality ought to be avoided as long as possible. Adams complained that Congress had provided too few funds for the foreign service. The United States badly needed first-class representatives at London, Paris, Madrid, and The Hague to forward intelligence. Hamilton was the slowest to reply and made the most involved explanation. He embedded in lengthy prose the suggestion that since "many of the best and ablest people" in the United States wanted an "intimate connection" with Great Britain, it might be better to side with her against Spain, navigation of the Mississippi was far more important than the British posts (a point made by the British cabinet), and more land possessions might never be desirable for the United States.

HAMILTON TIPS BRITISH INTELLIGENCE

Washington and Knox together planned a military expedition from Fort Washington (Cincinnati) to the Miami Villages (Fort Wayne) to check Indian raids south of the Ohio. The president asked Jefferson if Dorchester ought to be notified that the attacks were to be confined to raiding Indians and were not to touch British posts. The secretary of state said this was undesirable since it would certainly forewarn the Indians. The surprise presence of American troops in the Ohio region might also act as a deterrent to any moves planned by Dorchester against Spanish territory.

On August 20 General Arthur St. Clair, governor of the Northwest Territory, arrived in New York to discuss military plans with Knox and finance with Hamilton. The ubiquitous Beckwith was all eyes and ears to learn what was going on. Next day, while the president and secretary of state were in Rhode Island, Hamilton informed Beckwith of St. Clair's expedition. While Lord Dorchester himself did not receive the information until September 11, it was well within the bounds of Beckwith's capabilities to have sent the intelligence directly to British agents in the Ohio area. On August 24 Knox warned General Josiah Harmar, leader of the expedition, that "every possible precaution in the power of human foresight should be used to prevent surprise."

On November 10 Beckwith forwarded to Quebec a special intelligence report, rating St. Clair, Harmar, Wyllis, and Doughty the American officers in charge of the expedition. There was other information, but this dispatch was too late to be useful, for Harmar had already been ambushed and beaten. The man who supplied the information was a New Yorker experienced in military matters.

GOUVERNEUR MORRIS TRADUCED

Gouverneur Morris delivered the funeral eulogy over Hamilton in 1804. He might have enjoyed this more had he known what Hamilton had done to him in 1790. Just after the president left for Virginia, Hamilton talked to David Humphreys, Washington's special agent to Madrid, who had strict instructions to keep his mission secret at all costs. Humphreys, who was not too bright, reported to the president that he had had a very interesting conversation with

Hamilton and that he was glad to have his reasoning and to compare it with that "of other political characters. He said that Hamilton was not perfectly satisfied with the manner in which Morris had conducted the business in London" and had asked him to look into this while he was there. Humphreys complained that he did not see how he could do this and still keep himself secret.

In one of his interminable conversations with Beckwith, about September 25, Hamilton brought up his disapproval of Morris. Wording the conversation in such a way as to receive confirmation from Beckwith, he suggested that perhaps Morris had been so intimate with French Ambassador Luzerne in London that this might have brought about some reserve on the part of the British government. Beckwith said he had heard some of Morris' New York friends and relatives say that he had seen Luzerne and that Charles James Fox thought well of him. Hamilton picked this last name up in such a way as to extract from Beckwith the remark that "intimacies" with Fox, a member of the opposition, were not very desirable. Hamilton then indicated to Beckwith how much better it would be to have all negotiations transferred to New York— where he could keep an eye on them. Hamilton sent an arch letter to Washington on September 30:

> *I had lately a visit from a _certain_ _Gentleman_ the sole object of which was to make some observations of a delicate nature, concerning _another_ _Gentleman_ employed on a _particular_ _errand_; which, as they were doubtless intended for your ear, and (such as they are) ought to be known to you, it is of course my duty to communicate.*

> *He began (in a manner somewhat embarrassed which betrayed rather more than he intended to discover) by telling me that _in_ _different_ _companies_ where he had happened to be, in this City (a circumstance by the way very unlikely) he had heard it mentioned that that _other_ _Gentleman_ was upon terms of very great intimacy with the representatives of a certain Court at the one where he was employed and with the head of the party opposed to the [Prime] Minister; and he proceeded to say that if there were any symptoms of backwardness or coolness in the Minister, it had occurred to him that they might possibly be occasioned by such _an_ _intimacy_... If this should be the case (said he) you will readily imagine that it cannot be calculated to inspire confidence or to facilitate free communication... Man, after all is but man; and though the Minister has a great mind, and is as little likely as most men to entertain illiberal distrust and jealousies, yet there is no saying what might be the effect of such conduct upon him...*

Having provided this imaginative version of what Beckwith did not say,

Hamilton added that *he* had told Beckwith: "I have never heard a syllable, Sir, about the matter you mention." He then put into Beckwith's mouth a phrase, "trifles often mar great affairs," a variant of what Hamilton had previously said to Beckwith, when he urged that negotiations take place in New York. Washington had sources of information, not known to Hamilton, and the secretary got back a rather short note, dated Mount Vernon, October 10:

> *Your letter came duly to hand. For the information contained in it I thank you, as I shall do for all others of a similar nature. The motives, however, by which the author of the communication to you was actuated, although they may have been pure and in that case praiseworthy, do also (but it may be uncharitable to harbor the suspicion) admit of a different interpretation and by an easy and direct clue.*

Washington thus left Hamilton to think about what the president knew. On November 4 the president dropped a note to the secretary of war, expressing his concern lest General St. Clair might have made a premature disclosure to the British of General Harmar's movements in the Northwest Territory. On November 19 he wrote further that he had forebodings of disaster.

LONG ISLAND, RHODE ISLAND, AND PHILADELPHIA

Washington made two special tours in 1790, the first before his illness, through much of Long Island. From Brooklyn he rode on April 20 to Utrecht, remarking that the farmers there grew twenty-five to thirty bushels of corn to the acre, and thirty or more bushels of wheat and rye. "This was the effect of Dung from New York (about 10 cart loads to the acre)... The land after crossing the Hills between Brooklyn and Flat Bush is perfectly level... All that end of the Island is a rich black loam... The timber is chiefly Hickory and Oak, mixed here and there with locust and Sassafras trees, and in places with a good deal of Cedar." He spent the night at "a pretty good and decent house" in Jamaica.

From Jamaica he drove ten miles to South Hempstead. He noted there was not a tree or shrub on the road except some rather poor fruit trees. The soil was "thin and cold, and of course not productive, even in Grass." He rode down to the ocean, observing "the small bays, marshes and guts, into which the tide flows at all times." He also observed a type of social distinction which had begun to appear in America, in the form of guesthouses. The owners maintained theirs were private houses, accepting paying guests, rather than taverns or inns, kept by common innkeepers. Washington appeared unable to discern any real difference. General de Chastellux had earlier guessed that they thus avoided paying license fees.

At Brookhaven Washington turned north to the sound. There the soil was also poor and indifferent. He circled around to Huntington and Oyster Bay, "to the House of a Mr. Young (private and very neat and decent where we lodged)." He noted that for nearly five miles out of Smithtown there was a bed of white sand and no trees taller than 25 feet. At Glen Cove he examined a grist mill and two paper mills. From thence he rode to Flushing and Brooklyn, again commenting on the productivity of New York City's manure on the fields. In general he found that this nearly doubled the crops but he also noted the use of such green manure as clover and timothy, which was plowed into the soil. He wrote that Long Island "fences" were often "growing trees, with the use of dogwood and white oak predominating."

When Rhode Island joined the Union, Washington was glad to have another excuse for a trip. On August 15, the day after Congress adjourned, Washington picked up Jefferson, Governor Clinton, and three secretaries and sailed for Newport, through Long Island Sound. Washington's own diary is missing but a congressman from South Carolina, William L. Smith, supplied the deficiency with his notes: "As we entered the harbor [Newport], a salute was fired from the fort and some pieces on the wharves; at our landing we were received by the principal inhabitants of the town, and the clergy who, forming a procession, escorted us through a considerable concourse of citizens to the lodgings which had been prepared for us..."

The president and his party walked to the heights above, followed by a large number of townspeople. At four o'clock everyone marched to the town hall, Smith said, adding: "The dinner was well dished up, and conducted with regularity and decency; the company consisted of about eighty persons; after dinner some good toasts were drank: 'may the last be first'... The President gave 'The Town of Newport' and... Judge Marchant gave 'The man we love' which the company drank standing."

Everyone then followed the president while he took another walk around the town. Next morning after breakfast, he received an address from the city council, which apologized for the fact that Newport, having suffered a long trade depression, was unable to offer as much hospitality as other towns.

The presidential party took seven hours to sail from Newport to Providence, where Smith described the reception:

The same salute took place as at Newport, but the procession up to the tavern was more solemn and conducted with a much greater formality, having troops and music. The Governor of the State was so zealous in his respects that he jumped aboard the packet as soon as she got to the wharf to welcome the President to Providence. The President... The Governor... [Senator] Foster... Governor Clinton... Mr. Jefferson... [Justice] Blair... Colonel Humphreys, Maj. Jackson and Mr. Nelson... followed the principal inhabitants of Providence... making a long file, preceded by some troops and music; the doors and windows for the length of a mile were all crowded with ladies and spectators. When we arrived at the tavern, the President stood at the door, and the troops and procession passed and saluted. In the procession were three negro scrapers [fiddlers] making a horrible noise. We then sat down to a family dinner. After tea, just as the President was taking leave to go to bed, he was informed... that the students of the college had illuminated it, and would be highly flattered at the President's going to see it, which he politely agreed to do, though he never goes out at night, and it then rained a little, and was a disagreeable night. We now made a nocturnal procession to the college, which indeed was worth seeing, being very splendidly illuminated...

Smith concluded by giving the heavy schedule for the president's last day in Rhode Island:

Thursday morning began with a heavy rain and a cold, easterly wind. It cleared at nine o'clock, and then the President, accompanied as before, began a walk which continued until one o'clock and which completely fatigued the company which formed his escort. We walked all around the town, visited all the apartments of the college, went on the roof to view the beautiful and extensive prospect, walked to a place where a large Indiaman of 900 tons was on the docks, went on board her, returned to the town, stopped and drank wine and punch at Mr. Clarke's, Mr. Brown's, Gov. Turner's, and Gov. Bowen's, and then returned home. As soon as the President was rested, he received the addresses of the Cincinnati, the Rhode Island colleges, and the Town of Providence, and then went immediately to dinner at the Town Hall. The dinner was attended by 200 persons, and an immense crowd surrounded the hall. After dinner several toasts were drank: the second was "The President of the United States," at which the whole company, within and without, gave three huzzas and a long clapping of hands. The President then rose and drank the health of all the company; he afterwards gave "The Town of Providence."... At the conclusion... the President rose, and the whole company, with a considerable crowd of citizens, walked down the wharf, where he and his suite embarked for New York.

The president arrived back in New York late on August 21. Very likely he was not entirely displeased at being away while there was a great deal of packing going on at his house. The faithful and much overworked Tobias Lear, now married, had the task imposed on him of moving all the president's furniture and papers to the new capital at Philadelphia. He also had to get the Robert Morris house ready for his permanent residence while the president had a vacation at Mount Vernon. In the meantime Lear had requested Clement Biddle in Philadelphia to engage temporary rooms there for the president and his wife, the two grandchildren, two secretaries, two maids, and four white and four black servants. His sixteen horses had also to be accommodated.

Lear stressed that Philadelphia should have "as little ceremony and parade as may be possible, for the President wishes to command his own time, which these things always forbid in a greater or less degree, and they are to him fatiguing and often times painful. He wishes not to exclude himself from the sight or conversation of his fellow citizens, but their eagerness to shew their affection frequently imposes a heavy tax on him." Nonetheless, the Philadelphia Light Horse Troop was out, and there were cannon shots and fireworks and a formal dinner for the President and his wife on September 2. Although Martha Washington was ill, both had to attend another dinner for two hundred people on September 4, where there were bands, songs, and endless toasts.

THE NATIONAL CAPITAL

The bargaining over the residence and assumption bills brought public commotion and discussion, letters to the newspapers, cartoons, squibs, and hints of corruption. New York was particularly annoyed at Robert Morris, the Philadelphia financier, who was accused of snatching the national capital for his own economic benefit.

The final residence act provided that the permanent capital might be placed anywhere along the Potomac River, from the Eastern Branch (the Anacostia) to the Conococheague River. The latter was a small stream across the Blue Ridge Mountains, which George Washington had first visited in his youth. To the city people of New York, Boston, and Philadelphia, it had the sound of the wilderness. The president probably had the name inserted as a ruse to keep the location secret from speculators but it soon became a national joke. Many assumed it really meant that Philadelphia was to be the permanent capital, but they did not know George Washington, the skilled professional surveyor and amateur architect. When Congress adjourned, the president proceeded to have a look at potential sites.

The *Pennsylvania Mercury* contains a subsequent report from Georgetown, September 11: "The President of the United States, his lady and suite [arrived] on their way to Mount Vernon. The members of the Potowmack company of Alexandria, and this place, met their illustrious President at Mr. John Suter's. Notwithstanding the fatigue of a long journey, his Excellency proceeded to business respecting the navigation of the Patowmack." If, in the course of business and dinner, the president asked a great many questions on land ownership and values, the condition of the harbor, and general facilities available, no one was surprised, since all had read the act for the establishment of the capital on the river.

Two days later Jefferson and Madison reached Georgetown. After examining the area from the Eastern Branch to Great Falls, they held conversations with various landowners on the possibility of buying a modest acreage for the federal buildings. On October 12 the president returned to Georgetown, thereafter travelling nearly eighty miles to the Conococheague itself. Ostensibly he was looking at the Potomac River and its navigational problems but in reality he was giving a false scent as to the area where the capital might be placed. One of the few surviving records of the trip indicates that he was at Elizabethtown (Hagerstown) on October 20. Even in the wilderness he was given an address which was literate and felicitous. The citizens suggested that their village might be the capital of the United States:

> *We the inhabitants of Elizabeth Town... being deeply impressed with your illustrious character, and sensibly awake to your resplendent and innumerable virtues, hail you a hearty welcome.*
>
> *We are happy to find that, notwithstanding your perils, toils, and incessant cares and guardianship, you are still able to grant us this first, this greatest of all favors, your presence.*
>
> *We felicitate ourselves on your exploring our country—and, as you already reign in our hearts, we should think ourselves doubly blessed, could we have the honor to be included within your own especial command and jurisdiction—within the grand centre of virtues.*

While the record is lacking, it can be assumed that the one-time surveyor and town-planner of Alexandria also carefully studied the topography from Rock Creek to the Eastern Branch and Alexandria. Everyone in the area was inordinately curious as to the results but the president kept his counsel until he issued a proclamation in January.

MOUNT VERNON

Except for the Potomac trip, Washington was at Mount Vernon from about September 12 to November 22. He was still short of cash, for when Charles Carter sent a note asking for a loan, Washington replied that he himself had tried to borrow from "Mr. Carroll of Carrollton, as the most likely, being the most monied man I was acquainted with, but without success."

The Washingtons had a visitor shortly after their arrival, a cheerful young gourmet, Thomas Lee Shippen. He wrote his father who had served in the revolutionary army's medical service, that he had met "my two valuable friends Messrs. Jefferson and Madison on the eastern shore of Maryland... We waited all day for want of a boat to take us over, and I never knew two men more agreeable than they were. We talked and dined, and strolled, and rowed ourselves in boats, and feasted upon delicious crabs... Mann's Inn at Annapolis is certainly to be placed among the most excellent in the world. I never saw so fine a turtle or so well dressed a dish as he gave us [with] Old Madeira... to season it..."

On September 16 he wrote again to his father from Mount Vernon: "I have been here two days... I have been treated as usual with every most distinguished mark of kindness and attention. The President exercises it to a superlative degree... and Mrs. Washington is the very essence of kindness. Her soul seems to overflow with it and her happiness is in exact proportion to the number of objects upon which she can dispense her benefits."

The president had to work on a great many of his old headaches, which had arisen from his too amiable past acceptance of trustees and other duties. As executor he was still trying to settle the estate of a Captain Colville, who had died twenty-three years before, as well as the affairs of his stepson, Jack Custis, nine years dead. The longest-lived case was that of Colonel Joshua Fry, who had been killed in a fall from his horse thirty-six years before. Eighteen years later he obtained for Fry's heirs the land bounty promised by Dinwiddie. Washington had gone to considerable expense on this. He asked Benjamin Harrison, November 21, to see if he could collect the amount which had been due him for yet another eighteen years:

> It is a fact _well_ known to most of the Patentees that had it not been for my exertions and decided conduct, the proclamation of Governor Dinwiddie... would never have been recognized... If the Gentleman claiming under Joshua Fry Esquire inclines to pay what is justly due me, the enclosed list of balances, which is original... will show what my advances are for his proportion of the land. If he pays this sum with interest since the year 1772, when the patents issued were paid for, and the title

became perfect, it will be no more than what is due in <u>gratitude</u>, and to <u>justice</u>. If he inclines to pay the principal only, let him do it and the matter will be closed. Or, lastly, if he chuses to do neither, preferring to receive the patents without paying any thing, e'en then let them go forth, for I shall not appear in a Court of law for this…

Aside from routine correspondence with members of his cabinet, Washington concentrated heavily on his new house in Philadelphia. Here he was undoubtedly a trying husband, tenant, and chief, for he insisted on being his own interior decorator, builder, and steward. He had gone carefully over the Robert Morris house on his trip through Philadelphia. From then on numerous letters went off between September 5 and November 14 to Morris and Lear. His first letter to Lear assigned everyone his or her rooms:

First floor, two public rooms, and one for the upper servants.

Second floor, for Mrs. Washington, children and maids, leaving a small private dressing room and office for the President.

Third floor, one public room, one room for Mr. and Mrs. Lear, and two rooms for Washington's four to five male secretaries.

Garret, one room for the steward and wife, the rest for William and the other servants.

Over stable, assigned to groom and postilions.

Washington suggested building a back wing for a servants hall, with one or two rooms reserved for "servants who are coupled." In addition the smoke house might be more useful for servants than for smoking meat. Altogether some thirty people had to be squeezed in, while allowing some place for Washington to work and receive people. He asked Lear to see that his coach was repaired and ample firewood laid in. He wondered what to do with the washerwomen from New York who had families. He complained that the steward interfered with the cook's planning of meals; he thought she could make them "more tasty" if she had a freer hand.

Other letters followed. He reminded the Robert Morrises about putting in bow windows, getting the house painted, the back hall built, and the cow barn converted into stables. He was sorry it had to be done while they were still in the house. Washington was upset when Lear wrote from New York that people there had not commented too much on his moving into the house of the man everyone blamed for moving the capital to Philadelphia. Washington wrote back, in indignation, that the Philadelphia authorities had engaged the Morris house and he had had nothing to do with it. He worried further about the steward and his wife, feeling that their dining table was always as well loaded with liquors and fruits as his own. He had thought Samuel Fraunces (of Fraunces' Tavern) had been too expensive, but the new steward and his wife seemed even worse. He told Lear that he and Mrs. Morris had agreed to exchange mangles, since hers was already permanently attached in the house.

Lear, who had had to enter into extensive negotiations for the settlement of rent and other matters on the president's house in New York and to move eight servants and the president's furniture and fixtures to Philadelphia, was also instructed to look carefully into suitable schools for Washington's step-grandson, two nephews, and a niece. He was ordered to examine all the tradesmen in Philadelphia to find out where best to shop. On October 27 Washington acknowledged Lear's letters of October 6, 10, 14, and 17, the last two from Philadelphia advising the president he had arrived in good order. This caused the president to send up ample advice as to where to put each bit of furniture and all the ornaments. Washington added that he had not decided whether green or yellow curtains would look best in the hall.

By November 22 the president of the United States had assembled his wife, her two grandchildren, his secretaries and servants, carriage, and baggage wagons for a procession to Philadelphia. Four of the servants went by stage or boat, and the remainder, perhaps six, accompanied the Washingtons. A few miles below Baltimore, the president wrote an exasperated letter to Tobias Lear:

> *With some difficulty (from the most infamous roads that ever were seen) we have got to this place, and are waiting dinner; but have no expectation of reaching Baltimore to Night.*
>
> *Dunn has given such proofs of his want of skill in driving, that I find myself under the necessity of looking out for another Coachman. Before we got to Elizabeth Town we were obliged to take him from the coach and put him to the Waggon; this he turned over twice; and this Morning was much intoxicated. He has also got the Horses in a habit of stopping.*
>
> *Mrs. Washington's predilection for Jacob is as strong as my prejudices and fears are great. Yet in your enquiries after a Coachman ask something concerning Jacob. He wanted much it seems to return to us whilst we were in Philadelphia...*

Washington hurriedly sent the letter off by the regular stagecoach which was "at this instant starting." No time was lost by Lear and an assistant secretary.

They had an agreement prepared for another coachman, a Hessian, by the time the president reached the nation's new capital in November.

STATE OF THE UNION

Although the British had sent sufficient strength from Detroit to rout General Harmar on November 4 near the present Fort Wayne, the American commander had previously wrought great damage to the Miami villages. He destroyed the principal British trading posts of the area, three hundred loghouses and wigwams and many supplies. This show of strength was disturbing to the traders operating out of Detroit. The Indians looked to that fort for protection and support, and it was not going to be easy thereafter to maintain a policy of secret hostility to the United States, operating under a guise of friendship.

When Washington reached Philadelphia, no word had yet come of Harmar's defeat. He did have Morris' reports on the unwillingness of the British government to negotiate, and he well knew the extent of their support of Indian raids against the United States. He moved therefore to a stronger national policy in his brief address to Congress, December 8, on the State of the Union:

> *In meeting you again I feel much satisfaction in being able to repeat my congratulations on the favorable aspects which continue to distinguish our public Affairs. The abundant fruits of another year have blessed our country with plenty, and with the means of a flourishing commerce. The progress of public credit is witnessed by a considerable rise of American Stock abroad as well as at home and the revenues allotted for this and other national purposes have been productive beyond the calculations by which they were regulated...*

> *A loan of three million florins... has been completed in Holland...*

> *It has been heretofore known to Congress that frequent incursions have been made on our frontier settlements by certain banditti of Indians from the North West side of the Ohio. These, with some of the tribes dwelling on and near the Wabash, have of late been particularly active in their depredations; and being emboldened by the impunity of their crimes and aided by such parts of the neighboring tribes as could be seduced to join in the hostilities or afford them a retreat for their prisoners and plunder, they have, instead of listening to the humane overtures made on the part of the United States, renewed their violences with fresh alacrity and greater effect.*

The lives of a number of valuable citizens have thus been sacrificed, and some of them under circumstances peculiarly shocking; whilst others have been carried into a deplorable captivity.

I have accordingly authorized an expedition in which the regular troops in that quarter are combined with such drafts of Militia as were deemed sufficient. The event of the measure is yet unknown to me...

The disturbed situation of Europe, and particularly the critical posture of the great maritime powers, whilst it ought to make us more thankful for the general peace and security enjoyed by the United States, reminds us at the same time of the circumspection with which it becomes us to preserve these blessings. It requires also that we should not overlook the tendency of a war... to abridge the means of transporting our valuable productions to their proper markets. I recommend... such encouragements to our own Navigation as will render our commerce and agriculture less dependent on foreign bottoms...

The establishment of the Militia; of a mint; of Standards of weights and measures; of the Post Office and Post roads are subjects... which are abundantly urged by their own importance.

Lord Hawkesbury of the British Board of Trade, England's leading advocate of commercial and shipping restrictions against the United States, headed a committee on general policy towards this country. The preceding April 8 it had issued a secret report: "The Lords are of the opinion that, in a commercial view, it will be for the benefit of this country to prevent Vermont and Kentucky, from becoming dependent on the Government of the United States."

The president's message informed Congress that Kentucky had applied to be the fourteenth state. "The sentiments of warm attachment to the Union and its present Government, expressed by our fellow citizens of Kentucky, cannot fail to add an affectionate concern for their particular welfare..." There were some delays in forming a state constitution there. Vermont slipped in quietly as the fourteenth state in March 1791, and Kentucky became the fifteenth state in June 1792.

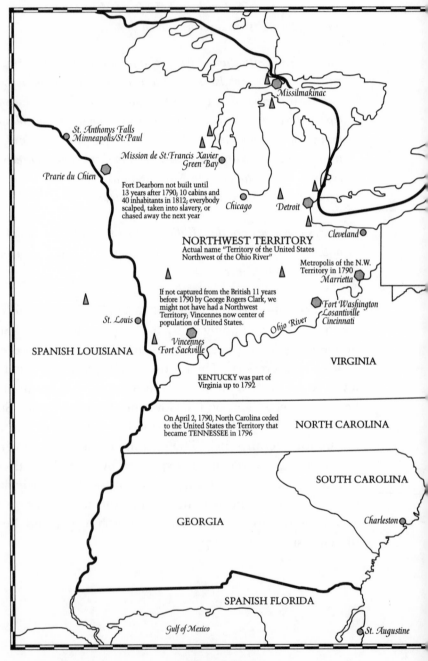

Missilmakinac

St. Anthonys Falls
Minneapolis/St.Paul

Mission de St.Francis Xavier
Green Bay

Prarie du Chien

Fort Dearborn not built until
13 years after 1790; 10 cabins and
40 inhabitants in 1812; everybody
scalped, taken into slavery, or
chased away the next year

Chicago

Detroit

Cleveland

NORTHWEST TERRITORY
Actual name "Territory of the United States
Northwest of the Ohio River"

Metropolis of the N.W.
Territory in 1790
Marrietta

If not captured from the British 11 years
before 1790 by George Rogers Clark, we
might not have had a Northwest
Territory; Vincennes now center of
population of United States.

Ohio River

Fort Washington
Losantiville
Cincinnati

St. Louis

Vincennes
Fort Sackville

SPANISH LOUISIANA

VIRGINIA

KENTUCKY was part of
Virginia up to 1792

On April 2, 1790, North Carolina ceded
to the United States the Territory that
became TENNESSEE in 1796

NORTH CAROLINA

SOUTH CAROLINA

GEORGIA

Charleston

SPANISH FLORIDA

Gulf of Mexico

St. Augustine

United States

CANADA

Quebec

Montreal

DISTRICT OF MAINE
Part of Massachusetts

NEW HAMPSHIRE

Vermont was part of
New York up to 1791

NEW YORK

Gloucester
Marblehead
Boston

MASSACHUSETTS

Providence
CONNECTICUT
Newport

PENNSYLVANIA

NEW JERSEY

New York City

— *Rhode Island and*
Providence Plantations

Philadelphia

MARYLAND

Baltimore

DELAWARE

Atlantic Ocean

——— *United States Boundary*

——— *State Boundaries*

◯ *Towns with* 1790 *population of* 5,000 *or more*

⬡ *Forts*

▲ *Indian Forts or Villages*

1790

EIGHT

PHILADELPHIA— THE OLD CAPITAL

1790–1791

T HE ELECTIONS THAT fall and winter provided a large turnover in
Congress. In the House of Representatives twenty-seven of the sixty-five
members were replaced. Five senators, some of whom had drawn only
a two-year term, retired, mostly involuntarily. Two of these were among the principal American contacts of Beckwith—Schuyler of New York and Johnson of
Connecticut. In informing Hamilton of Aaron Burr's election in place of his
father-in-law, James Tillary of New York wrote in January 1791: "[Burr] is
avowedly your enemy, & stands pledged to his party, for a reign of vindictive
declamation against your measures. The Chancellor [Robert Livingston] hates,
& would destroy you." Those who were retiring from office continued to vote
until March 4. The session accomplished much. On March 16 the president
gave David Humphreys in Europe a brief account of new legislation:

*Congress finished their session on the 3 of March, in the course of which they
received and granted the applications of Kentucky and Vermont for admission into
the Union; the former after August, 1792; and the latter immediately; they made
provision for the interest on the national debt, by laying a higher duty than that
which heretofore existed on spirituous liquors imported or manufactured; they
established a national Bank; they passed a law for certain measures to be taken
towards establishing a mint; and finished much other business of less importance,*

conducting on all occasions with great harmony and cordiality. In some few
instances, particularly in passing the law for higher duties mentioned above, and
more especially on the subject of the Bank, the line between the southern and eastern
interests appeared more strongly marked than could have been wished; the former
against and the latter in favor of these measures.

The tax on spirits, the foundation-stone of Hamilton's revenue system, was
extended to cover both imported and domestically manufactured spirits.
Even though the latter tax was small it was pretty unpopular, especially in the
western areas where government operations, state or local, were characteris-
tically limited.

Hamilton's proposal for a national bank, which passed the House by a wide
margin, brought a split between South and North, as well as the first open cabinet debate on the extent of federal powers under the Constitution.
Washington asked his three Virginia friends, Jefferson, Randolph, and
Madison, to give him their opinions. The first two provided written negative
legal opinions, and the third argued orally against the act. Madison, swinging
away from the positions he had taken in the *Federalist Papers,* declared in the
House that the Constitution was designed to protect the states by limiting the
power of the national government. The president, who had listened to all the
constitutional debates and had read the *Federalist Papers* with care, unhesitat-
ingly signed the bill into law two days later.

Because of the defeat of General Harmar and the continued Indian raids,
Congress at the end of the session voted to increase the standing army to
1,216 enlisted men. For economy's sake, their pay was cut from four to three
dollars a month. The president could get almost anything he really wanted
through Congress, except his unpopular militia proposals. He had asked for
a universal militia system, which had been used from the days of the first settlement. This was too much for Congress, which preferred a poorly paid small
army, which could enlist only society's dregs.

INDIANS

Washington, Jefferson, and Knox, in numerous memoranda and letters,
agreed that fair treatment of the Indians was a prerequisite for peaceful internal development. The new Constitution gave treaty-making powers to the federal government, which were considered to override all state and local laws.
The settled policy of the national government was to establish pacts with the
Indians under which white settlement was forbidden in Indian-held territories

and to license all trading with them. The aim was good in theory but difficult to enforce.

The Indians were divided into many tribes, ranging from the warlike and cannibal, to the gentle and domesticated. They were often at war with each other. Many were accustomed to migrating over hundreds of square miles, returning to small settlements in the winter. Hostile British and Spanish agents stirred many tribes to war. The state governments, often in opposition to the federal government, encouraged their citizens to extract land from the Indians. The frontiers were frequently overrun by criminals and unscrupulous American and British traders, who did not hesitate to murder Indians for gain. Innocent settlers were killed in retaliation. With a tiny army and a frontier stretching over 1,800 miles, policing was next to impossible.

Indian relations and treaty negotiations were under Knox's jurisdiction, thus giving the War Department an important voice in foreign policy. Here Washington, as he did with Europe, took a strong hand in all negotiations, especially when Indians came to see him in the capital.

Knox's extensive correspondence with Washington shows that Indian complaints of treaty violations or mistreatment were considered at length and seriously. The president signed letters to "Yockonahoma, great Medal Chief of Soonacoha, Yockehoopie, leading chief of Kaskooqua, Tobochoh, great Medal Chief of Congaltoo, Pooshemastubie, gorget Captain of Soungaro, and all the other medal and gorget Chiefs and Captains and Warriors of the Choctaw Nation" and to "Pearmingo, or the Mountain Leader, Head Warier and first Minister, and the other Chiefs and Warriors of the Chickasaw Nation." When the Senecas complained, Washington himself, after reading all the correspondence, speeches, and Knox's comments, wrote out a document of many pages which was signed by the president, the secretary of state, and the secretary of war:

> *The reply of the President of the United States, to the Speech of the Cornplanter, Half-town and Great-tree Chiefs and Counselors of the Seneka Nation of Indians.*
>
> *I the President of the United States, by my own mouth, and by a written Speech Signed with my own hand, and Sealed with the Seal of the United States, Speak to the Seneka nation, and desire their attention, and that they would keep this speech in remembrance of the friendship of the United States...*
>
> *I am not uninformed that the Six nations have been led into some difficulties with respect to the sale of their lands since the peace. But I must inform you that these arose before the present government of the United States was established, when the*

Separate States, and individuals under their authority, undertook to treat with the Indian tribes respecting the Sale of their lands.

But the case is now entirely altered—the general government only has the power to treat with the Indian nations...

Hear well, and let it be heard by every person in your nation, that the President of the United States declares that the general government considers itself bound to protect you in all the lands secured to you by the Treaty of Fort Stanwix...

It appears upon inquiry of the Governor of New York that John Livingston was not legally authorized to treat with you, and that everything he did with you has been declared null and void...

In the future you cannot be defrauded of your lands—you possess the right to sell, and the right of refusing to sell your lands...

When you may find it necessary to sell any part of your lands, the United States must be present by their agent, and will be your security that you shall not be defrauded...

The murders that have been committed upon some of your people, by the bad white men, I sincerely lament and reprobate...

The Senekas may be assured, that the rewards offered for apprehending the murderers will be continued until they are brought to trial...

The problem of frontier control was so difficult that friendly Christian Senecas were killed near Fort Pitt, while Cornplanter and the other chiefs were returning, by way of the fort, to their nation. Washington, Jefferson, and Knox were outraged. Cornplanter sent a pathetic letter to the president from Pittsburgh on March 17:

When we raised from the great Council of the thirteen fires, we mentioned that we meant to have a Council with the Chiefs of the bad angry Indians.

Father!

Your promise to me was, that you would keep all your people quiet—but since I came here I find that some of my people have been killed—the good, honest people who were here trading.

Father!

We hope you will not suffer all the good people to be killed; but your people are killing them as fast as they can...

Father!

Our father and ruler over all mankind, now speak and tell me, did you order these men to be killed?

Father!

Our word is pledged to you that we would endeavor to make peace with all the warrior nations—If we cannot do it, do not blame us—You struck the innocent men first—we hope you will not blame us, as your people have first broke good rules, but as for our people they are friendly and as firm as ever.

Father!

We must now acquaint you with the man's name who did this murder at Beaver Creek—Samuel Brady, formerly a captain in your army, and under your command—also a Balden...

The murders aroused anger among all the Indians, friendly, neutral, and hostile, as well as great anxiety among the settlers.

Some hostile Indians attacked whites who, in retaliation, struck back at friendly Indians, nearly killing Cornplanter in the process. From Knox's reports it appears that Brady, the original murderer, was rounded up by the Pennsylvania authorities and tried but acquitted. Federal troops scheduled to take part against the Indians under British control soon reached Pittsburgh and restored some sort of order.

Washington summed up the situation to Tobias Lear on April 3: "Until we can restrain the turbulence and disorderly conduct of our borders it will be in vain I fear to expect peace with the Indians, or that they will govern their own people better than we do ours." The following day he complained to Hamilton not only about disorderly frontier people but of the work of land speculators, as well as interferences by the state governments in Indian affairs. What was particularly awkward was that he had been negotiating to have the aid of the six nations against the hostile Indians north of the Ohio. The actions of a few frontier desperadoes might set all Indians raging against the Americans. When he wrote to Knox to approve the measures he was taking to protect Cornplanter and the friendly tribes, he also wrote Jefferson from Mount Vernon on April 4:

You will readily agree with me that the best interests of the United States require such intimation to be made to the Governor of Canada, either directly or indirectly, as may produce instructions to prevent the Indians receiving military aid or supplies from the British posts or garrisons. The notoriety of this assistance has already been such as renders inquiry into particulars unnecessary. Colonel Beckwith seems peculiarly designed to be the channel of an indirect intimation... I wish it may be suggested... that certain information has been received of large supplies of ammunition being delivered to the hostile Indians, from British posts, about the commencement of last campaign. And, as the United States have no other view in prosecuting the present war against the Indians, than, in the failure of negotiation, to procure by arms, peace and safety to the inhabitants of their frontier, they are equally surprised and disappointed at such an interference by the servants or subjects of a foreign State... as seems intended to protract the attainment of so just and reasonable an object.

Washington had appointed Arthur St. Clair, governor of the Northwest Territory, as major general in command of the American army. He made Major General Richard Butler commander of the six-months' levies, and Brigadier Charles Scott head of the militia. Knox was ordered to raise sufficient auxiliary troops for St. Clair to undertake an expedition against hostile Indians in the Northwest Territory. Because Congress did not approve an increase in the army until March 3, the force was exceedingly slow in being organized. In the meantime, during the spring and summer, Knox received many reports of the continuing activities of Simon Girty, a notorious renegade white, Alexander McKee, the British deputy Indian commissioner, and Joseph Brant, the Mohawk chief who had participated in the Cherry Valley massacre. Their names struck terror into the hearts of peaceful settlers as well as of peaceful Indians.

THE FEDERAL CITY

Immediately after New Year's Day 1791, the president and the secretary of state went over the measurements which Washington had taken along the Potomac and his initial plans for the federal district. On January 24 the president proclaimed the new federal territory, extending from Georgetown to the Eastern Branch of the Potomac. He noted that the latter boundary was to be temporary until Congress passed additional legislation, permitting him to extend it to Alexandria. In forwarding his proclamation to William Deakins and Benjamin Stoddert of Georgetown, Washington asked them to give it wide publicity. The president, at the same time, appointed Thomas Johnson and Daniel Carroll of Maryland, and David Stuart of Virginia, as the first commissioners of the district, along with Andrew Ellicott as surveyor.

To get cheap initial land for the federal buildings and to foil speculators, the president displayed some of his old military skill at moves to deceive. Maryland and Virginia had guaranteed initial funds of $192,000 for the federal capital. With this as a reserve, the president asked Deakins and Stoddert to ascertain, "in the most perfect secrecy," how much land they could purchase in their own name for federal use. Washington said that his mind was perfectly balanced between Carrollsburg and "the lands on the river, below and adjacent to Georgetown." Deakins and Stoddert were to investigate the prices of various parcels but always to stipulate that no final decision could be made for two weeks. This would give them time to consult the president. He also suggested his particular interest in the property of David Burnes, along the Potomac, on which the president's house was eventually placed.

On March 2 Washington instructed Pierre-Charles L'Enfant, artist-engineer, to lay out plans for the public buildings between the Potomac River and the road from Georgetown to the Eastern Branch. To divert attention from the land to the west, L'Enfant was instructed to begin his work to the east. Not long afterwards, Thomas Jefferson handed the president his own sketch of a proposed capital, which was considerably cruder than the plan for Alexandria, which Washington had drawn at the age of seventeen. Jefferson scrunched the government buildings into an area of less than three hundred acres, adding the outline of a town perhaps four times as large.

When the president reached Georgetown on March 28, he saw L'Enfant who, eleven days later, wrote to Hamilton to describe his joy at what had happened. L'Enfant said he was always being accused of wanting to do more than his instructions permitted. Looking over the federal district, he had done this "without compunction," surveying the entire area. When the president arrived, he suggested having it all for the capital "and was fortunate enough to see it meet with his approbation." Washington then directed him "to delineate a grand and general plan" and to have it ready by the time he returned in June. Washington's diary continued the story; he described his meeting with the competing groups of land owners:

> *Finding the interests of the Landholders about Georgetown and those about Carrollburg much at variance... I requested them to meet me at six o'clock this afternoon at my lodgings...*

> *To this meeting I represented that the contention in which they seemed engaged, did*

*not in my opinion comport either with the public interest or that of their own...
That neither the offer from Georgetown or Carrollburg, separately, was adequate to
the end of insuring the object. That both together did not comprehend more ground
nor would afford greater means than was required for the federal City; and that,
instead of contending which of the two should have it they had better, by combining
more offers make a common cause of it, and thereby secure it to the district; other
arguments were used to show the danger which might arise from delay and the good
effects that might proceed from a Union...*

*The parties to whom I addressed myself yesterday evening, having taken the matter
into consideration saw the propriety of my observations... and therefore mutually
agreed and entered into articles to surrender for public purposes, one half of the
land they severally possessed within bounds which were designated as necessary for
the City...*

*The business being thus happily finished and some directions given to the
Commissioners, the Surveyor and Engineer... I left Georgetown, dined in
Alexandria, and reached Mount Vernon in the evening.*

At Georgetown, "on the thirtieth day of March in the year of our Lord 1791
and the independence of the United States the fifteenth," the president
signed the proclamation extending the federal district to its full hundred
square miles. Alexandria, Hamburg, Georgetown, and Carrollburg were now
within the new territory. On April 4 he formally directed L'Enfant to plan a
new city for the more than ten square miles between Rock Creek and the
Eastern Branch. In forwarding the proclamation to the secretary of state,
Washington said that he had persuaded the owners, "even the obstinate Mr.
Burnes," to make all the land available, on condition that it be planned as a
city. He had asked L'Enfant to design the capital, to locate the proposed federal buildings, and to lay out lots and streets. Under his agreement with the
landholders, they were to own every other lot, alternately with the government, and to provide land for streets free of cost. Lands needed for public
purposes could be purchased for $71.50 an acre.

His April 8 letter to Hamilton indicated that L'Enfant had begun work at
once on the area which he described as "a most eligible one for to fix upon the
capital of this extensive empire." He found it extremely fatiguing "surveying at
so improper a season of the year." The area itself was a wilderness of forests and
mud, streams and swamps, with small areas of cleared farmland. Nonetheless he
persisted and in less than three months had ready an imaginative design for a
great capital of the future. He broke up the normal rectangles of planned

American towns, by diagonal avenues, intended to add variety, as well as to give more rapid access from one part of the city to another. Included was his "grand avenue," subsequently named for Pennsylvania, which swept from the Eastern Branch to Georgetown. On it he placed the Capitol, atop Jenkin's Hill, and the president's house, at the Burnes farm. L'Enfant had been at the siege of Savannah. Probably influenced by that city's design, he subsequently added fifteen rectangles or squares, one for each state, to provide a further attractive form for the capital.

A draft plan and description was ready for the president on June 22. On June 28 Washington, L'Enfant, and Andrew Ellicott rode from Georgetown to examine the area and determine the final location of the two principal government buildings. Washington approved as perfect L'Enfant's choice for the capitol but he moved the president's residence to a higher nearby point. He seems subsequently to have reduced the number of avenues and to have suggested the addition of a public market. Then, recognizing the grandeur of L'Enfant's design, he gave it enthusiastic approval. The capital was thus designed and on its way within a year of the congressional vote.

While Washington was in the south, various landholders had second thoughts and some refused to part with their land. It took only brief persuasion by Washington to see they might spoil everything. Pennsylvania, alarmed about the capital's move from Philadelphia, had introduced a bill to build a capitol and president's house in Philadelphia. Washington wrote in his diary: "They readily waived their objections and agreed to convey to the utmost extent of what was required." When all the deeds had been signed on June 29, Washington showed them L'Enfant's plan for the city, noting certain expected changes in it. He wrote: "It was with much pleasure that a general approbation of the measure seemed to pervade the whole."

On September 8 the district commissioners, at a meeting attended by Jefferson and Madison, named the capital the city of Washington, and the district, the territory of Columbia.

THE SOUTHERN TOUR

The president left Philadelphia on March 20 for a planned absence of about three-and-a-half months in the southern states, a trip which would include his work on the national capital. Accompanying him were his secretary, Major Jackson; five servants; eleven horses; and a chariot and baggage wagon. Although the roads south of Philadelphia were poor and rutted, the procession encountered no trouble until it tried to cross the Chesapeake Bay by the Rock

Hall ferry four days later. A great part of the day was spent loading two boats. The president wrote:

> *Unluckily, embarking on board of a borrowed Boat because she was the largest, I was in imminent danger, from the unskillfulness of the hands, and the dullness of her sailing, added to the darkness and the storminess of the night. For two hours after we hoisted Sail, the wind was light and ahead, the next hour was a stark calm, after which the wind sprung up at [Southeast] and increased until it blew a gale. About which time, and after 8 o'clock P.M., we made the mouth of Severn River (leading up to Annapolis) but the ignorance of the People on board with respect to the navigation of it, ran us aground, first on [Greenberry] point from which with much exertion and difficulty we got off; and then, having no knowledge of the Channel and the night being immensely dark with heavy and variable squalls of wind, constant lightning and tremendous thunder, we soon grounded again on what is called Horne's Point where, finding all efforts in vain, and not knowing where we were, we remained, not knowing what might happen, till morning.*

The president described his rescue in his diary of March 25: "Having lain all night in my Great Coat and Boots, in a berth not long enough for me by the head, or much cramped, we found ourselves in the morning within about one mile off Annapolis and still fast aground. Whilst we were preparing our small boat in order to land in it, a sailing Boat came to our assistance, in which with the baggage I had on board I landed" to a fifteen-gun salute.

The governor of Maryland, John Eager Howard, had attempted the preceding night to meet the president on his passage across the bay but was driven back by the weather and spent an anxious night wondering about the president's safety. Howard met Washington as soon as he arrived at Mann's Inn, where young Shippen had so much enjoyed his turtle. The governor took him to see St. John's College, with its eighty students, and then back to a public dinner at the inn. The following day the president dined at the governor's house and then attended a dancing assembly in the evening. On the 27th, the president left for Georgetown and discussions on the capital. On March 31 he reached Mount Vernon.

After looking over his farms for a week, the president departed for the south on April 7. Almost immediately he encountered a further unpleasant experience with eighteenth-century travel:

> *In attempting to cross the ferry at Colchester, with the four horses hitched to the Chariot, by the neglect of the person who stood before them, one of the leaders got overboard when the boat was in swimming water and 50 yards from the shore—*

with much difficulty he escaped drowning before he could be disengaged. His struggling frightened the others in such a manner that one after another and in quick succession they all got overboard, harnessed and fastened as they were, and with the utmost difficulty they were saved, and the Carriage escaped being dragged after them... Providentially, indeed miraculously, by the exertions of people who went off in boats and jumped into the River... no damaged was sustained.

Richmond was illuminated the night of April 11 in honor of the president. Washington inspected the canal, sluices, and locks of the James River Canal Company, which he had been instrumental in forming. He took time to sound out Edward Carrington, federal marshal for the state, as well as others, on the political sentiment of Virginia. He was assured that the violent opposition in the Virginia Assembly to the assumption of state debts and to the tax on domestic spirits, was not representative of what the people of the state felt. In general they were very favorably disposed to the federal government but they needed more explanations of the measures, in order to support them.

Washington was accompanied from Richmond to Petersburg by large parties on horseback, intending to do honor to the president of the United States. They succeeded in enveloping him the whole way in clouds of choking dust. He found that more escorts were eagerly waiting to do the same thing south of Petersburg. When they asked him what time he planned to leave in the morning, the president replied that he "should endeavor to do it before eight o'clock; but I did it a little after five, by which means I avoided the inconveniences above mentioned."

While circling from Virginia to Georgia and back, Washington repeatedly commented on the poorness of the soils, region, roads, and inns. The trip was often as rough as his frontier travels. By the time he got to North Carolina, violent spring rains had turned the dusty roads not to mud, but "water, so level are the roads." The inns he encountered were so dirty and disagreeable that he had to travel as far as Halifax to find a place where he could stay.

As he travelled farther south in North Carolina, he observed the first cotton as well as flax and the usual corn. He was a fascinated observer of tarrolling into barrels at Tarboro and Greenville. At New Bern, then the state capital, Washington had "good" lodgings. He attended a ball "at which there were abt. 70 ladies," at the governor's old palace, "a good brick building but now hastening to Ruins."

After New Bern Washington recorded that the inns were "indifferent" (his category for third-class), while the road from New Bern to Wilmington "passes through the most barren country I ever beheld." At Wilmington he had "very good" accommodations, his rare superlative. The town had "some good houses pretty compactly built." He examined the port which exported tobacco, corn, rice, flax seed, and pork. He attended a ball "at which there were 62 ladies—illuminations, Bonfires, etc."

Even indifferent inns disappeared as the president moved into South Carolina, where he was forced to accept private hospitality. The rice plantation of William Alston on the Waccamaw River was an oasis. Washington wrote: "His house which is large, new and elegantly furnished, stands on a sand hill, high for the Country, with his Rice fields below; the contrast of which with the lands back of it, and the Sand and piney barrens through which we had passed is scarcely to be conceived." At Alston's house he met Generals William Washington, a distant cousin, and William Moultrie, who had been famous in southern battles.

Washington travelled on to Georgetown where, he noted, many of the houses had been burned by the British. The town gave him a public dinner in the open and he then proceeded to a tea party with "50 ladies." Washington was further entertained at other plantations on his way to Charleston. That city, the most sophisticated in the south, had been looking forward with all the ardor of Boston to the president's visit but with much more careful preparations. He was met at Haddrel's Point by various officials who had come to get him "in a 12 oared barge rowed by 12 American Captains of Ships, most elegantly dressed. There were a great number of other Boats with Gentlemen and ladies in them; two Boats with Music; all of whom attended me across, and on the passage were met by a number of others. As we approached the town a salute with artillery commenced, and at the Wharf I was met by the Governor, the Lt. Governor... the two Senators of the State, Wardens of the City, Cincinnati, etc. and conducted to the Exchange where they passed by in procession; from thence I was conducted in like manner to my lodgings, after which I dined at the Governors (in what he called a private way) with 15 or 18 Gentlemen." His lodgings, in a fine old Charleston house, he pronounced "very good."

Washington stayed a full week in the city and thoroughly enjoyed it. On his second day he "was visited about 2 o'clock, by a great number of the most respectable ladies of Charleston—the first honor of the kind I had ever experienced and it was as flattering as it was singular." The following evening he went "to a very elegant dancing Assembly at the Exchange, at which were 256 elegantly dressed and handsome ladies." Washington failed to note in his diary that all the ladies wore ribbons with such legends as "Long live the President." The following evening he attended a concert, "at which there were at least 400 ladies, the number and appearance of which exceeded anything of the kind I had ever seen." Next night he danced at another ball at the governor's house "where there was a select Company of ladies." In their head-dresses were pictures of Washington or other references to him.

The president did not spend all his time dancing. He examined the fortifications of Charleston. In commenting on the 1780 battle in which Lincoln was captured, Washington thought that "the defense was noble and honorable, altho' the measure was undertaken upon wrong principles and impolitic." He visited the boys' orphan asylum, twice attended church services, rode through the town on horseback, found himself charmed by the view from Saint Michael's steeple, "the Gardens and green trees... adding much to the beauty of the prospect." He noted many good houses of brick or wood. "The inhabitants are wealthy, Gay and hospitable; appear happy and satisfied with the General Government." He wrote that Charleston's rice exports ranged from 80,000 to 120,000 barrels and tobacco from 5,000 to 8,000 hogsheads.

Savannah, much smaller than Charleston, had done its best to honor Washington, sending eight ships' captains to row him down the Savannah River. On his way he stopped to call on the widow of Nathanael Greene. Savannah was illuminated in his honor. On Friday, May 13, he attended "a dancing Assembly, at which there was about one hundred well-dressed and handsome ladies." There was a public dinner, attended by two hundred people, and fireworks. He inspected the defenses of Savannah, already largely obliterated, which made it impossible for him to judge how well d'Estaing and Lincoln had performed. The ladies of the town made a call on him after church on Sunday. He found walking in Savannah disagreeable because of the sand which filled the houses with dust when the wind blew. Three sides of the town were completely occupied by rice fields. Washington wrote that the principal exports were rice, tobacco, lumber, indigo, hemp, and cotton.

At Augusta, Georgia, a town described by the president as "well-laid out with wide and spacious streets," he was met by the governor, Edward Telfair, and the principal state officers. After dining at the governor's, he took "tea with many well-dressed ladies." The following day the citizens of the town gave a public dinner at the courthouse and, in the evening, Washington attended a ball "at the Academy." The following day he examined "the Ruins or rather small Remnant of the Works which had been erected by the British during the War and taken by the Americans." That same day he dined privately with the governor.

As he travelled north, Washington was rather depressed by the land, after the more luxuriant seacoast. "The whole Road [to Columbia, South Carolina]... is a pine barren of the worst sort, being hilly as well as poor. This circumstance added to the distance, length of the stages, want of water and heat of the day, foundered one of my horses very badly." Between Columbia and Camden lay "the most miserable pine barren I ever saw."

North of Camden Washington examined the areas where Greene fought Rawdon and Gates was beaten by Cornwallis. Of the former skirmish he wrote: "The ground had just been taken by [Greene] was well chosen, but he [was] not well established in it before he was attacked; which by capturing a Videt was, in some measure by surprise." On the latter he added: "As this was a night meeting of both Armies on their march, and altogether unexpected, each formed on the ground they met without any advantage in it on either side, it being level and open. Had Genl. Gates been 1/2 a mile further advanced, an impenetrable Swamp would have prevented the attack, which was made on him by the British Army, and afforded him time to have formed his owns plans, but having no information of Lord Cornwallis's designs, and perhaps not being apprised of this advantage it was not seized by him."

Not until Washington neared Charlotte, North Carolina, did the lands begin to lose their sandy appearance and "to assume a very rich look." Beyond Charlotte he noted the first meadows he had seen since he quit Virginia.

Washington was charmed by "the small but neat village" of Salem, North Carolina, a Moravian settlement. As he neared the town, according to its annals, he was serenaded with melodies, "played partly by trumpets and French horns, partly by trombones." Washington greeted everyone, as he always did, very affably, but the people were pleased that he was particularly attentive to the children who had come to see him. At dinner he said he would like some more music with his meal and this was quickly provided. The following evening he heard choral singing and instrumental music. He spent one more day in Salem than he had planned, partly to meet the governor of the state, but perhaps also because he enjoyed it so much.

Governor Martin of North Carolina confirmed what Washington had heard in Virginia, South Carolina, and Georgia. Opposition to the federal government was rapidly disappearing. Governor Martin supported, as did the governor of Georgia, the federal policy of peace and fair dealings with the Indians. This was of importance because both states bordered on Indian country. Washington later noted that, in his southern conversations, he found little opposition to the tax on domestic spirits, while almost no one had even mentioned the national bank act, which split his cabinet.

As soon as Washington crossed the Virginia line he summarized his none-too-enthusiastic impressions of southern conditions. His travels had taken him over more than 1,000 miles of North and South Carolina and Georgia. "Excepting the Towns (and some Gentlemens Seats along the Road from Charleston to Savannah) there is not within the view of the whole road... a single house which has anything of an elegant appearance... The accommodations... we found extremely indifferent... It is not easy to say on which road—the one I went or the one I came—the entertainment is most indifferent—but with truth it may be affirmed that both are bad."

Washington noted how much poor soil there was just inland from the sea, when it became "dead level and badly watered." In the low country, drainage and irrigation had made the soil productive for rice. Some land there was priced as high as $225 an acre whereas nearby piney soil sold for $1 an acre. Above the fall lines, land was often superior and capable of growing corn, tobacco, wheat, and hemp. In general, interior farms were too far from profitable markets. He thought inland water navigation could be widely developed at little cost. The rivers were great, with extensive lateral tributaries. The falls were low and easily bypassed by canals. With these, corn, tobacco, indigo, hemp, tar, pitch, timber, and other local products could be floated cheaply to market.

As Washington moved further north he noted that land and houses improved and the settlements were thicker. It took him a week to travel across Virginia to Mount Vernon. Next day, June 13, he dropped a note to Hamilton to say that his 1,700-mile trip had been uninterrupted by accidents, sickness, or bad weather. He had allowed eight days extra for "casualties," but he had not needed a single one of them. He planned to use the saved time to look over his farms.

In those happier days, the secretary of state had written the president on May 8: "The last week does not furnish one single public event worthy of communicating to you: so that I have only to say 'all is well.'" A week later Jefferson said: "We are still without any occurrence foreign or domestic worth mentioning to you."

Washington cleaned up a lot of business at Mount Vernon, left enough detailed written instructions to keep the whole staff at work till the snow fell, then set off for Georgetown to complete the business of the national capital. Still interested in seeing more, he decided to veer off into western Maryland and the Pennsylvania Dutch country. On June 30 he left Georgetown at 4 A.M. for Frederick, Maryland, covering the forty-three miles by sundown. The unexpected arrival of the president put the town into a frenzy. Citizens raced to ring the church bells and to load cannon. A band was hastily assembled to serenade him. The people asked if he could stay two days but he said he had to leave in the morning. Frederick managed to produce an address before he left, which they delivered practically at dawn, for the president set out at 7 A.M. for York, Pennsylvania.

As Washington moved north across Maryland and Pennsylvania, the contrast with the three southernmost states grew ever sharper. The president noted that, from Georgetown to Frederick, the soil was "rich and fine, the Country is

thicker settled and the farm Houses of a better kind than I expected to find."
North of Frederick "the lands... are remarkably fine... The farm houses are
good mostly of stone and the settlers compact, with good Barns and meadows."
He thought Hanover "a very pretty village with a number of good brick
houses... The country is exceedingly pleasant... The Country from York to
Lancaster is very fine, thick-settled, and well cultivated. About the ferry they are
extremely rich—the river Susquehanna at this place is more than a mile wide
with some pretty views on the banks of it."

Washington attended the Dutch Reformed Church, July 3, commenting
that as the sermon was "in a language not a word of which I understood, I was
in no danger of becoming a proselyte." The following day he celebrated
Independence Day with the good German people of Lancaster. By July 6 he
was back in Philadelphia. On July 28 he wrote a brief but cheerful account of
his trip to Gouverneur Morris: "In my late tour through the Southern States,
I experienced great satisfaction in seeing the good effects of the general government in that part of the Union... The Farmer, the Merchant and the
Mechanic have seen their several interests attended to, and from thence they
unite in placing a confidence in their representatives... Two or three years of
good crops, and a ready market for the produce of their lands, has put everyone in good humor; and, in some instances, they even impute to the government what is due only to the goodness of Providence."

CENSUS

In writing Morris, Washington corrected an earlier estimate he had sent him
of the population of the United States. "The estimate was then founded on
the ideas held out by the Gentlemen in Congress of the population of their
several States, each of whom, looking thro' a magnifying glass, would speak of
the greatest extent, to which there was any probability of their numbers reaching." He now indicated that the population would be just short of four million
but, as he had learned on his trip, many census officials had been negligent
in their counting, some people refused to report, thinking it was to be a base
for taxation, while others expressed some religious scruples against being
numbered. Europe, the president said, had always assumed that America had
a much smaller population. Now they might give her somewhat more weight
in the international scale.[*]

---

[*] These are rather rough estimates of the 1790 population of the main European powers:
Great Britain and Ireland, 14 million; France, 25 million; and Spain, 10 1/2 million.

AFFAIRS OF THE STATE

With the president being away from the capital for much of the first half of 1791, other founding fathers used the time to build up trouble for themselves and, subsequently, for Washington. Adams had been squelched by the Senate at its beginning. It consisted of only twenty-two members in its opening session. Not infrequently divided evenly, the vice-president cast the deciding vote, thereby always annoying eleven senators. Largely condemned to silence in his presiding role, the vice-president began writing for the newspapers. His long-winded "Discources on Davila," printed by the *Pennsylvania Gazette,* took a few critical flings at the French Revolution and the doctrine that one man was as good as another. Adams suddenly found himself the center of outraged cries that he, who had been so long at the Court of St. James', was a monarchist, aristocrat, and a hater of his own as well as the French Revolution. Adams complained that no one bothered to read what he had actually said.

It is not clear whether Jefferson's emotional reactions to events preceded or followed his migraine headaches. He had such headaches in May and may have had them in April. About April 5 he received Washington's plans for a great federal city, implying his faith in a strong national government. His own small plan was given short shrift. His July 10 letter to Monroe, flailing at "the federal town" and "certain schemes of manufactures," indicates that he was more upset than he indicated at the time. Not long afterwards, he began to fire at the leading figures of the government, omitting, in the initial stages, the president.

In late April or early May, having borrowed a copy of Thomas Paine's *Rights of Man,* which denounced Edmund Burke for attacking France and its revolution, Jefferson forwarded it, as requested, to the brother of a waiting printer. With it, he sent a note, welcoming its publication, adding a swipe at Adams' "political Heresies." The printer used this in his preface, joining to it praise of Jefferson. As a result of the ensuing uproar, the secretary of state wrote to the president to say that he was distressed that his letter had been used without permission. He himself was a good friend of Adams, in spite of his "apostasy to hereditary monarchy and nobility." In a polite letter to Adams, Jefferson explained how the situation had arisen. Adams met him openly, declaring that Jefferson was "wholly mistaken" as to the views ascribed to him. Jefferson then wrote Adams that he had not even had him in mind, a statement in direct contradiction to his letter to Washington.

Not long afterwards Jefferson and Madison went north to New York and New England, a trip which temporarily relieved Jefferson's headaches. Fortified by their belief in the extent of Virginia's sour opposition to many of the president's policies, the pair held conversations with leaders of similar thought in New York—George Clinton, Aaron Burr, and Robert Livingston. They also met with Philip Freneau, Madison's Princeton classmate. Leaving Madison in New York, Jefferson proceeded to Philadelphia. On July 10 he informed Madison that he proposed to "press on the President" the nomination of Paine, who had become a citizen of France, to be postmaster general of the United States. In August Freneau appeared in Philadelphia as translator for the Department of State. Along with this duty he edited the *National Gazette*, which was eventually to attack the president with fierce invectives. By July 28 Jefferson had added the names of the chief justice and the secretaries of the treasury and war, as plotting with Adams to overturn the government and Constitution, in order to have a king of America.

In the meantime Alexander Hamilton was engaged in actions and conversations of so complex a nature that they require a historian to unravel, nearly eighty-eight pages, much of it in fine print. These involved the apparent fabrication of documents by the secretary of the treasury.

RELATIONS WITH GREAT BRITAIN

Major Beckwith showed up in Philadelphia, not long after the government began its operations there. He settled into the same boarding house as Madison. This worried Jefferson who asked Madison to come and share his quarters. Beckwith also attended, quite freely, the president's receptions. He caused quite a lot of talk in New York and Philadelphia, because Sir John Temple, British counsel, wrote in April 1791 to the British foreign secretary: "Lord Dorchester has had one of his aides de Camp here and at Philadelphia, for the year past. The status of this Person about Congress hath indeed disgusted not a few who heretofore leaned towards Great Britain. An envoy, they say, from a Colony Governor… He can be considered in no other light than as a petty Spy!"

On the American side, the initial congressional bills for discrimination against British vessels had been a simple retaliation for Great Britain's restrictive practices. Washington's proposals, however, while they involved some of the same principles, had a far higher aim—the need to have an adequate merchant marine and fishing fleet for the national economy, as well as for the country's security. Senate and House had replied to the president that they would be prepared to support his requests with the necessary funds. Not long afterwards the president forwarded to Congress the correspondence of Gouverneur Morris with the British cabinet. His letter noted that the British government had declared "without scruple" that it did not mean to adhere to the treaty which it had signed.

Beckwith protested vigorously to Hamilton on February 16 that the president's messages had shown a French bias, they would prevent England from sending a minister to the United States, and they would check the "growing friendship" of Great Britain. Hamilton heard him without, as far as can be determined, raising a defense of the president. In private conversations in Philadelphia Beckwith declared that the trade of the United States was of no importance to Great Britain, a view which undoubtedly horrified the commercially minded British government when it reached London. The United States was, in fact, Britain's largest customer; British exports to the United States more than doubled from 1789 to 1791.

Beckwith's report to London on March 11 contained an appraisal of Washington and Jefferson:

> *The talents of General Washington are greatly overrated in the world. His public reputation has hitherto been supported by reserve, caution, temper, firmness, and a plain understanding, with a good choice of men around him; his present high station has lately become extremely embarrassing from a difference in the political opinion of the officers at the head of the executive departments... The great point of difference is on an English and a French connection; the gentleman at the head of the former, conceives the best interests of this country will be greatly promoted by a solid and permanent friendship with Great Britain... Mr. Jefferson is at the head of the latter, he is blindly devoted to a French interest... There are no lengths in his power to which he will not go to favor the interests of that kingdom.*

Beckwith's messages conveyed unintended warnings. Britain's carefully cherished commerce was being carelessly tossed around by a soldier-spy. There was also a growing danger in American commercial policy, which called for a diplomat rather than a soldier. The British government, not long after the receipt of Beckwith's dispatches, recalled George Hammond from the British Embassy at Madrid. He was ordered to proceed to Philadelphia as his majesty's minister. Washington and Jefferson had scored a first point.

Beckwith did not learn for some time of the British decision to establish a legation. He continued to try to influence policy, notably by suggesting to Hamilton a British "mediation" with the Indians. In essence, though it was not explained as such, the British would control the Indians west of the Ohio if Americans promised to stay out of this part of their territory. This proposal was too much even for Hamilton. He informed Beckwith that it was "inadmissible, and I could not submit such a paper to the President's consideration."

Though the British continued to refer such suggestions to Hamilton over the years, he was unshakable in his view that the United States was sovereign in the Northwest Territory. Beckwith, nonetheless, in further conversations with Hamilton in June and July attempted to persuade the secretary that the British government had nothing to do with the hostility of the Indians. Beckwith also protested against a law of Congress which located the new customs office for Vermont at Alburg, north of the British fortification which still existed in that state. Beckwith's last act, before leaving for London, was to forward to Hamilton a copy of an August 15 speech of Lord Dorchester to the Indians, which was supposed to indicate the pacific intentions of the British. In those parts which have been here underscored, they were quite to the contrary:

> When the King made peace and gave independence to the United States, he made a treaty in which he marked out a line between him and them... This line, which the King then marked out between him and the States, _even supposing the treaty had taken effect_, could never have prejudiced your rights. Brothers, the King's rights with respect to your territory were against the nations of Europe; these he resigned to the States. But the King never had any rights against you...

Dorchester's speech had been made to a group of confederated Indians at Quebec about six weeks after the British held extensive negotiations with them at the Maumee Rapids. That conference took an initial step towards the establishment of an extensive Indian buffer state. With no intended humor, the British government that winter, and the following spring, issued instructions and decrees for America, as though 1776 had never happened. They organized, on paper, a territory under British control, which was to cover the present states of Ohio, Indiana, Illinois, Michigan, parts of Minnesota, Vermont, and Pennsylvania, and nearly half of New York State.

FRENCH DEVELOPMENTS

Lafayette, not yet thirty, had taken the lead in the early stages of the French Revolution. As a member of the 1787 Assembly of Notables, he issued a call for the first French National Assembly. In 1789, as vice-president of the assembly, he secured passage of the Declaration of the Rights of Man. On March 17, 1790, he sent to Washington "a picture of the Bastille just as it looked a few days after I had ordered its demolition, with the main key of that fortress of despotism. It is a tribute which I owe... as a Missionary of Liberty to its Patriarch."

Lafayette was made head of the National Guard of Paris the day after the

Bastille fell. Shortly afterwards he designed the tricolore cockade of liberty. He subsequently rescued the queen from the Paris mobs and attempted to prevent the flight of the king and queen in 1791. Lafayette hoped to give France liberty and greater equality with orderly constitutional changes. As the Jacobin terror gained momentum, the moderate and liberal forces were swept aside. Lafayette himself, the following year, was declared an enemy to liberty and forced into exile.

The president and the secretary of state were warm in their sympathies with France but they viewed developments with different eyes. Washington, who had seen so much bloodshed, watched what was unfolding in France with realism and increasing apprehension. Jefferson gazed at the terror with equanimity and even joy. On the basis of almost the same information as Jefferson had, Washington wrote to Lafayette on July 24, 1791:

> *To a philanthropic mind, the happiness of 24 million [French] people cannot be indifferent... We must place a confidence in Providence... that right will ultimately be established. The tumultuous populace of large cities are ever to be dreaded. Their indiscriminate violence prostrates for the time all public authority, and its consequences are sometimes extensive and terrible. In Paris we may suppose these tumults are peculiarly disastrous at this time, when the public mind is in a ferment and when (as is always the case on such occasions) there are not wanting wicked and designing men, whose element is confusion, and who will not hesitate in destroying the public tranquillity to gain a favorite point. But until your Constitution is fixed, your government organized, and your representative Body organized, much tranquillity cannot be expected; for, until these things are done, those who are unfriendly to the revolution, will not quit the hope of bringing matters back to their former state.*

Thus, long before the real terror, Washington clearly foresaw the intense struggle that would develop between the forces of absolutism and the mobs led by evil men. Jefferson's mind, however, remained largely closed during the whole of the French Revolution. Four days previous to Washington's letter, he had written Edmund Pendleton: "The French revolution proceeds steadily, and is I think beyond the danger of accident of every kind. The success of that will ensure the progress of liberty in Europe, and its preservation here. The failure of that would have been a powerful argument with those who wish to introduce a king, lords & commons here, a sect which is all head and no body." Differences on foreign as well as domestic policy were basic to Jefferson's subsequent bitter hostility to Washington.

The French had been without a minister to the United States since the comte de Moustier had returned home in the autumn of 1789. On August 12, 1791, Jean-Baptiste Ternant presented his credentials to the president. The secretary of state was most unceremonious about this, dropping a note to the minister to say that he would be with the president in the early afternoon and Ternant could stop in at two-thirty.

Ternant had been an officer with Rochambeau's army and was probably hand-picked by Lafayette for his cordiality to America. When Washington and Jefferson subsequently left town, Hamilton called the French minister to his office to provide assurances almost the opposite of those he had given Beckwith—that any idea of a treaty of alliance with Great Britain was not admissible, and that the United States would insist on full rights for its shipping in the British West Indies.

STATE OF THE UNION

Washington appointed his nephew, George Augustine Washington, as overseer of Mount Vernon, when he went to New York. The younger George had been an aide to Lafayette, and the president usually referred to him as "the Major." Since he married Mrs. Washington's niece both Washingtons took a special interest in him. He had the family tuberculosis and Washington often warned him not to work too hard. When his health deteriorated, he was forced to travel to Warm Springs, where his uncles had once gone, to attempt a cure. Because of this, Washington made an emergency trip to Mount Vernon on September 15.

On October 7 he asked Tobias Lear in Philadelphia to get material ready for his third State of the Union address. He requested him to examine his speeches and messages to the preceding sessions of Congress, to note everything he had recommended and what Congress had passed. He was to check with the clerks of the Senate and House on the status of proposals which had not yet received approval. Washington received a reply from Lear on October 14 telling him that Congress was scheduled to convene on October 24, not on the last day of the month as he supposed. The president replied that he was "distressed" to hear this. "I had no more idea of this than its being doomsday." He said he would return as rapidly as possible to the capital. He set out on October 17, pausing just long enough at Georgetown to order the sale of lots for the federal city and to confer with Jefferson and Madison. He spent the night at Bladensburg, was up writing notes at 5:30 in the morning, and started for Philadelphia at 6 A.M. in a heavy storm. He reached the city on October 21.

On October 25 the president delivered his third annual message to this, the

Second Congress. The president expressed pride in "the progressive state of Agriculture, Manufactures, Commerce and Navigation... and the... new and decisive proofs of the increasing reputation and credit of the nation." Revenues were proving so buoyant that no new taxes would be needed. The entire public stock issue of the Bank of the United States was sold in a single day. Most of the old holders of the domestic debt had subscribed to the new issues. The United States floated with ease a loan of eight and a half million florins in Amsterdam.

The president urged action on his past recommendations. The country needed a proper militia act and magazines and arsenals. More and better roads were required, especially new roads to the West and crossing outwards from the main northern and southern routes. Small change was scarce; a mint was urgently wanted. Provision was needed for the opening up and sale of public lands, at reasonable prices, to new farmers.

Indian affairs, he noted, were difficult. The government had concluded preliminary treaties with the Cherokees and Six Nations but many other tribes were still hostile. It was essential that the United States adopt, towards all Indians, a fair and enlightened policy, corresponding to its own principles of religion and philanthropy. They ought to have an impartial administration of justice and their land titles guaranteed by treaties, which the United States would enforce on its own citizens. Hostile Indians should be pacified under "offensive operations... conducted as consistently as possible with the dictates of humanity." Such enterprises were now under way. "It is sincerely to be desired that all need of coercion, in future, may cease; and that an intimate intercourse may succeed; calculated to advance the happiness of the Indians, and to attach them firmly to the United States."

NINE

REELECTION

1791–1792

WHEN CONGRESS, ALARMED by General Harmar's 1790 defeat, added to the ill-paid army, the secretary of war and the commanding general had severe organizational problems. Neither had direct experience with Indian warfare. Supplies for the western offensive had to be assembled in Philadelphia, Pittsburgh, and other staging areas for transport by wagon and boat to Fort Washington at what is now Cincinnati. The late passage of the act delayed the recruiting of regulars and militia. Desertions among the additions were frequent.

It was not until September 21, six months after the act was signed, that St. Clair was able to report to Knox that he had assembled 849 regulars and 1,538 militia, and was ready to start his campaign. Thereafter the reports by Knox and St. Clair expressed remarkable optimism about the anticipated results. St. Clair told Knox that he did not expect he would have to fight more than 1,200 or 1,500 Indians and he was sure of success. Knox, in turn, wrote to Washington that he presumed St. Clair's troops would be superior to any possible enemy force that could be assembled.

As St. Clair proceeded north, only fragmentary and delayed reports reached Philadelphia. As Washington had found when he was a frontier fighter, bad news always travelled fast. Reports of a disaster reached Philadelphia by various routes, well before St. Clair's own version arrived on December 9. This announced that he had reached Fort Washington with "the remains of my army." The mortified president learned that his defeat near the present Fort Wayne had been comparable to that of Braddock. Casualties numbered over 900 out of 1,400 Americans in battle. The survivors abandoned their guns and equipment and fled in panic to the Ohio River.

When Congress assembled three days later, the president gave them St. Clair's full report. He added that he had asked the secretary of war to provide complete information on all steps taken by his administration to secure peace with the Indians. The fact that nothing was concealed turned out to be wise. There was a good deal of "murmuring" in the country. Knox's and St. Clair's reputations suffered, but there was little criticism of the president. St. Clair resigned as commanding officer but retained his governorship of the Northwest Territory. A subsequent congressional inquiry did not attempt to place the blame on any person.

As Washington had learned during the revolution, it was easier to get Congress to improve the army after a defeat. Although Jefferson disapproved, Congress voted the first organic act for the United States army in March. This established a Legion of the United States, consisting of four infantry regiments, and cavalry and artillery battalions, with an authorized strength of around 4,500 officers and men. Hamilton and Knox estimated that the cost per year of the additional forces would be more than $650,000. Whatever his enemies thought of Hamilton, he was not lacking in courage. He proposed to Congress that the whole expense be covered by new taxes. Congress, which had been imposing so many imposts, balked at this suggestion. Fortunately the country's economy was developing rapidly. Government revenues for 1792 increased by more than enough to cover the additional military expenditures. Hamilton's November estimates indicated that the year's tax receipts would be $4.3 million, a sum ample to cover the civil list, payments on the national debt, and the revised budget of the secretary of war.

The president had a difficult time finding the right man to command the new army. By this time the surviving revolutionary generals were aging and often ill. Washington went over and over lists of those who might be competent and in good enough health to undertake a severe western campaign. After much consultation he made a choice which surprised many. On April 9, 1792, he sent to the Senate the name of Anthony Wayne, hero of Germantown and Stony Point, as major general and commanding officer of the troops of the United States. Wayne accepted this task with considerable reluctance, but he proved to be one of Washington's most fortunate appointments. He had once borne the name "Mad Anthony" for his impetuosity in attack, but this time he organized and trained the army with such caution and patience that there were to be many complaints of his inaction. In the end his policy was justified by success. Earlier, on October 31, Washington had nominated William Henry Harrison as ensign of the first Virginia regiment. Harrison subsequently became Wayne's aide, a first step on his long course upward to the presidency.

FAMILY PROBLEMS

Washington had always to turn from critical affairs of state to those of his relatives. Since the estate of his brother, Samuel, was insolvent, the president assisted in bringing up his three youngest surviving children. Although he could ill afford it, he dug into his own pockets for the education of Samuel's two sons, George Steptoe and Lawrence. He got them out of scrapes, complained of their extravagance, transferred them from school in Georgetown to Alexandria, and then to college in Philadelphia. Their sister, Harriott, a good-natured but careless child, was an especial source of worry to the president. He had hoped to leave her under the care of Fanny Washington, Martha's niece and wife of his manager, but this became too difficult when her husband grew very ill. The president did what he could, sending Harriott to his sister or to other relatives. He also took time to give advice freely and sometimes humorously. He wrote her on October 30, 1791:

I have received your letter of the 21st. Instant, and shall always be glad to hear from you...

At present I could plead a better excuse for curtailing my letter to you than you had for shortening of yours to me, having a multitude of business before me while you have nothing to do and delayed it until your Cousin was on the point of sending it to the Post-Office. I make this remark for no other reason than to shew you it is better to offer no excuse than a bad one... Occupied as my time now is, and must be during the sitting of Congress, I nevertheless will endeavor to indulcate upon your mind the delicacy and danger of that period to which you are arrived under peculiar circumstances. You are just entering into the state of womanhood, without the watchful eye of a Mother to admonish, or the protecting aid of a Father to advise and defend you; you may not be sensible that you are at this moment about to be stamped with that character which will adhere to you through life; the consequence of which you have not perhaps attended to, but be assured it is of the utmost importance that you should.

Your cousins with whom you live are well qualified to give you advice... but if you are disobliging, self-willed, and untowardly, it is hardly to be expected that they will engage themselves in unpleasant disputes with you, especially Fanny, whose mild and placid temper will not permit her to exceed the limits of wholesome admiration or gentle rebuke. Think then to what dangers a giddy girl of 15 or 16 must be exposed in circumstances like these. To be under little or no control may be pleasing to a mind that does not reflect, but this pleasure cannot be of long duration...
Your fortune is small; supply the want of it then with a well cultivated mind; with dispositions to industry and frugality; with gentleness of manners, obliging temper, and such qualifications as will attract notice, and recommend you to a happy establishment for life....

Harriott as an orphan had no easy time, being shifted around from step-mother to uncle to aunt and to cousins, some of whom had little money to spare for her needs. She developed such an engaging way of appealing to the president, whenever she needed anything, that her "dear uncle," as she called him, always came through with her requested clothes, books, music, and finally, wedding dress.

WASHINGTON, THE FEDERAL CITY

Washington's nieces and nephews always assured their uncle they would follow his counsel at all times, whether they subsequently did so or not. The president also handed out good advice to emotional cabinet officers, as well as artists, who often paid him the same lip service. In the designer of the capital city he came up against a temperament too difficult to manage, though he explained to his district commissioners how to handle genius.

The commissioners very well understood the president's interest in the new capital and his desire to be consulted on every point. He did complain in April 1792 that they need not have sent him the specifications for the stone bridge between Georgetown and Washington, for he was a busy man, but the commissioners nonetheless continued to inform him of everything. This was to the good, since the president had superb taste and little would have been accomplished without his full support.

Washington, after choosing L'Enfant to lay out the capital, backed him in giving "imagination its full scope" and enthusiastically approved his subsequent draft plan. As everyone soon discovered, L'Enfant wanted to drive through to his objectives, without regard to the law, his superiors, or cost considerations. The commissioners squabbled often with him. The president, far from the scene, was repeatedly called upon to intervene. The first disagreement came when L'Enfant flatly refused to let his plans be used by the commissioners at the first public sale of lots because he did not wish to encourage speculators. They complained to the president that they could not sell the lots if no one could see what he was buying. Washington replied to them through David Stuart on November 21, 1791:

It is much to be regretted, however common the case is, that men who possess talents which fit them for peculiar purposes should almost invariably be under the influence of an untoward disposition... by which they plague all those with whom they are concerned. But I did not expect to meet with such perverseness in Major L'Enfant as his late conduct exhibited.

Since my first knowledge of this Gentleman's abilities in the line of his profession, I have received him not only as a scientific man but one who added considerable taste to professional knowledge; and that, for such employment as his is now engaged in... he was better qualified than any one who had come within my knowledge...

I had no doubts, at the same time, that this was the light in which he considered himself; and of course that he would be so tenacious of his plans as to conceive they would be marred if they underwent any change or alteration... The feelings of such Men are always alive, and where their assistance is essential, it is policy to humour them or put on the appearance of doing it...

As he was to do the following year with Hamilton and Jefferson, Washington tried various tactics to soothe L'Enfant. He wrote a letter praising him and saying that his design was splendid. He pointed out, however, that the district commissioners were authorized by the law and the president to carry out the design and get the city going.

He had hardly dispatched this letter when more complaints reached him. Daniel Carroll, nephew of one of the commissioners, wrote that L'Enfant had abruptly threatened to pull down a house he was building, claiming that it intruded onto a platted but nonexistent street. Washington tried to soothe Carroll, L'Enfant, and the commissioners, but further letters arrived saying that L'Enfant had gone ahead and torn down the house. Carroll threatened to take him to court. Washington wrote the commissioners: "You are as sensible as I am of his value to us. But this has its limits, and there is a point beyond which he might be overvalued." He wrote a strong letter to L'Enfant, saying: "Having the beauty and regularity of your plan only in view, you pursue it as if every person and thing was *obliged* to yield to it." He insisted that L'Enfant heed both the law and the commissioners. He suggested to the latter that they see if there were some way to gratify L'Enfant's pride and ambition, while keeping a curb on him. He noted that he thought Carroll had been equally to blame with L'Enfant in not waiting for the architect's street plats. He urged everyone to try to adjust the disputes among themselves.

More letters reached Washington that winter on L'Enfant's intractable nature. The president finally took the trouble to send his private secretary, Tobias Lear, to Washington, but L'Enfant brushed him off with the remark that he had heard enough talk on the subject. This ended the president's patience, and L'Enfant was dismissed. He ordered Andrew Ellicott to proceed with the engraving of L'Enfant's plans and to lay out the principal streets and lots. Washington complained that Ellicott's wages of five dollars a day, including Sundays, were high but they had better get on with the job. He proposed that Congress pay a proper fee to L'Enfant for his work.

Washington was frequently in and out of Georgetown in 1792. He anxiously looked at the designs for the buildings which had been submitted in open competition. On July 30 he wrote Tobias Lear from Mount Vernon: "I found at Georgetown many well conceived and ingenious plans for the Public buildings in the New City: it was a pleasure indeed to find, in an infant Country, such a display of architectural abilities." He had selected James Hoban's plan for "The President's House" and men were already at work digging the cellars. Hoban was to supervise the work and also assist on the capitol. Washington probably did not know that one design he rejected was submitted anonymously by Jefferson. Washington also mentioned that two or three "elegant" drawings had been submitted for the capitol. On January 31, 1793, he wrote the commissioners that he liked Dr. William Thornton's plan best. "The Grandeur, Simplicity and Beauty of the exterior; the propriety with which the apartments are distributed; and the economy in the mass of the whole structure will, I doubt not, give it a preference in your eyes, as it has done in mine." The commissioners voted to accept it.

AMERICAN AGRICULTURAL SURVEY

The president had corresponded for several years with Arthur Young, the British agricultural expert. He continued this during his presidency, exchanging additional letters with Sir John Sinclair and James Anderson, Scottish agricultural writers and economists. Sinclair became president and Young secretary of the first British Board of Agriculture in 1793. Washington was so interested in their promotion of scientific agriculture and dissemination of information that he subsequently recommended to Congress that the United States establish a similar board. The inquiries by Young and to some extent, Sinclair, led to the first general, if rather haphazard, survey of American agriculture.

In early January 1791 Young asked the president for detailed information on American farming. He wanted to know the prices of lands and the portions of typical farms which were arable, pasture, and woodland. He inquired on yields of the principal grains, vegetables, and grasses. He requested the prices of farm animals and of marketed produce such as meat, butter, and cheese. Since the subject was dear to Washington's heart, he sent a circular letter to men he considered knowledgeable, asking them to make as detailed inquiries as they could.

Individual reports surviving among the president's papers cover Pennsylvania, New Jersey, southern Maryland, and northern Virginia. The reporters, who included Thomas Jefferson and David Stuart in Virginia, Richard Peters in Pennsylvania, and Thomas Johnson in Maryland, usually made very detailed replies. In general they were quite shocked at what they found. Jefferson said that agriculture practices in Charlottesville were "slovenly." David Stuart reported that he had never had a high regard for Virginia farming but after going over the situation his opinion was "certainly much lower than it was." He used almost the same phrase as Jefferson, speaking of the Northern Neck's "slovenly farmers." Thomas Johnson, who had been Maryland's governor, made one of the more interesting surveys. He, along with others, complained that farmers kept so few records they could not answer questions intelligently. He had therefore to do most of the work himself. He made careful comparisons of well-managed farms, where there was intensive cultivation and heavy manuring, and general Maryland practices. The yields in the former case were three to four times as much. His report on Montgomery County said that much of the land had been worn out by tobacco. Farming practices were so poor that no surplus food would be available for the federal city.

Washington read all the letters before forwarding copies to Young. He accompanied them with comments of his own. His letters of December 5, 1791, and June 18–21, 1792, indicated that he thought the area from Virginia to Pennsylvania best suited for agriculture, from the point of view of soil and climate. From what he had read of English soil, American land was inferior along the seacoast, but sixty to a hundred miles inland some of the world's richest agricultural areas were to be found. The Shenandoah Valley was one of the great agrarian regions of the world. Pennsylvania had the best managed agriculture in the Union, but it could well stand improvement.

Washington commented on the difference between the English intensive and the American extensive cultivation of land. This arose because laborers were better paid and fed than in England. "An English farmer must entertain a contemptible opinion of our husbandry, or a horrid idea of our lands, when he shall be informed that no more than 8 or 10 bushels of Wheat is the yield per acre; but this low produce may be ascribed… to a cause… namely, that the aim of the farmers in this Country (if they can be called farmers) is not to make the most from the land, which is, or has been cheap, but the most of the labour, which is dear, the consequence of which has been, much ground has been *scratched* over and none cultivated or improved as it ought to have been; Whereas a farmer in England, where land is dear and labour cheap, finds it to his interest to improve and cultivate highly… It requires time to conquer bad habits, and hardly anything short of necessity is able to accomplish it. That necessity is being approached by pretty rapid strides."

Young was so impressed that he asked the president for permission to reproduce his letters in the *Annals of Agriculture.* Washington replied that he had been writing as a friend. He would prefer that they not be published, especially as there were many strictures on his countrymen's practices.

FOREIGN INTERCOURSE

Although a few members of Congress regarded an American foreign service as tarnation foolishness, the Senate approved the president's recommended appointments to Madrid, London, Paris, and The Hague. His selections as chiefs of mission, along with Wayne as army commander, were among the most important of his administration.

George Hammond presented his credentials as the first minister from the Court of St. James' on November 11, 1791, after being assured that the president had selected a man for London. Washington's proposed nominee was Thomas Pinckney of South Carolina. In this, as in other diplomatic appointments, Washington informed but did not consult Jefferson about his choice. Pinckney had the broadest foreign education of any American diplomat. Before the revolution he had attended Westminster and Oxford. He also read law in London and passed a year of study in France. He returned to South Carolina to serve in the continental line and then as his state's governor. About all that could be said against his appointment was that he had no diplomatic experience but in this he was comparable to Franklin, Adams, and Jefferson when they took their posts.

Washington had to be sure of Pinckney's acceptance before sending his name to the Senate. It took several weeks to hear from Charleston. When Pinckney agreed to serve, Washington informed Jefferson that he was also nominating Gouverneur Morris to Paris and shifting William Short to the Netherlands. He sent the names to the Senate on December 9. Jefferson was most unhappy about Morris for he had hoped that his protégé, Short, would have the job.

The nominations brought lengthy debates in the Senate where some felt that there should be no diplomatic missions, others objected to The Hague alone, while several senators denounced Morris. In the end all were confirmed. On January 11 Washington sent to the Senate Jefferson's letter informing him that Spain, having agreed to discuss the navigation of the Mississippi, had requested that a commissioner be sent to Madrid. William Short, in addition to his Dutch duties, was designated one of two commissioners, along with William Carmichael, the American chargé at Madrid.

Gouverneur Morris was to be unique in being the only diplomat to stay in Paris through the whole Terror. In consequence Washington was probably the best informed chief of state at this period. Morris' information was invaluable as the continent broke into savage war and the stability of the new American nation was threatened by both Britain and France. The relatively narrow margin by which Morris was confirmed (16–11), plus the suspicions which Hamilton had once planted in Washington's mind, compelled the president to write him a friendly but forthright letter on January 28, 1792:

> *The official communications from the Secretary of State… will convey to you the evidence of my nomination, and appointment of you to… the Court of France; and my assurance that both were made with all my heart… I wish I could add that the advice and consent flowed from a similar source… Candour forbids it, and friendship requires that I should assign the cause…*

> *Whilst your abilities… were adduced and asserted on the one hand; you were charged, on the other hand with levity and imprudence of conversation and conduct… In France you were considered a favourer of Aristocracy, and unfriendly to its Revolution (I suppose they meant Constitution.)… That in England you indiscreetly communicated the purport of your Mission in the first instance to the Minister of France, who… gave it the appearance of a movement through his Court. This… added to close intercourse with the opposition Members, occasioned distrust to the Ministry…*

> *But not to go further into detail, I will place the ideas of your political adversaries in the light which their arguments have presented them to me… That the promptitude, with which your lively and brilliant imagination is displayed, allows too little time for deliberation… In a word, that it is indispensably necessary that*

more circumspection should be observed by our representatives abroad, than they conceive you are inclined to adopt...

In this statement... I give you a proof of my friendship... I have the confidence (supposing the allegations to be founded in whole or in part) that you would find no difficulty... to effect a change and thereby silence, in the most unequivocal and satisfactory manner, your political opponents...

Of my good opinion, and of my friendship and regard, you may be assured...

In June Washington hinted to Morris that, in the normal course of events, what he wrote would be communicated to the secretary of state. However, there might arise certain questions which of necessity should be for the president's eyes alone. Morris, in his discretion, was authorized to report directly and privately to him.

The British minister had arrived with rigid instructions. He was to fight any move to discriminate against British trade. Permission was given to initiate discussions about a commercial treaty but not to take further action without London's approval. He was ordered to point out to the Americans all their treaty violations. Hammond set out almost immediately to collect the facts on such alleged breaches but he took several months to do so.

Late in the winter he handed a document to Jefferson outlining all the errors of the Americans. A few days later, March 6, 1792, he wrote to his Foreign Office: "This statement will be found... to contain a body of proof so complete and substantial as to preclude the possibility of cavil and contradiction on the part of this government."

Jefferson never saw this comment by Hammond but he did have the paper. The secretary of state had been studying the peace treaty for years, and he had been in London to discuss the debt. He had already assembled a formidable documentation on the laws of the thirteen states. He added copiously to his files after receiving Hammond's letter. He spent much of the spring of 1792 drawing up a polemical but factual rebuttal. This quoted innumerable authorities on international law, acts of parliament directed against America, the laws of each of the states, and the negotiations over many years to obtain the frontier posts. Hamilton, when he read it, objected to some of its blunter statements. Jefferson accepted a few changes but refused to make more. Washington, after reading Hamilton's critique, overruled him. Jefferson delivered his letter to Hammond about the first of June.

Hammond acknowledged its receipt saying that he would send it to London. He assured Jefferson he had not intentionally misstated any facts. Jefferson and

Hammond thereafter had a long talk, in which the British minister said that the idea that his country had committed the first infractions would be entirely new to his ministry.

Hammond held an entirely different conversation with Hamilton at about the same time. He had not liked the "acrimonious" reply and complained to Hamilton of Jefferson's "extraordinary performance." Hammond reported to London: "After lamenting the intemperate violence of his colleague, Mr. Hamilton assured me that this letter was very far from meeting his approbation, or from containing a faithful exposition of the sentiments of this government. He added that at the time of our conversation the president had not had an opportunity of perusing this representation: For having returned from Virginia in the morning only on which it had been delivered to me, he had relied on Mr. Jefferson's assurance, that it was conformable to the opinions of the other members of the executive government."

The statement to Hammond was a flat lie on Hamilton's part. The president had read and approved the document and thereby made it the official view of the United States government. In spite of repeated subsequent inquiries by Jefferson, the only response that Hammond ever gave was that London was studying his document.

FIRST VETO

The completion of the first census required, in accordance with the Constitution, reapportionment of the House of Representatives. With this came fights in both Houses. The House had 69 members but the Constitution permitted an increase to 120. Each state wanted a little more than its share and New England managed proportionally to get the most. The bill passed the Senate by but one vote and the House by two votes. When it reached Washington's desk in March 1792, it was one of the first congressional acts seriously to disturb him. His general inclination was to accept compromises worked out in Congress but this one appeared unfair. Washington consulted the four members of the cabinet as to the act's constitutionality. Hamilton wrote a rather hasty opinion saying that he had not read the bill but it appeared to be permitted by the Constitution. Jefferson studied the bill more carefully. He did not go so far as to declare it absolutely unconstitutional but that it was, to say the least, "an inconvenient expression of its words," by giving several states more representation than one per thirty thousand, which is permitted by the organic document. Jefferson, by law, mathematics, and logic, was clearly in the right. The president followed his advice and returned it to

Congress unsigned, briefly giving his reasons. A new act was passed on a more equitable basis. This was one of many instances, as Washington later pointed out to Jefferson, in which his advice prevailed over that of Hamilton.

FAREWELL ADDRESS

Washington had optimistically hoped that, in one term, he could get the new government on its way and then retire. A clear hankering to be president was evident on the parts of Adams, Jay, Jefferson, Hamilton, Madison, and others while Washington wanted a peaceful life for his remaining years. None of the five main possible successors believed any of the other four as suitable as Washington, nor that the United States was yet strong enough to walk alone.

Washington talked with members of his cabinet on his desire to retire from office. He also discussed it with James Madison, whom he had always trusted, not realizing that the Philip Freneau who had so severely attacked his administration had been selected because he was Madison's old Princeton friend.

On May 20, 1792, Washington wrote Madison to ask his advice and help in drafting a farewell address to the American people. He summarized his thoughts, much of their substance appearing later in his farewell of 1796. Washington wrote that he wanted to tell Americans

that we are all the Children of the same country; a Country great and rich in itself; capable, and promising to be, as prosperous and happy as any the Annals of history have ever brought to our view. That our interests, however diversified in local and smaller matters, are the same in all the great and essential concerns of the Nation. That the extent of our Country, the diversity of our climate and soil, and the various productions of the States consequent to both, are such as to make one part not only convenient, but perhaps indispensably necessary to the other part; and may render the whole, at no distant period, one of the most independent in the world. That the established government being the work of our own hands, with the seeds of amendment grafted in the Constitution, may by wisdom, good dispositions, and mutual allowances, aided by experience, bring it as near to perfection as any human institution ever approximated; and therefore, the only strife among us ought be, who should be foremost in facilitating and finally accomplishing such great and desirable objects; by giving every possible support, and cement to the Union. That however necessary it may be to keep a watchful eye over public servants and public measures, yet there ought to be limits to it; for suspicions unfounded, and jealousies too lively, are irritating to honest feelings; and oftentimes are productive of more evil than good.

Madison drafted several paragraphs for Washington but in the end the president was prevailed upon to accept a second term.

PANIC

The crisis in the money market in the spring of 1793 cannot be classified as the first of the business cycles which made a roller coaster of America's economic development. The United States was, in fact, reaping the combined benefits of a strong government and financial system, together with a high level of European demand for its products. The panic, however, shook the country's confidence in Hamilton and the administration; the opposition made the most of it.

William Duer, Hamilton's old associate, had quit the Treasury to engage in speculation. Duer used remarkably advanced techniques, rather like those employed in New York in the 1920s. He borrowed on an ever-expanding scale, paying higher and higher interest to the public, who were delighted to lend money to him. He pyramided his profits into more speculations, and he supported the market for his stock, while also selling short.

In January 1792 security prices fell abruptly. Duer was ruined and in prison by March. Many persons and institutions were dragged under, including Hamilton's own society for establishing useful manufactures, but the panic itself was short-lived.

Hamilton acted promptly to establish the Treasury's first open-market operations. Backed by cash and borrowings to the amount of $200,000, he successfully intervened to support the government's bonds and credit. He was attacked unmercifully for this, the *New York Journal* maintaining that he had substituted "the golden dreams of speculation" for the sacred words: "liberty and independence."

EXCISE TAX

The 1791 tax on domestically manufactured spirits turned out to be one of the most troublesome of the new imposts. It is difficult to write about from a modern point of view since the uproar concerned an excise of as little as two cents a quart on whisky distilled from domestic grain. It was originally proposed, as preferable to a land tax, by Madison, who had started out as a good federalist but had fallen under the thumb and spell of Jefferson. The latter made the most of the tax, weeping over the poor "ploughman" who supposedly had to pay it, though a plowman's land tax would have been worse.

On March 6, 1792, Hamilton submitted to the House of Representatives a "Report on the Difficulties in the Execution of the Act Laying Duties on Distilled Spirits." It was, in part, a hilarious comment on human foibles, which demolished every argument against the tax, except that it was not easy to collect. Hamilton took account of the many petitions against the act which had been submitted to the House. He noted that those who opposed it said that the tax contravened the principles of liberty, injured morals, and was ruining the distilling business.

Hamilton obviously enjoyed writing portions of it. He said that he could not quite grasp how an internal tax on "a consumable commodity [was] inconsistent with the genius of free government," while an import duty on the same commodity was not. He showed that the tax was higher on foreign whiskey, gin, or rum, and thus was a protective stimulus to the domestic industry. He could not see how filling out tax forms was such a hardship, since the distiller knew what he was doing and the government even gave him his ledger book. He said that the objection that an oath required on reports could hardly be said to be ruining morals, since he was sure most people were not committing perjury. He did not understand the complaints from western Pennsylvanians that the tax bore particularly hard on them. If so, they must be drinking too much and they ought to drink less. Their statement that they had to make the grain into spirits to save transport costs to distant markets made no sense as an objection since the consumer, not the farmer, paid the tax. The Pennsylvanians said they had little cash but Hamilton, as treasurer of the United States, noted that he was sending five times as much money to the area for its protection as he was getting back in excise receipts.

Hamilton summed up his whole argument by noting that, on the average, a family of six would consume about sixteen gallons of spirits a year, on which they would pay only a little over a dollar and a quarter in taxes. The federal government did not tax their lands, houses, or stock. Hamilton did, however, recommend to Congress administrative changes in the law to make it less objectionable.

In spite of Hamilton's reasoned statements, petitioning opposition in western Pennsylvania erupted into a small rebellion in the summer of 1792. Revenue officers were threatened with mayhem. When Hamilton reported this to the president at Mount Vernon, Washington replied on September 7: "Such conduct in any of the Citizens of the United States, under any circumstances that can well be received, would be exceedingly reprehensible; but when it comes from a part of the Community for whose protection the money arising from the Tax was principally designed, it is truly unaccountable, and the spirit of it much to be regretted." The president said he approved of the steps taken by Hamilton to get evidence against the offenders, in order to prosecute them in federal courts. He added: "But if, notwithstanding, opposition is still given to the execution of the Law, I have no hesitation in declaring, if the evidence of it is clear and unequivocal, that I shall, however reluctantly I exercise them, exert all the legal powers with which the Executive is invested, to check so daring and unwarrantable a spirit. It is my duty to see the Laws executed: to permit them to be trampled upon with impunity would be repugnant to it; nor can the Government longer remain a passive spectator of the contempt with which they are treated. Forbearance… seems to have had no other effect than to increase the disorder."

On September 15 a thunderous proclamation came from "George Washington, President of the United States," calling on "all persons whom it may concern, to refrain and desist from unlawful combinations and proceedings whatsoever having for object or tending to obstruct the operation of the laws aforesaid; inasmuch as all lawful ways and means will be strictly put in execution for bringing to justice the infractors thereof… "

In sending the proclamation to Jefferson for the signature of the secretary of state, he said that he knew that his actions would be "severely criticized; but I shall disregard any animadversions upon my conduct when I am called upon by the nature of my office, to discharge what I conceive to be a duty, and none, in my opinion, is more important than to carry the Laws of the United States into effect." To Hamilton he wrote that he expected strictures, but he added, what he did not say to Jefferson, that the government ought to use regular army troops only as a last resort, "otherwise there would be a cry at once 'the Cat is let out; we now see for what purpose an Army was raised… '"

Some of the riotous leaders were indicted and brought to trial. For a while peace returned to western Pennsylvania. However, the opposition to the government later found a chance to revive the disorder and more trouble came in Washington's second term.

JEFFERSON'S COUNTER-REVOLUTION

When Jefferson read the new Constitution in Paris, his first appraisal was unenthusiastic. He missed Virginia's savage ratification fight where Patrick Henry, George Mason, Richard Henry Lee, and James Monroe lined up against Washington and Madison. An oft-reiterated complaint of the opposition was that the Constitution had no Bill of Rights, but when this was proposed by Washington and passed quickly by Congress, Virginia took nearly two years to ratify it. The objections were far deeper; many Virginians had a fundamentalist desire to maintain the state just as it was, a view quite different from that held by Virginia's greatest son.

Washington's influence had been responsible for the margin by which the state ratified the Constitution but this did not remove the fears of the national government which had been duly reported to him by Dr. Stuart. Most basic was apprehension that federal power might try to control or abolish slavery. There was a great uproar in Virginia in 1790, when the representatives debated a Quaker memorial, asking for the suppression of the slave trade. Another grievance was the use of federal courts to collect private debts due the British. The federal tax program and the assumption of state debts were a constant source of complaint from those who ill understood them.

When Jefferson returned from Paris to Virginia, the views he heard may have influenced his reluctance to enter Washington's cabinet. When he joined the administration, he sat with three men, Washington, Knox, and Hamilton, who had fought for freedom side by side at Harlem, White Plains, Trenton, Princeton, Brandywine, Monmouth, and Yorktown. Jefferson wrote that he soon found himself to be almost the only republican in governing circles. He defined the word as a belief that each state would "remain independent as to internal matters, and the whole form a single nation as to what was foreign only." What moved Jefferson to eventual frenzy was the sweep of Washington's national economic program. Washington believed that the country, stimulated and aided by an active federal government, should move forward in agriculture, commerce, industry, science, education, manufacturing, transport, and communications. Defense should be national, with a permanent American army. Jefferson, on the other hand, felt that farmers "are alone to be relied on for expressing the proper American sentiments." He was against banks and even paper money, feeling that gold and silver alone had value. Road building was too much even for a state government; Virginia, he thought, handled this properly by giving the function to the counties. A militia could do everything better than a trained army and would be much cheaper. In short, he wanted an ideal of farmer-philosophers watching over happy plantations and slaves.

A further fundamental divergence lay in Jefferson's lack of Washington's abounding faith in God and humanity. He persistently maintained that the people would elect corrupt men to Congress, the federal power in turn would corrupt the states, and all would end in tyranny. Washington's views, as he expressed them in his draft inaugural address of 1789, were that "this Constitution is really, in its formation, a government of the people; that is to say, a government in which all power is derived from them, and at stated periods reverts to them... The election of the different branches of Congress by the

Freeman… is the pivot on which turns the first Wheel of government… The exercise of this right to election seems to be so regulated as to afford less opportunity for corruption and influence than has usually been incident to popular governments. Nor can the members of Congress exempt themselves from the consequences of any unjust and tyrannical acts they may impose on others. For in a short time they will mingle with the people… Their re-election must always depend upon the good reputation they shall have maintained in the judgment of their fellow citizens… No government before introduced among mankind ever contained so many checks and such efficacious restraints to prevent it from degenerating into any species of oppression."

Jefferson saw conspiracy and intrigue in many government actions which were entirely well intended. Even as an old man he would repeat charges that von Steuben and Knox had conspired to set up a monarchy, that the Cincinnati was part of the plot, and that he alone had saved the republic. Washington suffered Jefferson during his four years in the cabinet with endless courtesy and patience although the secretary of state, orally and by letter, traduced his policies and vilified his motives. Along the way Jefferson was joined by James Madison, who had done so much to build the national government, as well as by James Monroe. Their home state of Virginia could not swing an election, but Jefferson found other allies farther south, and such New York supporters as Aaron Burr, George Clinton, and the Sons of St. Tammany. It took little calculation to show that the South and New York State with the extra votes given the South for its slaves would have enough electoral votes to capture the presidency.

In May of 1792 Jefferson wrote to the president, expostulating against his wish to retire at the end of his first term. Jefferson's plea that he continue in office probably arose from his fear that a successor would be much less "republican." He added a fervent though polite attack on the principal measures of the administration which, he said, were causing great public distress and worry. He implied that the president had nothing to do with the financial measures adopted by the government nor did he know of the stockjobbing and bribery in Congress, the split between North and South, and the move within the government to monarchy.

When he received the letter, Washington extracted the attacks on his policy and forwarded them to Hamilton with a statement that they represented the views of people not too friendly to the government, "among whom may be classed my neighbour and quondam friend, Colo. Mason." Hamilton made a strong and effective reply to Washington which ran many pages.

He demolished Jefferson's objection to the excise tax as an aristocratic concept by noting that there was, perhaps, "no article of more general and equal consumption than distilled spirits." He suggested that the Jeffersonian opposition was Tory and conservative while the government was Whig and progressive in its program. He added that the idea that anyone wanted a monarchy in the United States "is one of those visionary things, that none but madmen could meditate and that no wise man will believe."

In this letter, Hamilton pleaded with the president to remain in office, for enemies to the administration were making strenuous efforts to gain control of the government. The attorney general, Edmund Randolph, also urged him to serve a second term. If he did not, there would probably be civil war and Washington would be called on to suppress it.

While considering whether to remain in office, the president appealed to Hamilton, Jefferson, and Randolph to stop all dissension and bickering and to work for the common good. His letters to Jefferson and Hamilton were very similar but he made slight shifts of emphasis. He wrote Jefferson on August 23: "My earnest wish, and my fondest hope, therefore is, that instead of wounding suspicions, and irritable charges, there may be liberal allowances, mutual forbearances, and temporizing yieldings on all sides... Without them every thing must rub; the Wheels of Government will clog; our enemies will triumph, and by throwing their weight into the disaffected scale, may accomplish the ruin of the goodly fabric we have been erecting." He added that the many attacks on the government had filled him "with painful sensations; and cannot fail, I think, of producing unhappy consequences at home and abroad." In expressing similar sentiments to Hamilton, he added: "I cannot prevail on myself to believe that these measures are as yet the deliberate acts of a determined party." He hoped that "healing measures" would be applied everywhere in the Union.

Hamilton's reply was conciliatory, saying that he felt he was the deeply injured party but he would try to be as forbearing as possible. He thought the best thing would be for himself and Jefferson to quit the cabinet and thus give the president a free hand. He had recently, for the first time, begun a strong counterattack on subversive forces working to destroy the national government. He could not for the present recede but if Washington worked out a plan of reconciliation, he would at once desist. Jefferson, on the other hand, sent an insolent letter.

Jefferson said Washington had been duped by Hamilton on the assumption-capital issue, he denied that he had ever intrigued against the government, and he reiterated that Washington's financial system had corrupted the legislature. Congress had deserted the people, while the administration and Congress had subverted the Constitution and had even assumed power to legislate for the general welfare. He said that the long list of Treasury appointments throughout the nation (who had been almost entirely selected by the president) were an additional source of corruption. He defended his hiring of a State Department clerk to edit a paper attacking the government, adding that Hamilton's career was "a tissue of machinations" against the liberties of his adopted country.

The summer and fall of 1792 saw severe press attacks on Hamilton and Adams as well as Hamilton's counterattacks on Jefferson. The latter kept his hands clean of actual newspaper writing, but he had a host of others to do the work, including Freneau, Madison, and Monroe. No one emerged from the press debate, which took place under Latin pen names, with credit, and all concerned did great disservice to Washington. In the course of it, one Jeffersonian called Hamilton a "cowardly assassin," Monroe flung in an oblique reference to Hamilton's extramarital activities, Hamilton and William Smith were caustic about Jefferson's war record, while Hamilton made an obscene reference in print to Jefferson. The secretary of the treasury was always unsurpassed on the attack. In a strong position, pleading from a successful policy, he drove Jefferson into a frenzy. He described him as substituting "national disunion, National insignificance, Public disorder and discredit" for union, respectability, and order. On September 29, as "Catullus," he skewered the secretary of state:

> *Mr. Jefferson has hitherto been distinguished as the quiet, modest, retiring philosopher—as the plain simple unambitious republican. He shall now for the first time be regarded as the intriguing incendiary...*

> *There is always a first time when characters studious of artful disguises are unveiled; when the vizor of stoicism is plucked from the brow of the Epicurean; when the plain garb of Quaker simplicity is stripped from the concealed voluptuary; when Caesar coyly refusing the proffered diadem, is seen to be Caesar rejecting the trappings, but tenaciously grasping the substance of imperial domination.*

STATE OF THE UNION

The usual cheerful tone of Washington's earlier annual messages to Congress was replaced by a more somber note in his fourth report, delivered on November 6, 1792:

> *It is some abatement of the satisfaction with which I meet you on the present occasion that, in felicitating you on a continuance of the National prosperity*

generally, I am not able to add to it information that the Indian hostilities, which have for some time past distressed our western frontiers, have terminated.

Reiterated endeavors toward effecting a pacification have hitherto issued only in new and outrageous methods of persevering hostility... Besides the continuation of hostile appearances among the tribes North of the Ohio, some threatening symptoms have of late been revived among some of those south of it...

I have reason to believe that every practicable exertion has been made (pursuant to the provision by law for that purpose) to be prepared for the alternative of a prosecution of the war, in the event of a failure of pacific overtures. A large proportion of the troops authorized to be raised, has been recruited, though the number is still incomplete. And pains have been taken to discipline and put them in condition for the particular kind of service to be performed. A delay of operations (besides being dictated by the measures which we are pursuing towards a pacific termination of the war) has been in itself deemed preferable to immature efforts...

In looking forward to the future expense of the operations... I derive consolation from the information I receive that the product of the revenues for the present year, is likely to supersede the necessity of additional burthens on the community, for the service of the ensuing year.

I cannot dismiss the subject of Indian affairs without again recommending... laws for restraining the commission of outrages upon the Indians; without which all pacific plans must prove nugatory... If, in addition, an eligible plan could be devised for promoting civilization among the friendly tribes and for carrying on trade with them... under regulations calculated to protect them from imposition and extortion, its influence in cementing their interests with ours could not but be considerable.

Measures have been taken for employing some artists from abroad to aid in the establishment of our mint... Provision has been made of the requisite buildings... There has also been a small beginning in the coinage of half-dimes; the want of small coins in circulation calling the first attention to them.

The adoption of a constitution for the State of Kentucky has been notified to me.

Three new loans have been effected, each for three millions of florins—one at Antwerp... and the other two at Amsterdam... The rates of these loans and the circumstances under which they have been made, are confirmations of the high state of our credit abroad.

THE 1792 ELECTION

As the second presidential election approached, the Jefferson faction turned its fire from Hamilton to Adams. Not until the election was over did Jefferson's friends attack the president, who had been largely spared from direct bludgeoning.

It was not customary at that period for candidates for the presidency and vice-presidency to campaign. Neither Washington nor Adams did so. Nonetheless, the political enemies of both were exceedingly busy. They included a large number of Southerners plus Aaron Burr of New York and John Hancock and Samuel Adams in Massachusetts. Washington regarded the election as a test of confidence in his policies and he admitted that he would feel chagrin if there were a substantial decline in his previous unanimous electoral support.

The Jeffersonians chose George Clinton, who had fought the Constitution, as their candidate for vice-president. Adams, more pessimistic by nature than Washington, thought at one point that he would be defeated.

In 1788 only ten states voted in the national elections. In 1792 five additional states chose electors. Washington received all 132 electoral votes for president. John Adams lost three southern states and New York to Clinton, plus Kentucky to Jefferson. He, nonetheless, had a comfortable majority of seventy-seven, a stronger vote of confidence than he had received in 1788.

TEN

FOREIGN AND
DOMESTIC STORMS

1792–1793

FRANKLIN HAD BEEN a fascinated watcher at the first Paris balloon ascension of 1783. Early in 1785 Jean-Pierre Blanchard, a Frenchman, and John Jeffries, an American physician, floated across the English channel. Washington read the initial reports from Paris with interest. On April 4, 1784, he wrote to General du Portail in France: "I have only news paper Accts. of the Air Balloons, to which I do not know what credence to give; as the tales related of them are marvellous, and lead us to expect that our friends at Paris, in a little time, will come flying thro' the air, instead of ploughing the Ocean to get to America." Washington's curiosity was finally satisfied when Blanchard appeared in Philadelphia near the end of his first term. On January 9, 1793, the president, attended by the secretary of state, went to the grounds at Walnut and Fourth Streets, to see Blanchard make his ascension. A large crowd of Philadelphians attended. The president handed Blanchard a special passport requesting every citizen to give him aid and friendship. Blanchard, displaying French and American flags from his balloon, rose in the air and soared over the Delaware. He landed less than an hour later in Woodbury, New Jersey, from which he returned to call on the president that evening.

MOUNT VERNON

The president, compelled by his unanimous countrymen to serve one more term, did relatively little public or private grumbling. The intensity of his feelings appeared in the extraordinary series of letters he sent to Mount Vernon from Philadelphia, beginning in October 1792 when he knew he would serve again, and continuing through June of 1793. More than 30 letters of instruction went out in his hand, most of them to his manager, Anthony Whiting. These were of such length that they would make a book of perhaps 150 pages. They displayed Washington's hope that by correspondence he could produce nearly as good management of the various Mount Vernon farms, as if he were there personally. Not until late spring did he learn that Whiting, like his previous manager, had been dying of tuberculosis during the period.

The letters indicate vividly that Washington had a photographic memory of the more than twelve square miles he owned on the Potomac. He knew also the individual capacities of his overseers, hired hands, indentured servants, and many of his slaves. He required weekly reports from his manager and overseers, and he had an eye for discrepancies.

In writing to Mount Vernon he explained how he accomplished a vast amount of work, suggesting that everyone else do the same. His manager was instructed to get a notebook and put down each Washington order so that he could check whether or not it was done. In preparing reports and letters, he was to make out a list of everything he wanted to tell the president and it would then be as easy for him as for Washington to write so many. The weekly orders from Philadelphia were so numerous and varied that it would have taken a corps of clerks to record and check them. Washington remembered them all, but not the poor manager. The president, who could address the nation gracefully, tended to lapse into clichés in writing his farm employees: "There is a season for all things; many a mickle makes a muckle; do not put off till tomorrow what you can do today; a penny saved is a penny got."

An index to the Whiting letters refers to such topics as water and wells; hospitality to Mount Vernon visitors; hedges, fences, and gates; grass, grain, and meadows; quarters and outhouses; barns and threshing; timber cutting; taxes; roads; thefts; house painting; censuses of stock; erosion and conservation of soil; fallow culture; the building of an icehouse and an experimental garden; protection of buildings against fire; the improvement of the fisheries; and work at the flour mill. From time to time Mrs. Washington added queries as to whether the potash was collected for the soap, why the seamstresses were making fewer shirts each week than when she was home, and what happened to the cart that had been ordered for one of her farms.

About the end of 1792, the president took time to design a barn and sheds, with their construction specifications, for the Dogue Run farm. The following year he described the plan to Arthur Young as "well calculated, it is conceived, for getting grain out of the straw more expeditiously than is the usual mode of threshing. There are good sheds... sufficient to cover 30 work horses and Oxen."

The president, when he was at Mount Vernon, had shared George Augustine Washington's agony as he coughed his health and life away. The younger George had at length gone to the house of his father-in-law, Burwell Bassett, in the autumn of 1792. In January Basset, Mrs. Washington's brother-in-law, died; George Augustine followed him to the grave the next month, two losses which greatly distressed Washington and his wife. The president, on February 24, 1793 (approximately the day he received a moving appeal from Madame de Lafayette for help for her imprisoned husband), wrote Frances Washington:

My dear Fanny: To you, who so well knew the affectionate regard I had for our departed friend, it is unnecessary to describe the sorrow with which I was afflicted at the news of his death... To express this sorrow with the force I feel it, would answer no other purpose than to revive in your breast, that poignancy of anguish, which, by this time, I hope is abated...

The object of the present letter is to convey in your mind the warmest assurances of my love, friendship, and disposition to serve you; These also I profess to have in an eminent degree, for your Children.

What plan you have contemplated... is unknown to me; and therefore I add, that the one which strikes me most favorably, by being best calculated to promote the interest of yourself and Children, is to return to your old habitation at Mount Vernon. You can go no place where you will be more welcome, nor to any where you can live at less expence, or trouble...

You might bring my niece, Harriet Washington, with you for a Companion; whose conduct, I hear with pleasure, has given much satisfaction to my sister... My affectionate regards attend you and your Children; and I shall always be your sincere friend...

Eventually Washington did over a house he owned in Alexandria for her occupancy. While he was still working on her problems, he received a warning from Dr. Craik that the successor overseer of Mount Vernon, Anthony Whiting, was quite ill and spitting blood. By June Whiting too was dying and Washington had to make a hasty trip to Mount Vernon, and found his affairs in bad order. He was soon recalled to Philadelphia by the French declaration of war against the Netherlands, Britain, and Spain. He appointed as temporary overseer one of a large supply of nephews, Howell Lewis, who had been an assistant secretary to the president.

INAUGURATION

As soon as it was certain that Washington would serve another term, the Jeffersonians opened up with violent attacks on him. These, to an extraordinary degree, were to parallel the abuse which France heaped on Washington during much of the period from 1793–1797.

The first move was a series of resolutions introduced in the House of Representatives by William Branch Giles of Virginia. These had been drafted in strong terms by Jefferson but were modified in the course of discussion. Several of them called on the president as well as Hamilton for information, thus making clear that the distinction previously maintained between the secretary of the treasury and the president had now been breached. The resolves accused Hamilton in effect of having violated the laws by manipulating the foreign loans entrusted to his care. Jefferson's draft resolution that Hamilton be dismissed from office and the Treasury be broken into two parts was never offered. The resolves failed completely, with only Madison and the Virginia delegation, together with a few other congressmen, voting for them. Even so, the main objective, to introduce into the country a suspicion as to the integrity of the administration, had been achieved.

The president's sixty-first birthday reception, February 22, 1793, a day which had long been celebrated by all Americans, was attacked by Freneau as a symbol of "royal pomp and power." The presidential diaries for that day noted: "The House of Representatives waited upon the President at 12 o'clock, in a body (excepting those who were opposed thereto,) to congratulate him on the anniversary of his birth." The president, who found ceremonies tedious, decided to take his second oath of office simply, within the Senate chamber, rather than before the people as he had done in 1789. Tobias Lear recorded in Washington's diary for March 4:

> *At 12 o'clock the President went to the Senate Chamber to take the oath of office prescribed by the Constitution. The members of the Senate were present—and such of the House of Representatives as had not left the City—the Heads of the Departments—the foreign Ministers—and as large a number of other persons as could press into the Senate Chamber and adjacent Rooms. The oath was*

*administered by Judge Cushing—previous to which the president made the
following short address to the Spectators:*

"Fellow Citizens

*"I am again called upon by the voice of my Country to execute the functions of
its Chief Magistrate. When the occasion proper for it shall arrive, I shall
endeavour to express the high sense I entertain of this distinguished honor, and
of the confidence which has been reposed in me by the people of United America.*

*"Previous to the execution of any official Act of the President, the Constitution
requires an Oath of Office. This oath I am now about to take—and in your
presence—that if it shall be found during my administration of the Government,
I have in any instance violated willingly, or knowingly, the injunctions thereof, I
may (besides incurring Constitutional punishment) be subject to the upbraiding
of all who are now witnesses of the present solemn Ceremony."*

After the oath was administered the President withdrew from the Senate
Chamber, and returned to his own house. The President, on this occasion,
went alone in his carriage to the Senate Chamber—on his return he was preceded by the Marshal of the District and the High Sheriff of the County with
their deputies, who had convened at the Senate Chamber to prevent any disturbance or inconvenience that might arise from the Crowd.

Senate and House recessed until December 2, leaving the president to direct
the nation through a critical period. Much of Washington's work in the next
weeks concerned preparations for peace negotiations with the Indians north of
the Ohio River. A group of leading Philadelphia Quakers suggested that, because
of their long and good relations with the Indians, they send a delegation with the
official commissioners. The president gratefully accepted their offer.

Before he started for Mount Vernon, Washington had word that the
Indians, backed by the British, were insisting that all Americans leave the
Northwest Territory. He also had the news that Louis XVI had been executed,
and he heard from Gouverneur Morris that France was mobilizing an army to
attack Great Britain.

In no optimistic mood, with his personal affairs in disorder, the president
left for Mount Vernon on March 27. At Georgetown he took time to try to settle a continuing squabble between Andrew Ellicott, engineer for Washington
City, and the district commissioners. After hearing on April 12 from Hamilton
and Jefferson that France had declared war on England, Spain, and Holland,
he set out next day for Philadelphia. He wrote to the cabinet that the United

States should observe "Strict neutrality" and every effort should be made to prevent American privateers from embroiling the country in war. On April 17 he was back in Philadelphia to find his desk piled high with trouble.

NEUTRALITY

Washington returned with a resolve to prevent any action by American citizens, or others, which would bring the United States into a European war and thus destroy the country's growing economic and political strength. Members of the cabinet as well as the chief justice had worked on a proclamation for the president to study on his return. Randolph and Jefferson both disliked the word "neutrality," which was not used, though almost everyone soon called the proclamation by that name. In its final version, Washington asked all citizens to observe "impartial" conduct towards the belligerents, declaring those who violated the proclamation to be outside the protection of the government and subject to legal prosecution. The proclamation became the organic basis of America's historic policy of neutrality in European wars, broken in the nineteenth century only when Madison was in office. On the day that he signed the proclamation, April 22, 1793, Washington outlined to a friendly English admirer, the Earl of Buchan, his basic arguments for its existence:

The favorable wishes which your Lordship has expressed for the prosperity of this young and rising Country, cannot but be gratefully received by all its Citizens... One means to... its happiness is very judiciously portrayed in the following words of your letter "to be little heard of in the great world of Politics." These words I can assure your Lordship are expressive of my sentiments... I believe it is the sincere wish of United America to have nothing to do with the political intrigues or squabbles of European Nations; but on the contrary to exchange commodities and live in peace with all the inhabitants of the Earth... To administer justice to, and receive it from every power with whom they are connected will, I hope, be always found the most prominent feature in the Administration of this Country... Under such a system... the agriculture and Mechanical Arts, the wealth and population of these States will increase with that degree of rapidity as to baffle all calculation...

I take the liberty of sending you the Plan of a new City... designed for the permanent seat of the Government; we are... deeply engaged and far advanced in extending the inland navigation of the River on which it stands... In 10 years, if left undisturbed, we shall open a connection by water with all the Lakes Northward and Westward of us... and an inland navigation in a very few years more from

Rhode Island to Georgia… To these may be added the erection of Bridges over considerable Rivers, and the commencement of Turnpike roads…

GENET

In 1793 France renewed its efforts to reinstitute Vergennes' old plan, similar to that of Great Britain: to confine the United States to the Alleghenies. The first diplomatic agent of republican France was Edmond Charles Genet, just thirty, who had been his country's representative at St. Petersburg, until he was expelled by Russia as an emissary from revolutionary France. Genet was ordered to America, with instructions to organize attacks on Spanish-held Louisiana and Florida, to stimulate French privateer assaults on British shipping in the Atlantic and the Caribbean, and to establish French admiralty courts in American coastal states. He was also instructed to recruit American troops and seamen for the French forces. To finance and manage these schemes he was directed to apply to the secretary of the treasury for advance payments on the French war loans and to the secretary of war for guns. Genet landed at Charleston on April 8 and proceeded to commission the four armed privateers, which the French consul had purchased. He ordered the establishment of a French admiralty court in the city, empowered to condemn and sell all British ships taken at sea. Washington soon had word at Mount Vernon that preparations were under way by a foreign power to use American territory as a war base. Before Genet left Charleston, Senator Ralph Izard of South Carolina warned him that Jefferson and Madison were two ambitious men. They would work with him, so long as he furthered their interests, but would quickly drop him, if things went wrong.

John Marshall, who lived through the events, vividly described America's first reactions to Genet. The French declaration of war, he wrote, "restored full vivacity to a flame, which a peace of ten years had not been able to extinguish. A great majority of the American people deemed it criminal to remain unconcerned spectators of a conflict between their ancient enemy and republican France. The feeling upon this occasion was almost universal… Disregarding totally the circumstances which led to the rupture… and that the actual hostilities were first commenced by France, the war was confidently and generally pronounced a war of aggression on the part of Great Britain." Marshall noted that "extravagant marks of public attachment [such] as had never before been lavished on a foreign minister," were shown to Genet at Charleston and these continued on his way north to Philadelphia. At the capital, on May 16, Genet was welcomed with "transports of joy by the great majority of the inhabitants."

Two days later the minister presented his credentials to the president, whose desk had been burdened for weeks with reports of French violations of American sovereignty and laws. There were now three warring powers, operating with near impunity, in a peaceful neutral country.

JEFFERSON VERSUS WASHINGTON

In one of his final appraisals of the American government, Beckwith reported to London that the secretary of state "is blindly devoted to a French influence... and there are no lengths in his power to which he will not go to favor the interests of that kingdom." With the arrival of a minister from revolutionary France, Jefferson now began a policy of calculated deception and treachery which only his innate timidity and Washington's masterly control kept from bringing disaster to the country. The secretary soon developed his own definition of neutrality as "fair" when it favored France, whereas the president's aim was to meet all foreign intrigues with equal firmness. During his last months in the cabinet, Jefferson spoke on distinct levels, to the president with one voice, to Washington's opponents with another. Hardly any cabinet secret was safe, since he duly reported the substance of the discussions to Madison and Monroe. Genet later complained that the secretary of state conversed also with him in a private language and he found it and his public utterances hard to disentangle.

On May 5 Jefferson wrote Monroe: "All the old spirit of 1776 is kindling... A French frigate took a British prize off the capes of Delaware the other day, and sent her here. Upon her coming into sight thousands & thousands of the yeomanry of the city crowded and covered the wharves... When the British colours were seen reversed, & the French flying above them they burst into peals of exultation." Ten days later, the secretary of state informed the French minister that the vessel had been seized in American waters, in violation of American laws, and he was ordered to release the ship to the British.

On May 8 Jefferson wrote an ostensibly private letter, introducing Dr. Enoch Edwards to Jean-Pierre Brissot de Warville, leader of the Girondin party, which had forced an aggressive foreign war to offset economic and political difficulties at home. The secretary of state said: "We too have our aristocrats and monocrats, and as they float on the surface, they shew much... For their particular description, I refer you to Edwards... I continue eternally attached to the principles of your revolution. I hope it will end in the establishment of some firm government, friendly to liberty & capable of maintaining it. If it does not, I feel that the zealous apostles of English despotism will increase the number of its disciples."

Jefferson also requested Genet to forward to the French interior minister, a letter from James Madison, enthusiastically accepting honorary French citizenship and wishing France a triumph over all her enemies. Jefferson wrote Madison that his letter was precisely right in tone, though it was, in fact, a contemptuous disavowal of the president's neutrality proclamation.

The actions of the Philadelphia mobs, particularly those who cheered the capture of the British ship, were heady for the secretary and Genet. It is not hard to see Jefferson in Genet's early dispatch to Paris: "The voice of the people continues to neutralize the declaration of neutrality of President Washington." Jefferson was generally delighted with Genet in the first stages of their collaboration. On May 19 he wrote Madison: "It is impossible for anything to be more affectionate, more magnanimous than the purport of his mission... In short he offers everything and asks nothing." Eight days later, much annoyed, he reported to Madison that Hamilton suspected a trap in Genet's offer to negotiate a commercial treaty.

As the records now show, Genet hoped to subordinate the American economy to French interests. Genet was subsequently to report that Jefferson filled his mind with suspicions of the "monarchists" and "aristocrats" in the American government, whom Genet came to hate. While neither Jefferson nor Genet were trustworthy in their reports of conversations, the latter's 1797 letter to the former secretary, referring to what he said about the president, has a ring of truth: "You always spoke to me that unfortunately that excellent man was controlled by the English and the aristocrats, that you were the only one in the Cabinet who still took an interest in France, but that your voice was entirely powerless; that the people, however, was for us, that your friends would have a majority in the next Congress."

In June and July Genet handed to Jefferson a series of notes, which still rank as among the most insulting ever given an American secretary of state by a foreign diplomat. Genet said that neither "the public nor the private opinions of the President" were sufficient for him to change his course, for the government seemed to be directed by foreign (i.e., British) influence. He refused to comply with the president's orders against arming French warships or privateers in American ports. He asserted that France would alone determine whether her consuls acted as admiralty judges. He suggested that the president call Congress into session. He threw in phrases about America's "cowardly" abandonment of her friends. In July Genet wrote to France to complain that old man Washington ("le vieux Washington") was interfering with him "in a thousand ways." He had therefore determined secretly to order Congress to reassemble in Philadelphia.

Jefferson's duplicity reached its first peak in late June and early July when he compromised the president's neutrality policy as well as his own negotiations with Spain. On June 30 Jefferson asked the American commissioners at Madrid to protest vigorously against Spanish support of hostile Indian attacks in the south. The commissioners were to point out to the Spanish court: "We love peace and we value peace... We abhor the follies of war... Unmeddling with the affairs of other nations... we have, with sincere and particular dispositions, courted and cultivated the friendship of Spain."

Six days later the secretary of state extended his cooperation to Genet's plan to seize Spanish Louisiana. Genet informed Jefferson that he was sending a French agent, André Michaux, to Kentucky, to enlist Americans for war against Spain's territories. He mentioned that there were two Americans, George Rogers Clark and Benjamin Logan, who had been made French generals and would do the actual recruiting. Genet stated that he was issuing proclamations from the United States, encouraging the inhabitants of Louisiana and Canada to revolt. The secretary noted in his diary that the minister said he was telling these things, not to the secretary of state, but to "Mr. Jeff." The latter told Genet that the Americans might be hanged, if caught on Spanish territory, but "leaving out that article I did not care what insurrections might be excited in Louisiana." At Genet's request, Jefferson gave Michaux a letter of introduction to the governor of Kentucky, in which he noted that Michaux stood in high favor with Genet, implying that he also stood well with the American government. In July, when Washington asked Jefferson to supply him with an account of all his written and oral communications with Genet, the available evidence indicates that Jefferson failed to disclose his Louisiana-Canada conversation to the president.

FALL OF GENET

On order of the president, backed in full by his cabinet, Jefferson gave Genet a courteous refusal on the part of the United States to repay the French loan in advance or to provide arms. Genet persisted nonetheless with his demands. Thereafter the presidential diaries noted repeated instances of Genet's disregard of American laws and neutrality. Complaints were met with countercomplaints that American courts were interfering with French consuls, who were empowered to judge prizes. Genet protested that American marshals, acting "in the name of the President," had been outrageous in preventing the French from arming vessels.

The crucial test came for the government on June 22 when the president, according to his diary, received a letter from Governor Mifflin of Pennsylvania which "stated that a vessel called the *Little Sarah*, prize to the frigate *Ambuscade*, was equipping and fitting out as a privateer." This was being done in Philadelphia, almost under the president's nose. Washington asked the governor to investigate and report as soon as possible to the federal authorities. Two days later the president set out for a hasty trip to Mount Vernon because of the critical illness of his manager there. He returned to the capital on July 11, after Whiting's death, to face his severest diplomatic crisis.

On July 4 Hamilton received reliable word that the *Little Sarah*, renamed *Little Democrat*, had been heavily armed. The following day he met with Jefferson and Knox, who agreed that the cabinet should request the state's governor to prevent her sailing. Mifflin learned quickly that the ship was, in fact, ready to depart. He sent Alexander Dallas, secretary of the Governor's Council, to Genet late on the night of July 6 to warn him not to let the ship leave. Genet, in a rage, threatened to appeal at once to Congress and the sovereign people of the country. He said the ship would sail.

That same day Genet had gained Jefferson's cooperation in his Louisiana venture. During the conversation Genet informed the secretary that he intended to send two armed privateers to assist the enterprise. Jefferson did not record whether Genet mentioned that the *Little Sarah* was to be one of the two, but this was not hard to guess. The day after the dispute with Dallas, the secretary of state called on the French minister. Exactly what happened will never be known but it is clear that there was a violent altercation. Jefferson subsequently prepared two highly variant versions of the discussions. He wrote one immediately afterward on July 7 for Madison: "Never, in my opinion, was so calamitous an appointment made, as that of the present Minister of F. Here. Hot headed, all imagination, no judgment, Passionate & even indecent towards the [president] in his written as well as verbal communications, talking of appeals from him to Congress, from them to the people, urging the most unreasonable & groundless propositions & in the most dictatorial style &c.&c.&c. If ever it should be necessary to lay his communications before Congress or the public, they will excite universal indignation."

During the conversation Genet refused to delay the ship's departure until the president returned to the city, but he informed Jefferson that the *Little Sarah* might not be ready to sail. He added that any attempt to stop her by force would be met with force. He hinted too that a French fleet was about to arrive in American waters. Jefferson then persuaded the Pennsylvania governor to restrain the state militia, by assuring him the ship would not be ready to sail before the president arrived.

In his *Anas*, Jefferson noted a version of the conversation with Genet, which he gave to Mifflin, and which undoubtedly was similar to the report he subsequently gave the president. He said that Genet had talked so much he found it impossible to state the particulars of what he said. He added: "He did, in some part of his declamation to me, drop the idea of publishing a narrative or statement of transactions; but he did not on that, nor ever did on any other occasions in my presence, use disrespectful expressions of the President."

On July 8 there was a conference attended by the secretaries of state, treasury, and war, together with the governor of Pennsylvania. Hamilton, Knox, and Mifflin argued that the president's orders to stop the departure of vessels armed in the United States should be firmly supported. Mifflin proposed to send state militia to Mud Island, below Philadelphia, and Knox agreed to supply them with federal guns. Jefferson pleaded against this policy, fearful that the French would fire back. He claimed that France was "a most friendly nation" which was supporting "the most sacred cause that ever man was engaged in." The secretary of state managed to stymie action long enough for the *Little Sarah* to move downriver past Mud Island. He then took to his bed with a high fever and was still there when the president arrived in the capital on July 11. As soon as Washington read the correspondence, he wrote Jefferson:

> *What is to be done in the case of the <u>Little Sarah</u>, now at Chester. Is the Minister of the French Republic to set the Acts of this Government at defiance <u>with impunity</u>? and then threaten the Executive with an appeal to the people? What must the World think of such conduct, and of the Government of the U. States in submitting to it?*
>
> *These are serious questions. Circumstances press for decision, and as you have had time to consider them (upon me they come unexpected) I wish to know your opinion upon them, even before tomorrow, for the Vessel may then be gone.*

Jefferson pleaded with Genet to detain the ship until the president could study the legal problems, but the ship sailed to sea. Hamilton and Knox asked the president to request that France recall Genet immediately.

During the many crises of 1793, Knox, the huge secretary of war, was as fearlessly solid in international affairs as he had been on the battlefield. Throughout, and for the rest of his time in the cabinet, he was the president's strongest bulwark. His energetic attempt to prevent the escape of the *Little Sarah* risked Washington's displeasure, because he had given federal guns to state militia. Although the president on his return thought it an unfortunate precedent for other states, he approved the measure. Knox went farther than any other cabinet member in proposing the immediate suspension of Genet's functions. Knox's views greatly displeased Jefferson who called him a "fool" in his diary notes.

The cabinet struggled and fought, supposedly in secret, in the last days of July and the hot early days of August with the problems of France and Genet. Hamilton and Knox proposed that all correspondence with Genet be made public but Jefferson demurred. He suggested that this would set off a popularity contest between the president and the French minister: he gave his real reason to Madison—that such a revelation would weaken their faction in the country. The cabinet unanimously agreed that the French government be asked to recall Genet; all members but Jefferson wanted this to be peremptory. Jefferson suggested the request be made "with great delicacy." When the question arose as to whether Genet should be informed, Knox was for first telling him and then kicking him out of the country, whereas Jefferson thought it best not even to inform him, since "little differences" between friendly governments could be ironed out directly.

In the end Jefferson had to write to Gouverneur Morris to ask France to recall Genet. After a delay he also informed Genet that he was to be dismissed. Genet fired back in the press with a loud salvo against Jefferson. In the meantime, he had encouraged his consuls at New York and Boston to bring ashore forces from French warships to prevent American marshals from placing prizes under American jurisdiction.

By November, the president and Hamilton had swung over to Knox's view that Genet should be asked to leave the country. Jefferson opposed this, suggesting that Genet might not be willing to go. In the end, radical political changes in France caused that country to replace its minister.

THE HOT SUMMER AND FALL

The eleven months from June 1793 to April 1794 were the most perilous of Washington's presidency. In addition to trouble with France, almost everything else went wrong. The United States had no navy and its tiny army was almost entirely concentrated in the Ohio Valley. The country was far more sharply divided politically than during the revolution. In all the major seaports and in western villages, Jacobin clubs shouted for America to support France in its war. Hugh Brackenridge, in a July 4 speech in western Pennsylvania, declared that if France asked for American heroes and privateers, the United States should reply: "You shall have them... Our voice of war shall be heard with yours." On Bastille Day, Governor Mifflin, though his own authority had been defied by France, attended a dinner with Genet where speeches and toasts implied that those who would separate America from France were "Arnolds" and "traitors." The Jeffersonian press was soon calling

Washington a double-dealer and traitor; one cartoon placed the president's head under a guillotine and Philip Freneau composed a funeral dirge for George Washington.

While mobs shouted for war with England, the British government formulated policies which made it nearly impossible for the president to pursue a course of peaceful neutrality, General Wayne, from the field, wrote to Knox on July 2 that not only were the British using every tactic to prevent the American peace commissioners from treating with the northwest Indians, but they were sending agents to the southern Indians, in order to bring them into general league against the United States. A little later he reported that hundreds of Cherokees and Creeks were proceeding north to the Maumee Valley to meet British agents. These intrigues were directed by John Graves Simcoe, lieutenant governor of upper Canada. Simcoe had fought the Americans all during the revolution and had been captured by Washington at Yorktown. Not long before he had declared that he was determined once more to meet Washington on the field of battle and this time to defeat him. By the end of the year, the failure of peace negotiations made it clear that General Wayne would have to take the offensive against the Indians and risk war with England.

In June the British government issued an order-in-council, which provided for the seizure of all American ships carrying goods to France. This was reinforced in the autumn when the French Caribbean possessions were made a special target. Secret orders were issued to the Royal Navy in the West Indies, and their ships soon rounded up more than 250 American merchant vessels. Many of these were condemned in admiralty courts and their crews left penniless and starving.

Additional trouble for the president came from the South, where relations with both Spain and the Indians were critical. The hard-working Knox frequently brought to the president's desk his immense correspondence from American governors and agents in the area. A portion of the Creek nation was warring with other parts, the Cherokees were fighting the Creeks, while both engaged in raids on American settlements. Spanish agents continually worked to stir up the tribes to war on the Americans. As a further fillip to trouble, the French consul at Charleston organized a Franco-American expedition to proceed overland to attack Spanish settlements in Florida.

A number of Americans were in foreign pay. William Smith, the vice-president's son-in-law, was a French political and commercial agent, employed to press for money and arms for France. The second in command of the American army, General James Wilkinson, was in Spanish pay. Wilkinson tipped off the Spanish commissioners in Philadelphia that the French planned to invade their territory and that George Rogers Clark had been made a French general for this purpose. The Spaniards complained at once to the secretary of state. At the president's order, Jefferson, who had helped to promote the plot, was forced to write to the governor of Kentucky to warn him not to help the French. The governor replied that he did not understand why Jefferson should interfere when America's friends wanted to attack Spanish tyrants. To old and trusted friends, Washington reviewed his troubles with candid humor. He wrote Henry Lee, Virginia's governor, on July 21:

I should have thanked you at an earlier period for your obliging letter... had it not come to my hands only a day or two before I set out for Mount Vernon; and at a time when I was much hurried, and indeed very much perplexed with the disputes, memorials and what not, with which the Government were pestered by one or other of the petulant representatives of the powers at War: and because, since my return... I have been more than ever overwhelmed with their complaints. In a word, the trouble they give is hardly to be described.

The communications in your letter were pleasing and grateful to me; for, although I have done no public act with which my mind upbraids me, yet it is highly satisfactory to learn that the things which I do (of an interesting tendency to the peace and happiness of this Country) are generally approved...

That there are in this, as well as in all other Countries, discontented characters, I well know; as also that these characters are actuated by very different views: Some good... some bad, and (if I might be allowed to use so harsh an expression) diabolical; inasmuch as they are not only meant to impede the measures of that Government generally, but...to destroy the confidence, which it is necessary for the people to place... in their public servants; for in this light I consider myself, whilst I am an occupant of office; and if they were to go further and call me their slave, (during this period) I would not dispute the point.

But in what will this abuse terminate? The result, as it respects myself, I care not; for I have a consolation within, that no earthly efforts can deprive me of, and that is that neither ambitious nor interested motives have influenced my conduct. The arrows of malevolence, therefore, however barbed and well pointed, never can reach the most vulnerable part of me... The publications in Freneau's and [Bache's] papers are outrages on common decency; and they progress in that style, in proportion as their pieces are treated with contempt...

As we are told that you have exchanged the rugged and dangerous field of Mars, for the soft and pleasurable bed of Venus, I do in this, as I shall in every thing you may pursue like unto it good and laudable, wish you all imaginable success and happiness.

Earlier in the year Lee had asked Washington whether he should accept an offer to become a general in the French revolutionary army. The president, writing privately, warned him that conditions in France were too troubled and that he did not think it would be a very opportune time to go. Lee, instead, married Ann Hill Carter, who was to produce Robert E. Lee, who would vainly attempt to destroy the nation his father had worked so hard to build.

YELLOW FEVER

John Adams wrote to a friend in 1808 that if yellow fever had not appeared, the president would have been hauled out of his house in 1793 and roughly treated by the Philadelphia mobs, but this seems an Adams exaggeration. The epidemic did, however, bring government and politics almost to a halt. During its height, Martha Washington proved more strong-minded than the president for she forced him out of the city.

Philadelphia had been overwhelmed by French refugees from Santo Domingo where the fever flourished. A cabinet meeting in early July, while Washington was still out of town, discussed a letter from Henry Lee, which mentioned that the governor of South Carolina was worried that the French were bringing epidemic diseases from the West Indies. He asked for advice. The cabinet, having no information, did not take the letter seriously.

Yellow fever was first diagnosed by Dr. Benjamin Rush on August 19 as the cause of a number of deaths near the Philadelphia waterfront. Rush, who noted that mosquitoes were very troublesome that month, attributed the outbreak to rotting coffee brought from the West Indies. Washington's first written mention of the epidemic was contained in an August 23 letter to his temporary Mount Vernon manager, Howell Lewis, in which he said that Philadelphia was "very sickly and numbers dying daily." That same day Rush wrote his wife that the fever had taken a sudden and "alarming" spread and people were fleeing the city. He issued a statement on the disease to the public. It appeared in the *American Daily Advertiser* about the time the paper printed an unsigned letter recommending the use of oil on all stagnant waters to control the increase of mosquitoes expected after heavy August rains.

Alexander Hamilton and his wife both came down with the disease in early September. It was the secretary of the treasury who subsequently led a move for a more rational treatment of the disease than that used by Dr. Rush. Hamilton's old West Indies boyhood friend, Ned Stevens, to whom he disclosed his ambitions at fourteen, had settled into a Philadelphia medical practice, after taking an Edinburgh degree. Stevens' treatment was an essentially modern one, in which, where there is no specifically known cure, all support is given to nature. Yellow fever is highly debilitating and dehydrating; Stevens recommended that the patient stay quietly in bed, keep serene, and receive good nursing care, and that he eat well and drink many liquids, including Madeira. He recommended peppermint oils to relieve vomiting. Stevens deplored excessive evacuations which reduced the body's liquid. The Alexander Hamiltons recovered relatively quickly under Stevens' care.

Dr. Rush, assisted by various physicians and orderlies, sometimes treated as many as 150 patients a day. He used an entirely different procedure. He gave his patients severe purges more fit for a horse than a man. In addition, he bled them to excess, occasionally drawing more blood in five days than the amount normally contained in an adult human body. Both processes greatly increased debilitation and dehydration. There is no way to estimate how many deaths his methods caused but his letters to his wife contain the names (not all of them his patients) of 120 persons who died, including his sister, several of his student physicians, and numerous old friends. Others, outside his direct care, followed the Rush methods he gave out freely to the newspapers.

On September 11 Hamilton published a letter in the *Federal Gazette* and *Philadelphia Daily Advertiser* strongly praising Dr. Stevens' methods. As the disease spread and panic grew, Hamilton's letter was increasingly used to prove that Rush was wrong. In a final rationalization Rush stated he was being persecuted for having "republican" principles for which he could never be forgiven by such people as Hamilton.

The president, in late August, had written to his proposed new manager for Mount Vernon, William Pearce, that he planned to be at his farms on September 20. He asked Pearce to meet him there. Although the epidemic spread and the death rate went up sharply, the president decided to keep to his schedule. He suggested to his wife that she take her two grandchildren and proceed ahead of him to Mount Vernon. Martha Washington drew herself up to her five feet and announced that she would not leave the president in danger and the children would stay right there with him. He surrendered; on September 10 he climbed into the carriage with his wife and the children, and headed for Mount Vernon. On September 25, sounding a bit sheepish, he told the story to Tobias Lear. The president's departure meant that members of the cabinet, including Jefferson, and most government staffs, soon followed.

While at Mount Vernon, Washington's main concern was how he could get the government to function again and where Congress should meet. He made numerous constitutional inquiries to his widely scattered cabinet as well as to James Madison and the speaker of the House; he received sharply divergent advice in reply. In the end he decided to rent a house in Germantown, in ample time to prepare his fifth annual State of the Union message. With the first frosts the epidemic suddenly halted. On November 24 Washington wrote to Burges Ball that the fever had apparently entirely ceased in the city and he was now spending considerable time there. Shortly afterwards he was back in his old house.

During this period he outlined topics for Congress, which indicated that he had a lot on his mind—the western posts, British sea measures, negotiations with Spain, squabbles with Genet, American captives at Algiers, failure to attain peace with the Western Indians, troubles in Georgia and the Southwest, and a need for increased defense measures. His keynote point was to be: "The times are critical, and much temper and cool deliberate reflection is necessary to maintain Peace with dignity and safety to the United States." Washington had written Richard Henry Lee on October 24 to say that those who were attempting to subvert the government's peaceful measures were not genuinely concerned with France, nor liberty, for if war came they "would be among the first and loudest of the clamourers against the expense and impolicy of the measure."

STATE OF THE UNION

In view of the multiple problems to be presented to Congress, the president decided to cover many of them in separate messages. On December 3, 1793, at noon, Washington delivered his fifth annual message, his most forceful to date. He gracefully thanked the American people for their "affectionate partiality" in choosing him again for office, in spite of his "earnest wish for retirement."

He then stated bluntly that he intended to keep the country out of war. He had issued a neutrality proclamation, designed not only to keep Americans from committing belligerent acts but to impress on foreign nations that the United States was entitled to all the immunities of neutrality. He had not hesitated to prevent France from arming vessels within the United States, nor from retaining British merchant vessels captured within American territorial waters. He urged Congress to strengthen the federal laws in order to prevent *all* persons within the United States from committing hostile acts, assuming judicial powers, or organizing military expeditions. He continued:

I cannot recommend to your notice measures for the fulfillment of <u>our</u> duties to the rest of the world, without again pressing upon you the necessity of placing ourselves in a state of complete defence, and of exacting from <u>them</u> the fulfillment of their <u>duties</u> towards <u>us</u>. The United States ought not to indulge a persuasion that... they will forever keep at a distance those painful appeals to arms, with which the history of every other nation bounds. There is a rank due to the United States among Nations, which will be withheld, if not absolutely lost, by the reputation of weakness. If we desire to avoid insult, we must be able to repel it; if we desire to secure peace, one of the most powerful instruments of our rising prosperity, it must be known, that we are at all times, ready for War.

Two days later the president sent to Congress a special message on relations with France and Great Britain. With respect to the former, he wrote: "It is with extreme concern I have to inform you, that the proceedings of the person whom they have unfortunately appointed their Minister plenipotentiary here, have breathed nothing of the friendly spirit of the nation which sent him; their tendency on the contrary, has been to involve us in War abroad, and discord and anarchy at home... The papers now communicated, will more particularly apprize you of these transactions."

With reference to London, the president said: "The British Government, having undertaken by orders to the Commanders of their armed vessels, to restrain generally our commerce in Corn and other provisions to their own ports and those of their friends, the instructions now communicated were immediately forwarded to our Minister at that Court... I may expect to learn the result... in time to make it known to the Legislature during their present Session."

On December 16 the president delivered a further message on Spain. While, he said, his commissioners were treating at Madrid, the agents of their government were exciting "the hostilities threatened and exercised by the southern Indians on our border... It could not be conceived we would submit to the scalping knife and tomahawk of the savage without any resistance. I thought it time therefore to know... the views of their sovereign, and despatched a special messenger with instructions to our Commissioners, which are among the papers now communicated."

The president, in vigorous command of the foreign relations of the United States, proceeded, for the rest of the month, to dispatch messages to his manager and overseer at Mount Vernon. Included were complete plans for all major crops on his Mount Vernon farms for each of the years 1794 to 1799. If he could hold the peace, he would be back there to direct the last half of his six-year plan.

ELEVEN

PEACE IN THE WEST

1794

T HE PRESIDENT HAD expressed to Congress his feeling that a real, rather than a "fair," neutrality was "the powerful instrument of our rising prosperity." In an era where economic indices were few, the president could not know in the fullest detail the scope of the country's economic growth during his administration. His extensive travels and repeated conversations with members of Congress from various states, however, gave him a pretty good concept of it. In addition his Treasury reports showed that government revenue in 1793 was nearly two-and-a-half times the annual rate of 1789. By the end of 1793 gross national product had shown a gain of nearly 50 percent. Although the youthful population was growing with remarkable rapidity, real income per capita rose by an average of 9 percent a year.

Late in 1793 Jefferson reported to Madison that "the market," as he called the cost of living, had been going steadily upward in Philadelphia. Madison's boardinghouse charges would be higher at the new session of Congress. Jefferson blamed Hamilton for juggling the government bond market in order to raise prices and tax the farmer. In reality the American farmer was the principal beneficiary of the price rises of the 1790s, which seem to have been induced entirely by external causes. The revolution in France and the outbreak of a general European war brought food and raw material shortages and a constant rise in European demand. In consequence prices of American

exports increased much more rapidly than those of imports of European manufactured goods and West Indies tropical products. The terms of trade
became increasingly favorable for the United States. The effects were noticeable in several individual economic indices of the period. By 1793 Americans
were importing eight times as much coffee and nearly four times as much
sugar as in 1789; an indeterminate portion of this was, however, for re-export.
In a single year, excises paid on domestic whiskey jumped by nearly 60 percent, although some of the increase may have come from a better collection
of the tax. In 1789, after more than 170 years of settlement, the United States
had only 75 post offices; in the next four years, 131 were added. Government
revenues, thus far, generally covered the growth in military expenditures and
allowed for a planned further increase.

Even so the tax system was so light on the American farmer that
Washington could write to Sir John Sinclair on July 20, 1794: "Your system of
Agriculture, it must be confessed, is in a stile superior and of course much
more expensive than ours; but when the balance at the end of the year is
struck, by deducting [your] taxes, poor rates, and incidental charges of every
kind from the produce of the land in the two Countries, no doubt can remain
in which Scale it is to be found."

One person much hurt by the rising prosperity was the president himself.
His annual allowance of $25,000 to cover all the expenses of the presidency,
including rent, entertainment, secretaries, and domestic staff, remained
fixed, while prices continued to rise. In his last term, Washington's real
income was cut by a third and he had to sell land to meet his expenses.
Although he found a new manager for his Mount Vernon farms, William
Pearce, who turned out to be more competent than many of his previous managers, he complained that his farm income and outgo just about balanced.

Washington had trouble, like leaders of underdeveloped countries, in
finding men to fill positions with the government. His rigid standard precluded many, those whom he nominated frequently declined for various reasons—health or family, a preference for being important in their own state,
or, in the case of Supreme Court justices, an unwillingness to ride circuit. With
the growth of the pro-French faction in American politics, the field of choice
further narrowed. Out of necessity Washington picked Edmund Randolph,
his old friend and attorney, as secretary of state in place of Jefferson who
resigned at the end of the year. Randolph had at least the advantage of having sat through all the cabinet crises, but as secretary of state he was to be a
largely negative factor. William Bradford was appointed attorney general in
his place.

END OF GENET

Jefferson's old friend, Brissot de Warville, who had plunged France into war with England, was guillotined at the end of October 1793. Genet, a Girondin, in consequence lost his basis of political support in France. Even without the American request for his recall, he could not have lasted long.

On February 21 Jean Fauchet, the new French minister, arrived in Philadelphia with a group of aides and an order for the arrest of Genet and his return to France. David Cobb remarked that Genet would soon have been a head shorter, if the president had not offered him asylum. In 1797 Genet, still angry at Jefferson, wrote him: "Robespierre, acting upon your denunciations alone, [gave] orders not to allow me to arrive alive in Paris... This bloody request was rejected by Washington who declared that he had asked for my recall and not for my punishment; but Randolph, your friend... added confidentially that I still had many friends." Genet soon courted and married Cornelia Clinton, the daughter of the governor of New York.

On February 22, 1794, Washington's sixty-second birthday, Fauchet presented his credentials to the president. That evening, with Washington and members of the cabinet, he attended the Philadelphia Assembly Ball, held annually on the president's birthday. Fauchet was as much an intriguer as the other French diplomats who had been stationed in America, but his was a more subtle approach. He soon recalled the commissions given out by Genet, notably to George Rogers Clark, thus reducing the possibility that the United States would be involved in war with Spain.

JOHN JAY, SPECIAL MINISTER

In his 1793 and 1794 diaries the president made copious notes of correspondence handed him by members of the cabinet. He followed General Wayne's activities in the West with the closest attention. He wrote of the work of Clark in promoting the invasion of Louisiana, the intrigues of Simcoe, and the general disaffection to the federal government in Kentucky.

Washington also made summaries of reports from his diplomatic and other agents abroad, many quite unpleasant. On December 11, 1793, he wrote: "Letter... from Edwd. Church, Lisbon 8 October 93... thinks that sooner or later to *crush the U.S.* is the determination of Engd. & Spain... [Lisbon] October 12 containing the disagreeably important intelligence of a truce having taken place between Portugal and Algiers for 12 months—thro' the mediation of G. B. The Algerine fleet has therefore sailed out into the Atlantic...

Four American vessels have been captured... The view of the English being the injury of the U.S." The president shortly afterwards wrote that Portugal, alone of the European powers, had made a friendly gesture, in offering to convoy American ships, in spite of protests handed to the Portuguese court by the Spanish and British ambassadors.

On January 21 Washington had a letter from Thomas Pinckney, in which he quoted Lord Grenville, British foreign secretary, as assuring him that the government and people of Great Britain wanted to keep "on good terms" with the United States. Any illegal seizures of American ships in the Caribbean would be fully prosecuted. In January Britain did, in fact, greatly modify the earlier orders-in-council but the news took a long time to reach Philadelphia. In February the president started to receive reports of the many American ships that had been captured in the Caribbean. On March 25 he forwarded to Congress letters from the American consul at St. Eustatia, which stated that as many as 250 ships had been seized.

Ominous reports from Canada also reached the president. On March 10 Governor George Clinton of New York forwarded an account of a belligerent speech by Lord Dorchester to the Northwest Indians on February 10. The Canadian governor, recently returned from England, said that all efforts by Great Britain to establish peace had failed, and she and the United States would soon be at war. The Indians could then set their own terms within the neutral area which Britain would establish.

Although Dorchester's threat was real, and was soon followed by the establishment of a British fort on the Maumenee, the president viewed the situation with a far more experienced eye than most of his countrymen. He was aware that the British army under the Duke of York had suffered a defeat in the Netherlands, while the Royal Navy had been driven from Toulon. He wrote to Clinton on March 31 to say that the combined powers in Europe had suffered "disappointments." Lord Dorchester had reflected "the Sentiments of the British Cabinet at the period he was instructed. Foiled as that Ministry has been, whether it may not have changed its tone, as it respects us, is problematical." The United States should, nonetheless, be ready for any event. He asked Clinton to send agents to northern New York and Canada to obtain intelligence of British regular and militia troops, the state of the Canadian government, the opinions and dispositions of the Canadians, and to forward reports on American settlements and strength in the North.

General Knox, who accurately reflected Washington's thinking, wrote to General Wayne on March 31 stating that, following the January 8 changes in the British orders-in-council, there was "some hope that compensation and satisfaction will be made for the damages and injuries we have sustained..." In consequence, Wayne was directed to abstain "from every step or measure which could possibly be construed into any aggression on your part against either Spain or England... You are to consider that we are at peace with Great Britain and Spain and to act accordingly."

In Congress both Federalists and Jeffersonians lost their heads, temporarily, in reacting to the sea captures and Dorchester's speech. In early January Madison had introduced resolutions for commercial discrimination against Great Britain but these got nowhere. In the heat of the passionate feelings aroused by British policy, Madison had better luck with efforts to shut off foreign trade, a proposal similar to the futile and disastrous embargoes which Jefferson and Madison were to push forward in the early 1800s. Both Houses of Congress overwhelmingly voted a thirty-day stoppage of freight shipments from American ports. This hit American shipping severely while placing intolerable administrative burdens on the president. The questions poured onto his desk. Were state governors required to enforce federal orders? Should cutters take the news to southern ports? Could the British and French ministers be permitted to send out dispatches? Were passengers permitted to leave for the French West Indies? Were fishing vessels included in the order? Would ships in ballast be allowed to depart? Congress had passed the law, but the president was supposed to answer all the questions, his three lawyers in the cabinet not being very helpful.

Madison's embargo aroused furious approval and disapproval. The new French minister reported in admiration to Paris that Madison was "the Robespierre" of the American government. He was referred to as "Mr. Mad" by a disgruntled constituent of Senator King. Government forces and Jeffersonians thereafter split widely on the next steps to be taken. The Federalists followed Washington's views that arming for peace was the best assurance of keeping it. They introduced bills to establish the first navy under the new Constitution, to fortify the coastal cities, to increase the armed forces, to strengthen the militia, and to increase the number of arsenals. Madison, Monroe, and others of their party fought against these measures but went down to easy defeat. In turn, they attempted to break off intercourse with Great Britain and to sequester all debts owed to the British until she should yield.

The president had already advised Knox that he thought an agreement could be obtained with London. It is not possible entirely to reconstruct the subsequent events which led to the appointment of John Jay, particularly when the president kept his counsel even from his secretary of state. On March 12 Senator Ellsworth, representing several members of the Senate, called on the president to suggest that he send a special envoy to Great Britain. Ellsworth proposed Hamilton as the man best qualified for the mission. In one of his rare disclosures of opinion, Washington said that, while he had confidence in Hamilton, many in the country did not and he would have to take account of this. Two days later Edmund Randolph suggested that the president send an assistant to Pinckney to work on legal and other aspects of the British seizures.

The embargo took effect on March 26. On April 7 Senator King of New York called on the British minister, George Hammond, who stated a bit wryly that not many people came to his house these days and he was glad to see him. Hammond was encouraging. He wanted to see a special envoy proceed to London, for he too hoped for peace and friendly commercial intercourse between the two countries. He informed King that he did not believe that the Dorchester speech could possibly have had the approval of the British government. As proof, he pointed out that the orders-in-council, which had aroused so great a storm in America, were quickly revoked.

It was clear that an envoy extraordinary would have to be of high rank within the government to make the mission impressive. This left the choice among the vice-president, who was never seriously considered, the chief justice, and Hamilton. On April 14 Hamilton wrote the president, outlining his views of the problem in relation to Great Britain. In a forthright way, he said that there were too many objections in the country to his appointment. He strongly urged the chief justice for the position.

While this was going on, the secretary of state, probably with the nudging of Fauchet, endeavored to push Madison forward as special envoy, but this idea got nowhere. James Monroe, in a letter which the president clearly regarded as impertinent, wrote him on April 8 to say that sending Hamilton would be "injurious to the public interest." Washington replied the next day: "I request, if you are possessed of any facts or information, which would disqualify Colo. Hamilton... that you would be so obliging as to communicate them to me in writing... Colo. Hamilton and others have been mentioned and have occurred to me as an Envoy for endeavoring by negotiation, to avert the horrors of War. No one... is yet absolutely decided on in my mind... As I alone am responsible for a proper nomination, it certainly behooves me to name such an one as, in my judgment, combines the requisites for a mission so peculiarly interesting to the peace and happiness of this country."

On April 15, the day after his receipt of Hamilton's declination, the president sent a note to the chief justice, who by this time was well apprised of the situation and knew what was behind the invitation: "At as early hour this morning, as you can make convenient to yourself, I should be glad to see you. At eight o'clock we breakfast. Then, or after, as suits you best, I will expect to have the satisfaction of conversing with you on an interesting subject."

Jay, devoutly religious and possessing an integrity as great as the president's, was thoroughly realistic. He knew that he was being given the most difficult assignment of Washington's administration, the country was deeply divided, and too many persons wanted no treaty and no peace. He accepted, with feelings which he expressed to his wife: "I feel the impulse of duty strongly... On an occasion so important, I ought to follow its dictates, and commit myself to the care and kindness of that Providence, in which we both have the highest reason to repose the most absolute confidence."

On April 16 Washington sent a message to the Senate: "Peace ought to be pursued with unremitted zeal, before the last resource, which has so often been the scourge of nations and cannot fail to check the advanced prosperity of the United States, is contemplated; I have thought proper to nominate, and do hereby nominate John Jay, as Envoy Extraordinary of the United States to his Britannic Majesty."

The appointment of Jay set off a wild storm among a minority in the country. Jay was hanged or burned in effigy and denounced on the Senate floor. Washington was excoriated in the Jeffersonian press, being even accused of trying to spirit the chief justice out of the country so that he could not, as required by the Constitution, preside at the president's impeachment trial. Neither Washington nor Jay was ruffled, but Mrs. Jay had hard work to bear the attacks with the composure her husband encouraged her to show.

Before Jay accepted his mission, he noted to Washington that the turbulence in Congress had to be kept under control. He was in no position to negotiate if Congress cut off all trade with Britain and refused payment on commercial debts. The bill to break off intercourse with Britain passed the House; it was beaten in the Senate on April 28 by the veto of Vice-President Adams. This was the high point reached by those who wanted to interfere with the president's peaceful negotiations. A Senate bill to stop paying debts to Britain got only the votes of Virginia's senators. The embargo, after being extended a month, died unlamented in May.

Between April 19, when he issued his commission to John Jay, and May 6 the president worked intensively on instructions for the mission. These were contained in the official directive signed by Edmund Randolph. The letter, although long, was remarkably clear and simple. The president observed that "the solemnity of a special mission" bore the fullest evidence to the British that he wanted "to repel war, for which we are not disposed, and into which the necessity of vindicating our honor and our property may, but can alone drive us and at the same time, to assert, with dignity and firmness, our rights, and our title to reparation for past injuries."

Although the British minister had told Senator King that he did not believe there was the slightest chance that Parliament would vote compensation for seized American ships, the president made this the first order of business for Jay. If, and only if, this point were granted by Great Britain, Jay was directed, in point of order, then "to draw to a conclusion all points of difference between the United States and Great Britain, concerning the treaty of peace." Jay was especially urged to point out that retention of the posts, and the employment of British agents to stir up Indians, brought "much bloodshed on our frontiers."

The instructions reiterated that "vexations and spoilations" of American commerce were to be kept entirely separate from discussions of the 1783 treaty. Any settlement with respect to the latter was not to influence the former. If all these points were agreed to, then Jay, entirely at his discretion, was authorized but not directed to "listen to," or even broach the subject of a commercial treaty, as well as numerous related points, ranging from fisheries to control of piracy.

On May 12 Jay sailed from New York for London. The Society of St. Tammany at its dinner that day gave two not quite contradictory toasts: success to the Jay mission and success to the armies of France. While Jay was on his way across the seas, General Wayne reported further menacing developments in letters to the secretary of war:

> It wou'd appear, that there is a perfect understanding & a constant communication between the Spanish Commandant at post <u>St. Louis</u> on the Mississippi, and the British at Detroit... The Spaniards... have taken post at the Chickasaw Bluffs... There are five Spanish Gallies now at the Mouth of the Ohio, carrying a Number of large Cannon, & Sixty men each. [May 26]

> Recent and well authenticated intelligence [indicates that I] may eventually have to oppose a Heterogeneous Army composed of British troops, the Militia of Detroit & all the Hostile Indians NW of the Ohio; now assembling at Roche de Bout at the foot of the Rapids of the Miami... under the Command of the Famous Governor Simcoe... His taking post in the Centre of the Hostile Indians & so far advanced within our acknowledged limits is most certainly an Aggression... [May 30]

Although letters took a long time to reach Quebec, one of the earliest fruits of Jay's arrival in London was a July 5 British government reprimand to Lord Dorchester, so sharp in tone that he offered his resignation. The Canadian governor was directed to pull back immediately from the new post established at Roche de Bout, since the government expected to settle all issues with Mr. Jay.

In the meantime, Knox on June 7 had authorized Wayne to attack the Roche de Bout post, if necessary, but to treat the British and Spaniards with every courtesy. Knox, speaking for the president, added that he was convinced the British did not want war and he therefore hoped that "Mr. Jay… will be able to adjust all differences in an amicable and satisfactory manner."

JAMES MONROE, ENVOY EXTRAORDINARY

Within two months of his arrival in Philadelphia, Fauchet asked the secretary of state to recall Gouverneur Morris, the American minister, who had been a valuable and trusted informant to the president during the Reign of Terror. This placed Washington in a dilemma since he knew that the pro-French faction would want one of their adherents in the post. He at once asked Jay whether he would consent to be the permanent minister at London so that he could transfer Thomas Pinckney to Paris. Jay declined, and Washington offered the French post to Robert Livingston, the chancellor of New York. After Livingston refused, there was a wild scramble for the appointment. Hamilton suggested to the president that he ship Randolph to Paris, but this did not seem desirable. Randolph, in turn, pushed for Aaron Burr or James Monroe. In the end, Monroe was selected. This removed from the Senate an opponent of the president's policies but placed him in a position where he could damage his efforts to secure a British peace.

While Monroe was waiting to sail from Baltimore, Washington passed through the city on June 19. He tried to send a note by Monroe to Morris "to assure you that my confidence in, and friendship and regard for you, remains undiminished." Finding it had missed the ship, Washington wrote a longer letter from Mount Vernon on June 25, adding an appraisal of the political situation at home: "The affairs of this country *cannot go amiss*. There are so many *watchful guardians of them*, and such *infallible guides*, that one is at no loss for a director at every turn."

By the time Monroe got to Paris, Robespierre had been guillotined and there was some delay in accepting his credentials. Finally on August 15, while Jay was locked in strenuous negotiations with Lord Grenville, Monroe delivered a rapturous address to the French Convention, praising "the noble career of France… Whilst the fortitude, magnanimity and heroic valor of her troops command the admiration and applause of the astonished world, the wisdom and firmness of her councils unite equally in securing the happiest result." Monroe added that all America offered France "the most decided proof of her sincere attachment to the liberty, prosperity and happiness of the French Republic."

When the speech was completed, the president of the Convention embraced Citizen Monroe and kissed him on both cheeks. While neither the English cabinet nor public viewed these antics with any favor, Lord Grenville confined himself to an ironic little note, saying he was sure Jay did not envy Monroe. If, he implied, Monroe enjoyed being kissed in public, the British government could not very well object.

On September 25 the secretary of state, Edmund Randolph, who had vigorously opposed Washington's wish to instruct Jay to negotiate a treaty, wrote to Monroe: "Notwithstanding all the pompous expectations, announced in the gazettes, of compensation to the merchants, the prospect of it is, in my judgment, illusory; and I do not entertain the most distant hope of the surrender of the western posts. Thus the old exasperations continue, and new ones are daily added. Judge then how indispensable it is that you should keep the French republic in good humor with us."

OTHER DIPLOMATS

On May 27, when Washington nominated Monroe for Paris, he also sent to the Senate the name of William Short, minister at The Hague and commissioner to Spain, to be minister at Madrid. Short, the first American career diplomat, had served as Jefferson's secretary at Paris. Two days later, his voice shaking with pleasure, the presiding officer, John Adams, read a message from the president:

United States 29 May 1794

Gentlemen of the Senate

I nominate John Quincy Adams, of Massachusetts, to be Minister Resident of the United States of America, to their high mightinesses the States general of the United Netherlands.

The Senate cheerfully and unanimously confirmed the nomination of Adams to the post which his father had held as the first United States minister.

The great expansion of American shipping and foreign trade brought with it a widened need for consuls. Presidential appointments were made that year to Gibraltar, Leghorn, Bremen, Amsterdam, Teneriffe, St. Petersburg, and Dublin.

HAMILTON'S TROUBLES

Samuel Flagg Bemis' *Jay's Treaty* maintained what is probably the oddest thesis ever put forth by a historian that, in 1794, Hamilton dominated American foreign relations, military affairs, and fiscal policy. The Washington presidential papers, which Bemis indicates in his bibliography he failed to examine, disclose, instead, that Hamilton was a rather apathetic administrator, who received sharp chastisement from Washington.

In his directives to Jay, the president largely ignored Hamilton's advice, since he thought a commercial treaty of minor importance in relation to the overriding issue of peace. When Congress recommenced an earlier inquest as to whether Hamilton had violated laws providing for the use of foreign loans only for payments on foreign debt, whereas some funds had been transferred to the Bank of the United States, Hamilton asked Washington for a letter stating that he had approved all the transactions. He got little satisfaction from the President who replied on April 8:

> *I cannot charge my memory with all the particulars which have passed between us, relative to the disposition of the money borrowed. Your letters, however, and my answers... speak for themselves...*

> *As to verbal communications, I am satisfied and... I do not doubt that it was substantially as you have stated in the annexed paper, that I have approved of the measures which you, from time to time, have proposed to me for disposing of the Loans, upon the condition that what was to be done by you, should be agreeable to the Laws.*

Since the statement with its last critical phrase went to Congress and was made public, it provided Jefferson and Madison an opportunity to jeer privately at the supposed ignorance of the president on fiscal matters. In fact Washington had so clear a memory that he wrote to Hamilton on April 22: "I wish to have some explanation of your letter of yesterday... [as to] whether the appropriation now proposed... will not in some measure be contrary to the appropriation contained in my power of the 8th of August 1793."

The president had advised nieces and nephews that no excuse was better than a weak one. The secretary of the treasury replied the next day: "When I wrote my letter of the 21st instant I had entirely forgotten the existence of your two powers of the 8 of August, owing probably to the effect upon my memory of my sickness which soon after ensued." Hamilton referred to the "embarrassments" he would encounter if he did not do things in his way. The president replied: "It may be well for you to state to me what the embarrassments are which you suppose will arise." Hamilton produced a very long statement which Washington answered by a short note on April 27. Hamilton was directed to follow the instructions of August 8. The president added that he would have no objections whatever if Hamilton went to Congress to explain the "embarrassments which you consider as probable."

On July 2 Hamilton was blasted by the president, in reply to a letter he wrote concerning compensation to the British for vessels seized by the French in American waters. This was a matter which Congress had rejected: "My understanding… of this business… differs very widely from your interpretation of it." He pointed out that Congress had not approved, his was a constitutional presidency, he had been exceedingly careful to give an opinion only to the British, and he could not stretch his powers, as Hamilton recommended. The only thing for him to do was to tell the British minister that Jay was authorized to discuss the matter in London.

Even on appointments within the Treasury Department, Hamilton was given little discretion by the president. In a letter of June 24, Hamilton suggested a nominee for the minor post of collector at Hampton, Virginia, adding the names of those who had forwarded recommendations. The president replied that he was going to Virginia, and he would discuss the matter with the governor of the state.

THE RISE OF SECRETARY KNOX

In the critical years, the strongest man of the cabinet was the secretary of war, who was much too sensible to try to dominate his colleagues. Knox was a gifted and totally loyal administrator who followed the president's instructions and wishes as closely as possible. His great hulk absorbed any amount of work, even the crushing load imposed upon him in 1794. A check of the presidential diaries for the first half of the year indicates the president saw or corresponded with Knox about four times as often as with Hamilton and nearly always on much more complex business.

Knox administered within his department a great deal of what were considered to be foreign affairs. He had worked out treaties with the Creeks and Cherokees, which had been duly ratified by the Senate. He was endlessly engaged in establishing federal authority in the West under Indian treaties of the Confederation. He managed an extended, if weak, army-militia system along the frontiers, in cooperation with the state governors. He directed the Legion of the United States, the American army operating north of the Ohio.

He controlled a network of agents employed to pacify the Indians or to provide intelligence.

In 1794 Knox rose to his full strength. He had complete confidence in the president's judgment that there would be peace with Great Britain. His instructions to the army and to his agents were to avoid aggression and trouble at any cost. At the same time the congressional votes to expand the army, to establish a navy, and to provide defenses for the country's seaports, greatly increased his responsibilities.

On March 18 Knox made an effective suggestion to the president. He noted that, in general, the operations of the federal government had lessened the "patronage... influence... and dignity" of the state governors. The president had also frequently imposed on them "unpleasant duties" in enforcing federal neutrality laws. He suggested that it might "be a conciliatory and grateful measure to them, as Commanders of their Militia, to be the agents of the United States, in a certain degree, of the proposed fortifications... The Engineers might be directed to consult and take the opinions of the Governors upon the points most proper to be fortified... The Governors might also be requested to appoint some suitable person to superintend the erection of the works and also of the mounting of such Cannon... as are to be furnished by the respective States... By an arrangement of this sort it is conceived that the Governors would be kindly brought to act by system to support the general government."

Washington approved this plan, and the governors, many of whom had been revolutionary officers, responded with enthusiasm. Two states, Pennsylvania and New York, went so far, in fact, as to pass special acts for their defense, thus raising embarrassing constitutional questions. In New York, General von Steuben, long in retirement, volunteered a plan for fortifying the city of New York. He was subsequently appointed by the state as chairman of a committee to provide for northern defenses. Undoubtedly Knox's proposal influenced the subsequent hearty support to Washington from nearby governors, when he moved to break an insurrection in western Pennsylvania.

Both the president and Knox were anxious to have Indian delegations visit the capital that year, and many came. On June 14 the president wrote in his diary: "Had a meeting with the Chiefs of the Cherokee Indians, now in Philadelphia, at my house. The Secretaries of State, Treasury & War & Colo. Pickering were present. The great pipe was smoked by all. Delivered a speech to them in writing. Several of them spoke & after having eaten and drunk plentifully of cake & wine, they departed seemingly well pleased... being referred to Genl. Knox for further communication."

On July 11 the president received Paimingo, chief of the Chickasaws, and other chiefs. According to John Quincy Adams, who was present, a peace pipe, twelve to fifteen feet long, was brought out and everyone took whiffs from it. The president read a speech which was interpreted sentence by sentence. Then all had wine, punch, and cake. A few days later, at Knox's request, the president formally presented them with signed commissions.

Knox, in addition to handling armories, army, fortifications, and Indians, also worked on the authorized navy. He provided information and recommendations with great speed, and the president acted on them with decision. Following Indian attacks in Tennessee, Knox wrote the president that regular troops ought to be sent there but they could not be spared from Wayne. He therefore proposed that the president call into service the local militia, to be paid by federal funds and supplied with federal arms. On April 12 Washington wrote: "Your report dated the 11th instant, respecting the defense of Mero district is approved, and the Governor of the South Western Territory may be authorized to carry it into effect."

On April 15 Knox submitted to the president the first formal proposal for an American naval force. After he had discussed the matter with numerous shipbuilders and former naval officers, Knox recommended a program for construction of four ships of forty-four guns and two of thirty-six. He expressed prices, rather curiously, in pounds rather than dollars. His first preliminary estimate was that the larger ships would cost £34,100 each and the smaller, £27,300. Knox added that since the government was "of the whole people and not just a part only" it seemed proper to distribute the building among the ports of Charleston, New York, Boston, Philadelphia, Baltimore, and Norfolk. The following day Washington wrote Knox: "As soon as the most important points on which the master-builders have differed, are settled... and you can obtain means for carrying the law into effect, it is my desire that the work may be entered upon without delay."

On June 3 the president nominated and the Senate confirmed the first six captains of the regular navy: John Barry, Samuel Nicholson, Silas Talbot, Joshua Barney, Richard Dale, and Thomas Truxton. All had been revolutionary naval heroes who were to supervise ship construction. On July 25, long before there could be any ships, the captains met and designed uniforms for officers of the navy and the marine corps. Knox struck out the proposed "embroidery" as not suitable for a republican fleet.

Knox, his small salaried income steadily cut by price increases, was forced to think of resigning in order to provide for his large family. He asked the president for leave of absence in August, assuring him that things were under control and Hamilton could manage such business as the department's staff could not handle. He left for Maine on August 8 and thus missed receiving a rather immodest dispatch from General Wayne, dated August 28, which had been the goal of years of planning by General Knox:

> *It's with infinite pleasure that I now announce to you the brilliant success of the Federal army under my command with the combined force of the Hostile Indians & a considerable number of the Volunteers & Militia of Detroit on the 20th Instant, on the Banks of the Miamis, in the vicinity of the British post & Garrison.*

At Fallen Timbers, the last battle of the revolutionary war, Wayne, immensely cautious in preparing against any possible enemy surprises, attacked with such sudden force and fury that in an hour's battle, the astounded Indian, British, and Canadian army was totally annihilated as a fighting force. More impressive was the fact that Wayne beat over 2,000 of the enemy with fewer than nine hundred men. The nearby British garrison watched, helpless, as Wayne destroyed all the cornfields, as well as the houses and stores of Colonel Alexander McKee, the British agent in Ohio. Among those who received Wayne's special mention for bravery was Lieutenant William Henry Harrison.

MOUNT VERNON AND OTHER PROBLEMS

Sounding faintly offended, though this was not his intention, the president on July 13 wrote to his new Mount Vernon manager, William Pearce, who had complained of his numerous instructions: "I am sensible that I express my wishes faster than they can be accomplished; but by keeping them steadily in view you will fulfill them as fast as time and seasons will permit and this is all I can expect or do desire; but in order that my directions, when given, may not escape you, read my letters over frequently... or take from them at the time they are received such parts by way of memoranda to refresh your memory, as are necessary." The letters to Mount Vernon, picturing his acres in his mind as he wrote his instructions, appear to have been Washington's principal diversion from presidential duties.

Family problems, some trivial, plagued Washington. He had forwarded detailed instructions to Pearce to prepare a house in Alexandria for Fanny Washington. She wrote to the president to say that the cellar was damp and needed paving. He asked Pearce to do this work, adding: "This job will afford another week for Davis and his attendants, when one man in this City would begin and finish it... in half a day." It was an accurate guess. Washington learned from a subsequent report that the job had required six days.

Burges Ball asked his uncle to send down from Philadelphia "2 or 3 bushels of Chocolate Shells such as we've frequently drank Chocolate at Mount Vernon, as my Wife thinks it agreed with her better than any other Breakfast." The president politely replied that he would order the chocolate and have it placed on a ship to Virginia.

The president was once more brought into the troubled estate and family problems of Samuel Washington, his long-dead brother. Samuel's son, George Steptoe, had eloped in Philadelphia, the preceding year, with Lucy Payne, thereafter bringing his bride to his father's house, Harewood, at Charles Town. In September Dr. David Stuart informed Washington that there was to be a forced sale of Samuel's properties. He suggested that the president lend the estate a thousand pounds to prevent this. Washington replied on September 21: "The estate of my brother Samuel being involved, and left under wretched management, has already proved a heavy tax on me. Land which I sold twenty years ago… falling into his hands, and he thereby becoming paymaster to me, has… sunk me more than £800. For the board, education, and other expenses of his two sons, I am in a further advance for it, upwards of £1000 more, besides the support of his daughter Harriot." He added that giving a further thousand pounds would be a great hardship for him. He thought that Samuel's two sons had been extravagant, they had a mistaken idea of what their property was worth, and they seemed not to be "sensible, I believe, of the inconveniency of the advances I have made for their accommodation." If every other resource failed, Stuart was directed, nonetheless, to lend the money. The president did not, at this time, know of a footnote to this story. Six days previously Lucy Washington's recently widowed sister, Dolley Todd, had married, at Harewood, a rather troublesome member of Congress, James Madison.

"CREATED FREE"

Washington viewed slavery as abhorrent as well as uneconomic. His was a troublesome dilemma for he owned more slaves than his land could support. He noted that their productivity was but a fraction of that of white labor in Philadelphia. Unlike Jefferson, he had long refused to sell any of his slaves, no matter how pressing his financial problems, in order to avoid breaking up families. Sometime in 1793, in the midst of all his other problems, he resolved on a solution for his dilemma. So far as can be determined, he confided the plan to free all his slaves only to his family and to Tobias Lear.

After Arthur Young informed Washington that many farmers in the British Isles wanted to settle in America, the president in December 1793 provided

Young with a detailed report of all his Potomac holdings. He expressed a desire to rent to good farmers all Mount Vernon farms, except for the land around the mansion house. On May 6, 1794, he sent a copy of the letter to Tobias Lear in England, indicating that he would also like to sell all his western land holdings. He asked Lear to inquire in England for potential buyers. He added his reasons for selling or leasing most of his properties:

> *I have no scruple to disclose to you, that my motives for these sales (as hath been, in part, expressed to Mr. Young) are to reduce my income... to specialties [contractual income] that the remainder of my days may, thereby, be more tranquil and free from cares; that I may be enabled (knowing precisely my dependence) to do as much good with it as the resource will admit; for although, in the estimation of the world, I possess a good and clear estate, yet so unproductive is it, that I am oftentimes ashamed to refuse aids which I cannot afford unless I were to sell part of it to answer the purpose. (Private) Besides these, I have another motive which makes me earnestly wish for the accomplishment of these things, it is indeed more powerful than all the rest, namely to liberate a certain species of property which I possess, very repugnantly to my own feelings; but which imperious necessity compels... until I can substitute some other expedient by which expenses not in my power to avoid (however well disposed I may be to do it) can be defrayed.*

In Washington's mind, judging by his final directives, the problem was far more complex than that of giving them freedom, suffering a capital loss, and then forgetting about them. The older or sick workers who could not support themselves were to have pensions or other assured support. Those who wanted to work as free laborers had to be given employment. Children were to be educated and taught trades in order to prepare them for the future.

Washington's plan, had he been able to carry it out while living, might have had an enormous impact on the future of American society. Death came before he could provide this leadership but his will ordered his plan for freedom to be carried to completion.

WESTERN INSURRECTION

While called the Whiskey Rebellion, its supposed cause, the tax of as little as two cents a quart on domestic whiskey, was the flimsiest of pretexts for revolt. Hamilton had already demolished the arguments from western Pennsylvania, by his jocular declaration that if the tax hit the people of the area harder than anywhere else in the Union, they ought to try to be more temperate.

The insurrection, which extended from western Pennsylvania through Kentucky, had multiple causes, not all ignoble. Even before the 1776 revolution, friction existed between "the West" and the East. There were not infrequent complaints that taxes flowed eastward and no corresponding government benefits returned. When officials did appear, there was even more indignation as debtors were made to pay, the lawless were jailed, and squatters were kicked off land not theirs.

The federal government, after 1789, became an especial target as it moved to assert its sovereign authority over Indian affairs. The lawless, who had been accustomed to defrauding Indians of their land and to shooting them at will, were increasingly checked by federal officers; this aroused cries for liberty and the rights of man. British, Spanish, and French agents took advantage of the situation and freely circulated propaganda along with money and arms. The Jacobin or democratic societies were especially active in promoting both war with Britain and secession from the United States. The societies focused their attention, and eventually murderous tactics, not on their real objectives but on minor and unarmed officials of the federal government, the collectors of the alcohol tax.

On February 24 the president, according to his diary, "signed a Proclamation, offering a reward of 200 dollars for apprehending certain unknown persons who violently entered the office of the Collector of Revenue for the Counties of Westmoreland and Fayette in Pennsylvania and forced from him his commission." He had earlier noted therein that the "Collector for Bourbon" (County) in Kentucky had been having trouble.

In July disorders suddenly spread. While Hamilton was en route to Albany, Knox reported to the president on July 26 that Governor Mifflin of Pennsylvania was taking steps to suppress "the commotion in Allegheny county." It was soon evident to the president from numerous reports that armed rebellion against the federal government had broken out. He had no hesitation in signing a powerful proclamation, on August 7, 1794:

> And whereas the said combinations, proceeding in a manner subversive equally of the just authority of Government and of the rights of individuals, have hitherto effected their dangerous and criminal purpose... by endeavors to deter those who might be so disposed, from accepting offices... through fear of injury to persons and property, and to compel those who had accepted such offices, by actual violence to surrender or forbear the execution of them; by circulating vindictive menaces... [and] injuring and destroying the property of persons who were understood to have complied [with the law]; by inciting cruel and humiliating punishments upon private citizens... appearing to be friends of the law; by

intercepting the public officers on the highway, abusing, assaulting, and otherwise ill-treating them; by going to their houses in the night, gaining admittance by force, and committing other outrages, employing for these unwarrantable purposes the agency of armed banditti...

And whereas... the endeavors of the executive officers to conciliate a compliance with the laws, by explanations, by forbearance and even by particular accommodations... have been disappointed of their effect by the machinations of persons whose industry to excite resistance has increased with every appearance of disposition among the people to relax in their opposition and acquiesce in the laws, insomuch that many persons in the said Western parts of Pennsylvania have at length been hardy enough to perpetrate acts which I am advised amount to treason, being overt acts of levying war against the United States; the said persons having... proceeded in arms to the house of John Neville, inspector of revenue... having repeatedly attacked the said house with the persons therein, wounding some of them; having seized David Lenox, marshal of the district of Pennsylvania, who previous thereto, had been fired upon, while in the execution of his duty, by a party of armed men...

The president then quoted the act authorizing him to call out the militia "to execute the laws of the Union, suppress insurrections, and repel invasion." He noted that Associate Supreme Court Justice Wilson had declared that the laws were being opposed by such combinations of force as to render the usual processes of law no longer effective. Washington had therefore determined to order out the militia, since "the very existence of Government" was involved. He called on all "insurgents" to return to their abodes by September 1 or face the consequences.

On August 10 Washington acknowledged receipt of Charles Mynn Thruston's report of deep trouble in Kentucky. That state was moving to have its own war with Spain. The president said that he knew that the Jacobin societies were spreading disaffection there, in spite of "the unwearied endeavors of the General government to accomplish... what they seem to have most at heart, viz., the navigation of the Mississippi." They would be "dissatisfied under any circumstances, and under every exertion of government (short of a war with Spain, which must eventually involve one with Great Britain)." In referring to the Pennsylvania insurrection, he added:

If the laws are to be trampled upon, with impunity, and a minority (a small one too) is to dictate to the majority, there is an end put, at one stroke, to republican government, and nothing but anarchy and confusion is to be expected thereafter; for Some other man, or society, may dislike another Law and oppose it with equal propriety until all Laws are prostrate, and everyone (the strongest I presume) will carve for himself.

The president added that he was sure there would be people around who would be horrified equally by law-breaking and efforts to enforce the laws. As it turned out, the best example was the secretary of state, Edmund Randolph. He doubted whether Justice Wilson's letter had legal validity since it mentioned no particular laws that were violated. He opposed the use of force, fearing this would disrupt the Union. It was especially bad policy, he said, to draw militia from one state to enforce federal laws in another. He was afraid that Kentucky would secede, while western Pennsylvania would not only destroy the federal forces but would then turn against Wayne's army in Ohio. He foresaw a simultaneous civil war and war with England.

Randolph stood quite alone in the cabinet. The president directed that the militia of Pennsylvania, Maryland, Virginia, and New Jersey stand by in readiness. Governor Henry Lee of Virginia responded, offering the fullest support to Washington in suppressing rebellion and pledging that the president could count on him to lead the state's militia in person. Lee added that Patrick Henry had been much hurt by a story carried to him that Washington believed him to be "a factious seditious character." Lee thought this was unfortunate, for Henry was not only an able man but was now well disposed to the federal government. Washington's August 26 letter thanked Lee for his support and asked him to assure Patrick Henry that he had always "respected and esteemed him." He would be delighted to have him in the federal government, in any employment that he regarded as suitable, subject only to certain established practices, such as not having too many appointments in particular areas from a single state.

After issuing his proclamation, the president dispatched the attorney general and two federal agents, along with two Pennsylvanians, representing the state's governor, to negotiate with the insurgents. They were to be assured of full amnesty provided they submitted within the time set by the proclamation. By early September negotiations had failed, and Washington called the militia to active duty on September 9.

On September 25 he issued a final proclamation:

Whereas, from a hope that the combinations against the Constitution and laws of the United States would yield to time and reflection, I thought it sufficient, in the first instance, rather to take measures for calling forth the militia than immediately to embody them; but the moment is now come... when every form of conciliation not inconsistent with the being of Government has been adopted, without effect; when the well-disposed in these countries are unable by their influence and example, to reclaim the wicked from their fury, and are compelled to associate in their own defense; when the proffered lenity has been perversely misinterpreted into an apprehension that citizens will march with reluctance; when the opportunity of examining the serious consequences of a treasonable opposition has been employed in propagating principles of anarchy, endeavoring through emissaries to alienate the friends of order from its support, and inviting enemies to perpetrate similar acts of insurrection; when it is manifest that violence would continue to be exercised upon every attempt to defend the laws; when, therefore, Government is set at defiance, the contest being whether a small proportion of the United States shall dictate to the whole Union, and at the expense of those who desire peace, indulge a desperate ambition.

Now, therefore, I GEORGE WASHINGTON, President of the United States, in obedience to that high and irresistible duty, consigned to me by the Constitution, "to take care that the laws be faithfully executed"; deploring that the American name should be sullied by the outrages of citizens on their own Government; commiserating such as remain obstinate from delusion; but resolved, in perfect reliance on that gracious Providence, which so signally displays its goodness towards this country, to reduce the refractory to a due subordination to the laws; do hereby declare and make known that, with a satisfaction which can be equaled only by the merits of the militia summoned into service from the States of New Jersey, Pennsylvania, Maryland, and Virginia, I have received intelligence of their patriotic alacrity, in obeying the call... that a force, which according to every reasonable expectation, is already in motion to the scene of disaffection...

That same day, Washington, on the basis of his intelligence reports, wrote to Burges Ball:

The Insurrection in the Western counties of this State is... the first <u>ripe fruit</u> of the Democratic Societies. I did not, I confess, expect their labors would come to maturity so soon; though I never had a doubt that such conduct would produce some such issue if it did not meet the frown of those who were well disposed to order and good government, in time; for can anything be more absurd, more arrogant, or more pernicious to the peace of Society, than for self-created bodies, forming themselves into <u>permanent</u> Censors, and under the shade of <u>Night</u>, in a conclave, resolving [that] the acts of Congress which have undergone the most deliberate and solemn discussion by the Representatives of the people... [are] unconstitutional [or] pregnant of mischief; and that all who vote contrary to their dogmas are actuated by selfish motives or under foreign influence; nay in plain terms are traitors to their Country... The Democratic Society of this place (from which the others have

*emanated) was instituted by Mr. Genet for the express purpose of dissension, and
to draw a line between the people and the government, after he found the Officers
of the latter would not yield to the hostile measures in which he wanted to embroil
this Country.*

THE COMMANDER IN CHIEF

General Washington's call to arms for defense of the Union met with an overwhelming response. It was the more impressive because Pennsylvania filled its
quota of half the troops entirely from volunteers. Altogether at least 15,000
men assembled, more Americans than Washington had ever commanded,
except for fleeting moments in the revolution. The governors of
Pennsylvania, New Jersey, and Virginia placed themselves directly under the
orders of the president. Well-known regiments such as the Philadelphia Light
Horse and the Jersey and Macpherson Blues appeared. The officers included
several revolutionary generals and colonels: Morgan, Lee, Irvine, and Hand.
No fewer than five officers were nephews of the president. Henry Lee, newly
created major general and second in command to Washington, wrote him
that the federal union had to be preserved "at the risk of our lives and fortunes." Marching through a sullen Virginia countryside to Cumberland,
Maryland, Lee there joined the troops of his neighboring state. Pennsylvania
and New Jersey troops went to a rendezvous at Carlisle, Pennsylvania.

On September 30 George Washington assumed his constitutional duties as
"Commander in Chief... of the Militia of the several States, when called in to
the actual service of the United States." At 10:30 that morning, accompanied
by Alexander Hamilton and his secretary-nephew, Bartholomew Dandridge,
he set out for Carlisle.

For the president, while the business was deadly serious, it was also something of an outing. He spent as much time looking at the economy of the
country as into military matters. The success of his call assured him that he
had a force more than sufficient to battle down the insurgents, who had
threatened to sweep across Pennsylvania and seize Philadelphia. Washington's
first night on the road was further cheered when Knox's chief clerk galloped
up with Wayne's dispatch announcing his great victory at Fallen Timbers.
Ohio was now safe, and Pennsylvania, he knew, soon would be.

On October 2 the president examined a canal, under construction, to con-
nect the Susquehanna and the Schuylkill Rivers. Its four brick locks he pronounced to be "admirably constructed." On October 13 he made diary notes
on the country as far as Williamsport, Pennsylvania. From Philadelphia to

Reading, he found the whole road "very pleasant" and the farms "tolerably well cultivated." From Reading to Lebanon: "The country is extremely fine—The lands rich—The agriculture good, as the buildings also are, especially their barns, which are large and fine and for the most part good." As far as Carlisle the lands were good but not so well cultivated as in the Pennsylvania Dutch country. Turning south to Shippensburg, he found "thin and dry soil," but where it was better, "[t]he improvements along the road were mean—The farms scattered; the houses but indifferent—and the husbandry apparently bad." As they continued to Williamsport, the president noticed consistently better farming.

As he travelled, Washington reviewed various detachments of forces marching west. Approaching Carlisle, he found the governors of Pennsylvania and New Jersey awaiting him, their cavalry and infantry drawn up in honor of the commander in chief. For six days he worked to organize the militia who had arrived "in a very disjointed and loose manner; or rather I ought to have said in urging General Mifflin to do it; as I no otherwise took the command of the troops than to press them forward, and to provide them with necessaries for their March." Here Washington established the ranking officers in command: Lee, Mifflin, and Richard Howell, New Jersey's governor. General Edward Hand, his old revolutionary adjutant general, was here given the same assignment in this new national force.

On October 9 two deputies from the insurgents, William Findley and David Redick, were interviewed by the president. He recorded in his diary that Findley remarked there was now more disposition to submit in the West but that it had been not just the excise law that was opposed but "all law, and Government." Redick said that those who supported the government had, in fear of their lives, slept with "their Arms by their bed sides every night." Findley reported that the people of western Pennsylvania had presumed that opposition to the tax was universal in the country, that no troops could therefore be raised, and that rumors of an army coming were false. As soon as its reality became apparent, many of the leaders of the insurrection signed a submission and received amnesty.

The president noted that he had tried every form of conciliation and used force as a last resort. Now great expense had been incurred, winter was approaching, and he had to have "the most unequivocal <u>proofs</u> of absolute submission." The army would otherwise proceed as planned. Next day the two deputies asked if they could assemble a meeting in the counties to discuss submission. The president said that he saw no objection if everyone were unarmed. They were to be sure no gun was fired since the troops would then be forced to act. The army, he assured them, was not there to execute the laws nor to institute military trials, but simply to support the authority of civilian judges and marshals.

On October 10 the Pennsylvania and New Jersey troops began their march for Bedford. The president spent two days seeing them off, then drove south to Cumberland. There he found that nearly 6,000 Maryland and Virginia troops were in Pennsylvania or approaching the area. He interviewed deputies from Fayette County, Pennsylvania, who informed him that the people in the West were "very much alarmed at the approach of the army; but though submission is professed, their principles remain the same; and that nothing but coercion will reclaim and bring them to a due and unequivocal submission to the Laws."

After fixing the southern army's marching routes to Bedford, the president set out for that town on October 19 accompanied by General Lee. He recorded in his diary that they travelled over a road "opened by troops under my command in the Autumn of 1758." That afternoon the president and the three state governors met in Bedford to review the situation with Judge Richard Peters (who had stolen the British naval signals in 1781) and the federal attorney for Pennsylvania. While he was there the president received a letter from John Jay expressing optimism that he would reach agreement in London. In forwarding it to the secretary of state, Washington said that he presumed there would have to be a good deal of "give and take" between Jay and Grenville.

On October 20, having arranged the routes of all the armies westward, the president pressed their officers "to prepare with all the Celerity in their power for a forward movement." The army was ordered to march on October 23. Washington thereupon handed the command to General Lee, with a letter to be read to the troops:

> There is but one point on which I think it proper to add a special recommendation. It is this, that every officer and soldier will constantly bear in mind that he comes to support the laws and that it would be peculiarly unbecoming in him to be in any way the infractor of them; that the essential principles of a free government confine the provinces of the Military to these two objects: first, to combat and subdue all who may be found in arms in opposition to the National will and authority; secondly, to aid and support the civil Magistrates in bringing offenders to justice. The dispensation of this justice belongs to the civil Magistrate and let it ever be our pride and our glory to leave the sacred deposit there unviolated... Being about to return to the seat of government, I cannot take my departure without conveying through you to the Army under your command the very high sense I entertain of the enlightened and patriotic zeal for the constitution and laws which has lead them cheerfully to quit their families and homes and the comforts of private life, to

perform a long and fatiguing march and to encounter and endure the hardships and privations of a Military life...

No citizens of the United States can ever be engaged in a service more important to the Country. It is nothing less than to consolidate and to preserve the blessings of that Revolution which, at much expense of blood and treasure, constituted us a free and independent Nation...

Days of heavy rain followed, falling on the troops moving west and the president travelling east. On October 26, after crossing the Susquehanna, he wrote Hamilton: "I rode yesterday thro' the rain from York Town to this place, and got twice in the height of it hung... on the rocks in the middle of the Susquehanna, but I did not feel half as much for my own situation as I did on acct. of the Troops on the Mountains, and of the effect the rain might have on the roads through the glades." He hoped that Hamilton had arranged to ship the two or three ringleaders, already captured, to Philadelphia "for their winter quarters." Hamilton almost daily reported to the president the progress of the army westward in spite of the rains.

By November 17 some 150 insurgents had been rounded up and turned over to the federal court for trial. At that time Lee and Hamilton concluded that, with most of the rebels having signed submissions or being under arrest, the disorders had been smashed. Hamilton soon found ample evidence that the Jacobin societies had been the principal instruments of revolt against the government. The troops gradually returned home, leaving a small garrison under General Daniel Morgan in the west. In December Lee and his troops returned to Virginia after learning that his efforts to support the Union and Washington had received the disapproval of the Virginia Assembly. The Jeffersonians had chosen a new governor in his place.

STATE OF THE UNION

The president hurriedly returned to Philadelphia to attend the opening session of Congress set for November 3. More than two weeks elapsed thereafter before Congress had a quorum. This gave the president time, now that the west was peaceful, to turn his attention to John Jay, to Mount Vernon, and to his annual message. To Jay he wrote at the beginning of November:

[Your letter] of the 5th of August dawns more favorably upon the success of your mission than any that had preceded it; and for the honor, dignity and interest of

this country; for your own reputation and glory; and for the peculiar pleasure and satisfaction I should derive from it, as well on private as on public considerations, no man more ardently wishes you <u>complete</u> success than I do... So to deserve success, by employing the means with which we are possessed to the best advantage, and trusting the rest to the all wise disposer, is all that an enlightened public and the virtuous and well-disposed part of the community, can well expect... Against the malignancy of the discontented, the turbulent and the vicious, no abilities, no exertions, nor the most unshaken integrity, are any safeguard.

As far as depends upon the Executive, measures preparatory for the worst, while it hopes for the best, will be pursued; and I shall endeavor to keep things in status quo, until your negotiation assumes a more decisive form, which I hope will soon be the case, as there are many hotheads and impetuous spirits among us, who can, with difficulty, be kept in bounds...

The Self-created societies... have been the fomenters of the Western disturbances but, fortunately, they have precipitated a crisis for which they were not prepared... This has afforded an occasion for the people of this country... to show their attachment to the Constitution and the laws; for I believe that five times the number of militia that was required, would have come forward, if it had been necessary...

A subsequent note to Jay on December 18 pointed out that "the western insurrection has terminated highly honorably for this country... without spilling a drop of blood. In the eyes of foreigners among us, this affair stands in a high point of view."

On November 2 the president resumed his long weekly letters to his Mount Vernon manager. This letter made clear that William Pearce, more than any of the long preceding line to whom he had entrusted his affairs, had won his full confidence: "As the accident I met with in June last, prevented my riding about my farms when I was last at home, I should have been very glad to have made another visit to it, in the course of last month, knowing if I did not do it then, it would not be in my power to do it before April, as Congress will, more than probably, sit till March, and the roads during that month will be in no condition to travel. The perfect confidence, however, which I place in your care, judgment and integrity, makes me quite easy under the disappointment, which I should not have been, if my affairs were in the hands of a person of whom I did not entertain the same favorable opinion." There followed a summary of the main objectives he hoped to achieve by his six-year plan for Mount Vernon, together with numerous detailed suggestions.

On November 19, at noon, Washington delivered his sixth annual message on the state of the Union. The president, strong in his success, delivered his speech with such force and feeling that his highly critical audience heard him with "the utmost reverence and attention." He praised General Wayne for his victory and announced the first successful coinage by the United States mint (which had sent a silver dollar to him while he was with the troops). He noted that lawless American marauders on Creek lands had been thrown out through the efforts of the United States and Georgia. A proposed settlement at what is now Erie, Pennsylvania, had been stopped at the request of the Six Nations, in order to bring them to a peaceful feeling.

On the western insurrection, Washington was, as he had informed Jay he intended to be, "prolix." His was a thorough and documented account of the origin and course of the revolt. He threw down the gauntlet, in stronger terms than he had ever used publicly, to those of the opposition who, claiming to be democratic or republican, were, in fact, neither. He spoke of the "self-created societies," operating among the law-abiding citizens of western Pennsylvania, who stirred up the "vicious and turbulent," not over a particular law but against "all order." In high praise of the troops and of the cooperating states, the president said:

> *It has been a spectacle, displaying to the highest advantage, the value of republican Government, to behold the most and the least wealthy of our citizens, standing in the same ranks, as private soldiers; preeminently distinguished by being the army of the constitution, undeterred by a march of three hundred miles over rugged mountains, by the approach of an inclement season, or by any other discouragement...*

> *To every description, indeed, of citizens, let praise be given. But let them preserve in their affectionate vigilance over that precious depository of American happiness, the Constitution of the United States...*

> *Having thus fulfilled the engagement which I took, when I entered into office, "to the best of my ability to preserve, protect and defend the Constitution of the United States," on you gentlemen, and the people by whom you are deputed, I rely for support.*

George Thatcher, congressman from Maine, wrote his wife that, at this point of the speech, "I felt a strange mixture of passions that I cannot describe. Tears started into my eyes, and it was with difficulty I could suppress an involuntary effort to swear that I would support him." Elizabeth Smith shortly afterwards described her feelings; "It really seemed as tho' we were addressed by a far superior being than any here below."

Although the president was not to learn of it for months, John Jay and Lord

Grenville, a few hours before he delivered this message, had signed a treaty which declared that "there shall be a firm inviolable and universal peace, and a true and sincere friendship between His Britannic Majesty, His Heirs and Successors, and the United States of America." On December 14 Jay wrote to Tench Coxe, revenue commissioner of the Treasury: "The best disposition towards us prevails here... Next to the king, our President is more popular in this country than any man in it."

In 1765 when George Grenville introduced the Stamp Act which taxed the American colonies, his youngest son, William, was only five years old. At thirty-five, in an act of great statesmanship, William, Lord Grenville, thus terminated nearly thirty years of intervening hostility and bitterness. In America the document which he signed bears Jay's name but it might more aptly be called Grenville's treaty.

TWELVE

PEACE WITH
GREAT BRITAIN

1795

T WO DAYS AFTER delivering his annual message, Washington turned
to another vexing problem, relations with Spain. On November 21,
1794, he informed Congress that, while the American commissioners
at Madrid had made every effort to reach agreement, he had received intimations from Spain that they would prefer another negotiator. He was
amenable to this idea, in spite of his confidence in the Americans at Madrid.
He was therefore nominating "Thomas Pinckney, to be Envoy Extraordinary
of the U. S. to his Catholic majesty, for the purpose of negotiating of and concerning the navigation of the river Mississippi, and such other matters relative
to the confines of their territories and the intercourse to be had thereon, as
the mutual interests and general harmony of neighborhood and friendly
nations require should be precisely adjusted and regulated, and of and concerning the general commerce between the said United States and the
Kingdoms and Dominions of his said Catholic majesty."

Behind this clumsy verbiage lay the fact that Spain had been procrastinating for years. When, as an additional means of delay, Spain complained that
the American envoys were not of high enough rank, Washington took the
court at its word and dispatched the American minister at St. James' to
Madrid. Jay's letter of August 5 to the president, outlining the major points on
which agreement was expected with the British, had inserted a phrase "for

'there is a *tide* in human affairs,' of which every moment is precious." Jay added that this was for the president's "private satisfaction." This was an apparently prearranged signal from Jay to Washington to say the British would back American claims to navigation of the Mississippi, in which, by the 1783 treaty, they would share. If Spain made trouble, she would have no support from Canada. Washington's reply of November 1, carried by a friendly hand to London, said: "As it has been observed, there is a 'tide in human affairs' that ought always to be watched." Thus Pinckney was informed he was to proceed to Spain, in accordance with Jay's judgment. With the Spanish garrisons isolated, the president could lead from strength.

The president also took steps to keep the turbulent Kentuckians in line so they would not start a private war with Spain while Pinckney was en route to Madrid. He dispatched Colonel James Innes to the state capital to outline the long and serious efforts made by the federal government to secure the navigation of the Mississippi. On April 17, 1795, the secretary of state informed the president that Innes had sent a report from "Washington court-house... By a letter from the Governor of Kentucky to him, it is clear that his mission has been accepted most cordially and that it has had its full effect; as well proving its policy as engaging the Executive on the side of your measures. Shelby expresses himself in strains of high compliments to you for your exertion on the subject of the Mississippi." Randolph, in addition, mentioned that he had received a letter from Washington, Pennsylvania, which praised the good conduct of the army troops, stationed there because of the insurrection.

RESIGNATION OF KNOX

Henry Knox, risen from bookselling to head the American artillery, succeeded George Washington as commander of the fragment of the army which he left behind in December 1783. As secretary at war he became the first permanent member of Washington's cabinet, but soon his title changed from "at" to "of war." The ablest and most effective of all Washington's cabinet officers, he served the longest. He was as steadfastly loyal to country and president as he had been to country and general in the war. Before he retired, he provided the president with information on the progress of the navy (slow), the coastal fortifications (going forward well), and the size of the army. There were 3,629 noncommissioned and private men in the forces, of whom 369 were assigned to Atlantic forts. Most of the remainder were in Ohio. On December 29 Knox handed Washington a final report on Indian affairs:

To retrace the conduct of the Government of the United States toward the Indian tribes since the adoption of the present Constitution, cannot fail to afford satisfaction to every philosophic and humane mind. A constant solicitude appears to have existed in the Executive and Congress not only to form treaties of peace with the Indians upon principles of Justice, but to impart to them all the blessing of civilized life, of which their condition is susceptible. That a perseverance in such principles and conduct will reflect permanent honor upon the national character cannot be doubted. At the same time it must be acknowledged that the execution of the good intentions of the public, is frequently embarrassed with perplexing considerations.

The desires of too many frontier white people to seize by force or fraud the neighboring Indians' lands, has been and still continues to be an unceasing cause of jealousy and hatred on the part of the Indians... This appears to be a principal cause of Indian wars... An adequate police force seems to be wanting either to prevent or punish the depredations of the unruly. It would afford a considerable pleasure could the assertion be made on our part, that we have considered the murders of Indians the same as the murders of whites, and have punished them accordingly. This however is not the case. The irritated passions on account of savage cruelty are generally too keen in the places where trials are had, to convict and punish for the killing of an Indian... An adequate remedy ought to be provided...

It is certainly an evil to be involved in hostilities with tribes of savages amounting to two or three thousand, as is the case north west of the Ohio. But this evil would be greatly increased were a general Indian war to prevail south of the Ohio, the Indian warriors of the four nations in that quarter not being much short of fourteen thousand...

It seems that our own experience would demonstrate the propriety of endeavoring to preserve a pacific conduct in preference to a hostile one with the Indian tribes... There is a responsibility of our national character, that we should treat them with kindness and even liberality. It is a melancholy reflection that our modes of population have been more destructive to the Indian nations, than the conduct of the conquerors of Mexico and Peru. The evidence of this is the utter extirpation of nearly all the Indians in the most populous parts of the Union. A future historian may mark the causes of this destruction of the human race in sable colours. Although the present Government of the United States cannot with propriety be involved in the opprobrium, yet is seems necessary, however, in order to render their attention upon this subject strongly characteristic of their justice, that some powerful attempts should be made to tranquilize the frontiers...

Upon the most mature reflection... arising from the experience of several years, [the subscriber] humbly conceives all attempts to preserve peace with the Indians will be found inadequate, short of an arrangement somewhat like the following:

That a line of military posts... be established upon the frontiers within the Indian boundary and out of the jurisdiction of any State, provided consent can be obtained for the purpose from the Indian tribes [and] garrisoned with regular troops... If any murder or theft be committed upon any of the white Inhabitants by an Indian, [his] tribe shall be bound to deliver him to the nearest military post, in order to be tried and punished by Court Martial... All [white] persons who shall be assembled or embodied in arms on any lands belonging to Indians... for the purpose of warring against the Indians or of committing depredations upon any Indian town or persons or property, shall thereby become liable and subject to the rules and articles of War...

On December 30 Washington wrote to Knox to accept his resignation, wishing "that it was otherwise. I cannot suffer you, however to close your public service, without uniting with the satisfaction which must arise in your own mind from a conscious rectitude, my most perfect persuasion that you have deserved well of your Country. My personal knowledge of your exertions, while it authorizes me to hold this language, justifies the sincere friendship which I have ever borne for you, and which will accompany you in every situation of life, being with affectionate regards, always yours."

To replace Knox, Washington followed the policy, first established, rather unwillingly with Edmund Randolph, of promotion from within the government. Timothy Pickering, who had been Washington's rather ineffective quartermaster general during the revolution, was advanced from head of the post office to the War Department. Pickering, in little over four years at his previous job, had added thousands of miles of post roads and increased the country's post offices from 89 to 450. In addition to these duties, Pickering, whose benevolent attitude to the Indians was well known, was repeatedly chosen by the president, from 1789 onwards, as special peace commissioner to the Indians. In this work he reported directly to Henry Knox. A man of the utmost integrity, Pickering was highly qualified to complete Knox's efforts to establish peace with all the tribes. As secretary of war, Pickering proved so able that, in August, Washington also assigned him duties as secretary of state. This was a fast rise to responsibilities greater than those which had been borne by Jefferson, Hamilton, or Knox.

Pickering's clear and sharp reports to the president indicate that he possessed unusual administrative ability. In at least one area he improved on the methods of Knox, who was inclined to bundle up voluminous correspondence and send it, undigested, to the president. Pickering made summaries or abstracts, and where correspondence or proposed legislation was extensive, he pointed out the crucial points which required the president's reading. Washington expressed his gratification at this considerate approach. Pickering enlivened his letters to the president with dry New England humor: "The writer, David Campbell of the Southwestern territory, begged [this] might be presented; otherwise the Secretary of War would not have troubled the President with its perusal. It contains merely an eulogy on Gov. Blount... He aims at the poetic style, perhaps very properly, as poets deal in fiction." In reporting an officer's resignation, he added: "From the information heretofore received by the Secretary, the resignation is not to be regretted." He summed up his job to the British minister as long hours of drudgery, for pay so low he had to live on "mutton, mush and cold water."

On January 8 and 9, just after Pickering assumed office, the Senate ratified treaties with the Cherokees, the Six Nations, and the Oneida. The first had been negotiated by Knox, the latter two by Pickering, in the preceding year. Soon thereafter Wayne reported to the War Department that representatives of seven of the principal tribes north of the Ohio had requested peace talks. He added that British agents were at work, stirring up murders by Indians, and he feared that this would once again inflame Kentucky against the Union. Pickering prepared lengthy instructions to Wayne on his negotiations. The Indians were to be assured, above all, that they owned their land and that no American was permitted by law to purchase it, or otherwise come into its possession, without approval of the federal authorities. In March Pickering informed Wayne, in confidence, that the British had agreed to withdraw all garrisons from American territory.

HAMILTON ALSO

The Syrett edition of Hamilton's letters contains an undated, unaddressed note written by Hamilton in 1794, to someone in Europe, conceivably his sister-in-law, Angelica Church, saying that he was "heartily tired" of his situation in the cabinet and that he intended to resign. Before leaving he gave the president the unpleasant news that there would be a budget deficit for the year of more than $2 million and the Treasury would have to borrow to cover it. He informed Washington of an attempt by the French consul, J-B. Petri, at the direction of the French minister, to violate the American laws against arming privateers. He added: "I fear that agents of France have not ceased to countenance proceedings which not only contravene our neutrality but may prove a source of very serious expense to the United States."

Hamilton resigned effective January 31, 1795, and Washington wrote him two days later: "In every relation which you have borne to me, I have found that my confidence in your talents, exertions and integrity, has been well placed. I the more freely render this testimony of my approbation because I speak from opportunities of information which cannot deceive me, and which furnish satisfactory proof of your title to public regard. My most earnest wishes for your happiness will attend you in your retirement and you may assure yourself of the sincere esteem, regard and friendship of, dear Sir, your affectionate..." The president appointed as his successor, Hamilton's able and hard-working assistant, Oliver Wolcott, Jr., who was about the same age as Hamilton was when he was originally appointed.

THE JAY TREATY

On February 23, 1795, Jay replied to the president's November 1 letter, "Your remarks relative to my negotiations are just and kind. I assure you nothing on my part has been wanting to render the conclusion of them as consonant as was possible to your expectations and wishes. Perfectly apprised both of my duty and responsibility I determined not to permit my judgment to be influenced by any considerations but those of public good under the direction of my instructions."

The British foreign minister, Lord Grenville, received Jay promptly upon his arrival in London on June 15. He was soon dining with the cabinet, the prime minister, and the lord chancellor. King George III, clearly delighted that Washington had stood up so well to the French, was more than cordial. By July 21 Jay could inform the president that Simcoe had been ordered out of Ohio. He presumably did not hear of the cabinet's letter to Lord Dorchester, saying that the government expected to settle all issues with Mr. Jay, but the king himself told Jay he could count on a successful mission. By August 1 he had assurances that the British government would render "complete and impartial justice," in the case of the captured ships. Although the British minister at Philadelphia had expressed doubts that his government ever would pay damages, Grenville agreed that, where the processes of British law were insufficient, the government itself would pay the claims which were to be processed by a joint commission. This assured the first objective of the president.

The surrender of the British forts was easily negotiated but, as Jay wrote, the British could not avoid pressing the merchants' claims for American debts. Jay worked out a simple *quid pro quo* along exactly the line of the ship claims. The United States would pay, where American law processes failed. Jay, who hated slavery, described the southerners' claims to compensation for slaves who had escaped to freedom, as "odious." He simply ignored the matter.

The negotiations took five months. When the treaty was signed, Jay wrote to Lord Grenville: "To use an Indian figure, may the hatchet be buried for ever, and with it all the animosities which sharpened, and which threatened to redden it." Jay wrote of Grenville, as he might well have done of himself: "Few men would have persevered in such a dry, perplexing business, with so much patience and temper as [he] has done."

On March 6, 1795, Jay expressed to the president his considered opinion that the British government had been so persuaded of the inevitability of war, by the violent American clamors and the reception to Genet, that orders to prepare for it had gone to Lord Dorchester. The president's subsequent decision to send the chief justice of the United States to London was taken as proof of his firm desire for peace. "The perfect and universal confidence reposed in your personal character excluded every doubt of your being sincere." The British government had determined, therefore, "to give conciliation a fair experiment, by doing us substantial justice and by consenting to such arrangements favourable to us, as the national interests and habitual prejudices would admit… to admit us into their East and West India dominions, and into all their continental American territories, were decided deviations from their former policy, and tended to shock ancient prejudices… Whatever the American opinion of it may prove to be, the administration here think it very friendly to us; and it could not in the present moment have been made more so, without exciting great discontent and uneasiness in this country." Jay continued:

> *You have doubtless heard that the merchants concerned in the American trade gave me a dinner. The principal Cabinet Ministers were present, and about two hundred merchants. Many toasts were given. When 'The President of the United States' was given, it was proposed to be with three cheers, but they were prolonged (as if by preconcert, but evidently not so) to six.*

> *I have great reason to believe that the king, the Cabinet, and nation were never more unanimous in any system than that of conciliation with us…*

> *This system rests principally on their confidence in the uprightness, independence, and wisdom of your conduct… The idea which everywhere prevails is, that the quarrel between Britain and America was a family quarrel, and that it is time it*

should be made up. For my part, I am for making it up, and for cherishing this
disposition on their part by justice, benevolence, and good manners on ours. To cast
ourselves into the arms of this or any other nation, would be degrading, injurious
and puerile; nor, in my opinion, ought we to have any political connection with
any foreign power.

Two copies of the Grenville treaty were lost at sea, owing to action by French privateers. A third copy, after long delays, was delivered to the president on March 7. As he read it, he could clearly see the care with which Jay had followed his instructions and how much he had accomplished for the public good. First and foremost, he had achieved peace and British goodwill, the points nearest the president's heart. Second, the British agreed to make compensation for all seized vessels. Third, all British military posts were to be handed over to the United States in 1796, thus freeing the country of endless bloodshed and expense. Finally, financial claims on both sides were to go to two joint commissions. While this process was to take a long time, the United States paid $2.8 million to settle its prewar debts, and Great Britain handed over more than $10 million for the seized ships. Vague boundary lines were to be settled by a joint survey team and a joint commission. For the first time the British opened the West Indies to small American vessels and their East Indies ports to all American ships. Although potential sources of friction still remained between the United States and Great Britain, a maritime power at war, the British navy now became an important shield against aggressive France.

The Grenville treaty of 1795 provided a far more satisfactory recognition of American independence than the pact which Jay had negotiated thirteen years before. Europeans then expected that the thirteen former colonies could not hold together and would eventually fall into French or British hands. Now Great Britain conceded not only that the United States was entirely sovereign but was too strong ever to be a French or English satellite. The United States had become Britain's most important customer, as well as a vitally needed supplier of provisions to the West Indies, and food and raw materials to a Great Britain at war. Washington's peaceful measures in the Northwest clearly indicated that the United States had no desire to attack Canada, while, as a strong country, she would be an effective buffer against any threats to Canada from Spanish territories.

On March 3, just before Congress adjourned, the president issued a summons to the Senate to reconvene on June 8. He swore the secretary of state to secrecy on the treaty. With this diplomatic triumph in his pocket, the president could devote his mind to other matters.

A NATIONAL UNIVERSITY

Washington's work in promoting the James and Potomac River canals had brought him, in 1785, a Virginia grant of shares in the two canal companies. Since they had a face value of $32,000, he had been much embarrassed by the gift. He subsequently requested the governor and legislature to permit him to hold them in trust for educational institutions to be selected by him. This provision was ratified by the Virginia Assembly. The president's first annual message to Congress asked for federal aid to higher education and suggested the desirability of a national university. By 1794 Washington was telling John Adams that such a university had been long "talked of" but nothing had been done. What impelled Washington to further work on the matter was a proposal sent to John Adams to transfer the faculty of the University of Geneva to America because of disorders in Europe.

On January 28, 1795, Washington in a more refined manner wrote to the district commissioners to say that a university for the federal city "has frequently been the subject of conversation." He felt that it was a pity so many young Americans had to study in Europe where they were exposed to "principles unfriendly to republican government." He asked the commissioners to look into the cost and to draw up proposals.

On February 15 Thomas Jefferson wrote to the president about the Geneva proposal, indicating that its sponsorship had been turned down by the Virginia legislature. He suggested that the canal shares held by Washington might be used for this purpose. Washington replied on March 16 that he had never expected his shares to form more than part of the cost of a university and, in any case, "not to induce an entire college to emigrate." He now planned to donate his shares to a new national university which he preferred to have on the Virginia side of the federal territory. The central location within the Union would help bring together boys from all the states. The students would have the advantage of being able to study the operations of government. Washington could not resist inserting a little jollity at Jefferson's expense. He was not certain whether bringing the Genevans over was such a good idea for "having been at variance with the levelling party of their own country, the measure might be considered as an aristocratical movement by those who, without any just cause that I have been able to discover, are continually sounding the alarm bell of aristocracy."

On March 16 the president outlined his plans to Governor Robert Brooke of Virginia. He pointed out, as he had done to Jefferson, the desirability of having the fullest educational facilities at home, rather than sending young Americans abroad. He continued:

The time is therefore come, when a plan of Universal education ought to be adopted in the United States. Not only do the exigencies of public and private life demand it; but if it should ever be apprehended that prejudice would be entertained in one part of the Union against another; an efficacious remedy will be, to assemble the youth of every part under such circumstances, as will, by the freedom of intercourse and collision of sentiment, give to their minds the direction of truth, philanthropy, and mutual conciliation.

It has been represented, that a University, corresponding with these ideas, is contemplated to be built in the federal city; and that it will receive considerable endowments. This position is so eligible from its centrality, so convenient to Virginia, by whose legislature the shares were granted, and in which part of the federal district stands, and combines so many other conveniences, that I have determined to vest the Potomack shares in the University. [*]

The president then said that he thought it might be more agreeable to the Virginia legislature if his James River shares went to a college ("seminary") to be established within Virginia. From the college, students could proceed to further work at the national university. It would be better if all the shares were concentrated in a single institution but he wanted to "give a particular attention to Virginia," with these shares. The Virginia Assembly subsequently ducked the issue, requesting Washington to give them to such an institution as he saw fit. The shares eventually ended up as a portion of the endowment of what became Washington and Lee University.

WASHINGTON CITY

On May 24, Washington wrote to Alexander White, whom he had just appointed as commissioner of the District of Columbia:

The year 1800 will be soon upon us. The necessity therefore of hurrying on the public buildings, and other works of a public nature; and executing of them with economy; the propriety of preventing idleness in those who have day, or monthly wages, and

---

[*] From the history of Washington appearing in *The Georgetowner,* June 6, 1968: "November 13, 1874. Columbian College has opened as Columbian University this fall... It now seems unlikely we will ever see the federally sponsored university envisioned by John Quincy Adams, since there is a great deal of opposition to it, led by President Eliot of Harvard." This university was subsequently named for George Washington.

*imposition by others, who work by measure, by the piece, or by contract, and seeing
that all contracts are fulfilled, with good faith, are too obvious to dwell on, and are
not less important then to form plans, and establish rules for conducting and
bringing to a speedy and happy conclusion this great and arduous business.*

A severely troublesome problem of the capital site was its thick forests. The
avenues and streets in the L'Enfant plan had to be chopped out slowly, day by
day, with hand labor and axes. Even after several years, this work was far from
complete. From the descriptions of travellers who wandered through the
mazes in 1795 and 1796, it seems to have been a miracle that L'Enfant could
have penetrated some of the areas, have surveyed them so carefully and
quickly, and have dreamed of a better Versailles in such a wilderness.

To a certain extent Washington had pushed the enterprise, trusting to
heaven, nerve, and luck. Philadelphia, in the meantime, complacently went on
building a permanent house for the president. Since sales of individual lots in
Washington were slow, the commissioners had drawn in speculators, including
Robert Morris, under terms which would provide monthly construction money
for the capitol, president's house, and streets. The speculators were overextended; by September they were far behind in their payments and the commissioners begged Washington for help. He wrote to Morris on September 14
urging him to meet his commitments. He added: "There are many valuable
Stone cutters and other workmen now engaged; a number of laborers are
employed on the public buildings... Everything seems to progress as well as can
be reasonably expected under the embarrassments which have been encountered... Without the aid required... the workmen *must* be discharged... the
buildings will be left not only in a stagnant state but in a hurtful situation; involving consequences which are too obvious to need enumeration."

The last thing Washington wanted was to ask Congress for funds, for it would
revive all the old controversy as to where the capital should be. As the winter
drew on and there was a continuing shortage of money, Washington and the
commissioners agreed that an approach would have to be made to the state of
Maryland for loans to the federal government. The president said that if that
failed he would try Congress, because he did not intend to abandon the capital.

SALES OF WASHINGTON LANDS

Though benumbed by work, the president pursued with vigor his attempts to
sell his land holdings so that he could present to the nation a program leading to a voluntary abolition of slavery. As was only too soon to be evident, the

temper of Virginia and of the South in general with regard to the federal government and slavery, was too sour to be touched by anything but example.

The president's extensive acres were scattered through New York, Ohio, Pennsylvania, Maryland, Virginia, and Kentucky. He had never been a speculator, having held most of the land he began to acquire at eighteen until his presidency. Many farms had been settled on long leases or were in troubled areas, which made their sale difficult. There were no proper estate agents, and Washington had to pick from old friends or, from their recommendations, those who might persuade people to buy. Washington's correspondence was enormous to all points of the compass. It resulted that year in a reduction of a few thousand acres of his holdings but this was only a small beginning.

MONROE

When Jay wrote to Washington to express his own and the British displeasure at Monroe's behavior in Paris, Washington replied that perhaps Monroe's praise of France displeased the British but her enemy's stress over her American alliance might have helped to expedite Jay's negotiations.

The reactions to the Jay treaty by the American ministers at The Hague and in Paris were markedly different. Young John Quincy Adams wrote to Jay on January 9: "The value of peace and neutrality is nowhere more forcibly felt than at this moment in the country where I am. Its situation becomes more and more critical from day to day. In the terrible agitation between the dismal alternative of conquest or civil war, it feels at the same moment all the terrors of a torrent rushing from without, and a volcano bursting from within." Adams noted that bad weather alone seemed to be holding the French armies from their attack on Holland.

Monroe, on the other hand, wrote Jay of French uneasiness about the treaty. He demanded a copy for their government. Jay replied that the French did not seem to have the "confidence in the honor and good faith of the United States which they certainly merit." He pointed out the United States was entirely independent and sovereign and the agreement contained a clause stating that the pact did not affect any previous treaties, including the one with France. He had negotiated under the promise of secrecy, and it would not be becoming to deliver it without permission nor to have it submitted to the "judgment of the councils of a *foreign nation*." Not until late in the summer did Monroe receive the text, whereupon he set to work to defeat its major aims of peace and neutrality.

RATIFICATION OF THE JAY TREATY

Washington, that spring after the congressional adjournment, made a quick trip to Mount Vernon, returning to Philadelphia on May 2. There he found Randolph and Fauchet, the French minister, almost at sword's point. Randolph had informed James Monroe in Paris that Fauchet's behavior was terrible. He had raked up every charge he could find against the United States, which he presented in an "indecent" letter, a term employed by Jefferson in writing of Genet. The worst, however, was to come; in the middle of the Senate negotiations on the Jay treaty, a new French minister, Pierre Adet, appeared in Philadelphia to take Fauchet's place and to break the peace with England. Adet was to be the most ill-mannered of the ministers sent by France to America during Washington's presidency.

While the Senate was assembling, the Jeffersonian press bitterly attacked the president on the treaty, though none of the papers knew its provisions. Washington gave the Senate the documents on June 8, including the text of his instructions to Jay. Resolutions to make the treaty and its accompanying papers public were quickly voted down. The clause concerning commerce with the British West Indies, which permitted small American vessels for the first time to trade there but which forbade re-export of colonial products, including cotton, aroused much debate and many of the president's supporters found this provision objectionable. They resolved therefore to approve the treaty without this clause, while asking the president to hold further negotiations with Great Britain on the West Indies trade. During debate the southern states moved their objections to Jay for having failed to provide compensation for freed slaves, but only southern senators voted affirmatively. On June 24 the treaty carried, without the offending clause, by a vote of twenty to ten, with seven southern senators voting no.

About the first of July the secretary of state, possibly without the knowledge or approval of the president, provided the French minister with a copy of the Jay treaty. It appeared shortly thereafter, in full, in the Philadelphia opposition press, with the explanation that Senator Thomson Mason of Virginia had determined to give it out, in order to prevent false reports from circulating. The president himself was about ready to make it public but he was forestalled by a few days. Nevertheless, it was made to appear that a "patriot" had acted to let Americans know of a secret treaty, dangerous to their welfare.

Washington took advantage of the presence of the Senate in Philadelphia to make a number of appointments, including army officers and port collectors as well as consuls for Algiers, Tripoli, and Tunis. He also sent in the names of Benjamin Hawkins, George Clymer, and Andrew Pickens as commissioners to negotiate a treaty with the Creek Indians, who were causing much damage in Georgia and the Cumberland region.

John Jay returned to America to find that he had been elected governor of New York. He therefore resigned from the Supreme Court. In his place, Washington offered the nomination to John Rutledge, chief justice of South Carolina, but his reply could not reach the capital before the Senate adjourned.

ARMAGEDDON

Shortly after Jay was selected for his mission, Adams wrote to Jefferson that, while he did not expect Jay to achieve a brilliant success, he hoped that he could at least obtain peace. Like Washington, Adams tried a little humor on the former secretary of state. He said that a war would add $200 million to the national debt, force the building of a big army, and perhaps eventually bring in a monarchy: "Those who dread Monarchy and Aristocracy and at the same time advocate War are the most inconsistent of all Men."

Once the treaty terms were made public, there began a bitterly divisive struggle in America. It was a curious spectacle, for most of the old revolutionary generals and colonels lined up solidly for peace, while those who sought war included Madison and Jefferson who had never served in the armed forces.

The mobs again swung into action in the principal seaports. Jefferson reported to Madison on August 3: "Hamilton... spoke on its behalf in the meeting at New York, and his party carried a decision in favor of it by a small majority. But the Livingstonians appealed to stones & clubs and beat him & his party off the ground." The treaty and a British flag were burned in Charleston by a mob which included many Frenchmen. Other French joined a Philadelphia group in throwing rocks at the British minister's house after listening to inflammatory orations by followers of Jefferson.

Petitions poured in on the president from groups and individuals. It cannot be said that the American people did not read the treaty. From the length of many of the petitions, which took it apart clause by clause, it is clear that citizens read it in great detail. They also reviewed the Declaration of Independence and the Constitution, inserting therefrom appropriate phrases. The literary quality throughout the country was impressive. Many petitions noted that the Constitution required that Congress (i.e., both Houses) regulate commerce and therefore the representatives had also to approve the treaty. The president replied politely to most letters, saying that he had to do his constitutional duty and what he thought was right for the country. To those who were against, he added that he regretted the division of opinion; he thanked those who were for the treaty for their "approbation." Four of the petitions, three from the South, were scandalously abusive. The president marked them as "too rude" or "too indecent" to merit an answer. A highly emotional plea against the treaty came from Richmond, where the chairman of the meeting was George Wythe. The mayor of the city said that he was forwarding the document to the president "with pleasure."

An assessment of the petitions indicates that twenty-eight out of the forty against it were from the South, the bulk of them written in Virginia and South Carolina. Only a single voice of support for the president came from below the Potomac. General Daniel Morgan rallied the citizens of Frederick County in hearty approval of the treaty. It was probably about this time that the president made a remark later quoted by Edmund Randolph. If, said Washington, the North and South split, he intended to move to the North.

John Jay, who, of all the founding fathers, most nearly resembled Washington in strength of character, was subjected to unparalleled denunciations in the Jeffersonian portion of the press. He bore it with fortitude and a comment on its cause to James Duane on September 16:

> *The opposition to which you allude, except as to the degree of malignity, was not unexpected...*
>
> *The Constitution [is] a rock of offence to the Antifederalists; and the funding system, by affording support to the government, had become exceedingly obnoxious to that party. It was evident, then, That a treaty with Great Britain, by preventing war, would disappoint the Southern debtors of the receipts in full, which they flattered themselves from a war.*
>
> *That it would displease the French, by lessening our supposed dependence on them for protection against Great Britain, by diminishing their influence in our councils, and by making us friends with their enemies.*
>
> *That it would discontent the Antifederalists, by disarming them of their affected complaints against the government on account of the posts, and commerce, etc., and by giving additional strength to the administration.*
>
> *Hence there was reason to apprehend that a treaty with Great Britain would become a signal to the Antifederalists, the debtors, and the French, to unite their efforts to prevent its taking effect, and to embarrass its execution if ratified, and to conduct*

their opposition in a manner most injurious to the Constitution and to the administration...

Strenuous efforts will be made to gain *and* mislead *a majority of the House of Representatives at the ensuing session of Congress; and if they succeed, many perplexities and embarassments may be expected... While moral evil remains in the world it will constantly generate political ones.*

Jay put his finger on a major source of trouble, the House of Representatives. The southern vote there (and in the electoral college) was padded by the constitutional proviso that a slave was to count as three-fifths of a person, for the purpose of representation. In consequence fifteen congressmen represented slaves.

Jefferson, in a series of letters to Monroe in Paris, did all he could to encourage the French government to action by assuring Monroe the treaty was opposed by all the American people who would break it in the House. He wrote on September 6: "Mr. Jay's treaty has at length been made public. So general a burst of dissatisfaction never before appeared against any transaction. Those who understand the particular articles of it, condemn these articles. Those who do not understand them minutely, condemn it generally as wearing a hostile face to France. This last is the most numerous class, comprehending the whole body of the people, who have taken a greater interest in this transaction than they were ever known to do before. It has in my opinion completely demolished the monarchical party here... We do not know whether the President has signed it or not. If he has, it is much believed the H. of representatives will oppose it as constitutionally void, and thus bring on an embarrassing and critical state of government." Jefferson subsequently pushed Madison hard to defeat the treaty in the House, with the aid of southern members who held 43 percent of the seats.

TREATY OF GRENVILLE

General Anthony Wayne began negotiations for a peace treaty with the Northwest Indians in the spring of 1795. He reported to Pickering that the British were working to subvert the peace but that the Indians had lost all confidence in them after the Battle of Fallen Timbers, "because they remained idle spectators & saw their best and bravest Chiefs & Warriors slaughtered before their faces, and under their great Guns without attempting to assist them—hence they consider the British not only liars—but also Cowards."

After receipt of the Jay treaty, Pickering had given Wayne the confidential information that the British would evacuate their posts in the territory. Since the treaty was under a veil of secrecy, he could provide no further information until it was published. Wayne had therefore to negotiate in the dark until summer. He nonetheless satisfactorily concluded his treaty. On August 9 he wrote to the secretary of war: "It is with infinite pleasure I now inform you, that a treaty of peace between the United States of America & all the late hostile tribes of Indians North West of the Ohio, was Unanimously and Voluntarily agreed to, & chearfully signed by all the *Sachems* & *War Chiefs* of the respective Nations, on the 3rd & exchanged on the 7th Instant a copy of which I have now the honor to transmit."

Wayne added that he had seen the text of the Jay treaty in newspapers, which had just arrived, as well as the "violent and ungenerous attacks upon it... I however hope and trust... that our Great & virtuous President will once more save this Country from ruin, by ratifying that treaty... In the name of God what do these intemperate resolutions tend to? are they meant to provoke a War with Great Britain? where is our Marine or Naval force...? Will... the Virtuous thinking Citizens... wantonly precipitate & involve America in an unequal contest with a powerful Marine Nation, at a Crisis—when we are so ill prepared—to repel force by force, on that Element where she is clearly predominant! I believe not. At the same time I clearly foresee one very unpleasant consequence of those intemperate proceedings, i.e., a procrastination of the surrender of the Western posts & possibly—a renewal of the Indian War."

THE PRESIDENT SIGNS THE TREATY

Early in July American newspapers carried sketchy reports that the British, in expectation of grain shortages, had issued a new provision order to the Royal Navy. This permitted the navy to carry foreign grain ships, proceeding to France, into British ports where the cargo was to be purchased. The order was well within the letter but hardly within the spirit of the Jay treaty. John Trumbull, who had been Jay's secretary in London, protested to the British government in July that this was not a very politic move, while the treaty was under consideration, especially as the United States would be happy to sell directly any needed grain. The ministry assured Trumbull they intended to proceed with absolute fairness and to pay at once. The order was repealed not long afterwards.

Hamilton, out of the cabinet in 1795, turned from his previous apathy to great strength. He did more for the president during his ordeal over the treaty than any member of the government. At Washington's request, he examined every aspect of the treaty and wrote a powerful paper of great length, pointing out the treaty's many strengths and relatively few weaknesses. In his appraisal, Hamilton stated that the new British provision order, while not happily conceived, was within the existing law of nations as well as clause XVIII of the treaty. He strongly urged the president to sign. Hamilton forwarded his views to Washington, who received them a day or two before setting out for Mount Vernon.

Washington had also asked the secretary of state to appraise the treaty, in fullest detail. Randolph provided his own shorter report on July 12 which the president took with him to Mount Vernon on July 15. Randolph summarized the treaty as follows:

Advantages	Disadvantages
1. Old bickerings settled; except as to impressment and provisions	*1. Loss of Negroes*
2. Indian Wars at an end, at least those countenanced by G. Britain	*2. Assumption of debts due to creditors in certain cases*
3. New opportunities for extending trade in Canada	*3. The lands which may be taken from the U.S. by the indulgence of British settlers [within the restored bounds of the U.S.]*
4. Posts surrendered	*4. The situation of provisions*
5. Captures compensated	
6. Gr. Britain interested in securing to us the Mississippi	

Randolph noted that the treaty would secure peace, and the United States, in consequence, would not be "thrown into one set of European politics by an abhorrence of the outrages of another." He added that Jay had not exceeded his authority, there seemed little chance of obtaining a better treaty, and rejection would have a serious effect on national morale, while causing Britain to postpone the surrender of the posts. Finally, the twenty senators who had voted for it would be subjected to a savage public assault if the president rejected it.

Had the gods been kind to Edmund Randolph, they would have stopped his pen at this point but, with almost no transition, he inserted the sudden statement that "the order for capturing provisions is too irreconcileable with a state of harmony, for the treaty to be put into motion during its existence." He said that if there were no other way out, "the treaty ought to be absolutely broken up." He advised the president to take no further action. The war might end soon, people's passions would subside, and perhaps the British courts would order compensation for vessels previously seized. Negotiations could be resumed with Great Britain at some later date. The president should buy time by asking Randolph to tell the British minister that he would not sign the treaty until the order for recission had reached Philadelphia. Ratifications could then be exchanged at the American capital, if the president still wanted to sign it.

The secretary of state had placed strong doubts in Washington's mind on the provision order before he left for Mount Vernon. On the strength of this, Randolph, deliberately, or through a failure to understand, wrote on July 21 to the American legations in Europe to say that he believed that the president would not sign, so long as the order stood and perhaps never, even if it were repealed. At Mount Vernon, Washington read Hamilton's appraisal and compared it with Randolph's proposal to wreck the treaty. Shortly afterward, convinced by Hamilton that the British, while exasperating, were not willfully in violation of the treaty, the president changed his mind about the provision order and decided that he had no choice but to ratify, in the form that the Senate advised. On July 29 Washington informed the secretary of state that the violent opposition which had been manifested to the treaty would probably induce him to return rather quickly to the capital. Randolph was not to come to Mount Vernon, as he had planned to do. He continued:

> *I view the opposition which the treaty is receiving from the meetings in different parts of the union in a very serious light: not because there is more weight in any of the objections which are made to it, than were foreseen at first; for there are none in some of them; and gross misrepresentation in others; nor as it respects myself personally, for this shall have no influence on my conduct, plainly perceiving, and I am accordingly preparing my mind for it, the obloquy which disappointment and malice are collecting to heap upon me. But I am alarmed on account of the effect it may have on, and the advantage the French government may be disposed to make of the spirit which is at work to cherish a belief in them, that the treaty is calculated to favor G. Britain at their expence. Whether they believe or disbelieve these tales, the effect it will have on the nation, will be nearly the same; for whilst they are at war with that Power, it will... be their policy... to prevent us from being on good terms with G. B.*

On July 31 the Cabinet sent an urgent request to Washington to return to Philadelphia, the secretary of war privately adding that there was a "*special reason*" which made it desirable that he come "with all convenient speed." At the same time Washington wrote Randolph that "this government in relation to France and England may be compared to a Ship between the rocks of Scylla and Charybdis. If the Treaty is ratified, the partisans of the French (or rather of war and confusion) will excite them to hostile measures, or at least to unfriendly Sentiments; if it is not, there is no foreseeing *all* the consequences which may follow as it respects G. Britain." On August 1 Pickering wrote to Wayne to say that the president would ratify the treaty within a few days. On August 3 Washington informed Randolph that only "imperious" circumstances could shake his determination to sign the treaty.

Torrential rains delayed both the president's departure and his trip north. He found the roads muddied and flooded and bridges washed out. He arrived in Philadelphia on August 11 and was soon inquiring after Pickering's special reason. Pickering explained that the British minister had given him a copy of a Fauchet dispatch to Paris, which had been intercepted by the Royal Navy and forwarded to Philadelphia by the foreign office. Hammond, the British minister, had shown it to Oliver Wolcott, who, in turn, had consulted with Bradford and Pickering. It was soon clear to the president why he had been asked to return to town as soon as possible. The letter, which contained typical French praises of Jefferson, Madison, and Monroe, indicated that the secretary of state had made "valuable disclosures" to Fauchet. He added that Randolph, fearing civil and foreign war, had been very disturbed by the president's plan to issue a proclamation against the insurgents in western Pennsylvania. He suggested that Fauchet bribe certain persons in the state to forestall their cooperation with the federal government. The president read the letter and then indicated to the three cabinet members that they should continue to keep it secret.

Next day the cabinet met. Randolph introduced the memorial which he had sent to Mount Vernon, advising that the government tell the British minister that Washington would not sign the treaty. Many points needed adjustment and negotiation, and the British king was to be "invited" to consider them. The president asked the cabinet for their opinion.

Wolcott, Bradford, and Pickering advised him to sign immediately. Randolph, up to this time convinced that he had smashed the treaty, expostulated and protested. The president said that he would sign it without stipulation. He ordered Randolph so to inform the British minister in a memorandum. On August 14 Randolph delivered it to George Hammond, expressing his chagrin at having to do so. The minister was too polite to say that he knew that the president had entirely rewritten Randolph's original text. Hammond, who had been recalled to the foreign office, left for London with an assured peace. That same day Pickering wrote to Jay:

> *No man can be more anxious for the fate of the treaty with Great Britain than you; and the wanton abuse heaped upon you by enemies of their country, gives you a right to the earliest possible relief. The treaty will be ratified. This day the president finally sanctions a memorial announcing it to the British minister Mr. Hammond. The ratification will conform to the advice and consent of the Senate, unembarrassed with any other condition.*

On August 17 Jay replied to Pickering: "I think the President, with the blessing of Providence, will be able to carry his country safe through the storm, and see it anchored in peace and safety; if so, his life and character will have no parallel." On August 18 the president and secretary of state formally signed the treaty. A month later, still pursuing peace, the president wrote to Pickering to say that he had received the summary of the Wayne treaty with the northwest Indians. He asked him to dispatch at once the Indian agent in the Southwest to negotiate peace between the Cherokees and the Creeks. "It would be a pleasing circumstance not only to be enabled to say, at the meeting of Congress, that we were at peace with *all the Indian nations*, but by the mediations of the U States, we had settled the differences between the tribes above mentioned."

On August 19, in the presence of Pickering and Wolcott, Washington showed Randolph the Fauchet letter. There was discussion and some lame discourse by the secretary of state who then resigned. An additional burden for the president came when the attorney general, William Bradford, died four days later. The president encountered extraordinary difficulty for months in filling both posts. During the interim, Pickering handled, with great effectiveness, both the State and War Departments.

ABUSE OF THE PRESIDENT

Washington had written Hamilton in early July that he was greatly in need of relaxation. In addition he found the "intense" heat of Philadelphia "suffocating." He reported a "hot and disagreeable ride" to Mount Vernon from whence he was recalled to Philadelphia during another unpleasantly humid season. On September 8 he started once again for Mount Vernon for a month's rest, though he was not spared trouble while at home.

Hamilton, under the name "Camillus," had followed his private letter to the president with a series of brilliant articles in the *New York Argus* in defense of the treaty and in attack on the opposition. Washington praised the articles highly, while Jefferson wrote to Madison that Hamilton had become a "colossus" of the "anti-republican" (republican) forces. Hamilton squarely placed on Jefferson the blame for the general mob scenes and national disorders. He noted the immense abuse which had been heaped on Jay for his two successes, the peace and the ejection of a Jeffersonian from the governorship of New York. Hamilton won few southern hearts when he proclaimed that attempts by Virginia to lure back to slavery Negroes who had escaped to freedom during the revolution were "odious and immoral." He accused Virginia and South Carolina of deliberately evading, by acts of their legislatures, payments on private debts owing to British merchants, in violation of a national treaty. This forced the federal government to pay them, as a matter of honor, in order to regain the posts. Hamilton's arguments had a profound impact in the North; Jefferson, in alarm, wrote to Madison in September that he was even persuading many southerners of the treaty's merits.

During the period from the summer of 1795 through 1796, Jefferson managed an underground movement within the government, which operated against the treaty, even after its proclamation by the president had made it the supreme law of the land. He worked through Tench Coxe, commissioner of revenue in the Treasury, through whom he wrote letters to Monroe in vitriolic denunciation of the treaty. He urged Madison and other Virginia members of Congress to work to overthrow the peace. He also encouraged the Virginia Assembly, where his son-in-law was a member, to censure the president for having signed it.

The effectiveness of Hamilton was such that the Jeffersonian faction and press turned not on Hamilton, but on Washington with a savagery which would have been unbecoming in a jungle. Edmund Randolph wrote a number of harassing letters to the president, which Washington considered full of "innuendoes." He nonetheless gave Randolph permission to publish any and every letter he had written, even if private and confidential, or to quote anything he had said if they would help him to vindicate himself from the "suspicious" circumstances surrounding his resignation. Randolph, ungrateful, informed Madison on November 1 that Washington was a "Tiberius" and an "assassin." Washington dismissed Randolph's subsequent "vindication" as simply an "accusation."

In October the Jeffersonian press began an all-out assault on Washington's record as general and as president. That same month the *Aurora* of Philadelphia accused the president of having overdrawn his salary and asked for his impeachment. This information probably came from Tench Coxe. The distortions of fact here were remarkable. The president had been forced to move to a larger house in New York in 1790, and he then had to move his whole staff to Philadelphia at enormous expense. He received a Treasury advance to cover these extra expenses, which he subsequently covered from his own pocket, Congress having been too penurious to vote the necessary funds. In November a New York paper began printing the old forged Washington letters, prepared by the British at the beginning of the revolution, in which Washington was shown to have made treasonable comments. The French minister, Adet, eagerly seized on these and forwarded them to France as evidence of what Washington was really like.

In the midst of the uproar and after the Virginia Assembly had overwhelmingly adopted resolutions reflecting on the president and the treaty, the Maryland House and Senate, about November 27, unanimously passed a resolution condemning the "insinuations" and "invectives" of the Jeffersonians and expressing gratitude to Virginia's greatest son for his "*integrity, judgment, and patriotism.*" Washington replied to Governor John Stone on December 6:

> *At any time the expression of such a sentiment would have been considered as highly honorable and flattering; at the present, when the voice of malignancy is so high-toned, and no attempts are left unessayed to destroy all confidence in the Constituted authorities of this country, it is peculiarly grateful to my Sensibility; and coming spontaneously, and with the unanimity it has done, from so respectable a representation of the People, it adds weight as well as pleasure to the Act.*

> *I have long since resolved (for the present time at least) to let my calumniators proceed, without taking notice of their invectives myself, or by any other, with my participation or knowledge. Their views, I dare say, are readily perceived by the enlightened and well disposed part of the Community; and by the Records of my Administration and not by the voice of faction, I expect to be acquitted or condemned hereafter.*

STATE OF THE UNION

In spite of the abuse hurled at him, the president had so much good news to report that he made an unusually cheerful presentation of the state of the country on December 8, 1795:

> *I trust I do not deceive myself, while I indulge the persuasion, that I have never met*

you at any period when, more than at present, the situation of our public affairs has afforded just cause for mutual congratulation; and for inviting you to join with me in profound gratitude to the Author of all good, for the numerous and extraordinary blessings we enjoy.

The termination of the long, expensive and distressing war in which we have been engaged, with certain Indians Northwest of the Ohio, is placed in the option of the United States, by a treaty which the Commander of our Army has concluded... In the adjustment of the terms, the satisfaction of the Indians was deemed an object worthy no less of the policy than of the liberality of the United States, as the necessary basis of durable tranquillity...

The Creek and Cherokee Indians... have lately confirmed their pre-existing treaties with us, and were giving evidence of a sincere disposition to carry them into effect... But we have to lament, that the fair prospect in this quarter, has been once more clouded by wanton murders, which some Citizens of Georgia are represented to have recently perpetrated on hunting parties of the Creeks... Measures are persuing... to avert general hostility...

A letter from the Emperor of Morocco announces to me his recognition of our Treaty made with his Father... With peculiar satisfaction I add that information has been received from... Algiers... that the terms of a Treaty... authorize the expectation of a speedy peace, and the restoration of our unfortunate fellow-citizens from a grievous captivity.

The latest advices from our Envoy at the Court of Madrid, give moreover, the pleasing information that he had received assurances of a speedy and satisfactory conclusion of his negotiation...

A Treaty of Amity, Commerce and Navigation has been negotiated with Great Britain and... the Senate have advised and consented to its ratification... I have added my sanction...

If by prudence and moderation on every side, the extinguishment of all the causes of external discord, which have heretofore menaced our tranquillity, on terms compatible with our rights and honor, shall be the happy result—how firm, and how precious a foundation will have been laid for accelerating, maturing and establishing the prosperity of our country!

While many of the nations of Europe... have been involved in a contest, unusually bloody, exhausting and calamitous, in which the evils of foreign war have been aggravated by domestic convulsions and insurrection... [and] a scarcity of subsistence has embittered others' sufferings... our favored country, happy in a striking contrast, has enjoyed general tranquility... Our Agriculture, Commerce and Manufactures prosper beyond former example... Our population advances with a celerity which, exceeding the most sanguine calculations, proportionately augments our strength and resources, and guarantees our future security... With Governments founded on genuine principles of rational liberty, and with mild and wholesome laws, is it too much to say, that our country exhibits a spectacle of national happiness never surpassed if ever before equalled?

The president noted that he had pardoned all offenders in the western insurrection, including those who had been sentenced to death. Although it was his sworn duty to enforce the laws, it was also desirable to "mingle in the operations of government, every degree of moderation and tenderness, which the national justice, dignity and safety may permit."

Washington told Congress that he would forward separately the government's plans to provide fair treatment for the Indians, as well as reports on the progress made by the mint, and in the building of the navy and coastal fortifications. He added a final word to his countrymen: "Temperate discussion... and mutual forbearance where there is a difference of opinion, are too obvious and necessary for the peace, happiness and welfare of our country, to need any recommendations of mine."

FIRST PLACE

Lord Grenville had generously written to Jay after his departure: "You are happy in America if you can avoid, as I trust you will, the dangers of the war and the peace." He extended his sincere wishes for the country's prosperity.

Washington reported to his Mount Vernon manager during the year the price increases of one of the most important American exports, flour, as it moved from $8 to $10 and then to a record high of $12 a barrel. With the Jay treaty assuring peace and increasing shortages of food developing in the world, American exports rose by a third over the previous year. The American merchant marine had more than tripled in size since Washington assumed the presidency. In 1795 the fleet alone earned a larger sum in foreign exchange than the total value of all American exports in any year, when the states were colonies.

On a per capita basis the United States moved easily ahead of the mother country into first place in world trade. America's imports of goods and services in 1795 were 60 percent higher, per head, than those of the world's greatest commercial and industrial nation. While consumption was growing rapidly, it was clear that Americans were investing huge sums in shipping and insurance, fisheries and industries, canals and bridges, post offices and post roads, and schools and colleges. With the Indians at peace, hundreds of thousands of people began to move across the mountains into the land of milk and honey, carrying with them the Bible and the Constitution of the United States.

THIRTEEN

PEACE WITH SPAIN

1796

T HE LAST FOURTEEN months of Washington's presidency were triumphant on almost every front. Troubles with France, stimulated by
her American supporters, alone scarred the scene.

Washington began 1796 with a New Year's Day speech to the French minister, composed in all probability by his droll secretary of state. Citizen James
Monroe presented an American flag to the French Assembly, which ordered it
displayed alongside the tricolore. That body then voted to present a French flag
to the citizen representatives of the United States whom it persisted in trying to
label as the American government. Pickering deftly intercepted the presentation to Congress; the French minister agreed to hand it to the president. In his
speech Adet said that the flag was a symbol of terror to France's enemies but not
to those with whom she had established close relationships. The president
replied with disarming bombast. He referred to the French as "Wonderful
People! Ages to come will read with astonishment the history of your brilliant
exploits... [and your] interesting revolutionary movements." He concluded:

> *The transaction will be announced to Congress; and the colours will be deposited*
> *with the archives of the United States, which are at once the evidences and the*
> *memorials of their freedom and independence. May these be perpetual! and may the*
> *friendship of the two republics be commensurate with their existence.*

Nine days later the French minister discovered the significance of the paragraph indicating that the symbol of terror would be filed. He fired a furious but futile note of complaint to Pickering.

APPOINTMENTS

Finding the right man for office became increasingly irksome for the president. To add to his troubles, the chief justice, John Rutledge, who had been appointed *ad interim* to the Court while Congress was in recess, thereafter spent much of his time denouncing the Jay treaty. The Senate, which had ratified it by a vote of two to one, had no hesitation in booting him out of office. Since another judge had resigned, the president had to find two Supreme Court justices and two cabinet members from the limited supply of able personnel. He included, as a new potential appointee, Patrick Henry, who had swung to support of the Constitution while Madison turned away from it. Washington sounded out five men, including Henry, for the post of secretary of state. All declined, at least one saying he did not care to undergo the abuse heaped on the administration. In the end, Pickering, who had displayed great abilities and loyalty as head of the War Department (including the navy) and as acting secretary of state (including the foreign office, mint and patent office), got the job.

This left the war office open. Washington never tried to conceal from those whom he asked to take office that he had previously offered it to others. On January 20, 1796, he wrote to James McHenry, his aide during the revolution: " ...Will you suffer me to nominate you to the Office of Secretary of War? That I may give you evidence of the candour I have possessed above, I shall inform you that, for particular reasons (more fit for an oral, than a written communication) this office has been offered to Genl. Pinckney of So. Carolina, Colo. Carrington of Virginia, and Govr. Howard of Maryland, and that it would now give me sincere pleasure if you would fill it." McHenry accepted. This left the office of attorney general to fill. The president offered this post to John Marshall of Virginia. He declined, and Washington appointed Charles Lee, brother of Henry Lee, of a Virginia family noted for its devotion to the federal Union.

The appointments of Senator Oliver Ellsworth of Connecticut and Samuel Chase of Maryland as chief and associate justices completed Washington's most important assignments. It was noticeable that the president was increasingly forced to make most of his appointments from north of the Potomac in order to be sure of his men. The previous October 9 he had written to Edward

Carrington that it would be "an act of governmental suicide" to bring into high office a man "unfriendly to the Constitution and laws which are to be his guide."

TREATY WITH SPAIN

Next only to the Jay treaty, the agreement with Spain, officially known as the Treaty of San Lorenzo el Real but more usually called the Pinckney treaty, was the greatest diplomatic triumph of Washington's administration. It was gained by unorthodox methods, similar to those the president employed when he sent the chief justice to supercede the regular minister at London. Washington, in turn, transferred Pinckney to Madrid, as a special emissary to meet the procrastinating challenge of the Spanish government. The timing of his arrival was perfect; Pinckney appeared just as an aggressive French army was crashing into Spain. With assurances of secret British support in his Mississippi negotiations, Pinckney could lead from even greater strength than Jay.

Spain's astonishing first concession was a surrender of her previous claims to a large portion of present-day Alabama and Mississippi, as well as parts of Georgia, Tennessee, and Kentucky. Title to these areas had been transferred to the United States by Great Britain, in a secret clause of the 1783 treaty, but Spain had refused to recognize previous British claims thereto. The Mississippi River was divided between the United States and Spain. Americans were permitted to establish the trading post at New Orleans, which had been so much wanted by Kentucky. Spain agreed to withdraw all her garrisons from east of the Mississippi and north of the thirty-first parallel.

John Jay had sailed for London on May 12, 1794. Pinckney signed his treaty on October 27, 1795. In less than eighteen months, the president had broken forever the designs successively of Great Britain, France, and Spain to make the Alleghenies the western boundary for Americans. The sovereignty of the United States had more than tripled, with about 600,000 square miles added, covering parts or all of fourteen existing and future states. Today the world's most important agricultural and industrial area, it holds perhaps eighteen times the entire population of the country in 1790.

Wayne's Grenville treaty was unanimously ratified by the Senate in December 1795. On February 26, 1796, the president sent the Spanish treaty to the Senate which, six days later, also unanimously voted its approval. On March 1, having received a copy of the Grenville-Jay treaty signed by George III, the president formally proclaimed it in effect.

On April 8 the president transmitted to Congress the request of "the territory south of the Ohio" to be admitted as the sixteenth state. On June 1

Tennessee, now extending to the Mississippi, joined the Union. Andrew Jackson, the state's first congressman, was to be the last revolutionary war veteran to serve in the White House.

JEFFERSON

As the president moved from success to success, Thomas Jefferson, hidden away, endeavored with increasing emotion to block and baulk him, employing formidable weapons for the purpose. Virginia held nearly 20 percent of the seats in the House of Representatives. Aided by some New York and Pennsylvania votes, the deeper South, and the extra seats allotted for slaves, the democrats held a working majority in the lower chamber. Jefferson repeatedly urged Madison and his associates to use this power to wreck the Jay treaty. On March 27 he told Madison that the agreement was "a conspiracy with the enemies of our country," in which "the honor and faith of our nation are so grossly sacrificed." He had already added the Pinckney treaty to his proscribed list, writing to Madison, in early March, that the Spanish treaty "will have... eternal broils, instead of peace and friendship." Jefferson felt that Spain should have given up "vastly more," but it is difficult to see what else that country could have handed over, unless it were the crown jewels. Soon, with more accuracy than he intended, he was dividing Americans into "honest men" and "rogues."

Jefferson also kept up his correspondence with Monroe in Paris. He assured him that only Hamilton, in the entire United States, had the "effrontery" to defend the Jay treaty. The "public pulse" against it beat in more "universal union" than it had ever done since the Declaration of Independence.

While these intrigues were proceeding, the Jeffersonian press accused Washington of senility and of being both under British influence and subject to manipulation by his cabinet and Hamilton. In addition, Bache published in the *Aurora* a secret memorandum from the president to his cabinet, written just before he issued his 1793 neutrality proclamation.

This brought on the last known exchange of letters between Jefferson and Washington. The former, using a disclaimer that he was Bache's source, as an excuse for writing his letter of June 19, moved quickly to his real purpose which was to destroy the president's faith in Henry Lee. Lee had informed Washington two years earlier that Jefferson had been referring sarcastically to the president's advisers and to his supposed attachment to Great Britain. Washington replied to Lee that Jefferson's remarks seemed to be "enigmatical... or spoken ironically; and in that case they are too injurious to me, and have too little foundation in truth, to be ascribed to" the former secretary of state. When Jefferson heard of the Lee letter, he added Lee to his list of enemies. In writing Washington on June 19, 1796, he said of Lee:

> *I learn that this last has thought it worth his while to try to sow tares between you & me, by representing me as still engaged in the bustle of politics, & in turbulence & intrigue against the government. I never believed for a moment that this could make any impression on you, or that your knowledge of me would not outweigh the slander of an intriguer, dirtily employed in sifting the conversations of my table, where alone he could hear of me; and seeking to atone for his sins against you by his sins against another, who had never done him any other injury than that of declining his confidences... But enough of this miserable tergiversator, who ought indeed to have been of more truth, or less trusted by his country...*

Jefferson signed the letter in a Benjamin Rushlike manner: "With great & sincere esteem & respect." Washington replied on July 6 to the effect that he had never had any suspicion that Jefferson had given a cabinet secret to the press. He could easily "conjecture" the source (Randolph), and he knew that two Virginia congressmen had been bandying it about the halls of Congress. He then noted that the opposition press had used every opportunity to weaken the confidence of the people in the government by using existing documents, presented in a twisted form, as well as papers which had been forged for the purpose of publication. He continued:

> *It would not be frank, candid, or friendly to conceal, that your conduct has been represented as derogatory from that opinion I had conceived you entertained of me. That to your particular friends and connexions you have described, and they have denounced me, as a person under a dangerous influence; and that, if I would listen more to some other opinions, all would be well. My answer invariably has been that I had never discovered anything in the conduct of Mr. Jefferson to raise suspicions, in my mind, of his insincerity; that if he would retrace my public conduct while he was in the Administration, abundant proofs would occur to him, that truth and right decisions, were the sole objects of my pursuit; that there were as many instances within his own knowledge of my having decided against, as in favor of the person [Hamilton] evidently alluded to; and moreover, that I was no believer in the infallibility of the politics, or measures of any man living. In short, that I was no party man myself, and the first wish of my heart was, if parties did exist, to reconcile them.*
>
> *Until within the last year or two ago, I had no conception that Parties would, or*

even could go, the length I have been witness to; nor did I believe until lately, that it was within the bounds of probability, that, while I was using my utmost exertions to establish a national character of our own, independent, as far as our obligations and justice would permit, of every nation on earth; and wished, by steering a steady course, to preserve this Country from the horrors of a desolating war, that I should be accused of being the enemy of one Nation, and subject to the influence of another; and to prove it, that every act of my administration would be tortured, and the grossest and most insidious mis-representations of them be made (by giving one side only of a subject, and that too in such exaggerated and indecent terms as could scarcely be applied to a Nero; a notorious defaulter; or even to a common pickpocket). But enough of this; I have already gone farther in the expression of my feelings, than I intended.

Just before receiving this letter, Jefferson had written the most savage indictment of Washington and his administration which had yet appeared. He sent this to Phillip Mazzei, a French sympathizer living in French-occupied Tuscany. It would be difficult not to believe that Jefferson expected his letter to be published in Europe as, indeed, it soon was. He wrote on April 24:

The aspect of our politics has wonderfully changed since you left us. In place of that noble love of liberty, & republican government which carried us triumphantly thro' the war, an Anglican monarchical, & aristocritical party has sprung up, whose avowed object is to draw over us the substance, as they have already done the forms, of the British government. The main body of our citizens, however, remain true to their republican principles; the whole landed interest is republican, and so is a great mass of talents. Against us are the Executive, the Judiciary, two out of three branches of the legislature, all the officers of government, all who want to be officers; all timid men who prefer the calm of despotism to the boisterous sea of liberty, British merchants & Americans trading on British capitals, speculators & holders in the banks & public funds, a contrivance invented for the purpose of corruption, & for assimilating us in all things to the rotten as well as the sound parts of the British model. It would give you a fever were I to name to you the apostates who have gone over to these heresies, men who were Samsons in the field & Solomons in the Council, but who have had their heads shorn by the harlot England.

The letter, published in Italy at the end of the year, was reprinted in the French government's official newspaper, along with an editorial which declared it to be a complete justification for having broken diplomatic relations with the United States. This act, the paper further observed, was intended to effect "a triumph to the party of good republicans, the friends of

France," in the presidential elections. When Washington read the letter, which was reproduced by many American newspapers in 1797, he learned all that he needed to know of Jefferson.

THE MEANING OF THE WORDS

The Constitutional Convention of 1787 had proclaimed that "this Constitution for the United States of America" was ordained and established by "the people of the United States in order to form a more perfect Union, establish justice, insure domestic Tranquility, provide for the common defence, promote the general Welfare, and secure the blessings of Liberty to ourselves and our Posterity." To make certain that it was, in fact, the American people who ordained it by democratic process, the convention provided for its ratification not only by their representatives in Congress but by additional popularly elected special assemblies called for that purpose in each state. In transmitting the Constitution to Congress, the president of the convention, George Washington, wrote on September 17, 1787:

> *The friends of our country have long seen and desired, that the power of making war, peace, and treaties, of levying money and regulating commerce, and the correspondent executive and judicial authorities should be fully and effectually invested in the general government of the Union...*

> *It is obviously impracticable in the federal government of these States, to secure all rights of independent sovereignty to each, and yet provide for the interest and safety of all. Individuals entering into society, must give up a share of liberty to preserve the rest...*

> *In all our deliberations... we kept steadily in our view, that which appears to us the greatest interest of every true American, the consolidation of our Union, in which is involved our prosperity, felicity, safety, perhaps our national existence. This important consideration, seriously and deeply impressed on our minds, led each State in the Convention to be less rigid on points of inferior magnitude than might otherwise have been expected; and thus the Constitution, which we now present, is the result of a spirit of amity, and of that mutual deference and concession which the peculiarity of our political situation rendered indispensable.*

> *That it may promote the lasting welfare of that country so dear to us all, and secure her freedom and happiness, is our most ardent wish.*

In 1796 Jefferson began to diverge ever more sharply from Washington on the Constitution. To describe the Union he introduced, for the first time, the word "confederacy." Joined by Madison, who knew better, Jefferson began to call the Constitution a "compact" or, its slighter form, "pact." The transition from there to nullification and secession was easy and direct. Washington's Union, the "consolidation" of the American people into one nation, became the evil against which the sovereign and independent states were obliged to fight.

MADISON

In the months that followed Washington's message to the Senate on the Jay treaty, there was a marked shift in public opinion as the treaty's merits won increased acknowledgment. Even Benjamin Rush noted in January 1796: "All is peace in our country. General Washington is still esteemed by a great majority of our citizens and his treaty with Great Britain becomes less unpopular in proportion as it is understood." By March Rush was sure that the House of Representatives would vote its support.

Nonetheless the Democrats, under Madison, charged to the attack on the treaty, in confidence that they could overturn it. Their first assault took place on March 24, when, by a vote of sixty-two to thirty-seven, the House called for all the treaty papers, although this request was modified to exclude any documents the president considered "improper" to become public. Six days later the president replied with one of the bluntest statements he had ever sent to Congress:

> To admit... a right in the House of Representatives to demand, and to have as a matter of course, all the Papers respecting a negotiation with a foreign power, would be establishing a dangerous precedent.

> Having been a member of the General Convention and knowing the principles on which the Constitution was formed, I have ever entertained but one opinion on this subject... The power of making treaties is exclusively vested in the President, by and with the advice and consent of the Senate, provided two-thirds of the Senators present concur, and that every treaty so made, and promulgated, thenceforward became the Law of the Land.

> As therefore it is perfectly clear to my understanding, that the assent of the House of Representatives is not necessary to the validity of a treaty: as the treaty with Great Britain exhibits in itself all the objects requiring legislative provision; and on these the papers can throw no light: And as it is essential to the due administration of

government, that the boundaries fixed by the Constitution between the different
departments should be preserved: A just regard to the Constitution and to the duty
of my office, forbids a compliance with your request.

The president then forwarded to the Senate nominations for boundary commissioners under the Jay treaty, for which the House would have to vote funds.
The representatives blustered, threatened, and then asserted, by a vote of fifty-
seven to thirty-five, the right to pass on all treaties. At this point the voice of
the country began to be heard. A great Boston town meeting voted almost
unanimous approval of the treaty. Petitions and letters poured into the House,
in huge volume, asking the members to vote approval. "Washington and
Peace" became a byword.

For a month the debate continued; Madison found his supporters drifting
away, one by one. On April 30 a further vote was held. Although eighteen of
Virginia's representatives voted against the president, one congressman,
George Hancock of the Shenandoah Valley, sided with Washington.
Opponents from north of the Potomac, disturbed by the public clamor for the
treaty, deserted Madison in such numbers that the House, in committee of the
whole, voted forty-nine for and forty-nine against an appropriation. The
Speaker, on whom Madison had previously relied, broke the tie in favor of the
treaty.

The president had won, as Madison's twenty-five-vote majority shriveled
into a three-vote minority. Peace was secure; Madison was not to have his war
for another sixteen years. In June Jefferson complained to Monroe that "the
people" had overruled their representatives, who knew more than they did.

MONROE

The French minister had suggested to the president of the United States on
New Year's Day that France's flag was a symbol of terror. This was true in
Europe, as French armies swept across Belgium and the Netherlands and into
Germany, Austria, and Spain. Jefferson's new hero, "that wonderful man,"
Bonaparte, was leading a horde of pillaging French across the plains of Italy,
taking ransom from pope and princes alike. The Washington who had held
off the British empire for so many years was not terrorized, and, accordingly,
he was blindly hated by France.

In his generally hilarious 1798 comments on Monroe's defense of his
actions in France, Washington wrote that Monroe forwarded all complaints by
the French government to Philadelphia but delivered American protests

against French ship seizures so weakly they had no effect. Monroe's intrigues with "the French party" in the United States—Jefferson and Madison in Virginia, and Benjamin Bache and George Logan in Pennsylvania—finally forced the president to recall him. On July 2, 1796, three members of the cabinet urgently wrote to Washington at Mount Vernon:

> *We think the great interests of the United States require that they have near the French government some faithful organ… Our duty obliges us to be explicit. Altho' the present Minister plenipotentiary of the United States at Paris has been amply furnished with documents to explain the views and conduct of the United States, yet his own letters authorize us to say, that he has omitted to use them, and thereby exposed the U States to all the mischiefs which could flow from jealousies and erroneous conceptions of their conduct. Whether this dangerous omission arose from such an attachment to the cause of France… or from mistaken views of the latter, the evil is the same…*

> *In confirmation of our opinion of the expediency of recalling Mr. Monroe, we think the occasion requires that we communicate a private letter which came to our hands since you left Philadelphia. The letter corresponds with other intelligence of his political opinions and conduct. A minister who has thus made the notorious enemies of the whole system of government his confidential correspondents, in matters which affect the Government, cannot be relied on to do his duty to the latter. The private letter we received in confidence. Among other circumstances that will occur to your reflection, the anonymous letters from France to Thomas Blount and others are very noticeable… These… are proofs of sinister designs, and shew that the public interests are no longer safe in the hands of such men.*

> *The information contained in the confidential communication… on the project of the French Government relative to the Commerce of the U States, is confirmed by the open publication of the same substantially and more minutely in the News-papers.*

The letter, enclosed by the cabinet, had been written by Monroe to George Logan, forwarding material to be inserted in Bache's newspaper. Monroe promised to send further reports for this purpose. After consulting the attorney general, who was in Alexandria, Washington wrote to Pickering on July 8 to say he would recall him but he would have difficulty in finding a successor loyal to the government and acceptable to France. He again approached Patrick Henry and John Marshall, but neither were induced to go. Once again he turned to a Pinckney, Charles Cotesworth, brother of the minister at London. Pinckney accepted, but the French Directory subsequently refused to receive his credentials. Monroe, before his recall, informed the French government that there would be American presidential elections in 1796 and these would provide a leadership more friendly to France.

FRENCH WAR MEASURES

Spain, which had been fighting alongside Great Britain, had turned a flipflop. By 1796 she was allied with the French aggressor, this was to be the eventual undoing of the Spanish empire. For the United States its most immediate impact was a delay in surrender of the Spanish posts in Mississippi, but not in Tennessee and Alabama. Almost unnoticed, during the House flurry over the Jay treaty, was an amendment to it which the Senate ratified in 1796. It was presented as covering British traders in the Northwest Territory but so worded as to specify that the treaty would not affect or be affected by other commercial treaties which had been signed by the United States. This ensured that Britain would share the navigation of the Mississippi, as provided by the 1783 treaty. Spain did not like this at all but the clause assured warm British support for the United States, if there were to be any contest over the point. To this extent, therefore, the Jeffersonians were right in declaring that the United States had become, in fact, a limited ally of Great Britain.

In the meantime France increased her aggressive seizures of American merchant vessels, in a manner calculated to force the United States to war. Diplomatic relations were broken off towards the close of the year, the French foreign minister declaring to Monroe that the United States had become a vassal state of France's enemy. There were some 30,000 Frenchmen in the principal seaports of America, prepared to uphold France at all costs. The French resumed arming privateers in America to prey, not on British, but on American commerce.

France also resumed her dream of rebuilding a great empire in North America. She put pressure on Spain, weak and torn, to restore Louisiana to France. French agents, too, were busy in Canada and in French settlements in the Northwest Territory, planning to gain control of Canada, Louisiana, and all of the United States west of the Alleghenies. General Wayne, who had spent four arduous years fighting the British and Indians, wrote numerous dispatches to the War Department, outlining the activities of the country's newest enemies, operating under the orders of the French minister in Philadelphia.

On May 25, at the president's direction, McHenry informed Wayne that the government had positive and reliable intelligence that French spies were proceeding to Pittsburgh and the West, "to gain knowledge of our military posts in the Western country, and to encourage and stimulate the people in the quarter to secede from the Union, and form a political and separate connexion with a foreign power." He identified them as General Georges De Collot, Thomas Powers (a Frenchman of Irish descent), and a man named Warin, formerly an engineer in the American service. They expected to visit all the American posts in Kentucky and the Northwest, as well as the old French settlements of Vincennes and Ste. Genevieve.

Wayne soon confirmed that all three had been in Pittsburgh. He added that there was a fourth Frenchman, Constantin Volney, associated with them. Although neither Wayne nor McHenry knew it, Volney had just spent three weeks with Jefferson at Monticello, presumably not confining his discussions to philosophy. Wayne reported that De Collot carried with him "bushels" of introductory letters from leading Democrats in the Senate and House. Aaron Burr, who was to be associated with Wilkinson's future conspiracies, was among the writers. Wayne added that Judge Benjamin Sebastian of Kentucky was apparently also involved with the French and Spanish. Although Wayne could not know the details, subsequent documentation showed that Sebastian, Harry Innes, a federal judge of Kentucky; and George Nicholas were engaged in a conspiracy to turn Kentucky and Tennessee over to Spain.

Wayne reported that the French agents, who all spoke English fluently, were loud in their indiscretions. They denounced the Jay treaty everywhere, saying that it completely justified France's seizures of American ships. The agents described the president as "timid." They informed the Westerners that France was ready to force Spain to break the treaty opening the Mississippi and to return Louisiana to France. It was high time for that part of the United States west of the Alleghenies to secede from the Union, otherwise the Mississippi would be forever shut to them. Wayne particularly noted that De Collot was "busy in Electioneering for Mr. Jefferson & advises a *proper* choice of Electors for that purpose." He also wrote that the three principal agents issued a violent diatribe against the federal government in Kentucky. De Collot had then proceeded onward, making an accurate survey of defenses of the Ohio and of the Mississippi to the Kaskaskias River. Volney moved north to inspect the fortifications at Niagara, which would be of vital importance if France seized Quebec and the Saint Lawrence River.

Although Wayne, at the president's orders, made efforts to capture De Collot and his papers, the Frenchman escaped. Wayne did intercept letters from Adet which clearly showed that the mission had been sent for purposes of espionage, insurrection, and election intimidation.

THE FRIENDLY BRITISH

John Jay had reported from London that Washington was the foreigner most admired by the British people. Benjamin West was soon to hear from the king's own lips that this included George III as well. In the spring and summer of 1796 Washington had the new experience of being the subject of cordial enquiries on the part of Lords Dorchester and Cornwallis, as well as being toasted by British officers in Canada.

On May 13 Thomas Twining, returning to England after serving on the staff of Cornwallis, the governor general of India, called on the president. Mrs. Washington received him and engaged him in conversation. Twining reported: "The door opened and Mrs. Washington and myself rising, she said, 'The President,' and introduced me to him. Never did I feel more interest than at this moment, when I saw the tall, upright, venerable figure of this great man advancing towards me to take me by the hand. There was a seriousness in his manner which seemed to contribute to the impressive dignity of his person, without diminishing the confidence and ease, which the benevolence of his countenance and the kindness of his address inspired... So completely did he look the great and good man he really was, that I felt rather respect than awe in his presence. I mentioned the particular regard and respect with which Lord Cornwallis always spoke of him. He received this communication in the most courteous manner, inquired about his lordship and expressed for him much esteem." The president invited Twining to dinner but, to his distress, the latter had to decline because of another engagement.

Just before this visit, Washington and his secretary of war had discussed their approach to Lord Dorchester, requesting the formal surrender of all posts. The British had been understandably nervous at the loud cries of the Democrats, and had held them to a point where they could not be evacuated before June 1, the required treaty date. Not long afterwards McHenry sent a Captain Lewis (possibly Howell Lewis, the president's nephew) to Quebec with a letter to Dorchester. On June 27 the secretary of war wrote to the president at Mount Vernon, enclosing copies of the orders he had received from "Adjutant General Beckwith" (the old spy) for the evacuation of Fort Miamis, Detroit, Michilimackinac, Oswego, and Niagara. Next day he reported to Washington:

Capt. Lewis says he was treated with much civility by Lord Dorchester's family (staff). That the People seemed every where pleased at the prospect of a friendly intercourse with our Citizens. Lord Dorchester was particular in his inquiries respecting your health, and seemed pleased to learn that you were well and looked well. I believe his Lordship is himself about seventy. Lewis could have dined out for

a Month at Quebec. The first toast the King of Great Britain, the second,
invariably, the President.

Dorchester had resigned as governor of Canada after being reprimanded by
the British government for his actions in Ohio. He sailed for England and
retirement after ordering the graceful transfer of the posts he had worked so
long to hold.

In the meantime Wayne, on the frontier, had been worried that the
Chippewas and other tribes were again moving towards hostilities, stimulated
by the Canadian Indian department, which had been fearful that the
"Virulent Opposition" in Congress would cause the treaty to fail. As soon as it
was secure the British were prompt and magnanimous in handing over the
posts. On July 11 Wayne wrote to McHenry that his troops were now at Detroit
and Miamis. The British had been "polite and friendly" and had acted in a
manner "truly worthy to British Officers [doing] honor to them & the Nation
to which they belong." By August 28 Wayne himself was in Detroit. On
September 20 he reported that the posts of Michilimackinac, Niagara, and
Oswego had been transferred to the Americans "in the most polite, friendly &
accommodating Manner." He continued:

> *An event that must naturally afford the highest pleasure & satisfaction to every*
> *friend of order & good Government, & I trust will produce a conviction to the*
> *world—that the Measures adopted & pursued by that great & first of men, the*
> *President of the United States—were founded in Wisdom, & that the best interests*
> *of his country have been secured by that unshaken fortitude, Patriotism & Virtue,*
> *for which he is so universally & justly celebrated (a few Democrats excepted—&*
> *even they in their hearts must acknowledge his worth).*

On October 3 Wayne forwarded to McHenry a list of the Indian chiefs who
were proceeding to Philadelphia, "to see & converse with their great Father
the President of the United States of America, agreeably to the Unanimous
request of all the Chiefs who signed the Treaty of Green Ville." Accompanying
them were three army officers as interpreters for the tribes. On November 29
Washington received warriors from the Wyandots, Delawares, Shawanoes,
Ottawas, Chippewas, Potawtimes, Miamis, Weeas, Kickapoos, Piankashaws,
and Kaksaskias. In greeting them Washington referred to "my great warrior,
General Wayne." By then Wayne was seriously ill from overwork. He died in
Erie, Pennsylvania, on December 15, 1796.

Andrew Jackson, by Ralph Earl, elected to Congress 1796 and to the Senate in 1797, serving only to 1798, President 1829–1837. *(National Portrait Gallery)*

William Henry Harrison, by Rembrandt Peale, served in the Army 1791–1798, President 1841. *(National Portrait Gallery)*

By Amos Doolittle after Joseph Wright, shows the seals of the United States and the thirteen original States linked in strong union by Washington. *(Courtesy of Mount Vernon Ladies' Association of the Union)*

The Washington family by David Edwin after Edward Savage. *(Courtesy of Mount Vernon Ladies' Association of the Union)*

Bushrod Washington by Henry Benbridge; nephew of George Washington, who was appointed to the Supreme Court by President Adams in 1798. *(Courtesy of the Mount Vernon Ladies' Association of the Union)*

(Courtesy of John Melius, artist)

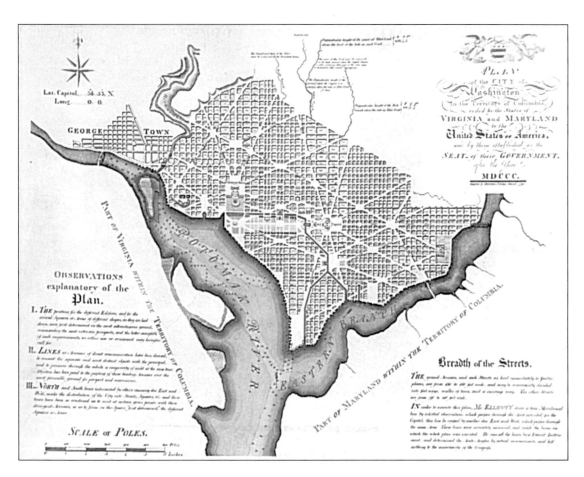

Plan of the city of Washington to be the federal capital in 1800.

Martha Washington, by Robert Field.
(Courtesy of the Mount Vernon Ladies'
Association of the Union)

Pastel portrait of
Martha Washington's
granddaughter, the
"Beautiful Nelly" Custis,
who married George
Washington's nephew,
Lawrence Lewis. *(Courtesy
of the Mount Vernon Ladies'
Association of the Union)*

Memorial Engraving *Pater Patriae* by Enoch Gridley after John Coles, Jr., and Edward Savage, circa 1800. *(Courtesy of the Mount Vernon Ladies' Association of the Union)*

LAFAYETTE

To Washington's continuing sorrow, Lafayette had been imprisoned since 1792 in a series of European fortresses, finally being incarcerated at Olmutz, Moravia. The president had a difficult role to play as an old friend of Lafayette and as chief of state. Washington and Lafayette were considered by the French government as enemies to France, while the European autocracies thought of Lafayette as a wild revolutionist who deserved imprisonment. Washington for years had requested his ministers, Morris, Monroe, and Pinckney, to make informal appeals to Franz II to permit Lafayette's release to the United States. In May 1796 Washington himself addressed a direct and moving request to the emperor to parole him, under any restrictions thought necessary.

The Marquise de Lafayette, having decided to appeal personally to the emperor to permit her and her daughters to join Lafayette in Olmutz prison, dispatched her fourteen-year-old son, George Washington, to the president with a note saying that she was placing "this dear child under the protection of the United States... and... the special protection of their President whose sentiments for his father are well known to me." Madame de Lafayette requested that her son be permitted to live an obscure life in America and to resume the education which had been stopped by the Reign of Terror.

Young Lafayette's arrival in Boston in early September 1795, with a tutor, Felix Frestel, placed Washington in what he considered to be an embarrassing dilemma. He wrote at once to Senator Cabot: "To express all the sensibility which has been excited in my breast by the receipt of young Fayettes letter, from the recollection of his fathers merits, services and sufferings, from my friend-ship for him, and from my wishes to become a *friend* and *father* to his Son, are unnecessary. Let me in a few words, declare that I *will be his friend;* but the man-ner of becoming so, considering the obnoxious light in which his father is viewed by the French government, and my own situation, as the Executive of the U. States, requires more time to consider... than I can bestow at present; the let-ters not having been in my hands more than an hour, and I myself on the point of setting out for Virginia..." Washington asked Cabot to assure young Lafayette that he would be a *"Father, friend, protector"* to him. He suggested that Cabot enroll Lafayette in Harvard, at Washington's expense, until he could plan his future more clearly. He pointed out that the president and the boy had to act with prudence because of difficult relations with France and the fact that his mother and many of his relatives had been imprisoned by the French govern-ment. In November the president sent young Lafayette a warm and affectionate letter, suggested that he proceed to New York, where Alexander Hamilton, his father's old friend, would take care of him until it was possible for the president to see him. By April the president's personal feelings for Lafayette and his son finally overruled any hesitation he had in regard to political consequences. George Lafayette and his tutor thereupon joined the Washington household, staying until news came of General Lafayette's release from prison.

LEAR AND CUSTIS

Tobias Lear, secretary to and friend of Washington, had left his post with the president not long after the sudden death of his first wife in 1793. His small son, Benjamin Lincoln, was placed in the care of Lear's mother while he went to Europe. When Lear settled in business in Georgetown in 1794, Washington offered him the post of district commissioner, which he declined. Washington continued to use him for various business matters including work with the Potomac Canal Company. On December 12, 1794, Washington asked Lear to get the master key to his papers from Fanny Washington, Mrs. Washington's widowed niece. The Alexandria widow and the Georgetown widower were married a few months later. Fanny Lear had the tuberculosis which had so long plagued the Washington family, and she died in March 1796, leaving Lear again a widower, this time with his own child and three stepchildren, Anna Maria, George Fayette, and Charles Washington. On March 30 the president and his wife wrote Lear:

> *Your former letters prepared us for the stroke, which that of the 25th instant announced; but it has fallen heavily notwithstanding...*

> *To say how much we loved, and esteemed our departed friend, is Unnecessary. She is now no more! but she must be happy, because her virtue has a claim to it.*

> *As you talked of coming to this place of business, let us press you to do so. The same room that serves Mr. Dandridge and Washington is large enough to receive a Bed also for you; and it is needless to add, we would be glad of your company. The change may be serviceable to you; and if our wishes were of any avail, they would induce you to make your stay here as long as your convenience would permit.*

> *At all times, and under all circumstances, we are, and ever shall remain, Your sincere and Affectionate friends*

> *G. Washington*
> *M. Washington*

In spite of his national problems, the president took a great deal of time and trouble to help Lear arrange for the care of the four children. He wrote to Burwell Bassett, Lear's brother-in-law, informing him that Lear had arrived in Philadelphia and they had had many conversations. At first Lear had wanted to keep all the children but he then decided that Maria, the daughter, should live with the Bassetts. The president said that he and his wife had always wanted to raise Fayette but now that the two boys had neither father nor mother, it seemed best to keep them together, at least until the president's forthcoming permanent retirement from government.

On June 3 the president wrote to Lear who had returned to Georgetown: "The chief design of my writing to you by this Post, is to inform you that your good Mother, and lovely son, arrived in this city on Tuesday evening; and left it yesterday about ten o'clock on their way to the Federal City. Mrs. Lear is very well, and Lincoln as sprightly as ever; but both disappointed at not meeting you here. It was with great difficulty a Carriage could be procured to take her on; for it so happened, that Congress closed their Session yesterday, that the members were struggling for, and bidding on each other for conveyances; and your Mother's anxious desire to get to you, would not permit her to wait. At length, after some unavailing attempts, Mr. [George Washington] Craik succeeded in getting a Carriage and a pair of horses, which I hope will take her safe down…"

Maria, also ill with tuberculosis, gave her stepgrandmother a difficult time. Martha Washington wrote Mary Lear on November 4:

As soon as we came to town the President sent Mr. Dandridge to enquire of the Minister of the Moravian church, if he could get Maria into the school at Bethlehem. I am sorry to tell you that the answer was that the school was full, so that it would be some time before she could be taken in. The President says he will write to Bethlehem and endeavor if its possible to get her in… I have been told there is a very good boarding school in Georgetown…

I was extremely sorry to be told, after Maria went from Mr. Law's, how ill she had behaved to you. Had I known it before, I should have reprimanded her very seriously. She has always been a spoiled child, as indeed they were all… I loved the child's mother and I love her. It gives me pain to think that a child as circumstanced as she is, should not have a disposition to make herself friends. Her youth will plead for her.

In addition to looking after Maria's welfare, the president took time to write to and about George Washington Custis, his wife's grandson, who was turning out to be a model of his father. Colonel George Washington had tried, with almost no success, to give John Parke Custis a good education. With rueful foresight the president wrote to Tobias Lear on November 20: "Washington Custis has got settled at Princeton College, and I think under favourable auspices, but the change from his former habits is so great and sudden; and his hours for study so much increased beyond what he has been accustomed to that though he promises to be attentive, it is easy to be perceived he is not at all reconciled to it yet. That of getting up an hour before day, to commence them, I will venture to pronounce not the least irksome to him."

ESTATE TROUBLES

In 1767 Washington's good nature had trapped him as executor of the Colville estate, bringing him thirty-one years of trouble. In 1796 Washington asked Bushrod Washington, his lawyer nephew, to make a final settlement of the business. His letter of February 10 to Bushrod referred to an "extraordinary devise" in the Colville will, adding that he hardly knew where to begin or end a story which had involved him in such "unexpected vexation and trouble." He continued:

> You must know then that in a visit to Colo. Thos. Colville on his death bed (an unlucky one I have ever since deemed it) he informed me, that he had appointed me one of his Executors. I told him that my numerous engagements of a similar kind, would not permit me to discharge the duties of one. He urged; I refused; he pressed again, assuring me that all the trouble would be taken off my hands by his wife and Mr. Jno. West (who married his niece) that he wished only for my name, and I would now and then only inquire how matters were conducted by those first named. Unwilling to make the last moments of a worthy and respectable character uneasy, I yielded to his request; and having done so I would not be worse than my word and qualified accordingly.

Washington then mentioned that he had gone off to the wars. Years later he returned to find Mrs. Colville and West dead and everything relating to the estate "enveloped in darkness." He thereupon engaged a lawyer to go through the whole of the papers so that a final settlement, for which he was responsible, might be made. The letter went on:

> I ought to have mentioned in an earlier part of this detail, that one of the first acts of the Executors was to publish in the English papers an extract of the Will of Colo.

Thos. Colville making the nearest relations of his Mother, the residuary legatees. The bequest and publication raised a host of claimants, one of whom, through the medium of General Howe, while he commanded the B. forces in America, <u>demanded</u> in an open impudent and imperious letter, which passed through the hands of that officer, the restitution of an Estate worth <u>Forty thousand</u> pounds which he said was the Surplus of the Estate and due to him; altho the very clause under which he claimed expressed a doubt of there being any surplus at all.

The president asked his nephew to submit the whole of the matter to the chancellor of Virginia so that the court could order a proper distribution based on the surplus, as finally calculated. Two more years of trouble were involved thereafter for Washington, including the writing of a reply to the clerk of the peace in Durham, England. He patiently explained to the clerk, on September 10, 1797, that it had been a long and trying business to find "the nearest relations of [Colville's] mother, by the names of Stott, Wills, Richardson and Catherine Smith, of Durham, or their descendants." The court of chancery of Virginia had now decreed a distribution. No doubt the heirs would be disappointed at the smallness of the amount involved, a little over $3,000. Washington had asked the Virginia court to determine it, for so many claims were handed in and many were either vague or "accompanied by such unjust and indecent insinuations" that only a court order could clear the mess up. Everyone in Durham now knew where to write to present their documents; he had "nothing more to do in the matter [himself]." Washington's share of the Colville estate correspondence ceased in 1798.

GILBERT STUART

A further unlucky event for Washington was the arrival in Philadelphia that winter of the portrait painter, Gilbert Stuart. Senator William Bingham of Pennsylvania and his wife had promised to present an oil of Washington to the Marquess of Lansdowne, the former British prime minister. On April 11, 1796, the president dropped a line to Stuart: "I am under promise to Mrs. Bingham to sit for you tomorrow at nine o'clock, and wishing to know if it be convenient to you that I should do so, and whether it shall be at your own house (as she talked of the State House), I send this to ask for information."

This was the only completed portrait of Washington which Stuart made directly from his subject and the result was disastrous. The face was devoid of all Washington's intelligence, charm, and humor, and aged far beyond his years. Benjamin Latrobe, the artist-architect, who saw him three months later, reported that "he is about 64 but appears some years younger." The stiff, ungainly figure was painted in later, as were the waxlike hands, by unskilled assistants of Stuart. The artist dashed off many copies of the Lansdowne and the unfinished Antheneum portrait, thereby providing a long line of American schoolchildren with an unpleasant image of the father of their country. The pitching of all Stuart portraits of Washington into Boston Harbor would be appropriate.

The comparison of Washington's real face to his portraits was noted by Charlotte Chambers. In writing her mother, February 21, 1795, about a visit to the Washingtons, she said, "The President, soon after, with that benignity peculiarly his own, advanced, and I arose to receive and return his compliments, with the respect and love my heart dictated." She added how little a portrait on the wall resembled him. The various pictures she had seen looked much more like each other than they did the president.

THE NATIONAL UNIVERSITY

In his last year in office, the president pushed, so far as his time allowed, his favorite object of a national university. By 1796 he had, perhaps because of Virginia's contumacy, decided that the university belonged in Washington, rather than in Alexandria. He was encouraged by reports from the district commissioners that investors and speculators intended to make substantial donations to the university. That year he selected a large site for it, west of the president's house, on which part of the present George Washington University is located. This included land that he owned and which he expected to give to the university as an addition to his Potomac Canal shares.

On July 16 Benjamin Latrobe visited Washington at Mount Vernon. He wrote that after breakfast next morning, the president talked for an hour: "His subject was principally the Establishment of the university at the Federal City. He mentioned the offer he had made of giving to it all the interest he had in the City on condition that it should go on in a given time, and complained that though magnificent offers had been made by many speculators for the same purpose there seemed to be no inclination to carry them into Effect." In December Washington entrusted Madison to carry legislation in the House, authorizing the university, for which he made a strong plea in his last address to Congress.

On September 15 Washington notified the governor of Virginia that he was presenting his James River Canal shares to Liberty Hall Academy in Lexington, Virginia. The institution changed its name to Washington Academy. It subsequently became Washington College and, in the course of time, Washington and (Robert S.) Lee University.

THE CITY OF WASHINGTON

Speculators, described by Washington as "men one day and mice the next," continued to give trouble to the Washington City commissioners. The commissioners' repeated appeals to Robert Morris and his associates were met by promises but no cash. The president approved of their alternate plans to advertise the sale of lots throughout the country and to apply for a loan in Holland, but he warned that the loan application in Europe would take six months to complete. He also endeavored to sound out a Philadelphia bank on the subject but without success.

Washington's letters repeatedly urged the commissioners to devote full time to their work and to live in the city itself. All preferred the amenities of Georgetown to the rigors of the capital's forests. On July 4, 1795, Washington wrote to commissioner Gustavus Scott:

> *I must be explicit in declaring that, not only to obviate the suspicions and jealousies which proceed from a residence of the Commissioners without the City, or in a remote corner of it, not only that they may be where the busy and important scenes are transacting and that they may be the judge of the conduct of others, not from <u>Reports Only</u>, but from ocular proof, as the surest guide to Economy and dispatch; Independent, I say of these considerations... I should view the Residence of the Commissioners... and their Officers... in some central part of it as a nest egg (pardon the expression) which will attract others...*

The finances of the city plagued the commissioners all summer; Washington told them it would be highly impolitic for him to go to Congress for money unless all else failed, since it would revive all the squabbles over the location of the capital. In November the president signed an application to Maryland for a loan; in December he added an urgent personal appeal to the state's governor for funds. On December 25, replying to Scott, who informed him that the Maryland Assembly was about to agree to a loan of $100,000 provided the commissioners personally guaranteed the federal government's note, Washington expressed his gratitude for Maryland's action but commented on the required endorsement: "The necessity of the case justified the obtaining of it on almost any terms, and the zeal of the commissioners... in making themselves liable for the amount, as it could not be had without, cannot fail of approbation... At the same time I must confess that the request has a very singular appearance, and will not, I should suppose, be very grateful to the feelings of Congress." He assured them they would suffer no loss.

THE FAREWELL ADDRESS

The president appears to have verbally informed John Adams in the spring that he would retire at the end of his second term. He gave the same assurance to John Jay by letter in May. No doubt others were told; his anticipated retirement was soon common knowledge, though the president made no formal announcement until September.

When Washington originally planned to retire at the end of his first term, he discussed a farewell address with Madison and gave him a letter indicating the topics he wanted to cover in a valedictory to the people. Madison drafted several introductory paragraphs for the proposed speech, based on their conversations and Washington's letter. Around February 1796, when Hamilton was in Philadelphia, Washington told him that he had been working on a proposed new valedictory, which he would like Hamilton to "redress."

Following his custom with state and private papers, and along the lines of his frequently repeated advice to farm managers and cabinet officers, the president made extensive notes of all the major points he intended to cover. Some of these were in the form of full paragraphs, others, brief outlines:

> *Cherish good faith, justice and peace with other nations:*
>   *1. Because religion and morality dictate it*
>   *2. Because policy dictates it.*
> *Our separation from Europe renders standing alliances inexpedient.*

In his first draft Washington quoted what Madison had said before he moved to the opposition, but this reference was subsequently removed. In preparing his outline the president wrote out his introductory paragraphs, added a rewrite of the Madison draft, and then introduced his major points. It was probably this outline which he showed to Hamilton and from which he expected to write his final paper. Subsequently he added to it his own draft of an address. Though this latter document was rather quickly written and not polished, it is often more moving than the final version:

> *I am every day more sensible that the increasing weight of years renders the private walks of it, in the shade of retirement, as necessary as they will be acceptable to me.*

May I be allowed to add that it will be among the highest as well as the purest enjoyments that can sweeten the remnant of my days, to partake, in a private station, in the midst of my fellow citizens, of that benign influence of good laws under a free Government, which has been the ultimate object of all my wishes, and... the happy reward of our cares and labours.

In contemplating the moment at which the curtain is to drop forever on the public scenes of my life... my sensations... do not permit me to suspend the deep acknowledgments required by the debt of Gratitude which I owe to my beloved country for the many honors it has conferred upon me... All the returns I have now to make will be in those vows which I shall carry with me to my retirement and to my grave, that Heaven may continue to favor the people of the United States with the choicest tokens of its benificence...

...I ask your indulgence while I express... the following most ardent wishes of my heart...

That party disputes, among all the friends and lovers of their country may subside, or, as the wisdom of Providence has ordained that men, on the same subjects, shall not always think alike, that charity and benevolence... may... banish... invectives...

That we may be always prepared for War, but never unsheath the sword except in self-defence, so long as Justice and our <u>essential</u> rights are preserved... If this country can remain in peace 20 years longer: and I devoutly pray that it may do so to the end of time; such in all probability will be its population, riches, and resources, when combined with its peculiarly happy and remote Situation... as to bid defiance, in a just cause, to any earthly power whatsoever.

That our Union may be as lasting as time; for while we are encircled in one band, we shall possess the strength of the giant and there will be none who can make us afraid...

... I leave you with undefiled hands, an uncorrupted heart, and with ardent vows to heaven for the welfare and happiness of that country in which I and my forefathers to the third or fourth progenitor drew our first breath.

When Hamilton reminded Washington in May that he had asked him to review the work and he would need time for it, the president put together all his notes and drafts, requesting Hamilton on May 15 to make a workable second draft from them. In late June Hamilton completed this, and at

Washington's request, went over the whole of the material with John Jay, who subsequently wrote the president about some matters he considered delicate.

It is not possible to determine how many times thereafter Washington rewrote the second draft. In a late August letter to Hamilton he referred to several intensive revisions. From then to the middle of September the paper had further reviews by the president as well as by the entire cabinet.

Washington was unsurpassed as editor and writer. He cut out masses of heavy paragraphs and phrases. He shifted material about, rewriting and transforming as he went. "Cherish good faith and justice towards, and peace and harmony with, all Nations" (Hamilton's version of Washington) became "Observe good faith and justice towards all Nations. Cultivate peace and harmony with all." The final Washington testament, Pauline in its injunction to keep the faith and to love one another, was also a powerful political document, warning against foreign intrigue and domestic anarchy and disunion.

Washington offered "unceasing vows that Heaven may continue to give you the choicest tokens of its beneficence—that your Union and brotherly affection may be sacredly maintained—that its administration in every department may be stamped with wisdom and virtue—that, in fine, the happiness of the people of these states, under the auspices of Liberty, may be made complete, by so careful a preservation and so prudent a use of this blessing as will acquire to them the glory of recommending it to the applause, the affection and adoption of every nation which is yet a stranger to it."

The Union and the Constitution—with its twin supports, religion and morality—had brought to America full independence, peace, liberty, tranquillity, and prosperity. Nevertheless there were grave dangers ahead. "Internal and external enemies... (though often covertly and insidiously)" would batter away against the national Union. He warned that parties were splitting up into northern, southern, and even western factions. In the West, great suspicions had been excited against the federal government which had now opened up the Mississippi River to the whole nation.

The president foresaw that mobs and factions would attempt to overthrow the constitutional government of all the people. Through them, "cunning, ambitious and unprincipled men will be enabled to subvert the power of the people and to usurp for themselves the reins of Government, destroying afterwards the very engines which have lifted them to unjust dominion." The spirit of faction, too, opened the highest councils of government "to foreign influence and corruption." "Habitual hatred, or habitual fondness" for foreign nations would make America, to some degree, "a slave" and provide "ambitious, corrupted, or deluded Citizens (who devote themselves to the favorite nation) facility to betray, or sacrifice the interests of their own country...

gilding, with the appearances of a virtuous sense of obligation, a commendable deference for public opinion, or a laudable zeal for public good, the base or foolish compliances of ambition, corruption or infatuation… Against the insidious wiles of foreign influence (I conjure you to believe me, fellow-Citizens) the jealousy of a free people ought to be <u>constantly</u> awake… Real patriots, who may resist the intrigues of the favourite, are liable to become suspected and odious, while its tools and dupes usurp the applause and confidence of the people, to surrender their interests."

Europe, he continued, had its own primary concerns having only a remote relation to those of the United States. "Why, by interweaving our destiny with that of any part of Europe, entangle our peace and prosperity in the toils of European ambition, rivalship, interest, humour, or caprice?" The neutrality proclamation had been the entire, open, and clear foundation of Washington's foreign policy. If it continued to be the basis of American policy, the United States would have entire "command of its own fortunes."

The president's diary for September 19 noted: "Address to the People of the United States was this day published in Claypoole's paper notifying my intention of declining being considered a Candidate for the Presidency of the United States of America… Left the City this morning on my way to Mount Vernon."

THE REACTIONS

Washington never conceived that his last farewell would be looked upon by his countrymen as if it had come from Mount Sinai. He expressed in it only the modest hope that "counsels from an old and affectionate friend… may be productive of some partial benefit, some occasional good; that they may now and then recur to moderate the fury of party spirit, to warn against the imposture of pretended patriotism." Nonetheless, for many Americans, the address, reproduced at the time from one end of the country to another by press and pamphlet and so often reprinted since, became almost as sacred as the Constitution itself.

The legislatures, in all cases unanimously, of Vermont, Rhode Island, Massachusetts, New Jersey, Pennsylvania, Delaware, Maryland, and North and South Carolina passed lengthy resolutions of praise for all aspects of Washington's conduct, as well as his final "paternal" advice to his countrymen. The warmest and most enthusiastic response came from Maryland, to which the city of Baltimore added its acclaim. Berkeley County in what is now West Virginia and Frederick County in Virginia also expressed their appreciation, first in prose, and then by ejecting their Jeffersonian representative from Congress. In his stead they chose General Daniel Morgan, who considered Democrats "a parsell of egg-sucking dogs." Abigail Adams wrote that his farewell found Washington "covered with glory... the first of heroes and greatest of benefactors to mankind." Jacob Hilzheimer expressed the hope that all good Americans would remember his words "to the end of time." Senator Cabot of Massachusetts, with Bostonian enthusiasm, declared the address to be "excellent." *The Times* of London said that Washington, the old revolutionist, was as far removed from the "wild and wicked revolutionists" of Europe as the "altar" was from "sacrilege."

Virginia did not quite ignore the Farewell Address but its assembly issued a resolution so brief, so grudging, and so sharply in contrast to Maryland's, that Washington, who responded warmly to messages from all the states and cities, answered Richmond: "Be pleased to accept my acknowledgment." Conspicuously absent from the state rolls were Georgia, Kentucky, and Tennessee, whose boundaries had been greatly widened by Washington's diplomacy. Madison thought the president's message, which asked for friendship with all nations, showed pro-British feelings and an unexpected "rancor" towards the French. Jefferson dismissed it as "the adieu." The French minister, in forwarding it to his foreign office, termed the address "insolent" and immoral.

THE 1796 ELECTION

The subsequent presidential election was a mess, in part because of the unfortunate constitutional provision whereby each elector had two votes. Both counted equally; the president-elect had to have a majority of half the electoral votes while the vice-president merely had to have the second highest total. Where letters took weeks to travel, it was difficult for the Federalist electors, in states as far apart as New Hampshire and South Carolina, to coordinate their plans in the brief period before the election.

The French played their part. In addition to his agents who electioneered for Jefferson in western Pennsylvania and Kentucky, the French minister issued a series of threatening letters in late October and in November, designed to sway the election. He timed his first letter just before Pennsylvanians went to the polls. The letters were ostensibly addressed to Pickering, the secretary of state, who received them after Bache had published them. Adet termed the proclamation of neutrality "insidious" and he called on Americans to unite to smash the Jay treaty. He threatened many evils if they did not do so. He denounced the Washington administration in the strongest terms, after claiming that the United States had violated its treaty with France. Until the United States returned to the alliance, France was breaking diplomatic relations, which would be restored only when the American government changed its neutral policy. "Let your government return to itself, and you will find in Frenchmen faithful friends and generous allies."

The Federalist candidates were John Adams, along with Pinckney who had not only secured the Spanish treaty but had the additional virtue of being a southerner. In both North and South, some electors hated to vote for both men, fearful that a tie would throw the election into the House of Representatives. In several states there were favorite sons or others who gained the approving votes of individual electors.

In the end no fewer than thirteen persons received votes, four Democratic and nine Federalist-Republicans. The total electoral vote was a triumph for the Federalists, who received more than a third of the votes south of the Potomac and 86 percent in the North. French activities were sufficient to give Pennsylvania to the Democrats by 235 popular votes. Except for this narrow popular margin in that state, the Federalists would have had almost every vote north of the Potomac.

The split in the vote among nine Federalists bore the fatal result that, while Adams was elected by a bare majority, Jefferson, with a minority, jogged in right behind him as vice-president. Adams himself had 80 percent of the electoral votes in the North, a sharp increase over his total in 1789 and 1793. Jefferson obtained only 15 percent of the electors above the Potomac, but this was sufficient to place him in an office, with limited responsibilities and unlimited opportunities for mischief.

THE STATE OF THE UNION

Washington returned from Mount Vernon to find awaiting him a French declaration of belligerency, accompanied by intolerable interference in America's internal affairs and elections. It was France's reply to the Farewell Address.

In that autumn crisis Washington consulted his cabinet as well as the two most experienced men outside the federal government, Hamilton and Governor Jay of New York. In asking Hamilton's advice he wrote on November 2: "There is in the conduct of the French government... an inconsistency, a duplicity, a delay, or a something else, which is unaccountable upon honorable grounds... As I have very high opinion of Mr. Jay's judgment, candor, honor and discretion… it would be very pleasing to me if you would shew him this letter… and let me have, for consideration, your joint opinion on the several matters therein stated." The president added that he was "fatigued with this and other matters which crowd upon me." Washington mentioned that the second letter from Adet to Pickering, issued a few days before his return, had been published in its entirety by "Claypool, at the government's suggestion." The Jeffersonian press had been giving it out piecemeal, and the government thought it best to make it known as a whole. Washington remarked that the French government was "disposed to play a high game. If other proofs were wanting, the *time* and *indelicate mode and stile*, of the present attack on the Executive, exhibited in this laboured performance, which is as unjust as it is voluminous, would leave no doubt as to the primary object it had in view."

Hamilton's advice to the president was judicious. He deplored Pickering's open reply to Adet in the newspapers, suggesting that it was undignified. The government should make such communications only to Congress. Complaints in regard to French actions ought to be presented to the French Directory by the American minister, in as calm and reasoned a manner as possible. Every possible effort should be made to secure peace. The United States should offer to negotiate all outstanding issues. Hamilton made it clear that France had certain justifiable causes of complaint; these should be adjusted by treaty, as had been done with Great Britain.

Washington, before writing Hamilton, had already determined to give Congress the whole story of the relations with France and to transmit a copy of all the documents to the American minister at Paris. He ordered Pickering to assemble material for a special message to follow his remarks on France in his State of the Union message.

On December 7, at noon, George Washington, with his cabinet in attendance, made his last address to the Congress. He stated that the House delay in voting for the Jay treaty "necessarily procrastinated the reception of the Posts stipulated to be delivered, beyond the date assigned for that event. As soon, however, as the Governor General of Canada could be addressed with propriety on the subject, arrangements were cordially and promptly concluded for their evacuation." American and British commissioners were already at work on the Canadian boundary and on compensation for the captured vessels.

The president said that, to protect "the active external Commerce" of the United States, a naval force was essential. "The most sincere neutrality is not a sufficient guard against the depredations of Nations at War. To secure respect to a Neutral flag, requires a Naval force, organized, and ready to vindicate it from insult or aggression. This may even prevent the necessity of going to War, by discouraging belligerent Powers from committing such violations of the rights of the Neutral party, as may, first or last, leave no other option."

The president then turned to the economic development of the country, adding further recommendations to those which he had previously proposed to Congress:

Congress have repeatedly, and not without success, directed their attention to the encouragement of Manufactures. The object is of too much consequence, not to insure a continuance of their efforts, in every way which shall appear eligible. As a general rule, manufactures on public account are inexpedient. But where the state of things in a Country leaves little hope that certain branches of Manufacture will, for a great length of time obtain; when these are of a nature essential to the furnishing and equipping of the public force in time of War, are not establishments for procuring them on public account, <u>to the extent of the ordinary demand for public services</u>, recommended by strong considerations of National policy, as an exception to the general rule?...

It will not be doubted that, with reference either to individual, or National Welfare, Agriculture is of primary importance. In proportion as Nations advance in population, and other circumstances of maturity, this truth becomes more apparent; and renders the cultivation of the Soil more and more an object of public patronage. Institutions for promoting it, grow up, supported by the public purse; and to what object can it be dedicated with greater propriety? Among the means which have been employed to this end, none have been attended with greater success than the establishment of Boards, composed of proper characters, charged with collecting and diffusing information, and enabled by premiums, and small pecuniary aids, to encourage and assist a spirit of discovery and improvement. This species of establishment contributes doubly to the increase of improvement, by stimulating to enterprise and experiment, and by drawing to a common centre, the results everywhere, of individual skill and observation; and spreading them thence over the whole Nation. Experience accordingly has shown that they are very cheap Instruments, of immense National benefits.

The Assembly to which I address myself, is too enlightened not to be fully sensible how much a flourishing state of the Arts and Sciences, contributes to National prosperity and reputation. True it is, that our Country, much to its honor, contains many Seminaries of learning, highly respectable and useful; but the funds upon which they rest, are too narrow to command the ablest Professors in the different departments of liberal knowledge, for the Institution contemplated, though they would be excellent auxiliaries.

Amongst the motives to such an Institution, the assimilation of the principles, opinions and manners of our Countrymen, by the common education of a portion of our Youth from every quarter, well deserves attention. The more homogeneous our Citizens can be made, in these particulars, the greater will be our prospect of permanent Union; and a primary object of such a National Institution should be, the education of our Youth in the science of <u>Government</u>. In a Republic, what species of knowledge can be equally important? and what duty, more pressing on its Legislature, than to patronize a plan for communicating it to those who are to be the future guardians of the liberties of the Country?

The Institution of a Military Academy is also recommended by cogent reasons. However pacific the general policy of a Nation may be, it ought never to be without an adequate stock of Military knowledge for emergencies... War might, often, not depend on its own choice... Whatever argument may be drawn from particular examples, superficially viewed, a thorough examination of the subject will evince, that the Art of War, is at once comprehensive and complicated; that it demands much previous study; and that the possession of it, in its most improved state, is always of great moment to the security of a Nation. This, therefore, ought to be a serious care of every Government; and for this purpose, an Academy, where a regular course of instruction is given, is an obvious expedient...

The Compensation to the Officers of the United States... appears to call for Legislative revision. The consequences of a defective provision are of serious import to the Government.

If private wealth is to supply the defect of the public contribution, it will greatly contract the sphere within which the selection of Characters for Office, is to be made; and will proportionately diminish the probability of a choice of Men, able as well as upright. Besides that it would be repugnant to the vital principles of our Government, virtually to exclude from public trusts, talents, virtues, unless accompanied by wealth.

The president then turned to France, where "circumstances of a very unwelcome nature have lately occurred. Our trade has suffered, and is suffering, extensive injuries in the West Indies, from the Cruisers and Agents of the French republic; and communications have been received from its minister here, which indicate that danger of a further disturbance of our Commerce, by its authority." He noted that he had been constant and sincere in his wish to have peace and harmony with France. "The wish remains unabated... Nor will I easily cease to cherish the expectations that a spirit of justice, candour and friendship on the part of the Republic will eventually ensure success."

The president noted that he would send a special message on the subject to Congress. In his subsequent January 4 directive to the secretary of state, Washington wrote: "I have no doubt you have taken care, and will continue to be assured of your facts; for as this business will certainly come before the public, not only the facts, but the candour also, the expression, and the force of every word will be examined with the most scrutinizing eye, and compared with everything that will admit of a different construction, and if there is the least ground for it, we shall be charged with unfairness, and an intention to impose on, and to mislead the public judgment."

REPLIES BY CONGRESS

It had been customary, throughout the first years of the republic, for each House to send a committee to thank the president for his message and to declare its sentiments on the various issues raised. The Senate quickly passed a warm-hearted message of gratitude for all Washington's services; this was delivered by John Adams on December 12. A similar message ran into trouble in the House, which shortly afterwards turned down the proposal for a national university by a single vote. Williams Branch Giles, a Virginia congressman, made a savage attack on the president. He asked that the reference to his "moderation, wisdom, and firmness" be stricken out. Giles said Washington lacked these qualities, and the United States was thereby being dragged into a calamitous crisis. He, for one, was glad the president was retiring from office. Giles' resolution received only twelve votes. On December 16 the House delivered an affectionate final message to the president.

FOURTEEN

MOUNT VERNON

1797–1798

DURING THE FEDERALIST era, 1789–1801, the United States achieved what appears to have been the most rapid rate of economic development of any country in history. George Washington, who left the presidency two-thirds of the way through this period, could take justifiable pride in the country's progress.

Between 1789 and 1796 the value of American exports quadrupled. In real terms—that is, deducting price rises—the 1796 export volume was up two and a half times. Gross national product rose a phenomenal average of nearly 30 percent a year. American per capita income was, in all probability, the highest in the world by 1801.

In 1796 the American merchant marine, which in colonial times, had been largely confined to the coastal and Caribbean trade, was sailing to most of the principal seaports of Europe, Africa, and Asia. The fleet had more than doubled in size; its earnings were up threefold. In 1789 the consular service consisted of a few agents only; by 1796 there was a worldwide network from Cadiz to St. Petersburg in Europe, and from Tangier to Calcutta and Canton in Africa and Asia.

Individual economic data showed impressive gains. The seventy-five post offices of 1789, all that existed after 182 years of settlement, had $29,000 in revenues. By 1801 there were 1,025 post offices; the great increase in the postal system's net revenues was devoted to a rapid expansion of the nation's post roads. Though proper data are lacking, it appears that wages rose much more rapidly than prices. John Adams complained that he paid his farm labor four times as much as he had given them earlier.

POLITICAL AND GEOGRAPHICAL GROWTH

The eleven states that formed the 1789 Union had increased to sixteen, stretching to the Mississippi. The country was extraordinarily youthful. The median age was sixteen in a population highly fecund. Although mortality rates were more than double those of today, the high birth rates carried the net population growth to around 3.5 percent a year. There were some 3.8 million Americans in 1789; nearly a million had been added by the time Washington returned to Mount Vernon. Younger sons and daughters were travelling by hundreds of thousands into new farms in western Pennsylvania, Virginia, and New York. Kentucky, Tennessee, and even far away Ohio were filling with energetic settlers.

The United States of America had become a thoroughly viable and vigorous country under strong leadership. An efficient and honest federal customs and revenue system operated to provide an increasing range of domestic and foreign services. The once bankrupt country had achieved the highest of the world's credit ratings in Amsterdam. A federal judiciary system, remarkably high in quality, was in operation in the national capital and in the sixteen states. The country had conducted its first census and established a mint, a decimal coinage system, and active copyright and patent offices. The federal government had greatly expanded the number of lighthouses, beacons, buoys, and public piers. There was a national sea-rescue system under the new coast guard. State and local road building added to the new national network of post roads, although the quality had apparently shown little improvement. The United States had its first national banking system and an efficient national army. A naval fleet was under construction. An imaginative new capital was well past the planning stage; major government buildings and private houses and hotels were pushing towards completion. The single diplomatic envoy at the capital, the representative of France, had been joined by several colleagues, as Great Britain, the Netherlands, Spain, and Portugal recognized the increasing importance of this newest republic. Nearly a dozen institutions of higher learning, many subsequently great universities, were established during Washington's presidency.

THE FINAL TWO MONTHS

As the end of his term approached, the Jeffersonians increased the fury of their attacks on the president. Thomas Paine's psychotic diatribe, which had been sponsored by Monroe, was published in Philadelphia in December. It was industriously circulated in the country, along with the French minister's aspersions on the administration. With relief in sight, Washington could view the situation with disdain in his January 8 letter to David Stuart:

> *A large party under real, or pretended fears of British influence, are moving heaven and earth to aid [French minister Adet] in his designs... Finding a Neutral conduct has been adopted, and would not be relinquished by those who administered the government, the next step was to try to rally the people... Several presses and many Scribblers have been employed... This not working as well as was expected, from a supposition that there was too much confidence, and perhaps personal regard for the present Chief Magistrate and his politics, the batteries latterly have been levelled at him particularly and personally and, although he is soon to become a private citizen, his opinions are to be knocked down, and his character reduced as low as they are capable of sinking it, even by resorting to absolute falsehoods. As an evidence whereof, and of the plan they are pursuing, I send you a letter from Mr. Paine to me, Printed in this City and disseminated with great industry. Others of a similar nature are also in circulation.*

> *To what lengths the French Directory will ultimately go, is difficult to say; but that they have been led to the present point by our own People, I have no doubt...*

As the attacks grew in intemperance, the people of Philadelphia determined to show Washington how much the great majority of the country loved and admired him. Weeks of planning and preparation went into the celebration of his last birthday as chief of state and government. According to Washington's diary, February 22 opened with rain, followed by a cloudy forenoon. Thereafter it was "clear and very fine." The whole city was on holiday. There were parades and the firing of cannon; all ships in the harbor were decorated with flags and pennants. Immense crowds gathered near the president's house to watch the dignitaries who called on him and his wife between noon and three—the vice-president, the cabinet, the diplomatic corps, members of the Senate and House, officers of the army and navy, and representatives of the Cincinnati.

That evening 1,200 persons attended a ball, which the president described as "elegant." Claypoole's newspaper expressed the opinion that for "Splendor, Taste and Elegance [it] was, perhaps, never excelled by any similar entertainment in the United States." James Iredell wrote to his wife that it was much too crowded and there was "such scrambling to go to supper that there was some danger of being squeezed to death." He reported that the applause for the president and his lady was so overwhelming that Mrs. Washington broke into tears and her husband found the tribute such that "his emotions were too powerful to be concealed."

The president was overburdened with business during his last two months in office, some of it time-consuming trivialities. A federal judiciary was established in Tennessee. Army officers were promoted. Consuls were nominated for North Africa, Italy, and Sweden. Patents were signed, including one for artist Charles Wilson Peale, who had developed "a new and useful improvement in making Bridges." Treaties with the Six Nations and the Cherokees were forwarded to the Senate and duly ratified. The president signed letters of credence for Minister John Quincy Adams, promoted from The Hague to Madrid, as well as David Humphreys, his old secretary, who became minister at Lisbon. On March 3, 1797, he nominated Anthony White to be surveyor of New Brunswick, New Jersey, and the Senate approved it the same day. This was Washington's last appointment to office but his work, thanks to the slowness of Congress, piled up to the end. He wrote to Jonathan Trumbull on March 3:

> When I add that, according to custom all the Acts of the Session, except two or three very unimportant Bills, have been presented to me within the last four days, _you_ will not be surprised at the pressure under which I write at present; but it must astonish _others_ who know that the Constitution allows the President ten days to deliberate on _each_ Bill that is brought before him, that he should be allowed by the Legislature less than half that time to consider _all_ the business of the Session; and in some instances, scarcely an hour to resolve the most important. But as the scene is closing with me, it is of little avail _now_ to let it be with murmurs.

On the afternoon of March 3 the Washingtons gave a dinner for the president-elect, the members of the cabinet who were to stay in office, and the diplomatic corps. That night the president of the United States slept very well.

MARCH 4, 1797

The president-elect, as he wrote his wife, had a very bad night, thinking he might very well faint next day in front of the whole world. The morning sight of a cheerful Washington, his face, according to Adams, "as serene and unclouded as the day," did nothing to aid his morale, for he thought the general was indicating how glad he was to be out of that office. Another observer, Charles Biddle, noted that Washington appeared happier than he had ever seen him before, while William Duer wrote that his face was "radiant."

President Adams was sworn in by the chief justice before Washington, Jefferson, the cabinet, the House and Senate, and all who could crowd into the chamber. Adams went through the ordeal very well after all. He made an excellent, strong, and forthright speech, echoing many of Washington's general principles of government as well as his Farewell Address. Without a trace of false sentimentality, Adams managed to be particularly graceful in referring to the "great example" of his predecessor in office. The whole occasion—the retirement of Washington, the easy transfer of power, and Adams' speech— brought tears to the eyes of almost everyone. The president noted that there was scarcely a dry eye to be seen anywhere, except for George Washington. The president was roundly cheered as he concluded his speech and moved through the throng. Jefferson waved to Washington to follow the president. Firmly but politely Washington indicated that the vice-president of the United States preceded a private citizen. The transfer of power was thus symbolically complete.

The former president called on the president, shortly after the speech, to wish him "a happy and successful and honorable" administration. Mrs. Washington had already told Adams how pleased she and her husband had been by his election, a remark which surprised the president-elect, coming as it did from a woman who had been notably discreet through the presidential years. Philadelphia gave a farewell dinner to Washington that afternoon. The Washingtons spent the next few days in packing and saying goodbye.

The Jeffersonian press hurled their final abuse at Washington, embellishing their insults by extolling John Adams. In England, however, there were other appraisals. On March 5, after acknowledging receipt of the Stuart portrait, Lord Lansdowne wrote to William Jackson: "I cannot express to you the satisfaction I have felt in seeing the forts given up... General Washington's conduct is beyond all praise. He has left a noble example to sovereigns and nations, present and to come. I beg you will mention both me and my sons to him in the most respectful terms possible. If I were not too old, I would go to Virginia to do him homage." Shortly afterwards his one-time enemy, George III, gave George Washington the most generous tribute of his career. The king told Benjamin West, the American painter who was a personal intimate, what he thought, in a conversation which West reported to Rufus King, the American minister, on May 3:

Mr. West said things respecting America had changed very much; that people who could not formerly find words of unkindness enough now talked in a different language; that the King had lately spoken in the most explicit manner of the wisdom of the American Gov. and of the abilities and great worth of the characters they produced and employed...

In regard to General Washington, he told him since his resignation that in his opinion "that act closing and finishing what had gone before and viewed in connection with it, placed him in a light the most distinguished of any man living, and that he thought him the greatest character of the age."

Although the former president was exceedingly anxious to get home, the logistics of moving family, house guests, servants, and an eight-year accumulation of papers, furniture, and general whatnots was complex. President Adams had agreed to occupy the Morris house, which the Washingtons previously rented. The former president himself wrote out a seven-page inventory of its contents. He informed Adams that he would leave all furniture for which the government had paid. He had originally planned to take the best of his own pieces home and sell the rest, but this seemed ungracious to Adams. He therefore offered to sell such contents of the house as he might want, but the new president eventually declined to buy any. Washington then sold at auction some of the pieces and gave others as presents to close friends. He asked Lear and Dandridge, his two secretaries, to see to the packing and shipment of all the rest. From Lear's letter to Washington, after his departure, it appears that they sent by sea to Mount Vernon more than 170 crates, boxes, trunks, and assorted packages of merchandise.

Early in the morning of March 9, with the temperature disagreeably cold, the Washingtons, Nelly Custis, George Lafayette, and his tutor, with assorted servants, carriages, and newly acquired horses, set out for the long journey to Mount Vernon. That evening Washington wrote to Lear from Chester: "On one side I am called upon to remember the Parrot, on the other to remember the dog. For my own part I should not much pine if both were forgot."

To add to the miseries of the bad roads, the bitter winds, and occasional snow, Mrs. Washington had a severe cold. In consequence, Washington tried to avoid all delaying ceremonies, but Baltimore, which had given him so hearty a welcome in 1789 and had since so ardently supported his presidency, could not be denied. The Washingtons were escorted into town by a troop of horse and, according to the Baltimore paper, were greeted by "as great a concourse of people as Baltimore ever witnessed." On alighting at the Fountain Inn, the General was saluted with reiterated and thundering huzzas from the spectators. The mayor and council delivered an address after which the Washingtons "dined and lodged" at the inn. On March 14 the couple drove through the city of Washington. The *Washington Gazette* reported next day:

Yesterday George Washington (God bless him) passed through the city on his way to Mount Vernon. When he reached the Capitol the company of Artillery, under the command of Captain Hoban, welcomed him by a discharge of cannon. After dining in the City, he was escorted to George Town by several of our most respectable Citizens. As he passed the President's house, a salute of 16 guns was fired by the said company and followed by repeated huzzas, dictated by hearts sensibly alive to his merits.

Washington dined in Washington with his wife's granddaughter, Eliza Law. The Washingtons spent the night with Martha Peter, another married granddaughter. Next day he received addresses from the city of Georgetown, as well as from its college, which had begun instruction the year he took the oath as president. The former president was welcomed at the Alexandria ferry by old friends and neighbors who escorted him to Mount Vernon. On March 19, four days after their arrival, Nelly Custis wrote to the wife of the secretary of the treasury that it had been a "fatiguing" trip. She added a sentence which Washington himself clearly dictated: "Grandpapa is very well and much pleased with being once more 'Farmer Washington.'"

MOUNT VERNON

Mrs. Washington's cold hung on until April but she recovered in the spring in her own house. The family's letters for the rest of the year had a note of good cheer, which was marred only by the death of Washington's sister, Betty Lewis, at the end of March. Mrs. Washington wrote that she and the general felt like children just released from school. They loved having old friends call but begrudged sparing any of their time for strangers, who dropped in to have a look at the general. The Washingtons, however, welcomed with interest three young Bourbon brothers who appeared on April 5, to stay four days. The Duc d'Orléans, once a Jacobin, was to be king of France thirty-three years later. Washington gave them a map and recommendations for their explorations in Kentucky and Tennessee.

On April 3 Washington sent a note to James McHenry, asking him occasionally to spare any news from the seat of government, which was "not contrary to the rules of your official duty to disclose." He added:

I find myself in the situation, nearly, of a young beginner, for although I have not houses to build (except one, which I must erect for the accommodation and security of my Military, Civil and private Papers which are voluminous, and may be interesting) yet I have not one or scarcely anything else about me that does not require considerable repairs. In a word I am already surrounded by Joiners, Masons, Painters, &ca. and such is my anxiety to get out of their hands, that I have scarcely a room to put a friend into or to set in myself, without the Music of hammers, or the odoriferous smell of Paint.

I am indebted to you for several unacknowledged letters; but ne'er mind that; go on as if you had them. You are at the source of information and can find many things to relate; while I have nothing to say, that could either inform or amuse a Secretary of War in Philadelphia.

I might tell him that I begin my diurnal course with the Sun; that if my hirelings are not in their place at that time I send them messages expressive of my sorrow for their indisposition; then having put these wheels in motion, I examine the state of things further; and the more they are probed, the deeper I find the wounds are, which my buildings have sustained by an absence and neglect of eight years; by the time I have accomplished these matters, breakfast, a little after seven o'clock... is ready. This over, I mount my horse and ride around my farms, which employs me until it is time to dress for dinner; at which I rarely miss seeing strange faces; come, as they say, out of respect to me. Pray, would not the word curiosity answer as well: and how different this, from having a few social friends at a cheerful board. The usual time of sitting at Table; a walk, and Tea, brings me within the dawn of Candlelight; previous to which, if not prevented by company, I resolve that, as soon as the glimmering taper supplies the place of the great luminary, I will retire to my writing Table and acknowledge the letters I have received; but when the lights are brought, I feel tired and disinclined to engage in this work, conceiving that the next night will do as well; the next comes and with it the same causes for postponement, and effect, and so on.

This will account for <u>your</u> letter remaining so long unacknowledged; and having given you the history of a day, it will serve for a year... but it may strike you that in this detail no mention is made of any portion of time allotted for reading; the remark would be just, for I have not looked into a book since I came home, nor shall be able to do it until I have discharged my Workmen; probably not before the nights grow longer; when possibly I may be looking in doomsday book...

Washington found not only that his buildings had been neglected but his farm production had greatly diminished. His 1797 yield of wool per sheep was less than half what it had been in 1789; he set about purchasing good rams to improve his breed. He did the same for his cattle, buying an expensive bull from John Threlkeld of Georgetown. In July he wrote to William Strickland, an English farmer who had made a tour of America, including Mount Vernon, to say that his observations of poor American fencing practices were just. He had tried in absentia to prevent the wasteful way his managers cut down trees to build fences, by asking them to plant living fences. They had not done as he directed; old as he was and even if he did not live to see them grow, he was determined to use cedars extensively, as natural fencing for his farms.

On July 31 Washington sent a note to Lear to say that the house was empty. "Unless someone pops in, unexpectedly—Mrs. Washington and I will do what I believe has not been done within the last twenty years by us—that is sit down to dinner by ourselves." Fortunately, the great majority of visitors who poured into Mount Vernon that summer and autumn for meals and, sometimes, bed, were old friends and relatives. They included the grand- and great-grandchildren of Martha, assorted nieces and nephews of the general, along with their children, as well as his great Virginia supporter, Henry Lee, and his wife and daughter. The Spanish and British ministers to Philadelphia appeared, as did various British treaty and colonial officials. In addition there were strangers whose names were listed as "a Mr. X" if Washington got the name or simply appeared as blank in his diary.

It was partly the mass of visitors but also the general's inherent kindness which led him to write on August 4 to the widowed Lawrence Lewis, whose mother had died in March, inviting him to make Mount Vernon his residence. He indicated that he could not pay him a salary as he was too overburdened with staff but he would be glad if, in return for bed and board for himself, a servant and a horse, Lawrence could take over some social and clerical duties. "As both your aunt and I are in the decline of life, and regular in our habits, especially in our hours of rising and going to bed, I require some person (fit and Proper) to ease me of the trouble of entertaining company, particularly of nights, as it is my inclination to retire (unless prevented by very particular company, always do retire) either to my bed, or to my study, soon after candle-light. In taking these duties (which hospitality obliges one to bestow on company) off my hands, it would render me a very acceptable service, and for a little time to come, only, an hour in the day, now and then, devoted to the recording of some Papers, which time would not allow me to complete before I left Philadelphia... If you have inclination for it [your other time] might be devoted to Reading, as I have a great many instructive books, on many subjects, as well as amusing ones..." Lawrence Lewis appeared on August 31 and helped the general until his death.

Washington declined an invitation to attend the marriage of another nephew, Lawrence Augustine Washington, saying that "as wedding assemblies are better calculated for those who are *coming in to,* than to those who are *going out of* life, you must accept the good wishes of your Aunt and myself in place of personal attendance, for I think it is not likely that either of us will ever be more than 25 miles from Mount Vernon again."

Washington, who had played so great a role in national and international affairs, now took particular interest in the growth and development of Alexandria and Washington. In a chatty June 26 note to David Humphreys at Lisbon, he wrote:

> *The Public Buildings in the Federal City go on well; one wing of the Capitol (with which Congress might make a very good shift) and the President's house, will be covered in this autumn, or to speak more correctly perhaps, the latter is now receiving its cover, and the former will be ready for it by that epoch. An elegant bridge is thrown over the Potomack at the Little Falls, and the navigation of the River above will be completed, nearly, this season; through which an immensity of Produce must flow to the Shipping Ports thereon.*

> *Alexandria you would scarcely know; so much has it increased since you [were] there; two entire Streets where Shallops then laded and unladed are extended into the River, and some of the best buildings in the Town erected on them. What were the commons are now all inclosed and many good houses placed on them.*

> *As my circle is now small, my information will be, of course, contracted; as Alexandria and the federal city will probably be the extent of my perambulations.*

When rumors reached Mount Vernon that Lafayette, after five years in prison, was about to be released, young George Washington Lafayette could not be restrained from returning to France. General Washington thought it imprudent to return on the basis of a rumor. He told young Lafayette that he could not be sure of conditions in France and his parents might very well be coming to America for refuge. On October 12 Washington rode to Georgetown with Lafayette and his tutor, Felix Frestal, in order to put them on the stage to New York. He accompanied their coach as far as the city of Washington. Having given them $300 to defray their return to France, Washington wrote to Alexander Hamilton in New York, asking him to procure their passage and to advance them any further funds they needed. As it turned out, young Lafayette's instincts were sound. His father, mother, and sister had been released into the hands of the American consul at Hamburg. Madame de Lafayette, who had spent much time in French and Austrian prisons, was too ill to travel to America. Young Lafayette joined his family in February.

LAWYER WASHINGTON

Washington complained that his lack of legal knowledge made the presidency particularly irksome. He was daily faced with intricate constitutional and international legal problems, with only a part-time lawyer, on a retainer basis, as his attorney general and counselor. When it came to land titles, however, his nearly fifty years of experience gave him as good knowledge as a member of the bar. When an overly smart attorney found what he thought to be a title flaw in land Washington had bought thirty-five years previously and subsequently sold, lawyer Washington got busy. To William Triplett, a purchaser of similar land, he wrote on September 24 to say that the testimony of the principal witness, Grafton Kirk, "is not *quite immaculate*, but so much the reverse as [he proves] to be always a ready witness upon all occasions." Washington never hesitated to get the best legal advice but he clearly hated paying lawyers. He asked two future Supreme Court justices, John Marshall and Bushrod Washington, to handle his case, if he had to appeal. He explained the situation to his nephew, Bushrod, in a letter of October 9, which was a mixture of irony, humor, legal language, and Latin and English puns:

> *Mr. Thomas Pearson, heir entail to Simon Pearson, his Brother, has brought suit… for the lands which the latter sold to Wm. Triplett, George Johnson and myself, five and thirty years ago.*

> *I understand from Colo. Simms, who is Pearson's Lawyer, that his complaint is founded upon some irregularity in the proceedings of the Jury, who met on the land to value the same, pursuant to a Writ of ad quod damnum. And the examination of the evidence to prove these irregularities went (for I attended) to the establishment of two points: 1st. that there was no survey of the premises in presence of the Jury, at the time of their enquiry into the value of the land and 2ly, that the said Jury did not explore it sufficiently to ascertain with exactness what the real value of the land was.*

> *This is the amount of Grafton Kirk's evidence, who was one of the jurors and who, from your practice in Fairfax county you may have learnt, is a rare hand at all obsolete claims that depend much on a good memory.*

> *Let me ask your opinion on the following points:*

> *Does the Law providing for the Docking of Entails, by a writ of ad quod damnum, make a survey in the presence of the Jury an essential part of the proceedings? The Writ itself (of which I retained a copy)… requires no such thing.*

Who is to judge of the mode by which a Jury on Oath is to report their Opinion of the value of the land, if they are not to do it themselves?...

Whether, as Simon was lawfully married and never legally divorced, the children of the woman, though begotten (no matter by whom) in the state of separation from him, is not a bar to the claim of Thomas?

What operation will the Act of Assembly of Virginia for Docking all entails. . . passed many years before the death of Simon Pearson, which happened only last Spring, have in this case...

Whether I had better interest myself in defending the suit, already commenced in the County court, or await the decision there and take it up in the dernier resort, if it should be adverse... I wish also... to be informed (confidentially) whether, in your opinion, Mr. Swan's demand for defending the suit [$200] is not unreasonable?...

You may think me an unprofitable applicant in asking opinions and requiring services of you without dousing my money, but pay day may come. If the case should go to the higher courts, I shall expect you to appear for me, and Mr. Marshall also...

P. S. Whether Colo. Simms has any thing in petto [up his sleeve] I am unable to say, I am told however, that he is sanguine and some add that he is to go snacks [divvy up the loot taken from Washington].

Washington made only a brief further reference in his correspondence to the suit, which presumably never got beyond the lower court.

GEORGE WASHINGTON CUSTIS

Martha Washington's grandson, born less than six months before her husband's Yorktown victory, grew to become his stepgrandfather's adolescent plague. He received Washington's best advice, always promised his faithful adherence to it, and as invariably defaulted. Custis was to be a double dropout, fit, as his stepgrandfather finally decided, only for the army. Custis entered the college at Princeton in 1796, to which the president addressed long letters of counsel and good cheer. On November 15 he forwarded ten dollars "to purchase a gown, if proper... I advise you not to provide this without first obtaining the approbation of your tutors; otherwise you may be distinguished more by folly, than by the dress." All Custis' letters to Washington have disappeared, probably owing to the indulgence of his grandmother or Washington heirs. Their general tenor, particularly as to how well he was doing, may be deduced from the president's constantly encouraging tone:

It affords me pleasure to hear that you are agreeably fixed; and I receive still more from the assurance you give of attending closely to your studies… Endeavor to conciliate the good will of all your fellow students, rendering them every act of kindness in your power. Be particularly obliging and attentive to your chambermate, Mr. [John] Forsyth [later Secretary of State], who, from the account I have of him, is an admirable young man and strongly impressed with the importance of a liberal and finished education. But above all, be obedient to your tutors, and in a particular manner, respect the president of the seminary who is both learned and good… Never let an indigent person ask, without receiving something, if you have the means, always recollecting in what light the widow's mite was viewed. (November 15, 1796)

You are now extending into that stage of life when good or bad habits are formed. When the mind will be turned to things useful and praiseworthy, or to dissipation and vice. Fix on whichever it may, it will stick by you… This admonition proceeds from the purest affection for you; but I do not mean by it, that you are to become a stoic, or to deprive yourself in the intervals of study of any recreations or manly exercise, which reason approves. 'Tis well to be on good terms with all your fellow-students, and I am pleased to hear you are so, but while a courteous behavior is due to all, select the most deserving only for your friendships and before this becomes intimate, weigh their dispositions and character well. I would guard you too, against imbibing hasty and unfavorable impressions of any one… To speak evil of any one, unless there is unequivocal proof of their deserving it, is an injury for which there is no adequate reparation… Keep in mind that scarcely any change would be agreeable to you at first from the sudden transition, and from never having been accustomed to shift or rough it. And, moreover, that if you meet with collegiate fare, it will be unmanly to complain. (November 28, 1796)

I presume you received my letter covering a ten dollar bill to pay for the gown, although it is not mentioned. To acknowledge the receipt of letters is always proper, to remove doubts of their miscarriage… The pleasure of hearing you were well, in good spirits, and progressing as we could wish in your studies, was communicated by your letter of the fourteenth… to your grandmama; but what gave me particular satisfaction, was to find you were going to commence a course of reading with Doctor Smith… 'tis to close application and constant perseverance, men of letters and science are indebted for their knowledge and usefulness… You… know how anxious all your friends are to see you enter upon the grand theatre of life, with the advantages of a highly cultivated mind, and a proper sense of your duties to God and man. (December 19, 1796)

Your letter of the 22n. inst. received. The affectionate sentiments contained in them are highly pleasing to me. But that which affords a still higher gratification is to hear that you are not only attentive to your studies but pleased with them also... (February 27, 1797)

It gives me singular pleasure to hear that your time has been so well employed during the last winter, and that you are so sensible of it yourself. (April 3, 1797)

The serene picture was suddenly shattered for the former president when, in May, he received a stern letter from the Reverend Samuel Stanhope Smith, president of the college. This has also not been found, but Washington's reply indicates its nature: "Your favor of the 18th instant was received by the last post, the contents of which, relative to Mr. Custis, filled my mind (as you naturally supposed it would) with extreme disquietude. From his infancy I have discovered an almost unconquerable disposition to indolence in everything that did not tend to his amusements; and have exhorted him in the most parental and friendly manner, often, to devote his time to more useful pursuits. His pride has been stimulated, and his family expectations and wishes have been urged as inducements thereto. In short, I could say nothing to him by way of admonition, encouragement, or advice, that has not been repeated over and over again."

Washington Custis followed up Smith's report with a long, remorseful letter, expressing his sorrow at his "late contest with the passions," apparently an outburst against the college authorities for trying to get him to study. Grandfather Washington sat down and wrote him on June 4: "Your letter... eased my mind of many unpleasant sensations and reflections on your account... If your sorrow and repentance for the disquietude occasioned by the preceding letter, your resolution to abandon the ideas which were therein expressed, are sincere, I shall not only heartily forgive, but will forget also, and bury in oblivion all that has passed... You must not suffer this resolution you have recently entered into, to operate as the mere result of a momentary impulse, occasioned by the letters you have received from hence."

On July 10, 1797, Washington wrote to Custis: "If it has been usual for the students of Nassau college to go to the balls on the anniversary of the Declaration of Independence, I see no reason why you should have avoided it, as no innocent amusement or reasonable expenditure will ever be withheld from you." Custis then developed a correspondence with a Yale tutor, who gave him advice on his studies, which were not in accord with those of Smith. Washington replied to Custis on July 23: "With regard to Mr. Z. Lewis, [he] was educated at Yale college, and as is natural, may be prejudiced in favor of the mode pursued at that seminary; but no college has turned out better scholars, or more estimable characters, than Nassau." He followed with another letter of August 29: "Your letter of the 21st instant... as usual, gave us pleasure to hear that you enjoyed good health, were progressing well in your studies and that you were on the road to promotion... I shall make all fears [that he would not return to Princeton after his vacation] yield to a firm persuasion that every day convinces you of the propriety and necessity of devoting your youthful days in the acquirement of that knowledge which will be advantageous, grateful and pleasing to you in your mature years, and may be the foundation of your use-fulness here and happiness hereafter. Your grandmamma.... has been a good deal indisposed by swelling on one side of her face but it is now much better. The rest of the family within doors are all well, and all unite in best regards to you, along with your sincere friend and affectionate... G. Washington."

His calm was once more interrupted by a series of letters from the president of Princeton. These no longer exist among the Washington files but his October 9 reply implies that Custis was asked to leave the college:

Dear and Revd. sir: I have duly received your several letters of last month; but as an expression of my regret at the conduct and behavior of young Custis would avail nothing, I shall not trouble you by the attempt.

I am persuaded that your conduct towards him, has been such as friendship inspired, and the duties of your important trust required. And, as you have seen, he will have himself only to upbraid for any consequences which may follow and this perhaps come too late.

Washington sent funds by young Lafayette to Smith to pay the final bills at Princeton. On January 7 he once more attempted to bring young Custis, now back at Mount Vernon, to a sense of order and discipline. He gave him a writ-ten memorandum, particularly asking him to stop wasting his time "running up and down stairs" and also engaging in "conversation any one who will talk to you." He then urged him to get up early and make it a habit. He was to engage in studies from breakfast till afternoon dinner. Thereafter he could walk till teatime and then resume his studies until bedtime. Above all he was to be punctual for meals, since the servants had "to be running here and there, and they know not where, to summon you." Saturdays he was to have for hunting or other relaxation.

These directives had little effect. On January 22, he informed Custis' step-father, Dr. Stuart, that he had been "disappointed and my mind much disturbed by his conduct." He asked Stuart to find out from him, while he was visiting his mother, what the boy really wanted to do. He himself had always thought Harvard was the best place in the country for him, since it was the largest institution and had the highest moral standards. Having him far away would be "a heart-rending stroke" for Mrs. Washington. He doubted that William and Mary would be satisfactory, even if Custis were placed in Bishop James Madison's own house. The following month, Washington conferred with an uncle, George Calvert of Annapolis. Calvert recommended St. John's College, assuring Washington there was little dissipation in the state capital, because of the "strictness of the police." Dr. Stuart agreed to enroll him there.

Once again grandpaternal letters went to Custis. On March 19 Washington wrote how pleased he was to find him "disposed to prosecute your studies with zeal and alacrity." His next letter said he was happy that "you are… going on well in your studies. Prosecute these with diligence and ardor and you will, sometime hence, be more sensible than now of the rich harvest you will gather from them." On May 10 he chided Custis for asking to whom he should apply for more money. "You were provided very plentifully… with necessaries when you left this house (two months ago only)… I am at a loss to discover what has given rise to so early a question. Surely you have not conceived that indulgence in dress or other extravagances are matters that were ever contemplated by me as objects of expense; and I hope they are not so by you." On June 15 he wrote: "It is now near five weeks since any person has heard from you… Knowing how apt your grandmamma is to suspect that you are sick, or that some accident has happened to you, how could you omit this?" When vacation time approached, Washington Custis finally cracked Washington's monumental patience by inquiring whether, now that he had completed a course in geometry, he was to quit school. Back went the answer from Mount Vernon on July 24: "Your… question… really astonishes me! For it would seem as if nothing I could say to you made more than a momentary impression. Did I not, before you went to that seminary, and since by letter, endeavor to fix indelibly on your mind, that the object for which you were sent there was to finish a course of education?" Washington's letter had induced Custis to leave his effects in Annapolis, while he came home for vacation. On August 13 the general wrote Stuart: "If you or Mrs. Stuart could, by indirect means, discover the State of Washington Custis's mind, it would be to be wished. He appears to be moped and stupid, says nothing, and is always in some hole or corner, excluded from Company. Before he left Annapolis, he wrote to me desiring to know whether he was to return there, or not, that he might pack up accordingly; I answered that I was astonished at the question! And that it appeared to me that nothing that could be said to him had the least effect. Whether this, by thwarting his views, is the cause of his present behavior, I know not." By September 6 he was writing the president of St. John's that Custis would be paying a brief visit to settle his accounts and pick up his books and clothing.

TROUBLES IN PHILADELPHIA

As John Adams' biographer, Page Smith, expressed it, the president had entered "into a goodly heritage. Washington had made the presidency a strong office and Adams intended to keep it so." Adams' inaugural address noted that for eight years the country had been administered by a citizen who, "by a long course of great actions" had brought "unexampled prosperity" and "the highest praise of foreign nations." After a brief recession in 1797, when peace hopes temporarily disappeared in Europe, the United States began to climb to yet higher prosperity.

John Adams had long and diversified experience. He had been in the Massachusetts legislature and the Continental Congress. He had achieved diplomatic triumphs in the Netherlands and France. For eight years he was Washington's loyal vice-president, thereafter as president, retaining Washington's entire cabinet, including Pickering and Wolcott, who had been in the federal government almost since its beginning. He could also rely on the remarkably able group of American diplomats abroad, who had been appointed by Washington. They included John Quincy Adams, considered by the first president to be the most competent of all.

There were offsets to these advantages. Adams did not have the stability and calm of his predecessor, and he realized he would never enjoy more than a fraction of Washington's popularity. In the crisis with France, now grown to dangerous proportions, he could count on the opposition of a large and powerful group of Jeffersonians, ready to thwart whatever he tried to do. His popularity with the Democrats, pleased as they were with the departure of Washington, lasted ten weeks. The president was surprised only that he escaped criticism that long. In the end, in trying to straddle the chasm between the Federalists and Democrats, he fell into the widening gap between them.

Adams later wrote his wife that the presidency was "a peck of troubles [arriving] in a large bundle of papers... every day." The reports from the legation in France were among the earliest to appear. Therein the president read the obsequious speech of Monroe to the French Directory, remarkable for its first person praise of France's revolution and aggressive armies. The farewell to Monroe, by the head of the Directory, was surly and insulting to the United States, but complimentary to the American minister, who represents "the true interests of your country. Depart with our regrets." The director refused to receive General Pinckney as a successor, threatened subsequently to place him under the jurisdiction of the police minister, and finally gave him written orders to leave the country. In European practice, this was the normal prelude to a declaration of war. Adams thereupon summoned Congress into special session. In his message of May 19, 1797, the president gave the full story but indicated that he intended to maintain the policies of Washington:

> *It is my sincere desire... to preserve peace and friendship with all nations: and believing that neither the honor nor the interests of the United States absolutely forbid the repetition of advances for securing these desirable objects with France, I shall institute a fresh attempt at negotiation, and shall not fail to promote and accelerate an accommodation on terms compatible with the rights, duties, interests and honor of the nation. If we have committed error, and these can be demonstrated, we shall be willing to correct them; if we have done injuries, we shall be willing on conviction to redress them; and equal measures of justice we have a right to expect from France and every other nation.*

On May 31, as evidence of his sincerity, Adams nominated General Pinckney, Francis Dana of Massachusetts, and John Marshall of Virginia "to be jointly and severally envoys extraordinary and ministers plenipotentiary to the French republic." When Dana was unable to go, Adams chose Jeffersonian Elbridge Gerry, an old personal friend, over the objections of his cabinet. Gerry had defended Monroe in correspondence with Adams and even urged the president to send him back to France. Adams replied that he thought Monroe was "dull and stupid." He denied Gerry's claim that France was republican, saying a republic there was likely to last as long as a snowball in a Philadelphia summer.

Adams' efforts to negotiate, while arming for defense, brought him into immediate conflict with the Democrats. Jefferson wrote to Madison to say that Adams wanted war and he himself would therefore work to defeat all defense measures. In subsequent letters Jefferson praised the "splendid" victories of Bonaparte as a deterrent to Adams' war plans. He reported conversations he held with the French spy, Constatin Volney. He repeatedly referred to the "folly" of Adams in calling Congress into session during a crisis. By June Jefferson was writing Aaron Burr that the president's speed had been "inflammatory," it was a declaration of war, and Adams wanted negotiations to fail, since two of his nominees were not "strongly attached" to the French alliance. "War then was intended." He called on Burr to rally the people of New York and the eastern states against the government. To Gerry, in expressing "infinite joy" at his appointment, Jefferson wrote that "peace even at the expense of [French] spoliations past & future," had to be secured. To Edward Rutledge he expressed the view that "Great Britain… is going down irrecoverably, & will sink us also, if we do not clear ourselves." It is well that Jefferson never knew that George III told the American minister in London how much he liked Adams' speech.

On June 28 James Monroe arrived in Philadelphia, indignant not at the French but at the American government. He was warmly greeted by Jefferson, who had been all impatience for his presence. On July 1 the vice-president sponsored a public dinner in his honor. Attending were some of Washington's enemies—Horatio Gates, Thomas Mifflin, and Aaron Burr. The presence of many Virginians caused a Federalist newspaper to refer to that state as the "land of debts," a reference to the fury of Virginians at having to pay what they had long owed to their English creditors. Jefferson himself had overdue more than $30,000 to his British creditors. His bitterness towards the federal government, the Jay treaty, and Great Britain had the same root causes as the attitude of other citizens of his state.

Thus publicly supported, Monroe began an open controversy with the secretary of state, from whom he demanded the reasons for his recall as minister to France. He received a forthright reply: "It is not true that removal from office implies actual misconduct. It may merely imply a want of ability." Pickering said that the president could not be expected to provide reasons for actions taken by his predecessor. At Adams' insistence, the cabinet informed Monroe that he could see the papers on his recall. Monroe, however, did not appear at Pickering's office to inspect the documents. On July 3, in the midst of these commotions, the president sent to the Senate an intercepted letter written to James Carey, an Indian agent, by William Blount, Democratic senator from Tennessee. It disclosed the surface of a conspiracy by western Democrats to attack Spanish possessions in the Southwest and Florida, with the aid of the British and Indians. Since Spain, at war with England, had heard of this plan, that country had been holding on to her last two posts on American soil. Blount asked Carey to inform the Indians that George Washington was responsible for their boundary problems. "This sort of talk will be throwing all the blame off me upon the late President, and as he is now out of office, it will be of no consequence how much the Indians blame him." Blount was not present when Jefferson read the letter to the Senate; upon his return, it was read again. Blount immediately departed the chamber and Philadelphia. On July 8 the Senate expelled him from office.

The two straightlaced Puritans in the president's house, John and Abigail, watched this sordidness and bore the press attacks with as much composure as they could muster. Adams at least had the satisfaction of seeing most of his recommended program for national defense, including twelve new frigates, succeed in Congress, in spite of Jefferson's determined opposition. The president was well aware of his activities, writing that Jefferson was "weak, confused, uninformed and ignorant." Mrs. Adams put it differently: "We are in perils by land, and we are in perils by sea, and in perils from false brethren."

"A TRICK SO DIRTY AND SHABBY"

Jefferson's Mazzei letter, severely blasting Washington, was published in the American press two months after Washington's retirement from office. "It became immediately," as John Marshall put it, "the subject of universal conversation." Since Washington subscribed to various newspapers, he had a copy in fairly short order. He made no mention of it in his correspondence. Jefferson, for his part, discussed with Madison, Monroe, and others, whether he should acknowledge the letter and what he should say in extenuation. Monroe urged him to avow it, while Madison thought it better to say and do nothing publicly. Jefferson followed the latter policy but privately disseminated the idea that he had been mistranslated or misquoted.

Whatever shred of faith Washington retained in Jefferson's integrity vanished after reading this letter written while Jefferson was professing esteem and attachment; from it the general learned that the vice-president was probably involved in a scheme to entrap him. In early October Washington received a letter from a stranger, John Langhorne of Warren, a small town south of Charlottesville. The writer praised Washington as "eminently just and virtuous" and commiserated with him for having borne such "unmerciful calumny." Washington returned a polite note of thanks on October 15. He said that attacks on a government elected "by the people" could result in no good and much evil for the country. He continued: "So far these attacks are aimed at me, personally, it is, I can assure you, Sir, a misconception if it be supposed I feel the venom of the darts. Within me, I have the consolation which proves an antidote against their utmost malignity, rendering my mind in the retirement I have long panted after, perfectly tranquil."

The arrival at a tiny post office of a letter from General Washington aroused much interest; this intensified when no one had heard of "Mr. Langhorne." The postmaster apparently asked the county clerk, John Nicholas, whether he knew anyone by that name. Nicholas said that there was a Mr. Langhorne in a neighboring county, who had fought in "Braddock's war" and might thereby have known Washington. In reporting to Washington, on November 18, Nicholas said that he asked a friend to deliver the letter to Mr. Langhorne. To his great surprise, it had been claimed by a county resident "closely connected with some of your greatest and bitterest enemies, as being intended for him, tho' his name was very different indeed from Langhorne... The only conclusion I can draw from this strange circumstance, is that certain men, who are resolved to stick at nothing to promote their wicked and inglorious views, have fallen on this last miserable deceptive means... to entrap you." He warned Washington to be exceedingly careful, for he knew the real dispositions towards him at "the headquarters of Jacobinism."

The name "Nicholas" had unpleasant connotations for Washington because of four brothers, John, George, Wilson, and Philip, devout Jeffersonians. John Nicholas, a congressman, had been a gadfly during the ratification of the Jay treaty. Washington consulted Dr. Stuart about John Nicholas, when the former stayed overnight at Mount Vernon on November 29. Having been assured by Stuart that this John Nicholas, a cousin, was a strong Federalist and "a respectable man," Washington wrote to express thanks for Nicholas' "obliging favour." He said that he had a high regard for his father, with whom he served in the Virginia Assembly and that he would be glad to see him if he were ever in the neighborhood of Mount Vernon. He forwarded copies of the Langhorne letter and his reply, asking Nicholas to find out whether there was any "nefarious plan" being developed at Charlottesville against the government. If he found nothing, he was to destroy the papers. He added that his only feeling about "Mr. Langhorne" had been that he was "a pedant who was desirous of displaying the powers of his pen."

On December 9 Nicholas forwarded to Washington a copy of a note, written by Peter Carr, in which he claimed to be "Mr. Langhorne" and "entitled to that letter." Nicholas added, in case Washington did not recognize the name, that Carr was "a favorite nephew of your very sincere friend Mr. Jefferson, raised and educated by himself from a child, a constant dependent and resident in his house from that period almost to the present; and entertaining sentiments, I do assure you of my own personal knowledge, very different indeed towards you from those contained in his letter." Nicholas sent a further report on February 22 which indicated he had not, as yet, been able to determine Jefferson's role in the attempted entrapment but the man who brought Carr's note and picked up the Langhorne letter was a Monticello servant. He learned that Jefferson encouraged and helped Monroe with his book attacking the former president. Nicholas had heard Jefferson say that Washington premeditated the destruction of Monroe, by appointing him minister to

France. Since Nicholas mentioned that he was a friend of Bushrod Washington, the general sent his March 8 reply to his nephew for review and an evaluation of Nicholas, adding that, knowing the political views of most of his family, he had little esteem for them. He was almost alone in his family in support of the government "but does not stand less firm on that account." Bushrod said that he had heard of "the virulence" of Peter Carr's feelings about Washington. He had therefore forwarded his uncle's letter, which follows, to Nicholas:

> *Nothing short of the Evidence you have adduced, corroborative of intimations which I had received long before, through another channel [General Lee], could have shaken my belief in the sincerity of a friendship which I had conceived was possessed for me by the person to whom you allude. But attempts to injure those who are supposed to stand well in the estimation of the People and are stumbling blocks in their way (by misrepresenting their political tenets), thereby to destroy all confidence in them, is one of the means by which the Government is to be assailed and the constitution destroyed. The conduct of the Party is systematized and everything that is opposed to its execution, will be sacrificed, without hesitation or remorse, if the end can be answered by it.*

> *If the person whom you <u>suspect</u>, was really the Author of the letter under the signature of John Langhorne, it is not at all surprising to me that the correspondence should have ended where it did; for the penetration of <u>that</u> <u>man</u> would have perceived at the first glance of the answer, that nothing was to be drawn from <u>that</u> mode of attack. In what form the next insidious attempts may appear, remains to be discovered. But as the attempts to explain away the constitution and weaken the government are so open... it is hardly to be expected that a resort to covert means to effect these ends, will be longer retarded...*

> *As to [Monroe's] propriety in exposing to public view his private instructions and correspondence with his own government, nothing need be said: for I should suppose that the measure must be reprobated by the well informed and intelligent of <u>all</u> <u>Nations</u>; and not less so by his abettors in this country, if they were not so blinded by Party views and determined at all hazards to catch at any thing that, in their opinion, will promote them. This mischievous and dangerous tendency of such a practice, is too glaring to require a comment.*

> *If the Executive, in the opinion of the gentlemen you have alluded to, is chargeable with "premeditating the destruction of Mr. Monroe in his appointment"... it is to be hoped that he will give it credit for its lenity to that Gentleman for having*

designated several others (not of the Senate) as victims to this, <u>before</u> the sacrifice of Mr. Monroe was ever in contemplation.

Somehow Jefferson's spies got word of Bushrod's role. In informing his uncle of this on August 7 Bushrod said there was a mention of him by Peter Carr in "Davis's paper of the 24th. July," calling him "an informer." He added that he well knew "that Mr. Langhorne was a scoundrel: but I did not suppose he would ever be so stupid as to provoke a publication of his own Villainy." John Nicholas, he continued, now wanted to publish an account of the whole affair. Washington replied on the 12th that, if Jefferson were the "real Author or abetter, it would be a pity not to expose him to Public execration, for attempting in so dishonorable a way to obtain a disclosure of Sentiments of which some advantage could be taken... If a *trick* so *dirty* and *shabby* as this is supposed to be, could be clearly proved, it would, in my opinion, be attended with a happy effect at this time." Washington warned, however, that unless it were not only fully substantiated and all documents in the case published, the report would recoil on the author.

The activities of the Jeffersonians were to react on themselves, since they brought Washington back to an active political role. He asked Bushrod and John Marshall, who were to sit for many years on the Supreme Court together, to come for an early conference at Mount Vernon. "The Crisis is important. The temper of the People of this State in many... places is so violent and outrageous, that I wish to converse with Genl. Marshall and yourself on the elections which must soon come."

FARM LIFE

If Mr. and Mrs. Washington felt they had too many strange guests, they seem to have made life more interesting for Martha's granddaughter, the happily disposed Nelly Custis. Her high spirits, Nelly later wrote, brought frequent hearty laughs from the general. Shortly after Christmas she informed Mrs. Wolcott: "We have spent our summer and autumn very happily here... Have had many agreeable visitors and are now contentedly sitting around our winter fireside, often speaking of and wishing to see again our good friends in Philadelphia, but never regretting its amusements or a life of ceremony. I stay very much at home, have not been to the city for two or three months... I never have a dull or lonesome hour..."

The general and his wife carried on a cheerful correspondence with Elizabeth Powel in Philadelphia. Washington had sold her his secretary-desk before leaving the city. She wrote him that, on opening it, she found a packet of love letters addressed to the president in a lady's handwriting. Lear had absolutely refused to touch them but she would see that he received them back in good order. He replied with thanks for her delicate handling of the matter; he was afraid that any reader might have been disappointed that Martha didn't write with more passion. On December 18 he asked his wife to tell Mrs. Powel that "neither his health nor his spirits were ever in greater flow, notwithstanding he is descending and has almost reached the bottom of the hill, or in other words, the shades below."

Washington's plan to free his slaves envisioned the sale of most of his western lands and the rental of his farms near Mount Vernon. In carrying out his 1793 plan, he undertook to establish centralized dwellings, barns, cribs, and storehouses at Union, Dogue Run, Muddy Hole, and River farms. He subsequently made repeated enquiries in England for suitable British migrants; in 1796 he also advertised the farms in various parts of the United States. The responses were not, on the whole, very encouraging. The applicants did not have the necessary knowledge or capital, or they could not use such large areas. In addition, as he discovered, uncleared western land, which could be bought cheaply, was more attractive than rented Virginia farms, even though they were fenced, cleared, settled, and in effective operation. Washington had therefore to turn back to managing his vast enterprises, with his usual difficulties in finding suitable overseers. In 1797 he drew up and studied an alternate plan to use his farms for grazing rather than crops.

Washington's supervision of more than twelve square miles of property was a heavy burden for a man of sixty-five. On December 3 he wrote to William Vans Murray, American minister to The Hague: "I rarely stir from home, never beyond Alexandria or the Federal city; indeed, if my inclinations were more extensive, my business would restrain them; for at no period of my life have I been more closely engaged... than during the months I have been home. Hardly a resident for the last five and twenty years at this place... I have found upon an examination into the state of my buildings that time and want of attention... have caused such depredations thereon and everything connected with them, and have so deranged all matters of private concern, that, what with the plague and trouble proceeding from the number of workmen I have been obliged to employ... I have been occupied from the 'rising of the sun to the setting of the same,' and which, as the wise man has said, 'may be all vanity and vexation of spirit,' but as I did not seek it as a source of happiness, but entered upon it as a case of necessity, a line may be drawn between his disappointments and mine."

He wrote to John Marshall on December 4: "A very severe winter has commenced. Since the first of November we have hardly experienced a moderate

Day; heavy rains following severe frosts have done more damage to the winter grain, now growing, than I ever recollect to have seen. At this moment and for several days past, all the Creeks and small waters are hard bound with Ice, and the Navigation of the River, if not entirely stopped is yet very much impeded by it."

Washington resumed various other duties. He followed closely the work of the Potomac Canal Company and did not hesitate to ask the governors of Maryland and Virginia for financial aid to keep the work going. His interest in the city of Washington remained keen though he himself had no further responsibility for the work. When he heard from Alexander White, a district commissioner, that the president thought the offices of cabinet members should be located near the capitol for the convenience of Congress, he replied on March 25 that his opinion, "as an individual is a matter of Moon-shine." He had placed the cabinet offices near the president's house for directly opposite reasons. The cabinet had to see the president daily. His officers constantly complained they could get no work done when Congress was in session. Senators and representatives dropped by so freely for conversation, or to ask for documents, that "they have been obliged, often, to go home and deny themselves, in order to transact the current business." After the commissioners declared that more houses should be built in the city for the accommodation of the government, Washington, even though overextended, engaged William Thornton to build two rental houses close by the capitol.

After the Washingtons learned that their old friend, Bryan Fairfax, now an Episcopal minister and eighth Lord Fairfax, was going to England on business, they took occasion on May 16 to renew their correspondence with his sister-in-law, Mrs. George Fairfax. Washington recalled the "happy moments, the happiest in my life, which I have enjoyed in your company… It is a matter of sore regret, when I cast my eyes toward Belvoir, which I often do, to reflect that the former inhabitants of it, with whom we lived in such harmony and friendship, no longer reside there." He and Martha strongly urged Mrs. Fairfax to return to her own country to pass her final years. As an inducement thereto, Washington added a report on how greatly the country had progressed during the years since she had left. A capital city was building on the Potomac which, "if the country keeps united, in a century might be of a magnitude inferior to few others in Europe… A situation not excelled for commanding prospect, good water, salubrious air, and safe harbor by any in the world; and where elegant buildings are erecting, and in forwardness, for the reception of Congress in the year 1800. Alexandria, within the last seven years (since the establishment of the General Government) has increased in buildings, in population, in the improvement of its Streets by well executed pavements, and in the extension of its wharves, in a manner of which you can have very little idea. This shew of prosperity... is owing... to the extension of the Inland navigation of the Potomack River; now cleared to Fort Cumberland... If this country can steer clear of European politics, stand firm on its bottom, and be wise and temperate in its government, it bids fair to be one of the greatest and happiest nations in the world."

WASHINGTON'S BIRTHDAY

The celebration of Washington's sixty-sixth birthday was as noteworthy for confusion as national joy. Alexandria honored it by the old-style calendar, whereby Washington was born February 11, 1731/32. As this date fell on a Sunday, the city held a birthday ball on February 12. Washington wrote in his diary that he and his family, presumably his wife and two stepgrandchildren, attended the dance.

A similar ball planned for February 22 in Philadelphia, caused the president and his lady to lose their aplomb. Abigail was furious that there should be a dance in honor of Washington, when there was now a new president. Adams thought it unfortunate that honor was to be paid to a private citizen. The Adamses sent a discourteously abrupt refusal. Jefferson, also invited, declared that there might be some sense in paying honor to General Washington but none to President Washington. As soon as he learned that Adams refused to attend, he also declined. Abigail Adams mistakenly thought the vice-president did this in deference to the president. Instead Jefferson was chortling at the fury of the Washingtonians and the discomfiture of the "Adamites."

On his birthday, Washington wrote to Senator Martin of North Carolina to thank him for forwarding some dramatic poetry. He added: "Lamentable and much to be regretted indeed it is, that in a crises like the present, when all hearts should be united and at their post, ready to rejoice at the good, or repel the evil which awaits us, that nothing but internal dissensions and political hostilities are to be found in the Councils of our common Country. Although no longer an Actor on this Theatre myself, I cannot but view these things with deep concern."

THE MONROE AND FAUCHET REPORTS

In 1796 and 1797, pamphlets and books were published which further extended the Franco-American attacks on the United States government. The most important were those written by James Monroe, Joseph Fauchet, the former French minister, William Duane, who went out of his way to defend the Mazzei letter by speech and pamphlet, and Albert Gallatin, a member of Congress.

On January 12 Washington requested Timothy Pickering to send him the works of Fauchet and Monroe. At the end of the month he wrote to acknowledge their receipt. He said that he had read Bache's "malignant falsehood… exhibited against you in the Aurora. Satisfied as I am of the motive and the end, intended to be answered by the publication, I have read with much gratification your explicit disavowal." He noted that Fauchet had accused him, Washington, of carrying on secret negotiations with "the Pretender" (Louis XVIII), who had sent a Mr. Antoine-Omer Talon to Philadelphia for that purpose. Washington called this an "impudent, wicked and groundless assertion." He could not remember any M. Talon, though it was always conceivable he might have been among the numerous strangers present at receptions.

When Monroe's lengthy treatise, greatly swelled by its inclusion of secret government dispatches, appeared, it bore a ponderous title which Jefferson had advised Monroe to shorten and improve: "A view of the conduct of the Executive in the foreign Affairs of the United States, connected with the Mission to the French Republic during the Years 1794, 5 & 6." The vice-president, after sending copies of the Paine letter and the Fauchet pamphlet to Virginia, informed Monroe that Bache would soon ship two or three hundred copies of his book to Richmond. He said that it was "irresistible" and that Fauchet had reinforced the story of Washington's "duplicity." Jefferson wrote to Madison that "Monroe's book is considered as masterly… and unanswerable."

Sometime that winter Washington read Monroe's publication and commented on it in the margins. Jefferson, in late years, tried to portray Washington as growing senile after 1793, but his mind was sharper than ever. By turns humorous and satirical, the former chief executive of the United States ripped James Monroe to pieces. Washington's masterpiece was not published for nearly a century thereafter. Because of its length, it is not possible to reproduce more than short extracts.

Monroe said that France and the United States had been in process of "being thrown wholly apart… Upon my arrival in Paris… I found that the work of alienation… had been carried further than I had before even suspected." Washington: "Why? Because one nation was seeking redress for violations and injuries committed by the other… If we had submitted to them without remonstrating, we should still have been their dear friends and Allies."

Monroe: "My first note to the committee of public safety… combatted copiously… the conduct of France in thus harassing our commerce against the stipulations of certain articles in our treaty." Washington: "But he finally told [the committee] (contrary to instructions) that if it was not convenient to comply... the Government and People of the U. States would give them up with pleasure..."

Monroe: "Such was my conduct upon the above occasion, and such the motives of it." Washington: "And extraordinary indeed it was!"

Monroe: "Had [the Jay] treaty then never passed... what might we not have expected from [France's] friendship?" Washington: "Nothing if she did not perceive some advantage to herself in granting it."

Monroe wrote that there had been "a spontaneous and almost universal disapprobation" of the Jay treaty "throughout the United States as soon as it was seen." Washington: "He should have said before it was seen; for it is a well known fact that the opposition from the French Party in the U.S. began... as soon as it was known that a Treaty had been concluded and before one article therein was known..."

Monroe: "With respect to the declaration that we were an independent people and had a right to decide for ourselves... I did not perceive how it applied..." Washington: "None are more dull than those who will not perceive."

Monroe wrote that he had considered resigning as minister to France, on which Washington scribbled: "Curious and laughable... His recall was a second death to him."

It is pointless to quote further from a Monroe who expressed himself in elephantine circumlocution. Washington's further observations were crisp and usually brief:

When a rational answer and good reason cannot be given, it is not unusual to be silent.

If the cap did not fit, why put it on?

What! Declare to the world in a public speech that we were going to treat with this and that Nation, and that France was to assist us! Insanity in the extreme!

Could this repeal be announced before it was known?

Declined for the best reason in the world because he had none that would bear the test of examination.

Self importance appears here.

Of all the mistakes he has made, and bold assertions, none stands more prominent than this.

None but a person incompetent to judge, or blinded by party views, could have misconstrued as he did. But had France a right to be acquainted with the Private instructions of our Ministers?

For this there is not better proof than his own opinion; whilst there is abundant evidence of his being a mere tool in the hands of the French government, cajoled and led always by unmeaning assurances.

As he has such a happy knack of determining, he ought not to have let this opportunity escape him.

Here is a pretty smart compliment paid himself, at the expense of the Administration; but the truth of the case is...

That is to say, if we would not press them to do us Justice, but have yielded to their violations, they would have aided us in every measure that would have cost them: Nothing.

The sufferings of our Citizens are always a secondary consideration when put in competition with the embarrassments of the French.

In his closing documentation, Monroe quoted the head of the French Directory as declaring that France would always welcome "loyal explanations... above all, citizen Minister, when they shall be made through you." Washington added: "The treatment of our minister, General Pinckney, is a pretty evidence of this. The thought of parting with Mr. Monroe was unsupportable by them."

XYZ AFFAIR

Washington received reports from Philadelphia, through Alexander White, that Democratic members of Congress had written to the French Directory to suggest that it refuse to receive the accredited ministers of the United States but "on the contrary, to menace us with hostile appearances, and they might rely on bringing the U. States to their feet." There was no subsequent evidence of this, although Democrats often wrote their friends in France, denouncing their country's policy. In this case, certainly, Jefferson did not sponsor such a scheme. In January he stated that Talleyrand, the foreign minister, had assured Joseph Letombe, the French consul-general at Philadelphia, that the American ministers had arrived safely in Paris and "they will be well received, & that every disposition exists on the side of France to accommodate their differences with us."

The American delegates, Marshall and Gerry, left the United States in July. While Jefferson and Monroe had been praising France for its friendship, that country had seized nearly 350 American ships, with a value in excess of $55 million. This figure was more than five times the amount of French monetary aid to America during the revolution. While thus engaged in piracy, the French government never failed to remind Americans of their ingratitude for France's earlier generosity.

On December 4 Washington wrote to John Marshall to express his appreciation of a letter announcing his safe arrival at The Hague and to say that the press had now reported that he was in Paris. He hoped he would have an honorable and successful mission. If, however, the French Directory proceeded on the assumption that the Federalist and Democratic parties were nearly equal in strength and that the latter would rally to the French standard, "they will greatly deceive themselves; for the Mass of our citizens require no more than to understand a question to decide it properly and an adverse conclusion of the Negotiation will effect this."

Thereafter, everyone from Adams and Washington to Jefferson and Madison waited with impatience to hear from Paris. A terrible silence followed. Washington grew anxious; he wrote the secretary of war on January 28: "Are there no accounts yet from our Envoys?" He followed with another enquiry on March 4: "Are our Commissioners guillotined? Or what else is the occasion of their Silence?" That same day the president opened the bulky coded reports of the mission. As they were deciphered, he read a tale of intrigue, deception, and greed, which approached in sordidness the affair of the diamond necklace, involving the queen and cardinal of France a few years before. Included were reports on Talleyrand's agents, denominated X, Y, and Z (Hottenguer, Bellamy, and D'Hauteville) and others, including a lady who was intended to charm the Americans out of their money. John Marshall himself wrote what is perhaps the best summary of the transactions for his biography of Washington:

> History will scarcely furnish the example of a nation, not absolutely degraded, which has received from a foreign power such open contumely, and undisguised insult, as were, on this occasion, suffered by the United States in the person of their ministers.
>
> It was insinuated that their being taken from the party which supported the measures of their own government furnished just cause for umbrage and, under

slight pretexts, the executive directory delayed to accredit them as the representatives of an independent nation. In this situation, they were assailed by persons... exhibiting sufficient evidence of the source from which their powers were derived, who, in direct and explicit terms, demanded money from the United States as the condition which must precede... any negotiation...

A decided negative was given to the preliminary required [Pinckney said, 'No! No! Not a sixpence.']... but they returned to the charge with wonderful perseverance... The immense power of France was painted in glowing colours, the humiliation of the house of Austria was stated, and the conquest of Britain was confidently anticipated... The fate of Venice was held up to warn her of the danger which awaited those who incurred the displeasure of the great republic. The ministers were assured that, if they believed their conduct would be approved in the United States, they were mistaken. The means which the Directory possessed, in that country, to excite odium against them, were great, and would unquestionably be employed...

This degrading intercourse was at length interrupted by the positive refusal of the envoys to hold any further communications with the persons employed in it.

Meanwhile, they urged the object of their mission with persevering but unavailing solicitude. The Directory still refused to acknowledge them in their public character; and [Talleyrand], at unofficial visits which they made him, renewed the demand which his agents had unsuccessfully pressed.

The American ministers made a last effort to execute the duties assigned to them. In a letter addressed to [Talleyrand], they entered at large into the explanations committed to them by their government, and illustrated, by a variety of facts, the uniform friendliness of its conduct to France. Notwithstanding the failure of this effort... they continued, with a passiveness which must search for its apology in their solicitude to demonstrate to the American people the real views of the French republic, to employ the only means in their power to avert the rupture which was threatened, and which appeared to be inevitable.

During these transactions, occasion was repeatedly taken to insult the American government; open war continued to be waged by the cruisers of France on American commerce; and the flag of the United States was a sufficient justification for the capture and condemnation of any vessel over which it waved.

At length, when the demonstration became complete, that the resolution of the American envoys was not less fixed, than their conduct had been guarded and temperate, various attempts were made to induce two of them voluntarily, to relinquish their station; on the failure of which they were ordered to quit the territories of the republic. As if to aggravate this national insult, the third, who had been selected from that party which was said to be friendly to France, was permitted to remain...

Marshall noted in a footnote that the masterly letter to Talleyrand, which he had drafted, had received a bitter and angry reply. The French government forwarded this to Bache, who had it before it reached the secretary of state in Philadelphia. Bache promptly published the reply but not the letter by the American mission.

Adams' first reaction was rage and a willingness to ask Congress to declare formally the state of war, which existed de facto. The president drafted a war message but with a divided cabinet and country, he decided on caution and to hold back the offensive dispatches. He informed Congress, March 19, 1798, that the mission had made every effort to bring about a pacific settlement with France but their attempts had been unsuccessful. He asked the Senate and House "to adopt with promptitude, decision and unanimity... measures... for the protection of our seafaring and commercial citizens, for the defense... of our territories... and to provide such efficient revenue as will be necessary to defray extraordinary expenses." He announced that he had authorized the arming of merchant vessels.

The vice-president told Madison that the president had delivered "an insane message." He informed Monroe that the Democrats would seek to override the authorization to arm merchant vessels and would introduce resolutions to adjourn Congress, so that no defensive measures might be passed. The Democrats needed to stall for time while France landed troops in England. In addition Jefferson wrote that he believed Adams had kept back the whole story, as too unfavorable for his war plans. His party would therefore call for all the secret papers of the American mission to Paris. The Bache-type press soon redoubled its attacks on Adams. So many threatening letters arrived at the president's house that Abigail Adams feared for her husband's safety.

In formal debate, at the beginning of April, the House took up a Democratic resolution asking the president to provide all relevant papers of the French mission. The president watched with interest as Federalists quietly added support. When the vote came, it was overwhelmingly in favor. The president, with ill-concealed satisfaction, forwarded to both Houses the whole of the story. The effects were shattering. The House Democrats attempted to stop their release but the Senate ordered the printing of 50,000 copies for distribution throughout the country.

PUBLIC REACTION

Washington's letter to Marshall had correctly anticipated what the feeling of the great mass of Americans would be, if the Directory broke off negotiations. A rush of support for the president brought him the highest degree of popularity ever achieved by an Adams. Addresses and letters poured in by the hundreds from town and country meetings, state legislatures, militia companies, old soldiers, Harvard, Princeton, and Dartmouth students, and the first president of the United States.

Joseph Hopkinson, son of Washington's old friend, Francis, having been asked to produce words to "The President's March," wrote "Hail Columbia," with its chorus, "firm united let us be, Rallying round our Liberty." With Mrs. Adams present, Gilbert Fox, accompanied by a chorus and orchestra, sang it in the Chestnut Street Theatre, to the enthusiastic shouts of the audience, who called for it again and again. On its last rendition the audience joined in. A few days later, when the president and his wife attended the theater, they were greeted with wild applause. The tune was again sung by the audience, band, and chorus. On May 9 Hopkinson sent a copy to Washington, saying that it was being played night after night, in theaters in New York as well as Philadelphia, "and men and boys sing it in the streets as they go." It became, in fact, a national serenade for John Adams.

Jefferson wrote that the XYZ message had produced "shock and dismay" among the Democrats. Several of them departed the House of Representatives to return home, while others rallied to Adams. On April 26 Congress authorized the establishment of a separate Navy Department, to which Adams appointed Benjamin Stoddert as its first secretary. Other measures, including the raising of 10,000 men for the army, as well as new taxes, passed Congress without much trouble.

Adams did not sponsor them, although he gladly signed two important measures for the national security. The first gave the president power, in case of war, to seize or deport all enemy aliens. Jefferson complained that this act seemed to be particularly directed at "Collot and Volney," the two French spies who had travelled through the West, drawing maps for France and electioneering for Jefferson. The pair quickly left the country, along with many other Frenchmen. A second act provided fines and imprisonment for those who engaged in insurrection or plots against the United States government, in seditious libel, or in hostile acts, on behalf of a foreign government, against the officers of the United States. In libel cases, a jury trial was required; malice and intent had to be proved by the government, and truth was a full defense. The first man indicted was Benjamin Bache.

John Marshall's masterly role in Paris won him wide popular acclaim in the United States. His June 18 arrival in Philadelphia was a signal for a popular demonstration greater than even Washington had received in the city. Jefferson, feeling the tide against him, had expected to leave the city but stayed for Marshall's arrival to see what intelligence he could acquire. Three days later he wrote Madison that Marshall "was received here with the utmost éclat. The Secretary of State and many carriages, with all the city cavalry, went to Frankfort to meet him, and on his arrival here in the evening, the bells rung till late at night, & immense crowds were collected to see & make part of the show, which was circuitously paraded through the streets."

Jefferson did not mention the dinner for Marshall which was attended by members of the Supreme Court, most congressmen, the Episcopal and Catholic bishops, and numerous others. Toasts were given to the president, the nation, General Washington, General Pinckney, the army, and the navy. It was Robert Goodloe Harper, congressman from South Carolina, who raised his glass and gave the famous words: "Millions for defense, but not one cent for tribute."

Jefferson's report to Madison noted an uproar in the press over Dr. George Logan, who had sailed for France and was reported to be a secret emissary "from the Jacobins here to solicit an army from France, instruct them as to their landing, & c. This extravagance produced a real panic among the citizens." Jefferson did not mention that Logan carried a letter of introduction from him. Shortly afterwards, the vice-president of the United States set out for Virginia, determined to bring the force of his state against the Constitution which he had sworn to protect and defend.

Adams, after ordering Gerry recalled from Paris, announced to Congress, June 21, that he would never send another minister to France "without assurances that he will be received, respected and honored as the representative of a great, free, powerful and independent nation." Talleyrand's eventual indirect reply, employing the president's own words, was to be the key by which Adams crowned the Washington peace policy with a French treaty.

On June 17 Washington, who had heard that the president planned an inspection trip to the federal city, where he was to move in 1800, politely asked him to make Mount Vernon his headquarters while in the area. He added: "I pray you to believe that no one has read the various approbatory Addresses, which I have done; nor are there any who more sincerely wish that your Administration of the Government may be easy, happy, and honorable to yourself, and prosperous for the Country."

A POLE VISITS MOUNT VERNON

Few of the hundreds of guests at Mount Vernon left useful surviving descriptions of family life there. A notable exception was Julian Niemcewicz, Polish poet, soldier, statesman, and dramatist, whom the Washingtons encountered rather accidentally in Washington city. He had been adjutant to General Kosciuszko, a former officer of Washington's revolutionary army, who subsequently led the Poles in an unsuccessful revolt against their Russian rulers. Niemcewicz recorded not only the domestic scene but Washington's reactions to the XYZ affair.

On May 19 the Washingtons left Mount Vernon for a week's visit to Martha's descendants. They spent a night at the house of David Stuart, whose wife had been the widow of John Custis. In Washington they spent several days at the houses of Martha's two granddaughters, Mrs. Thomas Peter and Mrs. Thomas Law. Niemcewicz was at the Law house. He recorded that he was struck dumb at meeting the general. He soon relaxed for Washington was very cheerful. When Law asked him if he had seen the account from New York of the duel in which the Democrat, Brockholst Livingston, killed John Jones, a Federalist, Washington replied: "They say that [Jones] shot off a piece of his nose. How could he miss it? You know Mr. Livingston's nose and what a first-rate target it is." Niemcewicz, who had much humor of his own, expressed his delight. His diary recorded that Martha Washington was "charming, bright and gay." Niemcewicz, in his turn, seems to have charmed the Washingtons who asked him to make an extended stay at Mount Vernon. In company with Law he arrived a few days later; thereafter he missed nothing.

"June 2... We arrived at the foot of a hill where the Washington properties begin. We took a road newly cut through a forest of oaks. Soon we discovered still another hill, at the top of which stood a rather spacious house, surmounted by a small cupola, with mezzanines and blinds painted in green... All kinds of trees, bushes, flowering plants, ornament the two sides of the court... Near the ends of the house are two groves of locusts... The ground where they are planted is a green carpet of the most beautiful velvet...

"We entered the house. General Washington was out on his farm. Madame appeared after a few minutes, welcomed us most graciously and had punch served. At two o'clock the General arrived, mounted on a gray horse. He shook our hand, dismounted, gave a cut of the whip to the horse, which went off by itself to the stable..."

While the general went to dress for dinner, Mrs. Washington took Niemcewicz on a tour of the house. After providing a minute description of the mansion, he wrote of "the most beautiful green" lawn to its front and "perhaps the most beautiful view in the world," from the piazza. The arrival of Nelly Custis diverted the poet's attention from the river. According to Washington's diary, Nelly was accompanied by a "Miss Lee of Greenspring." Niemcewicz said she "was not beautiful at all" but he was enchanted by Nelly: "A young woman of the greatest beauty... one of those celestial figures that nature produces only rarely, that the inspiration of painters has sometimes divined and that one cannot see without ecstasy. Her sweetness is equal to her beauty... She plays the harpsichord, sings, draws better than any woman in America or even in Europe."

That light June evening Washington took Niemcewicz around his gardens to complete his day: "The garden, the plantations, the house, their perfect form, show that a man born with natural taste can divine the beautiful without having seen the model. The General has never left America. After seeing his house and gardens one would say that he had seen the most beautiful examples of the great old houses of England..."

In the next couple of days, accompanied by Washington or Law, Niemcewicz rode over much of the land. He was astonished at the extent of the farms and the great fields of peas, rye, corn, wheat, flax, and alfalfa. He examined the flour mill, with its newly invented machine for aerating flour, and the large distillery, capable of turning out 12,000 gallons of whiskey (mainly rye) a year. He commented: "If this distillery produces poison for men, it offers in return the most delicate and succulent feed for pigs. They keep 150 of them of the guinea type ... [which are] so excessively bulky that they can hardly drag their big bellies on the ground. They looked to me like so many priors in our Dominican monasteries. We saw here and there flocks of sheep. The General has between six and seven hundred..." Niemcewicz examined his cattle, "super bull," Lafayette's jackasses, and some fifty mule descendants. Washington also showed him an ingenious plow which he had invented as well as the new octagonal barn that he had designed. From this point on (June 5) Niemcewicz turned increasingly to recording his impressions of the Washingtons:

At table, after the departure of the ladies, or else in the evening seated under the portico, he often talked with me for hours at a time. His favorite subject is agriculture, but he answered with kindness all questions that I put to him of the Revolution, the armies, etc. He has a prodigious memory. One time in the evening he listed all the rivers, lakes, creeks and the means to procure a communication between these waters, from Portsmouth as far as the Mississippi...

Since his retirement he has led a quiet and regular life. He gets up at 5 o'clock in the morning, reads or writes until seven. He breakfasts on tea and [corn muffins] spread with butter and honey. He then immediately goes on horseback to see the work in the fields; sometimes in the middle of a field he holds a council of war with Mr. Anderson [his manager]. He returns at two o'clock, dresses, and goes to dinner. If there are guests, he loves to chat after dinner with a glass of Madeira in his hand. After dinner he diligently reads the newspapers, of which he receives about ten of different kinds. He answers letters, etc. Tea at 7 o'clock; he chats until nine and then he goes to bed. Mrs. Washington is one of the most estimable persons that one could know, good, sweet, and extremely polite. She loves to talk, and talks very well about times past.

June 9. Mrs. Washington made me a gift of a china cup with her monogram and the names of the States of the United States. Miss Custis gave me my monogram in flowers, which she had herself painted...

June 13... On our return [from fishing] we found a notable and unexpected company from Alexandria. The table in the great hall was set with a Sèvres porcelain service with places for twenty. The General, in high spirits, was gracious and full of attention to everybody. Among the guests were the young Randolphs. I do not know whether both their ages would add up to 38 but they are already the parents of three children. Mrs. [William Fitzhugh], who in corpulence and girth gives way only to the late [Empress Catherine], was in a gay humor and had an enormous appetite. As she swept through one plate after another, her husband laughingly encouraged her with these words: 'Betsy, a little more, a little more.'

In the evening, after the departure of the company, the General, sitting with Mr. Law and me under the portico, read us a letter which he had just received from a friend [almost certainly John Marshall] in Paris. This letter, written with sense, dispassion and a sound knowledge of the situation in France and of the politics of those who rule her, gave us an opportunity for conversation about the wrongs suffered by America at French hands, and about the bloody struggle which might shortly break out between the two countries. This conversation aroused the passionate wrath of the venerable citizen and commander. I have never heard him speak with so much candor, nor with such heat.

"Whether we consider the injuries and plunder which our commerce is suffering (50 million dollars) or the affront to our national independence and dignity, in the rejection of our envoys, or whether we think on the oppression, ruin and final destruction of all free people, through this military government, everywhere we recognize the need to arm ourselves with a strength and zeal, equal to the dangers with which we are threatened. Continued patience and submission will not deliver

us, any more than submission delivered Venice or others. Submission is degrading. Rather than allow herself to be insulted to this degree, rather than having her freedom and independence trodden under foot, every American, including myself though old, will pour out the last drop of blood in his veins.

"They censure Mr. Adams for haste in deeds and excessive boldness in words; from the moment that I left the administration, I have not written a word to Mr. Adams [Washington did write four days later] nor have I yet received a word from him except the despatches which we have seen in our papers; I do not know what are those other sources of information on which he acts: with all this I am certain, as a reasonable and honest person and as a good American, that he cannot do other than he does. In his place, I would perhaps be less vehement in expression but I would prepare myself steadily and boldly in the same fashion."

The strong and noble feelings of this man pierced my heart with respect and emotion.

June 14. In the evening, for the last time, pretty Miss Custis sang and played on the harpsichord. The next day, having risen before the dawn, I walked for the last time about the green groves of Mount Vernon and looked out over the clear and beautiful Potomac river. Then, at six in the morning, with gratitude for the hospitable welcome and with sorrow, silent and unexpressed, I took my leave of the noble Washington, his worthy wife and the beautiful, good and kind Miss Custis. *

Niemcewicz had greatly pleased the family at Mount Vernon. He wrote a graceful letter of thanks from the "City of Washington." Washington's affectionate reply of June 18 said that "the pleasure this family derived from the favour of your company... could only be equaled by the regret we felt at parting with you." If his prayers for Poland's liberty had been answered, Niemcewicz would now be as happy under his own fig tree as the American people were. He hoped he would come again to Mount Vernon where they would try to show him attentions which would "alleviate the poignancy" of his feelings for Poland's tragedy. Washington thus indicated the tact and sympathy with which he and his family handled the despair gripping Niemcewicz after letters from Polish friends were delivered at Mount Vernon.

---

* Two translations exist from the original Polish, one by W. M. Kozlowski, the other by Metchie J. E. Budka. Both are used here, the latter more extensively. In neither is the English perfect, and each has received minor editing.

JULY 4, 1798

In the crisis years, 1775, 1787, and 1789, the nation turned, as a matter of course, to George Washington. President Adams in his June 22 answer to the invitation to stay at Mount Vernon, replied that Congress had authorized a great expansion in the army and he was faced with deciding whether to call on the old generals or to pull in "a younger set." Washington's name was worth more "than many an army." The secretary of war four days later asked if he would "accept the command of all our armies."

By chance the twenty-second anniversary of American independence turned out to be a hectic day for Washington. The nearest post office, Alexandria, was nine miles away. As president he had sent for letters on each post day but as a farmer he felt less need to do so. As a result the president's and secretary's letters did not reach him at Mount Vernon until July 3, a day when he was entertaining ten to dinner. With little time for reflection, he got up very early next morning to reply.

To Adams Washington wrote that when he left office, he had no idea there could ever be a threat of invasion but it seemed to be "reserved for intoxicated and lawless France... to slaughter its own citizens, and to disturb the peace of the World besides." He himself could not easily decide what he ought to do. In case of an "actual invasion by a formidable force, I certainly should not entrench myself under the cover of Age and retirement, if my services should be required by my country." Immediate preparations should be undertaken to repel invasion, if the government's information justified it. Yet he could not believe that the French would actually plan for an invasion "after such a uniform and unequivocal expression of the sense of the People, in all parts, to oppose them with their lives and fortunes."

Washington added that the "old set of Generals" would hardly be a suitable source of officers for an active army. Instead they should be chosen from the most "experienced and intelligent Officers of the late Army, without respect to Grade." The most important nominations would be in the general staff, and the heads of artillery, engineering, and hospitals.

To McHenry Washington wrote at greater length and with candor. He had entirely retired from public life; if he appeared once more therein, the opposition would denounce it as a "restless Act" by one who could not really leave power alone. He was convinced that no actual invasion would take place, even though French partisans in America had deluded the Directory into thinking that a show of force would lead to an uprising. The country might well want younger generals, particularly as the French always chose those "of juvenile years to lead their Armies" (Napoleon was twenty-eight). In addition, he was not himself convinced that his advanced age made it "advisable to commit so important a trust to my direction." He expanded further on the need for a good general staff. He added that the "pain" he would feel if, once more he had to accept a command, "cannot easily be expressed." He was prepared to help his country but only in case of an actual invasion or of knowledge of such "a design... as cannot be mistaken." Even then the country's call for his services had to be demonstrated to him "unequivocally." He would also have to be entirely free to select his staff.

Washington, having made his position clear, set off to celebrate Independence Day in Alexandria, in the uniform of general of the American revolutionary army. He arrived there at ten o'clock in the morning, presumably carrying with him the letters for mailing. He was escorted into town by troops and warmly cheered and greeted by the people in that strongly Federalist city. He watched the parades and celebrations. After attending Christ Church, he "dined in the Spring Gardens... with a large company of the Civil and Military of Fairfax County."

What he did not know was that the president, without awaiting his reply, had signed a commission, hastily ratified by the Senate, appointing George Washington "Lieutenant General and Commander-in-Chief of all the Armies raised or to be raised for the Service of the United States." In nominating him, the president reduced him a grade below the rank he held from 1775 to 1783.

The United States at the Close of the Federalist Period

FIFTEEN

COMMANDER IN CHIEF
OF THE ARMIES

J OHN ADAMS CONTINUED, in words, Washington's policy of building
the nation's strength as the surest means to peace, but his actions lagged
far behind. In nominating Washington to command, the president presumably intended to give France clear warning that the United States would
repel attack. For an extended time, however, he failed to produce the
expanded army, although required by law to do so. His unilateral decision to
send Washington's name to the Senate, without consulting anyone, annoyed
many of his supporters. Further dissension appeared when the Senate
attempted to restore Washington's previous rank. The president bluntly
rebuffed this by the statement that he was the constitutional commander in
chief of the armed forces.

Adams was aware of a move among the Federalists to make Hamilton commander of the army, if Washington refused, or second in line, if he accepted.
When it was apparent that the president would nominate Washington,
Hamilton wrote to him to express his willingness to be inspector general with
a line command. It is not clear to what extent Hamilton thereafter directly
engaged the support of Federalist senators but many put pressure on the secretaries of state and war to place him just below Washington. The first intimation of this reached Mount Vernon in July when Pickering informed
Washington that the president (who, with reason, mistrusted Hamilton)

appeared disinclined "to place Colo. Hamilton in what we think is his proper station, and that alone in which we suppose he will serve you: The Second to You; and Chief in your absence." Pickering said that even his political enemies "would repose more confidence in him than in any other military characters... The appointment of Colo. Hamilton... appears to me of such vast importance to the welfare of the country, that I am willing to risque any consequences of my frank and honest endeavours to secure it."

Washington replied at once that he did not know what the president thought but he himself certainly hoped Hamilton would be in the army. In his own mind, however, he wanted General Charles Cotesworth Pinckney as his second. "If the French should be so mad as openly and formidably to invade these United States... I conceive there can hardly be two opinions respecting their Plan, and that their operations will commence in the Southern quarter 1. because it is the weakest 2. because they will expect, from the tenor of the debates in Congress, to find more friends there 3. because there can be no doubt of their arming our own Negroes against us and 4. because they will be more contiguous to their Islands, and to Louisiana, if they should be possessed thereof, which they will be, if they can." He continued:

> *If these premises are just, the inference I am going to draw, from placing Colo. Hamilton over General Pinckney, is natural and obvious. The latter is an officer of high military repute; fond of the Profession, spirited, active and judicious; and much advanced in the estimation of the Public by his late Conduct as Minister and envoy at Paris. With these pretensions and being senior to Colo. Hamilton, he will not, I am morally certain, accept a junior appointment... His connections are numerous, powerful and more influential than any other in the three Southern States.*

Washington's reply was mailed in Alexandria by the coachman, who had been ordered to pick up the arriving James McHenry, secretary of war. McHenry, sent by Adams to Mount Vernon to deliver his letter and commission, proceeded to press on Washington, not the president's views, but those of Hamilton, Pickering, and himself. With Adams' letter, he also carried one from Hamilton which warned Washington that Adams knew little of military policy. The president believed in "routine [seniority,]" whereas active and energetic officers were needed for the new army. As if to confirm Hamilton's statements, Adams suggested as the order of senior officers: "Lincoln, Morgan, Knox, Hamilton, Gates, Pinckney, Lee, Carrington, Hand, Muhlenberg, Dayton, Burr, Brooks, Cobb, Smith."

The list was notable for its military ineptness and general tactlessness. Lincoln and Morgan were too old at sixty-five and sixty-four. The former, never a very competent general, seems to have been placed there because he was a Massachusetts man and a friend of Adams. Morgan was neither qualified for the second post nor was he in good health. He had, however, warmly supported Adams as a Federalist congressman from Virginia. Knox, younger but much more experienced than the first two, was placed third. Hamilton was well down the list. Two old enemies of Washington, Gates and Burr, were included. The last man, William Smith, was Adams' rather disreputable son-in-law, who had once been a French agent.

No record has been found of the discussions which took place between Washington and McHenry from July 11 to 14. An approximation can be deduced from what Washington wrote before and after the meeting. It is clear that the president's hasty action had placed him in a difficult position. If Washington refused his commission, it would be embarrassing for the president; if he accepted, he would be accused by the Democrats of once more wanting power. What he apparently did was to ask McHenry to inform the president of his many objections to serving. If he were to accept, it was to be clearly understood that he was not to be called to active service, except in a national emergency. He also had to have senior officers of judgment on whom he could fully rely. He emphasized that he did not want to interfere with the president's prerogatives of appointment but that none should receive a commission unless the commanding general found him suitable. In a memorandum which he gave McHenry, Washington suggested that there should be no hurry in appointing the senior officers or in calling them to active duty. The first task was to establish possibilities by consulting with the proposed nominees, to see if they would be available in a crisis. Orally, and probably in writing, he expressed his preference for Pinckney as senior major general, with Hamilton as inspector general and Knox as third major general. If any of the three declined, Washington's next choice was Henry Lee. The most important task, for the moment, as Washington saw it, was to commission recruiting officers to enlist men and field and company officers to train them.

In further work with McHenry, Washington provided from memory the names of more than fifty men in ten states, whom he considered as good officer material. He also suggested his preference for Edward Hand as adjutant general, Edward Carrington as quartermaster general, and Dr. James Craik as director of hospitals.

The precise nature of what McHenry advised the president on his return to Philadelphia cannot be established, but it is clear that Adams bears the responsibility for the next precipitous action. The House of Representatives had adjourned but the Senate waited for McHenry's return. Adams, contrary to Washington's advice, at once sent to the Senate for ratification the names of Hamilton as inspector general and major general, along with Pinckney and Knox as major generals. It is likely that McHenry failed to tell Adams, with sufficient precision, Washington's own preferences. None of the three officers was consulted on the matter.

In placing Hamilton first on the list, Adams clearly thought, and said so afterwards, that this did not give him a line command. McHenry and Pickering, on the other hand, believed that the order determined respective ranks. Clearly many in the Senate also thought so, for, as Knox later reported to Washington, voices were raised there in protest against his low seniority. Knox also wrote that the Senate was thereupon informed, presumably by the war office, that this had been Washington's choice and there could be no change. Adams added two major generals, Henry Lee and Edward Hand, to the list. He ignored Washington's request to make the latter his adjutant general and substituted his own son-in-law, William Smith.

In the meantime, Washington, not expecting Adams' action, wrote to Hamilton to explain candidly why he preferred Pinckney as his number two man. In any case, as he pointed out, the prerogative of choice rested with the president. The good of the country was all that mattered, and he himself wished that either Pinckney or Hamilton had been chosen in his stead. Two days later, Washington wrote to Knox. He said that he had intimations from Congress and the cabinet that they preferred Hamilton to all others for second in command. He himself, for the reasons he had given McHenry and Hamilton, preferred Pinckney. He hoped that the only contention among all would not be about rank but as to who would serve with the greatest zeal. He noted that he had discussed everything with the secretary of war, who would convey his views to the president for decision.

Hamilton's reply greatly surprised Washington, for he disparaged Pinckney and said he would not serve under him; it was too great a sacrifice. Hamilton also blasted McHenry as unfit for his office. The same post brought a long cry of outrage from Knox. This included a flat refusal to serve under either Hamilton or Pinckney. He said that he should have been "previously consulted on an arrangement in which my feelings and happiness have been so much wounded; or that I should not have been dragged forth to public view at all, to make the comparison so conspicuously odious." He was ready to shed his last drop of blood for the country but it would be a final touch of malignant irony if he were excluded from service by "a constant sense of public insult and injury." He had always held a high sense of friendship for Washington and believed that he stood well in his opinion, as friend and military man. Now he thought he had passed twenty years in "perfect delusion." While he had no official notifications from the secretary of war, his answer would be negative.

The president and McHenry had thus placed Washington in an extraordinarily difficult position. Washington had not wanted to serve at all, feeling that the place should go to "younger" men. He had been appointed without his knowledge or consent. Washington had been conspicuously reduced a grade. He had asked McHenry to see to it that no general officer was nominated until the main persons concerned had met with the president in Philadelphia. The army commander in chief now had two highly aggrieved men on his hands. Hamilton was furious with McHenry. He was soon to be equally so with Adams, when he found the president considered him number three on the list. Washington could not explain his own position to Knox without criticizing the president.

On August 9 Washington wrote to both Hamilton and to Knox. He expressed agreement with the former that McHenry had not shown capacity for his office. He had not received a single word as to the status of the army, nor what action had been taken since he had gone back to Philadelphia. He made no mention of Hamilton's position nor of his unwillingness to serve under Pinckney, knowing that nothing would keep Hamilton out. He sent him a copy of Knox's letter and his reply.

Washington wrote a very careful letter to his old artillery chief. Without in any way criticizing the president, he drafted it in a manner to enable Knox, if he read carefully between the lines, to understand what had happened. He himself, he wrote, had been hastily nominated without advance notice and it had been equally impossible for him to consult Knox. As for Hamilton, the appointment had been represented to him as Congress' most earnest wish, but it had not been made by him. He wanted all three to serve with equal heart. He did not think that New England should regard it as an outrage to have the "third" major general. All officers of that grade were of equal stature. Massachusetts, Knox's state, alone was to have two of the five major generals. He assured Knox that his friendship for him was as "warm and sincere" as ever.

The tempest grew worse when Knox went to see the president in Quincy, prior to receiving Washington's letters. There appears to be no record of their conversation but Knox was not in an amiable mood and Adams was not General Washington. The interview might have been worse for Adams, had Knox known that Adams had also placed him third in seniority. It is probable that Knox followed more or less the same argument he used with Washington. His previous rank and long service entitled him to far better treatment, and he should not be ordered to serve under officers, previously his juniors. The argument which carried most weight with Adams was that New England had been humiliated. That area would doubtless furnish a large proportion of the needed troops, but they were to have only a "third" major general.

During this period, Abigail Adams, the president's wife, was critically ill. Adams wrote that his "depression and anxiety" rendered him scarcely fit to think or to handle problems. Knox's agitation threw Adams into further loss of judgment. On August 14 the president wrote the secretary of war: "You may depend upon it, the five New England states will not patiently submit to the humiliation that has been meditated for them." General Knox was legally entitled to be first and Pinckney to be second. Hamilton must therefore be third. If General Washington would consent to this arrangement, the officers could be called to service.

McHenry was appalled by the president's letter. He had not adequately informed Adams of Washington's views: a) he preferred Pinckney, for urgent military and political considerations but b) the choice was up to the president. McHenry replied, with too little regard for the truth, that "the order of ranking proceeded originally and exclusively from General Washington." Adams answered that General Washington could have the presidency if he wished, but so long as he held the office, he would make the decisions. He had determined the order, and he did not intend to change. There had already been too many "intrigues" in the matter. McHenry protested against this last remark. Adams' reply indicated that he had guessed a good portion of the truth: "I have suspected that extraordinary pains were taken to impress upon your mind that the public opinion and the unanimous wish of the Federalists, was that General Hamilton might be first and even commander-in-chief; that you might express this opinion to General Washington more forcibly than I should have done and that this determined him to make the arrangement as he did." The arrangement, in fact, was McHenry's own.

The announcement that General Washington was once again commander of the army brought with it the usual upsurge in mail to Mount Vernon. Volunteers wanted to go immediately into service, many of them on Washington's staff. It was particularly gratifying to Washington to hear from old comrades or their sons: Tallmadge, Marshall, Carroll, Cadwalader, Nelson, and Izard. With the single exception of William Heth, he declined to consider any person as an aide until he entered on active duty.

Martha Washington and Nelly Custis were asked to be sponsors of the Alexandria regiments, which brought an amusing correspondence with the secretary of war. Washington wrote him on July 27:

> *The Greyheads of Alexandria, pretty numerous it seems, and composed of all the respectable old People of the place; having formed themselves into a Company [the Silver Greys] for the defense of the Town and its Vicinity, are in want of Colours: and it being intimated that the Presentation of them by Mrs. Washington would be*

flattering to them; I take the liberty of requesting the favour of you to have them made and sent to me. Handsome but not more expensive than becomes Republicans (but not Bachite Republicans) is required. If you think a Motto would be proper, the choice of one 'chaste and unassuming,' is left to your own judgment. Send the cost and the money shall be remitted by Yours always…

Nelly selected "Conquer or die" as the words for her volunteers' banner. McHenry told her that it was a pretty bloody motto for a young lady to choose. When her standard did not arrive from Philadelphia, Nelly grew impatient. She sent the secretary a letter, which was undoubtedly drafted by her "Grampa" who had used the same pun during the revolution. In it she said: "My troop are all uniformed and waiting for that Standard, which they are determined to defend with a bravery never excelled… I am afraid their patience (which is already *threadbare*) will be entirely *worn out*… Not having 'Conquer or Die' before their eyes… their patriotic ardor may be exchanged for a resolution… that it is better to stay at home."

WASHINGTON'S ILLNESS

Washington's request to have Tobias Lear commissioned as his aide, secretary, and lieutenant colonel took much time to win approval. It went to McHenry in Philadelphia who, in turn, had to forward it to the president in Quincy. Before this authorization "at length" reached Mount Vernon, the badly over-worked general had fallen into a critical illness. Washington on August 5 esti-mated his weight at 210 pounds, practically unchanged from the days he and his generals weighed themselves, fifteen years before. A few weeks later he was down to 190 pounds.

On August 27 Washington described the initial stages of his sickness to his nephew, Bushrod: "On the 18th at night I was seized with a [malarial] fever, of which I took little notice until the 21st; when I was obliged to call for the aid of Medicine; and with difficulty a remission thereof was so far effected, as to dose me all night on Thursday, with bark [quinine] which has stopped it, and weakness only remaining, will soon wear off, as my appetite is returning."

On August 30 Washington informed Lear that his appointment had been confirmed. He added that the secretary of war "having thrown a mass of Papers upon me which I have not looked into… I should be glad if you would now come and take your station. Yours always and affectionately." On September 3 he wrote McHenry that the War Department could not expect him to be as active as "you probably have counted on." His illness had made him "too much debilitated to attend much to business." Nonetheless he added several pages on the problems of the southern military district. Included were numerous directives and questions. On September 14 he informed Alexander Spotswood that he was down twenty pounds but his fever had gone and not returned. "I am recovering my flesh fast, nearly a pound and a half a day; at which rate if I should hold it for a twelve Month I shall be an overmatch for Major Willis."

General Washington increasingly complained of the difficult position in which he had been placed. The president was in Quincy for months, while the government drifted and decisions on the army command were changed and shifted. The cabinet tended to look to Washington for leadership but he was not the president and could not fill the vacuum. In turn the secretary of war was proving ineffectual and giving him no information. Though still weak, he wrote to McHenry on September 14:

No plan is yet decided on that I can discover for recruiting the augmented force, or even for appointing the officers therefor.

... It is for the Executive to account for this delay. Sufficient it is for me to regret, and I do regret it, sorely; because that spirit and enthusiasm which was inspired by the Dispatches from our Envoys... are evaporating fast... The law passed before the middle of July, was positive; and the middle of September has produced no fruit from it. This to me, is inconceivable.

I must once more, my dear McHenry, request that your correspondence with me, may be more full and communicative. You have a great deal of business I must acknowledge; but I scruple not to add, at the same time, that much of the important and interesting part of it will be transacted with the Commander in chief of the Armies of the U. States, from whom there ought to be no concealment or want of information. Short letters, therefore, taking no notice of suggestions or queries, are unsatisfactory and distressing. Considering the light in which I think my sacrifices have placed me, I should expect more attention from the Secretary of War, but from Mr. McHenry, as a friend and Coadjutor, I certainly shall look for it. Compare then my letter to you of the 3d inst., which I wrote in much pain, from the debilitated state into which the fever had thrown me, with your acknowledgment thereof dated the 7th, and judge yourself whether I could derive any satisfaction therefrom, on the score of business... Nor to this moment... and my asking the question in direct terms, what there was in the Report of Colo. North's nomination to the Office of Adjutant General, has there been the least notice taken of the matter since.

I will defer saying anything on the President's new arrangement of the three Major Generals until you have communicated the result of Colo. Hamilton's answer to me.

But in the name of the Army, what could have induced the nomination of Walton White to the rank of Brigadier... I formerly asked the same question with respect to Severe [Sevier] to which no reply was made.

White's name was placed in the list of Field Officers... merely as one that might be considered in that grade, when the general organization came on; but I had no idea when you left this place, that General Officers would be appointed at the time they were, for the Provisional Army... Of all the characters in the Revolutionary Army, I believe one more obnoxious to the Officers who composed it could not have been hit upon for a Genl. Officer than White, especially among those to the Southward, where he was best known, and celebrated for nothing but frivolity, dress, empty show, and something worse; in short for being a notorious [Liar]... As to [Sevier] the only exploit I ever heard of... was the murder of Indians.

What measures, if any, are pursuing, to provide Small Arms, I know not;... If any other article of foreign manufacture are needed, not a moment is to be lost in the Importation...

On September 16 Washington received from McHenry the determination the president had made with respect to the rankings of the three major generals. Washington replied that since this was only a private letter, he could take no action. He was informed that the cabinet would make a respectful representation to the president. Washington was not sure the president would change his mind and, therefore, he was prepared to return his commission. McHenry, much alarmed, wrote to Adams, who replied with a brief note to the effect that he had signed the three commissions on September 30. This action gave no one priority and settled nothing.

As soon as Washington heard that the president knew of his reactions, he wrote, September 25, a long, dignified, and respectful letter to Adams. He realized that what he had to say was "delicate." He had no desire whatever to lessen the power of the president nor to increase his own. Nonetheless his appointment to the command had placed him in a difficult position. He had not wanted it and accepted with "sorrow at being drawn from my retirement." He had explicitly declared to the secretary of war his express condition that the nominations of general officers must have his concurrence.

It had been Washington's understanding, when McHenry left Mount Vernon, that no general officers were to be nominated for some time.

Nonetheless the names of three officers had been sent to the Senate, in order, Hamilton, Pinckney, and Knox, and it was the Senate's understanding that this was the president's choice and that their commissions would so issue. Now Adams had reversed the first and last. The president had, further, nominated five brigadiers, one of whom had no military experience and another whose appointment had given "the greatest disgust." While Washington made no direct mention of the fact that Adams had appointed his own son-in-law as adjutant general, he noted that two nominations had gone forward without the least intimation to him. He would hope that the president would understand that all he aimed at in finding the ablest coadjutors, was the public good. If war broke out with France, conditions would be entirely different than in the revolution. From 1775 to 1781, the country had to buy time until it could train troops. Now the United States would have to move immediately to the attack, to prevent the French from gaining any foothold in the country. They would probably aim at the South because there were so many disaffected persons there and the area was near their Caribbean Islands. Working with McHenry, he had suggested certain arrangements with respect to the generals, hoping that everyone could meet with the president in Philadelphia, before final arrangements were made. He was subsequently presented with an accomplished fact. He had learned from many New England congressmen that they preferred Hamilton to Knox. The president had the prerogative of making any appointments he wished but he now wanted to change everything.

Washington further explained to Adams that he had especially wanted General Pinckney, for reasons he had previously given in detail to the secretary of war. He had never expected General Knox to make so many difficulties. Washington then pointed out that four months had gone by and there had not been a single recruit for the army nor any battalion officer appointed. If France were to attack the United States, he would have to meet veterans "with Militia or raw recruits; the consequence of which is not difficult to conceive or foretell." He concluded: "I have addressed you, Sir, with openness and candour, and I hope with respect, requesting to be informed whether your determination to reverse the order of the three Major Generals is final, and whether you mean to appoint another Adjutant General, without my consideration."

The president replied that any determination of ranks desired by Washington would be supported by him. He was instructing the secretary of war to commission whomever General Washington wished as adjutant general. Although the battle was thus technically over, the president thereafter displayed little enthusiasm for the army or for General Hamilton and Secretary McHenry.

The only happy note in the commotion was struck by General Pinckney. When Washington heard that Pinckney had reached New York, he wrote to Pickering, October 18, that he hoped "he will not play the second part of the difficulty created by General Knox." General Pinckney turned out to be the perfect southern gentleman. He said that he was delighted with the choice of Hamilton and would be pleased to serve under him. He intimated to General Knox that he would be glad to give way to him, so that he could be second. General Knox had since stated that he would not serve under Pinckney and he could not repeat the offer. Nevertheless if the president wished to change the ranks, he would neither be dissatisfied nor resign. Washington was highly pleased to find one general who placed his country first.

When the secretary of war asked Washington to attend a November conference of the senior generals, probably to be held in Trenton because of a renewed outbreak of yellow fever in Philadelphia, he replied on October 21:

> *I hardly think it will be in my power to attend... 1st because I am yet in a convalescent state (although perfectly recovered of the fever) so far at least as to avoid exposure and consequent Colds, 2dly, My Secretary (Mr. Lear) had had a severe fever, and is now very low... and 3dly, and principally, because I see no definitive ground to proceed upon... from anything that has hitherto appeared...*

> *If General Pinckney could be prevailed upon to remain with you, and there was a moral certainty of meeting Generals Hamilton and Knox, I would, maugre the inconveniences and hazard I might run, attempt to join them for the valuable purpose of projecting a Plan in concert with you...*

At the same time he wrote to Knox, who offered to serve as his aide, to plead for his reconsideration: "We shall have either no War or a severe contest with France; in either case, if you will allow me to express my opinion, this is the most eligible time for you to come forward. In the first case to assist with your council and aid in making judicious provisions and arrangements to avert it. In the other case, to share in the glory of defending your Country; and by making all secondary considerations yield to that great and primary object, display a mind superior to embarrassing punctilios, at so critical a moment as the present." Knox declined his commission, and Henry Lee became the third ranking major general of the American army.

VIRGINIA AND KENTUCKY RESOLVES

There was no mistaking the man Washington had in mind when he wrote to Colonel William Heth on July 18: "I think with you that all secret enemies to the peace and happiness of this Country should be unmasked, for it is better to meet two enemies in the open field than one coward behind the curtain." Generals Washington and Lee held similar views, for the latter wrote: "The real enemies of the Republic are Vice-President Jefferson and his henchmen. Like rodents they gnaw at the very foundations of our system of government at a time when our liberty itself is in peril."

Well hidden behind a protective curtain of secrecy, Jefferson was at work that summer, to see that his views would prevail or the Union perish. Making Wilson Nicholas his confidant, he drew up a series of resolutions designed to establish the states as superior to the federal government. Nullification of the federal laws was his first aim. Should this fail then it logically followed that a state could secede, even if this meant civil war and bloodshed. Jefferson's correspondence clearly indicated that he was prepared to go to the ultimate extreme of 1861. Nowhere in the wording does such a concept as "the people of the United States" appear. Instead, the Constitution is defined as a compact among states, who assigned certain defined powers to the general government, "reserving, each state to itself, the residuary mass of right to their own self-government... Whensoever the General Government assumes undelegated powers, its acts are unauthoritative, void and of no force." The state government alone could act for its citizens and not the people within the state.

Jefferson declared that the first unconstitutional act passed by Congress was "to punish frauds committed on the banks of the U.S." This act was void and of no force. The second was the sedition act which was also invalid. The third was control of alien immigration and emigration. Only the states had the right to admit or eject persons, not the national government. Fourth, "the power... to pay the debt and provide for the common defense and welfare... and to make all laws necessary" thereto, although in the Constitution, did not mean what the Constitution said. The federal government did not possess such rights. While, Jefferson continued, the people chose their representatives and had the right to change them this was not a sufficient defense for the Constitution. Where their representatives went beyond it, each state legislature had the right "to nullify of their own authority," whatever act had been passed by the people of the United States, in Congress assembled. The states, in communication with each other, were the sole authority "to judge in the last resort of the powers exercised" in the Constitution. Congress was a mere creature of a pact formed by the states.

The American people had already voted unconstitutional acts which were driving "these states into revolution and blood." In cooperation with their sister states, Virginia and Kentucky therefore declared "these acts void and of no force, and will each take measures of its own for providing that neither these acts, nor any others of the General Government, not plainly and intentionally authorized by the Constitution shall be exercised within their respective territories."

Although the resolves which Jefferson forwarded to Kentucky were modified, and references to war and bloodshed were stricken out, some even stronger language was used in the actual resolutions which passed the Kentucky legislature and were signed by the governor on November 16. Similar but more restrained resolves, prepared by Madison for the Virginia legislature, introduced the long-lived but ineffective doctrine of "interposition." So effectively did Jefferson conceal his part in the Kentucky action that it was to be nearly sixty years before his original words saw print. If he expected other states to swallow his constitutional line, he was disappointed. None joined Kentucky and Virginia. Eight legislatures denounced the resolves in varying degrees of horror. Maryland, as usual, was the most outspoken of all.

TO PHILADELPHIA

By the time General Washington started for his conference, frosts had killed the yellow-fever–bearing mosquitoes and the talks were reset for the national capital. Not yet fully recovered, Washington set out with Lear from Mount Vernon on November 5. Troops escorted him into Alexandria where a sixteen-gun salute was fired. Five Georgetown men carried him by yawl to their city, which rendered him honors. The Georgetown cavalry escorted him to Washington. There, having some business to transact, he stayed the night with his wife's granddaughter.

Baltimore turned out a cavalry escort, as well as the huge throngs which always greeted him when he passed through the city. As he proceeded north, he had another triumphant procession but not as fervid as he had experienced in going to the presidency. Once again the Philadelphia Light Horse escorted Washington into the capital and deposited him at his boarding house. Church bells rang as they had so often done when he came to the city. For the next three days all Philadelphia seems to have called on him, for he recorded in his diary that he had spent the time "receiving many visits."

On November 13 Washington had one unwelcome visitor when the Reverend Dr. Blackwell was announced. When he came downstairs, he found that he had been tricked; standing with Blackwell was George Logan, the self-appointed Jeffersonian emissary to France. Washington recognized him but failed to acknowledge his presence because he had used a cover in attempting to talk to him. Logan mentioned his own name as if it were not well known. Washington subsequently wrote that he offered Dr. Blackwell a chair, "the other took a seat at the same time. I addressed all my conversation to Dr. Blackwell, the other all his to me. I only gave negative or affirmative answers, as laconically as I could, excepting asking how Mrs. Logan did." When Blackwell rose to take his leave, Washington got up and went to the door, expecting Logan to follow. The latter stayed, however, and rambled on about meeting Lafayette, which "he had mentioned before... As I wished to get quit of him, I remained standing and showed the utmost inattention to what he was saying." When Logan mentioned that the purpose of his trip to France had been to improve relations, "this drew my attention more pointedly to what he was saying and induced me to remark that there was something very singular in this." Washington's comments grew sharper:

> *That he who could be viewed as a private character; unarmed with proper powers; and presumtively unknown in France; should suppose he could effect what these gentlemen of the first responsibility in our country, specially charged under the authority of the Government, were unable to do. With this observation, he seemed a little confounded; but recovering, said that not more than five persons had any knowledge of his going; that he was furnished by Mr. Jefferson and Mr. McKean with certificates of his citizenship. That Mr. Merlin, President of the Directory of France had discovered the greatest desire that France and America should be on the best terms. I answered that he was more fortunate than our Envoys, for they could neither be received nor heard by Mr. Merlin or the Directory. That if the Powers of France were serious... they [could] repeal the obnoxious arrets by which the commerce and Rights of the country had been invaded... A conduct like this would speak more forcibly than words... He said that the directory was apprehensive that this Country... was not well disposed towards France... I asked what better evidence could be given in refutation of this opinion, than its long suffering of the outrageous conduct of the Nation towards the U States. He said that the attempt at a Coalition of European Powers against France would come to nothing; that the Directory were under no apprehensions... and that Great Britain would have to contend alone; insinuating, as I conceived his object at the time to be, that we should be involved in a dangerous situation if we persisted in our hostile appearances. To this I finally replied that we were driven to these measures in self defense and asked him if the Directory looked upon us as worms; and not even allowed to turn when trod upon?... I hoped the*

Spirit of the country would never suffer itself to be injured with impunity by any
nation under the sun...

Awaiting Washington in Philadelphia was a memorandum from McHenry
proposing conferences with the secretaries of war and treasury but leaving the
subjects vague. Washington asked him to be more explicit so that he could
study the topics to be discussed. He thought it best they provide written data,
in advance for him to review. He added: "I find also that the documents
referred to in your letter of the 10st inst. did not accompany it. As these will
be necessary in forming an opinion... I must beg you to furnish me with them
without delay." He noted that six papers on the major dispositions of the
troops, artillery, and stores of the United States were missing as enclosures.

Washington did not comment on the long absence of the president, nor
did he make any further written remarks on the poor preparation of the War
Department for the conference. His diary records are scanty, indicating only
where he dined. It is not possible to determine when serious talks got under
way but it can be surmised that it was not at an early date. Not until the first
two weeks in December was there really hard work, with Washington confer-
ring from ten in the morning until late at night. During this period he
accepted no dinner invitations.

On December 8 the president delivered his annual address to Congress on
the state of the union. General Washington attended, flanked by Generals
Hamilton and Pinckney, as well as Colonel Lear. Adams hinted that he thought
France was moving towards a conciliatory policy, yet her warlike acts continued.
Nothing should cause the United States "to change or relax our measures of
defense. On the contrary, to extend and invigorate them is our true policy." The
United States still desired peace "but to send another emissary without more
definite assurances that he would be received would be an act of humiliation to
which the United States ought not to submit." Adams called for an increase in
the navy which had already done able service in protecting American commerce. He added a point at which Washington might well have raised an eye-
brow: "Various circumstances have concurred to delay the execution of the law
for augmenting the military establishment, among these the desire of obtaining
the fullest information to direct the best selection of officers. As this object will
now be speedily accomplished, it is expected that the raising and organizing of
the troops will proceed without obstacle and with effect."

Washington's final work consisted of two documents, more than 8,000 words
long, which he gave the secretary of war on December 13. He transmitted them
with a note: "I am really ashamed to offer the letters... with so many erasures,
etc., but it was not to be avoided unless I had remained so much longer as to

have allowed [Lear] time to copy the whole over again… My impatience to be on my return homewards on account of the Season—the Roads—and more especially the passage of the Susquehanna—would not admit of this."

Although his time had been short, Washington produced two of his most incisive state papers. After reviewing the problem of allocating officers to the states, he analyzed the whole of American relations with Europe and the compelling need for a defense system that would assure peace or, if France pushed to an extreme, a quick victory in war:

The law for augmenting the army is peremptory in it provisions… The voluntary suspension of execution could not be justified but by considerations of decisive cogency. The existence of any such considerations is unknown.

Nothing has been communicated respecting our foreign relations to induce the opinion that there has been any change… as to external danger, which dictates an abandonment of the policy of the law… It need not be examined how far it may be at any time prudent to relinquish measures of security… merely because there are probable symptoms of approaching accommodation… [These] may be ascribed to the measures of vigour adopted by the Government; and may be frustrated by a relaxation in those measures, affording an argument of weakness and irresolution… Hitherto nothing is discoverable in the conduct of France which ought to change or relax our measures of defense…

Though it may be true that some late occurrences have rendered the prospect of invasion by France less probable or more remote… Yet, duly considering the rapid vicissitudes of political and military events… it can never be wise to vary our measures of security with the continually varying aspect of European affairs… Standing, as it were, in the midst of falling empires, it should be our aim to assume a station and attitude, which will prevent us from being overwhelmed in their ruins…

It has been very properly the policy of our Government to cultivate peace. But in contemplating the possibility of our being driven to unqualified War, it will be wise to anticipate that frequently the most effectual way to defend is to attack. There may be imagined instances of very great moment to the permanent interests of this Country, which would certainly require a disciplined force. To raise and prepare such a force will always be a work of considerable time…

The sound conclusion, viewing the subject in every light, is conceived to be that no unavoidable delay ought to be incurred in appointing the whole of the Officers and raising the whole of the men, provided for by the act… It cannot be relied upon that troops will be raised and disciplined in less than a year. What may not another year produce? Happy will it be for us if we have so much time for preparation and ill-judged indeed if we do not make the most of it.

The general then made specific recommendations. He proposed that all officers hitherto selected be called immediately into active service and ordered to recruiting duty. General Washington then outlined a needed reorganization of the United States army. An engineer should report on all Great Lakes posts. The western army needed reinforcements. Artillery was to be located in the West and at eleven named seaports on the Atlantic. He selected five major points for new recruiting depots, as far away as possible from the larger cities. The army magazines were to be placed at three principal points, Springfield, Harpers Ferry, and Rocky Mount, as central to the three subdivisions of the country. He added four other towns, Pittsburgh, West Point, Trenton, and Fayetteville, for substations. He entered into detail on the organization of the infantry and cavalry regiments, clothing for the men (remarking there did not seem to be any), and rations. Washington noted how much the French armies depended on their artillery and engineers. He suggested numerous methods to improve the deficiencies of the American army in this regard.

On December 14, for the last time, General Washington left Philadelphia for home. In Chester that night he remembered that he had asked the secretary of war for the appointment of Washington Custis, as a cornet in Lawrence Lewis' regiment. He wrote the secretary to be sure to make no public announcement, until he had the approval of Mrs. Washington and Mrs. Stuart. The following day, held from crossing the Susquehanna by ice and winds, he turned to weightier matters. He informed McHenry that he intended to adhere to his original decision not to take command unless there were an emergency. The two senior officers could do the main work. He would like to see all southern states up to the Potomac under the command of Pinckney, aided by Wilkinson in Tennessee, and William Washington in South Carolina and Georgia. In the North Hamilton would be in immediate command, as well as in charge of the national recruiting drive. On December 19 Washington reached Washington, where he passed the night. He arrived at Mount Vernon the next day.

During Washington's stay in Philadelphia the most conspicuous absentee was the vice-president of the United States. He was expected, in his official station, to be present for the opening of Congress on December 3. Not daring to see General Washington in person, he remained in Charlottesville. On the day that Washington reached Washington, Thomas Jefferson started for the national capital, where he arrived three-and-a-half weeks late.

POLITICS

Although John Adams was to be negligent in carrying out his military recommendations, the general remained his most important political bulwark. Washington had occupied public offices almost continuously for fifty years. He had never been a politician on a party basis, but the attitude of many Virginians towards the federal government brought him into active political work. Aside from bandying doctrines of nullification and secession, Virginia had gone so far as to decree that no member of the state legislature could hold a post in the federal government. John Taylor, a Virginia state senator, who was nominated to a majority in the dragoons, explained to Washington his difficulty of choice. Washington strongly advised him to stay in the Senate where, as a Federalist, he was much more urgently needed.

From the middle of 1798 Washington actively urged the ablest Virginians to seek elective federal and state office. He well remembered that only one of the twenty-one Virginia senators and representatives supported his efforts to secure peace with Great Britain. His first aim was to capture a majority of the state delegation in the House of Representatives, as well as to increase Federalist representation in Virginia's legislature. In this work, the Lee brothers rallied to him, as did John Marshall, John Nicholas of Charlottesville, Daniel Morgan, and the old libertarian, Patrick Henry. Washington expressed his general political and military concerns to Bartholomew Dandridge. The latter, secretary to the American minister at The Hague, was offered an appointment in London as well as a captaincy in the army. Washington wrote that the choice between the diplomatic and military services had to be made by him:

Both are attended with uncertainties… The augmented Corps, in which you are appointed, are by Law, to exist no longer than the dispute with France shall continue; but how long this will continue, will require more wisdom than I possess to foretell; and you know, without information from me, what a bug-bear a standing Army (as a few regiments with us are called, though liable to be disbanded at any moment, by withholding the application for their support) is, in the eyes of all those who are continually raising Spectres and Hobgoblins, to affrighten themselves and to alarm the People: and how certain it is that ours (with their consent) will not exist a moment longer than it can be avoided by their endeavors; whether the cause which gives rise to it ceases, or not…

Lawrence Lewis is appointed Captn. in the Corps of light Dragoons… Washington Custis is made Cornet in Lewis's troops for it was found unpracticable to keep him longer at College... so great was his aversion to study... The Army, generally, will be very respectably officered.

The General Assembly of this State is in Session; and, by accounts of its proceedings, running into every kind of opposition to the measures of the General government, and into all the extravagant resolutions, which folly can devise...

Patrick Henry had declined the highest appointive offices in the federal government and had refused re-election as governor of Virginia. His political days, he often said, were finished forever. George Washington's appeal of January 15, 1799, changed his mind:

It would be a waste of time, to attempt to bring to the view of a person of your observation and discernment, the endeavors of a certain party among us, to disquiet the Public mind... with unfounded alarms...

Unfortunately, and extremely do I regret it, the State of Virginia has taken the lead in this opposition...

It has been said that the great mass of the Citizens of the State are well affected... to the General Government and the Union; and I am willing to believe it, nay do believe it: but how is this to be reconciled with their suffrages... both to Congress and their State Legislature...

One of the reasons assigned is, that the most respectable and best qualified characters amongst us, will not come forward...

Vain will it be to look for Peace and happiness, or for the security of liberty or property, if Civil discord should ensue; and what else can result from the policy of those among us who, by all the means in their power, are driving matters to extremity...

I come now, my good Sir, to the object of my letter, which is to express a hope, and an earnest wish, that you would come forward at the ensuing Elections (if not for Congress, which you may think would take you too long from home) as a candidate... in the General Assembly...

With great and very sincere regard and respect...

Henry did agree to run for the assembly and thereby gained Jefferson's malignant hatred. At one point Washington felt sure that he would win eleven of the nineteen Virginia seats in the House of Representatives. In the end eight Federalists were elected. In three additional districts, the election was so close as to give the Jeffersonians a scare. John Marshall became representative from Richmond and Henry Lee from the district which covered Washington's own Fairfax County. Lee's brother, Richard Bland, was elected as Fairfax delegate to the assembly at Richmond. Although disappointed at not attaining a majority, Washington had achieved a remarkable comeback for the national party, in the state where opposition was greatest.

Shortly after receiving news of Patrick Henry's defection, Jefferson remarked to Benjamin Rush in Philadelphia that only two men stood between him and the presidency: George Washington and Patrick Henry. Their deaths would make his election "*speedy* as well as *certain.*" On March 12, 1801, Rush reminded Jefferson of his grisly prophecy.

WASHINGTON'S BIRTHDAY

Lawrence Lewis did not accept his commission for reasons which Washington gave to the secretary of war: "The enclosed letter from Major Lawrence Lewis requires explanation and it is the purpose of this letter to give it. He had, it seems, been making overtures of Marriage to Miss Custis some time previous to the formation of the Augmented Corps... without any apparent impression, until she found he was arranged as a Captain in the Regiment of Light Dragoons, and was about to try his fortune in the Camp of Mars. This brought into activity those affections for him, which *before* she conceived were the result of friendship only. And I believe the condition of Marriage is, that he is to relinquish the field of Mars for the sport of Venus."

That year, 1799, when Washington was sixty-seven, he again had two attractive celebrations. Alexandria gave him "an elegant ball and supper" on the old style date, February 11. He was accompanied into town by three companies of dragoons who, with other troops, conducted maneuvers before the general.

Nelly Custis chose February 22 for her marriage, in special compliment to her stepgrandfather. The Reverend Thomas Davis of Alexandria appeared at Mount Vernon, in time for afternoon dinner. Washington's diary recorded that "Miss Custis was married about Candle light to Mr. Lawrence Lewis." Once again George and Martha Washington's blood relatives were united. Mount Vernon appears to have celebrated the event for an extended time. There were twelve guests for dinner on the 25th and eight more the following day. The bride's mother and three Stuart half-sisters and her sisters, Mrs. Lewis and Mrs. Peter, stayed at the mansion until March 3. It appears from the somewhat uncertain account in Washington's diary that another sister, Mrs. Law, was there for an even longer time. On March 5 the bride and groom went to Washington to spend a little over two weeks on their honeymoon.

The general, at sixty-seven, had more than enough to do, managing his extensive properties, keeping abreast of national and international politics, as well as the army, the inland navigation, and the city of Washington. He wrote McHenry on March 25 that he was still trying to get his affairs in order after his sixteen years' absence. "But this is not all, nor the worst, for being the Executor, the Administrator, and Trustee of and for other Estates, my greatest anxiety is to leave all these concerns in such a clear and distinct form, so that no reproach may attach itself to me, when I have taken my departure for the land of Spirits."

INLAND NAVIGATION

When Washington was twenty-two, his natural curiosity made him canoe down more than 170 miles of the Potomac. He began at a point just below Cumberland and continued within two miles of Great Falls, noting where channels might be cut or rocks dug out to permit boats to pass the falls and other obstacles to navigation. Forty-six years later, he was as keen as ever to see his early ideas move to completion.

On July 21 he wrote to Charles Carroll, the last to die of the Signers, hoping that all Potomac Company shareholders, including himself and Carroll, would attend the next meeting. He added:

> *Greatly is it to be regretted that an Undertaking productive of, or rather promising such immense advantages to the States of Maryland and Virginia… should be suffered to progress so limpingly, as this work has done for some years back.*

> *If this Navigation was completed, and it is susceptible of being so in a short time; and the Shenandoah opened… I would predict… that it would be found one of (if not) the most productive funds (with the least risk to the Stockholders) of any Legalized Institution in the United States…*

> *It might be as unjust as improper to censure the conduct of the Directors… but if the means can be obtained, I shall declare for having the residue of the Work executed by Contract…*

Washington attended the stockholders' meeting which prepared an appeal to

Maryland and Virginia for more capital funds. That night he spent with the Thomas Laws at their house near Jenkins Hill, atop of which the wing of Dr. Thornton's national capitol building was nearing completion.

On August 12 the general wrote to William Berkeley, treasurer of Virginia, to urge the state to come forward with financial help. "To dilate on the benefits which would result from improving the great *high way* which nature has marked out as the easiest and most direct communication with the Western World (maugre all the endeavours of Pennsylvania and New York to divert it into other Channels) would be a mere waste of time... But it must be acknowledged at the same time that habits and customs are not easily overcome. Consequently if the produce of the upper Ohio and the Lakes should settle in either of the channels above mentioned, it will require time as well as inconvenience, to bring it back to the course which nature has ordered... "

By December 1, Maryland, always more farsighted than Virginia, had subscribed to new funds for the canal. Washington wrote to Dr. Thornton: "I am glad to hear that the legislature of Maryland have acted favourably on the application made by the Potomac Company. Your information of this event is the first I had received. It is to be hoped that the Legislature of this State will 'go and do so likewise.' Neither would be backward in promoting this useful undertaking if the measure was impartially investigated and the welfare of the respective States duly considered."

The first part of the Potomac Company's work, the canal around the Great Falls, was completed in 1802. Other sections as far west as Harpers Ferry were finished a few years later. In 1828 Washington's organization was merged into the Chesapeake and Ohio Company, which, by 1850, had extended the canal from Georgetown as far as Cumberland. Thus George Washington's dream was completed 96 years after his canoe trip down the Potomac. Although never a profitable enterprise it served inland commerce for many years thereafter. Now part of the national park system, it is one of the most attractive of all monuments to the farseeing young colonel.

WASHINGTON, THE CAPITAL

Dr. William Thornton was a gifted and busy man. He was an inventor, painter, architect of the capitol, and commissioner of the territory of Columbia. In this last office, he worked night and day to get the city ready for the expected transfer of the government from Philadelphia in 1800. Dr. Thornton was also the physician who treated Tobias Lear as well as co-architect of the two houses which Washington ordered built on Capitol Hill. Washington admired, liked, and trusted Thornton and saw him frequently at Mount Vernon or in the federal city.

When Thornton queried him about the city's plan, Washington replied on June 1 that, since he had left the presidency, he had never intermeddled "in any public matter which did not immediately concern me." Thornton's question, however, seemed to refer to his own earlier directives "on which I presume my Letters were not as clear and explicit as it was my intention to be. I have no hesitation in declaring… that it has always been my invariable opinion, and remains still to be so, that no departure from the *Engraved* plan of the City ought to be allowed, unless *imperious* necessity should require it, or some great public good is to be promoted thereby." He added that the plan had been circulated throughout Europe, to induce purchasers to buy lots. They might well complain "of deception and injury," if the plans were arbitrarily changed without their knowledge.

Washington, jointly with Thornton, worked out designs for two elegant federal houses, with "united Doors in the Center, a Pediment in the roof and dormer windows on each side." The houses could be joined in the interior to form, if needed, a single house. Washington added a feature from Mount Vernon. This consisted of blowing fine sand on painted wooden exteriors, to give them the appearance of stone. The sand also acted as a preservative. In 1943 Ralph Cole Hall, an architect, and Stephen Dorsey, an architectural writer, after jointly examining Washington's plans, praised "the deep perception and judgment" of his designs.

As the buildings progressed, there was constant correspondence between Washington and Thornton. The general frequently came into town to inspect the work. On November 9 he examined them, then dined with the Thomas Laws and spent the night with the Peters at what became 2618 K Street. This was the last time that Washington slept in Washington. Nine days later he made a typical comment to Thornton: "I have no objection to Mr. Blagden's frequent calls for money; but I fear the work, which is not enumerated in the contract with him, is pretty smartly whipped up in the price of it."

Thornton continued to appeal to Washington's judgment on the city's development. On December 8 the general wrote him: "… I know not on what ground the Attorney General of the United States has founded the opinion communicated in your letter, of the insufficiency of the President's Powers to authorize the Commissioners of the City to accept a loan, for the purpose of carrying on the public works in that place. Under the original Act empowering the President to establish the permanent Seat of the Government on the Potomac, no doubt ever occurred to my mind, nor I believe to the Minds of any of the Officers thereof… of a want of this Power.

But by the obstructions continually thrown in its way, by *friends* or *enemies*, this City has had to pass through a fiery trial. Yet, I trust it will, ultimately, escape the Ordeal with éclat."

AGRICULTURE

On January 20, 1799, Washington wrote to Sir John Sinclair, the former head of the British Board of Agriculture: "No one is more impressed than I am with the importance of National encouragement to Agriculture. No one can approve more of such an Institution, as you have been the promoter of, than myself. Nor no one wishes more ardently than I do, to see such a measure adopted in the United States but we must look, I fear, to a more tranquil period for the accomplishment of it. Endeavouring in the meanwhile, to draw all the advantages we can from the labours of others." It was given to Lincoln, Washington's first great successor in office, to establish a small Bureau of Agriculture in 1862. Washington's dream of a national system of roads to unite the country and to promote western economic development, lay far longer in abeyance. For an extended period the Braddock and Forbes roads of 1755 and 1758 were the major connections to Ohio.

When his father died, George Washington inherited about 2,500 acres in Deep Run, in addition to his father's farm. He kept the former tract throughout most of his life, giving it to a nephew, Robert Lewis, in 1795. The additional lands he acquired from subsequent inheritance, purchase, or military service, he also held, for the most part. Occasionally, he exchanged properties for more convenient locations. At other times he sold lands to meet debts and obligations arising from his long periods of public service. Over the years his holdings increased until they totalled about ninety-six square miles. These lands were situated in New York, Pennsylvania, Maryland, Virginia, North Carolina, the District of Columbia, and the present states of West Virginia, Ohio, and Kentucky.

Washington's desire to sell large portions of this land, in order to free his slaves, had not been successful. In fact, his plan had become costly. He had resolved never to sell a slave who was to be freed. In his view at least half of the slaves were of no use to him but they had to be fed and clothed. He ran each year a large cash deficit which he estimated over several years to be in excess of $50,000. He was able to sell just enough acreage to break even.

LAST WILL

On July 9 George Washington drew up a will, disposing of the lands, shares, and other properties he possessed. With some exceptions, his wife was given a life interest in his property.

The next and most important provision was to free all his slaves, in a manner conforming to the laws of Virginia. Washington's will provided that all who were old or infirm were to be supported with full room, board, and clothing for the rest of their natural lives. Those who were not of age and had no parents were to be apprenticed to those who would teach them reading, writing, and a proper trade. He added: "And I do hereby expressly forbid the Sale or Transportation out of the said Commonwealth of Virginia, of any Slave I may die possessed of, under any pretense whatever. And I do moreover most pointedly, and most solemnly, enjoin it upon my Executors... to see that *this* clause respecting Slaves, and every part thereof, be religiously fulfilled... without evasion, neglect or delay... particularly as it respects the aged and infirm; seeing that a regular and permanent fund be established for their Support as long as there are subjects requiring it; not trusting to the uncertain provision to be made by individuals."

Succeeding clauses were devoted to education. Washington had been contributing an annuity to the Alexandria Academy for the education of orphans. In lieu thereof, he bequeathed the academy twenty shares in the Bank of Alexandria. He confirmed his previous donation of one hundred James River Company shares to the institution which was to become Washington and Lee University. A final educational clause looked to the great national university which Washington had planned for years. When he first laid his proposal before Congress, the opposition press severely attacked it. The congressional bill authorizing the acceptance of donations, was defeated by a single vote, thanks to Virginia's congressmen. Washington's will repeated and extended remarks which he had so often made:

> *It has been my ardent wish to see a plan... to spread systematic ideas through all parts of this rising Empire, thereby to do away with local attachments and State prejudices... from our National Councils. Looking anxiously forward to the accomplishment of so desirable an object... my mind has not been able to contemplate any plan more likely to effect the measure than the establishment of a UNIVERSITY... for education in... literature, in arts and sciences, in acquiring knowledge in the principles of Politics and good Government; and (a matter of infinite Importance in my judgment) by associating with each other, and forming friendships in juvenile years, to be enabled to free themselves from those local*

prejudices and habitual jealousies which... when carried to excess, are never failing sources of disquietude to the Public mind, and pregnant of mischievous consequences to this country.

For the establishment of a university in the territory of Columbia, Washington bequeathed the fifty Potomac Company shares, which had originally cost the state of Virginia $43,000. Washington had confidence in the future of the enterprise if it were well managed, and he expected the profits to be large and the value of the shares to increase. His will provided that all dividends be reinvested in bank stocks and added to the principal until the institution was established and the funds were needed.

The history of Washington's plan after his death is one of America's ironies. He assumed that the federal government would give such a national university a fostering hand. Jefferson ignored the proposal. Madison took up the suggestion with Congress in 1809 and 1815 but got nowhere. In 1816, Benjamin Latrobe, remembering Washington's enthusiasm and expecting a success for Madison's efforts, made an elegant sketch and design for the university to be located on the Mall, southeast of the president's house. The proposal was not acted upon, and Jefferson appropriated Latrobe's general design for the University of Virginia. The shares eventually became worthless. Some amends were made, six years after the Civil War, when Columbia College, in the nation's capital, was renamed the George Washington University.

Washington's further individual bequests were in excess of fifty, although a few were tokens of esteem rather than of value. Around forty nieces and nephews, grandnieces and nephews, and Martha Washington's four grandchildren shared in the estate. The most important bequest was to Bushrod Washington, associate justice of the Supreme Court, who received the Mount Vernon mansion house, 4,000 acres around it, and all of Washington's papers and books. Lawrence Lewis, married to Martha's granddaughter, got title to the 2,000-acre Dogue Run farm, on which Woodlawn was later built. Charles and George Washington, as grandnephews of both George and Martha Washington, were given a 2,077-acre tract, subsequently known as Collingwood. A portion of this, 360 acres, was reserved for their stepfather, Tobias Lear, as a lifetime free tenancy. Washington Custis was bequeathed approximately 1,200 acres near Alexandria, not far from his father's estate, which came to be known as Arlington. With the exception of certain other specific bequests, the remaining property was divided into twenty-four parts which were assigned, after the sales of property, to various heirs, some included in the preceding distribution. This portion Washington estimated as worth $530,000. He made no attempt to evaluate the whole estate.

A little over two months after he wrote his will, Washington informed Lawrence and Nelly Lewis that he was leaving them the Dogue Run farm. They had expressed a desire to settle near the general, who would be happy to rent them the property, so that they could build a house there. They would thus not have to buy expensive land but still have assurance that the rented property would pass to them as a gift, if they gave no displeasure to their uncle. Washington hastily added a reassurance that he had no reason to expect this, it was just his way of making certain about everything.

UNITED STATES ARMY

Although Washington had made it clear that he would not assume an active command until an emergency developed, he was nonetheless overworked and sometimes overwhelmed with army business. On February 25 he wrote to Hamilton that he thought the delay in recruiting was "unaccountable; and baffles all conjecture on reasonable grounds." If the winter were thus allowed to pass idly away, there would soon be heavy demands for agricultural workers and recruiting would be greatly hampered. The army would have to pick up "the riff-raff of the Country and the Scape gallowses of the large Cities." He followed this on March 25 with a forthright letter to Secretary of War McHenry:

> *You will not only consider this letter as a private one, but as a friendly one from G:W to J:M. And if the sentiments which you will find in it are delivered with more freedom and candour than are agreeable, say so; not by implication only, but in explicit language; and I will promise to offend no more...*

> *Thus premising, let me, in the name and behalf of the Officers who have been appointed, ask what keeps back the Commissions; and arrests the Recruiting Service? Be assured that both, among the friends of Government, excite astonishment and discontent. Blame is on every mind, but it is not known where to fix it. Some attach it to the P., some to the S. of W., and some, fertile in invention, seek for other causes. Many of the appointed Officers have quit their former occupations... Others, who were about to enter into business... stand suspended... Applications are made by numbers to me, to know what the cause of the delay is, what they are to expect, and what they ought to do.*

> *What could I say? Am I not kept in as much ignorance as they are themselves? Am I advised of any new appointments?... Any of the views or designs of the Government relatively to the Army?... Nothing short of a high sense of the Amor*

Patriae could have placed me in my present situation; and though I stand bound by, and will obey the call of my Country whenever it is made… none will regret the event with more poignancy…

I have been thus full, as it relates to myself, in order to shew you that information in all matters of a military nature, are necessary for my Government; thereby having a prospective view of things, I may prepare accordingly; and not, though detached from the Army until the exigencies of our Affairs may require my presence with it, appear as a person just dropped from the clouds, when I take the Command: nor will it, without doing great violence to the concerns of others, equally with my own, be in my power to "take up my bed and walk" at an unexpected requirement…

The augmented Corps… must have been intended as a well organized and disciplined body of Men… Will this be the case if the enemy should invade this Country? Far from it! What better, in the first instance, are Regiments so composed than Militia?

The two Major Generals and myself were called to Philadelphia in November last, and there detained five weeks very inconveniently to all of us, at an inclement season, in wading through volumes of applications and recommendations to Military Appointments; and I will venture to say that it was executed with as much assiduity and under as little influence of favor or prejudice, as a work of that sort… ever was accomplished; and what has followed? Why any member of Congress who had a friend to serve, or prejudice to indulge could set them at nought?

Thus prodded, McHenry issued a release to the gazettes, which explained that officers would be paid from the date of acceptance of their commission. On April 23 Washington wrote to the secretary to say that this had removed one cause of discontent among those who had quit their occupations, "but if these Officers are not speedily employed in the Recruiting Service, a clamour will soon arise in another quarter, for it will be asked why they are in actual pay and unemployed." In a subsequent private letter to Hamilton, Washington expressed agreement with Hamilton's argument for the promotion of Brigadier James Wilkinson, who had been commander of the American army. Having seen this letter, McHenry then asked Washington to give him a formal recommendation. Washington replied on July 7:

I am always willing to give publicity to any statement, which I have expressed in this way, if circumstances should require or render it proper. But as the appointment of other Officers of high rank has been made, not only without my recommendation but even without my knowledge, I cannot see the necessity... of my writing an official letter... Permit me, moreover to say that it would seem as if when doubts or difficulties present themselves, I am called upon to sanction the measure and thereby take a responsibility upon myself: and, in other cases, to which no blame may be attached, my opinions and inclinations are not consulted.

From great issues Washington was pulled back into trivia—the complaints of Washington Custis. The commander in chief wrote one week later to the secretary of war: "The young Cornet (in my family) is anxious to receive his Military equipments. Daily fruitless enquiries are made of me to know when they may be expected. Perhaps if you were to jog Mr. Francis, the *Purveyor*, the sooner they might be *Purveyed*, and the young gentleman gratified."

In 1798 Washington accepted two months active-duty pay, a little over $500 a month. On September 14, 1799, he declined the offer of the secretary of war to add a further sum, since he was living at Mount Vernon. He noted, however, the troubles his "inactive" command had brought him that year: "Applicants, recommenders of applicants, and seekers of information, with their servants and horses (appear at Mount Vernon) to aid in the consumption of my forage, and what, to me, is more valuable, my time." He would nonetheless draw only actual expenses, since he did not want those "who are always on the lookout for something to cavil at," to be able to say he was enjoying a lucrative retirement.

A remarkable feature of Washington's tenure as army chief was his sound advice on naval matters. He recommended to the secretary of the navy, on September 26, 1798, the establishment of a federal naval shipyard in the territory of Columbia. The opening of navigation of the Potomac, beyond tidewater, would provide, he said, the best naval timber in the country. Above the head of the Potomac was "an abundant supply of the largest and best white pine trees for Masts... No part of the U.S. affords better cedar and locust than the lands about this River. You know that iron of the best quality can be furnished from the works on the river, and as cheap as from any part of the U.S., and the establishment of a public foundry and Armory [at Harpers Ferry] will afford no small advantage in arming the ships. The articles of Tar, Pitch, live Oak, can be brought here upon as good terms as to any place North of this." Washington also noted that hemp could probably be grown cheaply and easily in the Ohio Valley. The government should encourage this, to avoid foreign dependence. He further advocated careful soundings of the Potomac and the deepening of its channels, in order to accommodate ships of the line.

The secretary of the navy followed Washington's advice and established a navy yard, which was subsequently destroyed during Madison's war.

The same letter pointed out how the national capital could be made impregnable to sea attack. "Should proper works be erected on Digge's Point… it would not be in the power of all the navies in Europe to pass that place… for every vessel, in passing up the River, must, from the course of the channel (and the channel is so narrow as to admit of but one vessel going abreast) present her bows to that point long before she comes within gun shot of it, and continue in that direction until she comes directly under the point, from whence shot may be thrown upon her deck, almost in perpendicular direction. Should she be so fortunate as to pass the works, she must expose her stern to the fire from them, as far as the shot can reach. Thus exposed to be raked fore and aft, for such a distance, without once being able to bring her broadside to bear upon the fort, you can readily see how impossible it will be for a vessel to pass this point; provided it be properly fortified and well supplied. And what makes it more important is that it cannot be attacked by land with any prospect of success… From the heights about Cedar Point… no Vessel can enter the River undiscovered, and by means of signals established on the prominent Eminences between that place and the site just mentioned, and the Federal City, notice thereof and of the number and descriptions of the Vessels may be conveyed to those places in a few minutes." Jefferson established a feeble fort at this point which Madison and Monroe continued to keep weak and useless. The British fleet easily captured it and the city of Alexandria in 1814.

One other point was made by the commanding general to the secretary of the navy: "If the British are resolved to keep up armed Vessels on the lakes, I presume it will be expedient for us to do the same; but in time of peace a better way, in my opinion, is for neither one to have any." Years later this became a firm pillar of Anglo-Canadian-American policy.

In September Washington received the news that General Pinckney, in charge of the army south of the Potomac, had taken his critically ill wife to Newport for her health. In consequence, Washington, the only high-ranking officer south of Philadelphia, had to assume aspects of command in September and October which he could otherwise have avoided. Most of it concerned instructions to three regiments, who were establishing cantonments and building new barracks at Harpers Ferry, or elsewhere. This involved extensive correspondence with the commanding officer of the regiments, the governor of Maryland, and others.

Washington's final letter on military affairs was written to Hamilton, who had forwarded to the secretary of war an overly elaborate plan for a national military academy. On December 12 he noted: "The Establishment of an Institution of this kind… has ever been considered by me as an Object of primary importance to this Country; and while I was in the Chair of Government, I omitted no opportunity of recommending it, in my public Speeches, and otherways, to the attention of the Legislature." He did not propose now, to go into the details of such a plan.

INTERNATIONAL DEVELOPMENTS

On February 18, 1799, the president of the United States transmitted to the Senate the nomination of William Vans Murray, American minister at The Hague, to be minister plenipotentiary to the French republic. Enclosed with the nomination was a letter from Talleyrand to the secretary of the French legation at The Hague, which declared that the French government would receive a minister from the United States "with the respect due to the representative of a free, independent and powerful nation." This phrase was the condition which, Adams had previously informed Congress, had to be met before he sent the French another minister. Under senatorial pressure, Adams subsequently made Murray one of three commissioners.

Adams had consulted no one on this measure and kept the Cabinet and Senate in the dark. Long afterwards, Timothy Pickering, secretary of state, surmised, probably correctly, that it was Adams' own idea, as a way to outflank Jefferson and win the Democrats over to his administration. He succeeded only in turning many horrified supporters against him. Jefferson, in reading the message to the Senate, noted the "mortification" and "dismay" of the Federalist senators. He immediately issued to Madison and Monroe the official party line. The Federalists had been concealing all along the true position of France. The French had always wanted peace, the Democrats were right, and it had been only provocation on the part of the United States which had caused trouble. With such a line, Adams could gain nothing politically. A few days previously Jefferson had written of the burden of defense, that the existing budget was already costing one-third the value of American exports and would soon take half. In fact, the then total federal expenditure was less than 10 percent of American exports and shipping earnings and perhaps a little over 1 percent of the gross national product. Once Adams announced peaceful overtures, the Jeffersonians returned with renewed angry attacks on any American defense system.

Washington viewed Adams' impetuous gesture with great concern. He wrote to the secretary of state on March 3 that he had been

informed there had been no __direct__ overture from the Government of France… On the *contrary that Mr. Talleyrand was playing the same loose and round-about game he had attempted the year before with our Envoys; and which, as in that case, might mean anything or nothing, as would subserve his purpose best. Had we approached the ante-chamber of this Gentleman when he opened the door to us and <u>there</u> waited for a formal invitation into the Interior, the Governments would have met upon equal ground; and we might have advanced, or receded, according to circumstances. In plainer words, had we said to Mr. Talleyrand, through the channel of his communication, we still are, as we always have been ready to settle by fair Negotiation, all differences… upon open, just and honourable terms; and it rests with the Directory (after the indignities with which <u>our</u> attempts to effect this, have been treated, if they are equally sincere) to come forward in an unequivocal manner, and prove it by their acts. Such conduct would have shown a dignified willingness on our part to Negotiate; and would have tested their sincerity, on the other. Under my present view of the subject, this would have been the course I should have pursued; keeping equally in view the horrors of War, and the dignity of the Government.*

Jefferson returned to Charlottesville in March to work on national and state elections. By this time he was counting on Pennsylvania to go Democratic which, with the South, would be sufficient to carry him to the presidency. The intrusion of Patrick Henry in support of the Federalists was particularly galling to him. He wrote on May 21 that whenever a man wanted public office, "a rottenness begins in his conduct. Mr. Henry has taken the field openly; but our legislature is filled with too great a mass of talents and principle to be now swayed by him… Still I fear something from his intriguing and cajoling talents, for which he is still more remarkable than for his eloquence." The elections of Patrick Henry and eight Federalist congressmen Jefferson found "extremely to be regretted."

Patrick Henry died on June 6, to the shock of Washington. Ten days later he wrote to John Marshall: "In the Death of Mr. Henry… not only Virginia but our country at large has sustained a very serious loss. I sincerely lament his death as a friend; and the loss of his eminent talents as a Patriot I consider as peculiarly unfortunate at this critical junction of our affairs." Yet Washington sensed there had been a move to moderation, even in the South. To the painter, John Trumbull, who was in London (and whom he asked to give his best respects to Benjamin West) Washington wrote on June 25: "The public mind has changed, and is yet changing every day with respect to French principles. The people begin to see clearly that the words and actions of the governing powers of that Nation can not be reconciled… The late changes in the Congressional Representation sufficiently evince this: for of the two sent from the State of Georgia, one certain, some say both are Federal characters; of six from South

Carolina, five are decidedly so; of ten from North Carolina, seven may be counted upon; and of nineteen from this state (Virginia) eight are certain, a ninth doubtful, and, but for some egregious mismanagement, eleven supporters of Governmental measures would have been elected." Washington also wrote:

> *No well informed and unprejudiced man, who has viewed with attention the conduct of the French Government since the Revolution in that Country, can mistake its objects or the tendency of the ambitious plans it is pursuing. Yet, strange as it seems, a party, and a powerful one too, among us, affect to believe that the measures of it are dictated by a principle of self preservation; that the outrages of which the Directory are guilty, proceed from dire necessity; that it wishes to be upon the most friendly and amicable terms with the United States; that it will be the fault of the latter if this is not the case; that the defensive measures which this Country have adopted, are not only unnecessary and expensive, but have the tendency to produce the evil which, to deprecate, is mere pretence, because War with France they say is the wish of this Government; that on the Militia we should rest our Security... [All this is done] with all the arts of sophistry, and no regard to truth, decency or respect to characters, public or private, who happen to differ from themselves in Politics...*

The dissensions within the Federalist party brought many leaders to look for another candidate in 1800. Washington seemed to be the one man who could again unite the country and save the Union. John Trumbull's brother, Jonathan, governor of Connecticut, was one of the first to sound out the general on the subject. Washington replied forcefully on July 21:

> *It would be a matter of sore regret to me if I could believe that a serious thought was turned towards me as his successor; not only as it respects my ardent wishes to pass through the vale of life in retirement... unless called upon to defend my country... but on public grounds also... I am thoroughly convinced I should not draw a <u>single</u> vote from the Anti-federal side; and of course should stand on no stronger ground than any other Federal character, well supported; and when I should become a mark for the shafts of envenomed malice, and the basest calumny to fire at; when I should be charged not only with irresolution, but with concealed ambition, which waits only on occasion to blaze out; in short, with dotage and imbecility. All this... ought to be like dust in the balance when put in competition with a <u>great</u> public good... But as no problem is better defined in my mind than that principle, not men, is now, and will be, the object of contention... Any other respectable Federal character would receive the same suffrages that I should; at my time of life (verging towards three score and ten) I should expose myself without rendering any essential*

service to my Country, or answering the end contemplated. Prudence on my part must arrest any attempt at the well meant, but mistaken views of my friends, to introduce me again into the chair of Government.

Washington then took up a problem which sorely vexed the Cabinet and everyone concerned with the operations of government in crisis: the fact that the president was so long away from the capital. He "would give him to understand that his long absence from the Government in the present critical conjecture, affords matter for severe animadversion by the friends of government, who speak of it and set it down as a favourable omen for themselves. It has been suggested to me to make this Communication; but I have declined it, conceiving that it would be better received from a private character, more in the habits of social intercourse and friendship."

In a further letter on August 11 to the secretary of war, Washington referred to various matters, including the charges by the Jeffersonian press that federal officials had been receiving bribes:

I think you wisemen of the East have got yourselves in a hobble... Whom will you offend?... But to be serious, I think the nomination and Appointment of Ambassadors to treat with France would, in any event, have been liable to unpleasant reflections... and, in the present state of matters in Europe, must be exceedingly embarrassing. The President has a choice of difficulties... If he pursues the line he marked out, all the consequences cannot be foreseen. If he relinquished it, it will be said to be of a piece with all the other Acts of the Administration; unmeaning if not wicked, deceptions & ca... and will arm the opposition with fresh weapons to commence new attacks upon the Government... I come now to the Scene of Bribery.

And pray, my good sir, what part of the $800,000 have come to your share? As you are high in Office, I hope you did not disgrace yourself in the acceptance of a paltry bribe. A $100,000 perhaps. But here again I become serious. There can be no medium between the reward and punishment of an editor who shall publish such things as Duane has been doing for sometime past... I hope and expect that the Prosecutors will probe this matter to the bottom.

Is the President returned to the seat of Government? When will he return? His absence (I mention it from the best motives) gives much discontent to the friends of government, while its enemies chuckle at it...

In the meantime, keeping his hand entirely secret, the vice-president further dabbled in treasonable activities by declaring the right of any state to secede, the doctrine by which Jefferson was to father the eventual civil war. In once more dispatching Wilson Nicholas to Kentucky to induce its pliant legislature to pass further resolutions, Jefferson wrote, September 5, asking Kentucky to reply to the many states who had denounced the earlier Virginia and Kentucky resolves. He complained bitterly that they had, in effect, endorsed the work of the national Congress and their actions were therefore unconstitutional. Kentucky should protest vigorously, "*reserving* the right to make this palpable violation of the federal compact the ground of doing in future what we might now rightfully do," that is to secede from the Union. Jefferson used the term "scission" rather than secession. Virginia would never surrender "the rights of self-government." Rather, as he had pointed out a few days earlier to Madison, we ought to "sever ourselves" from the Union.

While Jefferson was plotting to dissolve the Union and reports reached Philadelphia that Virginians were arming in defiance of the federal government, the president stayed quietly in Quincy from March to October. That year saw more revolutionary changes in France as most of the Directory were overthrown and the Terror briefly renewed. To numerous Federalists this French instability made it even less desirable that a mission proceed. In October the president reached Trenton where he stayed temporarily to avoid yet another yellow fever epidemic in the capital. As Pickering reported to Washington, October 24, the president ordered the secretary of the navy to prepare a frigate to carry the two American commissioners to France. Adams told the secretary that he had not consulted the cabinet because his mind was "unchangeable."

When Washington heard from Hamilton of the presidential decision, he replied on October 27: "I was surprised at the *measure*, how much more so at the manner of it? This business seems to have commenced in an evil hour, and under unfavourable auspices; and I wish mischief may not tread in all its steps, and be the final result of the measure. A wide door was open, through which a retreat might have been made from the first faux-pas; the shutting of which, to those who are not behind the Curtain, and are as little acquainted with the Secrets of the Cabinet as I am, is, from the present aspect of European affairs, incomprehensible." He wrote in a somewhat similar vein to McHenry, expressing the hope that "good will come from the Mission, which is about to depart... These are my wishes, and no one is more ardent in them; but I see nothing in the *present* aspect of European Affairs on which to build them. Nor no possible evil under the same circumstances, that could result from delay in forwarding it."

On November 10 McHenry replied with a long, gloomy, and as events turned out, quite accurate appraisal of the political situation. It was to be the last letter of importance on national affairs which Washington received.

McHenry explained that the French mission had been appointed without consultation with Congress. Most of the Federalist members disapproved. They regarded the move as ill timed, made on too slight grounds, and likely to be hurtful to the United States. In addition, Adams' action tended to encourage French and Jeffersonian principles. That summer, members of the Cabinet had written to the president, pointing out that the changes in the Directory and the successes of the British and their allies made it desirable to suspend the mission. The president made no reply but on his arrival simply ordered the Cabinet to prepare instructions for the mission, which was to depart on November 3. Three of the Cabinet, the secretaries of state, treasury, and war, regarded the move as "impolitic and unwise." The president, in consequence, was highly displeased with them, and there was a probability one or more would be dismissed. In McHenry's view, "good and able" substitutes could easily be found, but this would not remedy the evil. The mission had become such "an apple of discord" among the Federalists as to jeopardize the ensuing election for the presidency. Pennsylvania had already gone Democratic. The Jeffersonians were making progress elsewhere.

McHenry could see only danger ahead. The secretaries of state and treasury, able men both, had been made "cyphers... I see rocks and quicksands on all sides and the administration as a sinking ship. It will depend... upon the President whether she is to weather or go down." On November 17 Washington replied:

> *Your confidential and interesting letter... came duly and safely to hand. With the contents of which I have been stricken dumb; and I believe it is better that I should remain mute than express any sentiment on the important matters which are related therein.*

> *I have, for sometime past, viewed the political concerns of the United States with an anxious and painful eye. They appear to me, to be moving by hasty strides to some awful crisis; but in what they will result, that Being, who sees, foresees, and directs all things, alone can tell. The Vessel is afloat, or very nearly so, and considering myself as a Passenger only, I shall trust to the Mariners whose duty it is to watch, to steer it into a safe Port.*

On December 6 the Virginia legislature, where James Madison was a delegate, elected James Monroe as governor. Not long afterwards they steered through an act to give all Virginia's electoral votes to the man having the majority of votes in the state. He would clearly be Thomas Jefferson, facing a divided party under a nominal leader, John Adams.

THE FINAL AUTUMN

In late August 1799 Mrs. Washington fell seriously ill with malaria. She was in bed for several weeks. During this period Washington heard of the death of Charles, his brother. He wrote to Burgess Ball on September 22: "I was the *first*, and am now the *last*, of my father's Children by the second marriage who remain. When I shall be called upon to follow them, is known only to the giver of life. When the summons comes I shall endeavour to obey it with a good grace."

After Martha's recovery life was generally cheerful at Mount Vernon. On November 12 the general wrote to the managers of the Alexandria dances: "Mrs. Washington and myself have been honoured with your polite invitation to the Assemblies in Alexandria this winter; and thank you for this mark of attention. But alas! our dancing days are no more; we wish, however, all those who relish so agreeable and innocent an amusement, all the pleasure the season will afford them." Five days later he rode the nine miles to Christ Church, Alexandria, for his last church service.

Thereafter there was frequent company at Mount Vernon, largely family or old friends. These included Doctors Craik and Stuart and Colonel Carrington with their wives. On November 27 Dr. Craik was summoned from Alexandria; that morning Nelly Lewis gave birth to a daughter, Frances, who was the general's great-niece and his wife's great-granddaughter. Thirteen days earlier Martha Peter had given birth in the city of Washington to Mrs. Washington's great-grandson, John Parke Custis Peter.

On December 7 Washington rode to Mount Eagle to dine with Lord Fairfax, his friend of more than fifty years. On December 9 Howell Lewis and his wife set out for home, and Lawrence Lewis and Washington Custis for New Kent, none of the four thinking they would never again see George Washington. Lawrence Lewis later recalled the last sight of his uncle: "It was a bright, frosty morning. He had taken his usual ride, and the clear healthy flush on his cheeks and his sprightly manner brought the remark from both of us that we had never seen the General look so well. I have sometimes thought him decidedly the handsomest man I ever saw; and when in a lively mood, so full of pleasantry, so agreeable to all with whom he associated, that I could hardly realize he was the same Washington whose dignity awed all who approached him."

On December 13 three Fairfaxes, two Washington relatives, and John Herbert dined at Mount Vernon. That night the general noticed "a large circle around the Moon." Next morning "about 10 o'clock it began to snow, soon after to Hail and then to a settled cold Rain." In spite of the bad weather, Washington went out on horseback for his usual farm inspection. A little after three he returned to the mansion house, his neck wet and snow on his hair. Since dinner was waiting he went to the table without stopping to change. The following morning there was a heavy snow and Washington stayed indoors. He complained of a sore throat but nonetheless walked out on the grounds in the afternoon. That evening Lear noticed that he was hoarse but "he made light of it, as he would never take anything to carry off a cold, always observing 'let it go as it came.'"

In the evening General and Mrs. Washington sat with Lear, reading the newspapers which had come from the post office. About nine Mrs. Washington went upstairs to see how her granddaughter was doing. The general, Lear noted, "was very cheerful; and when he met with anything which he thought diverting or interesting, he would read it aloud as well as his hoarseness would permit. He desired me to read to him the debates of the Virginia Assembly on the election of a Senator and Governor; which I did and, on hearing Mr. Madison's observations respecting Mr. Monroe, he appeared much affected and spoke with some degree of asperity on the subject... On his retiring to bed, he appeared in perfect health, excepting the cold before mentioned, which he considered as trifling, and he had been remarkably cheerful all the evening."

Sometime before four in the morning of December 14 Washington awakened his wife to tell her he had a chill and fever and was very sick. Mrs. Washington noticed that he could scarcely speak and that he breathed with the greatest difficulty. Much alarmed, she wanted to get up and awaken the household but he told her not to leave her bed or she might catch cold. As soon as a servant appeared to light a fire in the early morning, Mrs. Washington sent for Lear, asking him to order George Rawlins, the farm overseer, to come to the house. Lear after looking at the general, ordered a servant to ride with all possible speed to Alexandria, to bring Dr. Craik to Mount Vernon.

Lear and Martha Washington, while waiting, prepared a drink to soothe his throat "but he could not swallow a drop. Whenever he attempted it he appeared to be distressed, convulsed and almost suffocated." When the overseer appeared, the general ordered himself bled according to the medical custom of the times. Mrs. Washington was worried about this, not thinking it proper and tried to stop it. She asked him to take only a little blood. At her entreaty, Rawlins desisted after drawing a half pint. Mrs. Washington then asked Lear to send for Dr. Gustavus Brown of Port Tobacco, Maryland, whom Dr. Craik had recommended if he were not available.

Dr. Craik appeared at Mount Vernon in midmorning. Dr. Brown arrived at 3:30 in the afternoon and Dr. Elisha Cullen Dick, summoned from Alexandria by Dr. Craik, joined them shortly afterwards. There has been, since that time, an endless but unnecessary controversy over Washington's medical treatment.* Before his colleagues arrived, Dr. Craik, his intimate friend since the French and Indian War, "employed two copious bleedings; a blister was applied to the part affected, two moderate doses of calomel were given, an injection was administered which operated on the lower intestines, but all without perceptible advantage." There was further bloodletting in the afternoon as well as administration of a strong emetic. These treatments, while very uncomfortable for the patient, may have hastened but did not affect the final outcome of the illness.

Dr. Dick, the last to arrive, at once favorably impressed his older colleagues with his diagnostic knowledge. As Brown subsequently wrote Craik: "You remember how, by his clear reasoning and evident knowledge of certain symptoms, he assured us it was not really quinsy, which we supposed it to be, but a violent inflammation of the membranes of the throat, which it had almost closed, and which, if not immediately arrested, would result in death."

Dr. Brown noted also that Dr. Dick proposed to halt further bleeding, as a means to conserve Washington's remaining strength. Dr. Dick himself on January 10, 1800, reported to Thomas Semmes, his further counsel: "I proposed to perforate the trachea as a means of prolonging life, and of affording time for the removal of the obstruction to respiration in the larynx, which threatened speedy dissolution." He would take all responsibility for failure. Dr. Craik appears to have at first agreed but was finally persuaded by Dr. Brown to oppose the measure.

Although he could scarcely speak, Washington's mind remained clear to the end and his politeness as natural as ever. He noticed that Christopher, his servant, had been standing all day and he motioned to him to sit. He asked Mrs. Washington to bring his two wills to the bed. After looking at them, he ordered one put in the fire, giving her the other. He informed Lear that he was dying and asked him to arrange all his military papers and accounts. He asked if Lear had any final question. He said he could think of nothing except to hope that it was not fatal. Washington smiled and said that it was the debt

---

* Dr. Heinz H. E. Scheidenmandel of Annandale, Virginia, made the first persuasive diagnosis in his "Did George Washington Die of Quinsy?" (Arch. Otolaryngol; 102: 519–521, September 1976). Dr. Scheidenmandel wrote: "The clinical findings in George Washington's case are identical to those produced by acute epiglotitis... a fearsome entity that does not respond well to medical treatment and that can lead to death within a few hours. It requires emergency tracheotomy or intubation in almost every case. If Dr. Dick would have prevailed, a rapidly performed tracheotomy or possibly cricothyreostomy would have led to immediate total airway obtrusion in his by then advanced case, and an airway would have to have been established within three to five minutes to avoid cardiac arrest." The epiglottis is the leaf-shaped plate of cartilage at the root of the tongue which covers the trachea when swallowing.

that all must pay. When the physicians once more appeared to look at their patient, he essayed his last little joke. After making several attempts to speak, he prayed them not to give themselves any further trouble.

Washington's final moments were subsequently recorded by Lear:

> *About ten o'clock he made several attempts to speak to me before he could effect it. At length he said, "I am just going. Have me decently buried, and do not let my body be put into the vault in less than three days after I am dead." I bowed assent for I could not speak. He then looked at me again and said "Do you understand me?" I replied, "Yes Sir." "It is well," said he. About ten minutes before he expired his breathing became much easier. He lay quietly. He withdrew his hand from mine and felt his own pulse. I spoke to Dr. Craik who sat by the fire. He came to the bedside. The General's hand fell from his wrist. I took it in mine and laid it upon my breast. Dr. Craik put his hand on his eyes and he expired without a struggle or Sigh. While we were fixed in silent grief, Mrs. Washington, who was sitting at the foot of the bed asked, with a firm and collected voice, "Is he gone?" I could not speak but held up my hand as a signal that he was. "It is well" said she in a plain voice. "All is now over. I have no more trials to pass through. I shall soon follow him."*

MARTHA WASHINGTON

It had been less than twenty-seven hours since Martha Washington had seen her husband, cheerful and happy, as she sat with him in the quiet Mount Vernon parlor. "Taught," as she subsequently wrote the president of the United States, "by the great example, which I have so long had before me," she bore his sudden death with Christian fortitude. It was she the following morning who asked Lear to order the coffin from Alexandria. She also requested that a door be placed on the family vault rather than having it sealed, repeating that she would soon follow him. Mrs. Washington gave instructions as to all the family and old friends who were to be invited to the funeral. She read the will and asked Lear to notify all executors. Soon letters poured out from Mount Vernon to the president of the United States, Generals Hamilton and Pinckney, members of the Washington family, the Laws, Peters, Howell Lewises and Lawrence Lewis, and Washington Custis.

On the afternoon of December 18, burial took place in the old family vault at Mount Vernon. Eleven pieces of artillery and a schooner had been sent from Alexandria to fire minute guns. Five clergymen, three Episcopal and two Presbyterian, were present, led by the Reverend Thomas Davis and including the Reverend Lord Fairfax. There were troops, cavalry, and foot, and a large delegation of Masons. After Davis read the Episcopal burial service and delivered a short eulogy, the Masons conducted their ceremony and the body of George Washington was placed in the vault. The mourners then retired to the Mount Vernon mansion house for the refreshments which Mrs. Washington had ordered.

Martha Washington's composure held until letters reached her from her old friends, John and Abigail Adams. The president's wife later learned through Lear that, although their letters were not long, it had taken Mrs. Washington two hours to read them through her tears. It was to Abigail Adams that Martha finally poured out her anguish. Martha Washington was given the grace, however, to be able to console those who mourned with her. The governor of Connecticut, Jonathan Trumbull, when writing, enclosed extracts of the moving letter he had received from her husband when his own father, the revolutionary governor of Connecticut, had died. Martha Washington replied on January 15, 1800, in phrases strongly reminiscent of her husband.

When the mind is deeply afflicted by those irreparable losses which are incident to humanity, the good Christian will submit without repining to the dispensations of Divine Providence, and look for consolation to that Being who alone can pour balm into the bleeding heart, and who has promised to be the widow's God. But in the severest trials, we find some alleviation to our grief in the sympathy of sincere friends; and I should not do justice to my sensibility, was I not to acknowledge that your kind letter of condolence of the 30th of December was grateful to my feeling. I well knew the affectionate regard which my dear deceased husband always entertained for you, and therefore conceive of what you have given of what was written to you on a former melancholy occasion, is truly applicable to this. The loss is ours; the gain is his.

For myself, I have only to go with humble submission to the will of that God who giveth and who taketh away, looking forward with faith and hope to the moment when I shall be again united with the partner of my life. But, while I continue on earth, my prayers will be offered up for the welfare and happiness of my friends, among whom you will always be numbered, being, Dear Sir, Your sincere and afflicted friend...

On November 11 of that year Mrs. Washington wrote to Mrs. Tobias Lear, Sr., to say that she had often been ill and never expected to be well, as long as she was in this world. On May 24, 1802, Martha Washington, who had also served her country with grace and distinction, was laid to rest beside the general in the Mount Vernon vault.

EPILOGUE

LATE IN THE summer of 1798, the American minister to The Hague, William Vans Murray, wrote to the secretary of war in Philadelphia: "The energy and great respectability of the United States have produced a State of Things in the Directory at Paris, from which we may see the rights of neutral Nations, in general, respected. It would dilate every artery in you to see the glory which is spreading over the U. S. at this moment in the eyes of Europe... She plants her foot with firmness—France recoils... Be firm and persevering... France will recoil, we shall triumph."

President Adams had indicated he thought that General Washington's name was worth many army divisions and perhaps it was to France. It was to be the navy, founded by Washington and Knox, on which Adams primarily relied. American frigates and armed privateers drove the French from the coastal areas of the United States, while navy squadrons also patrolled the Caribbean. More than eighty French armed ships were captured in less than two years. By September 1800 France had recoiled and concluded a convention with the United States, which restored the peaceful *status quo ante*. The question of reparations for ship seizures by France was still unsettled when Adams left office.

With the United States at peace with all the world, her 1801 exports reached a level four times as high as those of 1789. The country that year attained a per capita income greater than it was to enjoy for about seventy years. The twelve federalist years had shown an average increase in America's gross national product of nearly 20 percent per annum.

In 1801 Jefferson, who loathed the revolution's military heroes, moved into the presidency, thanks to the extra electoral and lower House votes given the South for its slaves. In turn the electoral machinery in the southern states was closely controlled within the state by the slave-owning coastal sections, which held a disproportionate share of the seats in the state legislatures.

Jefferson proceeded, as rapidly as feasible, to demolish the financial and military strength, of the national government. He also began an unsuccessful assault on the federal judiciary. The army and foreign service were greatly reduced in size and the navy practically junked. With the savings Jefferson used the federal budget as a sharply depressing deflationary device. Excess receipts were devoted to reducing the national debt rather than to developing the country's resources. In 1803 when Napoleon handed Jefferson what Henry Adams correctly termed his "trebly invalid" title to Louisiana, its "bargain" price was largely at the expense of American shipowners who received only trifling sums for their heavy losses. The new lands were added by Jefferson to the nation as slave territory.

After a temporary peace, the European powers resumed their war in 1803. This time, with American defense forces cut to the bone, the belligerents could afford to ignore the American president. He did make an attempt to revive a "navy" with the building of small boats, armed with one or two guns. He added to this feeble threat an embargo on American exports. Established at the end of 1807, it had limited effect on the belligerents but it nearly ruined the American economy. The embargo was dropped as Jefferson was leaving office. At the end of eight years America's per capita income was down by a third.

Things grew worse under Madison. Unlike Jefferson, he occasionally announced that there ought to be a constitutional amendment to permit the government to assist the country's economic development. This was rhetoric to cover his failure to use the powers already existing. In taking office in 1809, Madison moved once more to reduce defense expenditures which, by 1811, he had cut a further 22 percent. By then he had also destroyed the national bank and had begun a series of attacks against the Indians, which eventually brought the country into conflict with most of the tribes from Wisconsin to Florida. The Indians complained that their "great father, Washington" had promised them perpetual peace and the solemn observance of their treaties. Nonetheless there were more than twenty major battles with them from 1811 to the end of Madison's presidency.

In 1814, after hearing of the burning of Washington by the British, Philadelphia diarist Thomas Cope recalled that "with an empty treasury—six frigates and no army—we declared war against a nation... possessing the greatest naval force ever known... having more than one thousand ships of war..." Jefferson had written Kosciusko, ten days after the declaration of war: "Our present enemy will have the sea to herself, while we shall be equally predominant on the land... We have nothing to fear from their armies." Two months later, the British were in possession of Mackinac, Detroit, and Chicago, all American troops in the area having been killed or captured. Jefferson recommended to Madison that he shoot General Hull, who had been given orders from Washington to seize upper Canada with 1,500 militia. Further American attempts to attack that country were thrown back repeatedly and, it must be added, comically.

In August 1814 the war reached its climax of ineptness when the Royal Navy chased Jefferson's gunboats up the Potomac and Patuxent rivers. The president had provided no effective defense, and he and Monroe scampered ignominiously, much as Jefferson had done in 1781, to hide from the small British army which captured Washington and burned the principal public buildings. By the time Madison and Monroe returned to the capital, they found that other forces had captured Alexandria. At this point the British retired from the Washington area, having punished Madison for the burning of the capital of upper Canada.

By 1814 America's export and shipping earnings were down to 15 percent of what they had been when Adams left office in 1801. Per capita income had dropped sharply. The one continual series giving an indication of general prosperity, the consumption of coffee and sugar, declined by two-thirds in fourteen years. In the four war and postwar years, 1812–1815, the deficit in the federal budget of $68 million was slightly larger than the entire federal government expenditures in the twelve Federalist years. Thus the party of limited or no national government had engaged in reckless war and a feckless waste of lives and resources. This was a sharp reversal of the Washington-Adams era of frugal government and rapid economic growth in the private sector. Never again would the federal government operate so efficiently.

By the time Monroe, the least competent of the Virginia dynasts, had finished his first term in 1821, slavery had metastasized up both banks of the Mississippi, as far as Missouri. The great dreams of George Washington of permanent national union, continuous economic growth, and the abolition of slavery were now safely buried.

INDEX